New Dimensions in Spirituality, Religion, and Aging

D1552691

New Dimensions in Spirituality, Religion, and Aging expands the traditional focus of religiosity to include and evaluate recent research and discoveries on the role of secular spirituality in the aging process. Contributors examine the ways conventional religion and other forms of spirituality affect human development, health and longevity, and they demonstrate how myth-creation enables humans to make meaning in their lives. Taken together, the book points to further research to enhance current knowledge, approaches to care, and social policies.

Vern L. Bengtson is Research Professor in the USC Edward R. Roybal Institute on Aging at the University of Southern California (USC). Prior to his current appointment, Dr. Bengtson held the AARP/University Chair at USC and was past president of Gerontological Society of America. He is a MERIT awardee from the National Institutes of Health. He has written extensively on theories of aging, sociology of aging, and religion, publishing 17 books and over 250 research papers.

Merril Silverstein is Marjorie Cantor Professor of Aging Studies and the inaugural holder of the Marjorie Cantor Chair in Aging Studies at Syracuse University. Dr. Silverstein's research has focused on aging in the context of family life in over 150 research publications, with added emphases on life course and international perspectives. He is a Brookdale Fellow and Fulbright Senior Scholar, and between 2010–2014 served as editor-in-chief of *Journal of Gerontology: Social Sciences*.

New Dimensions in Spirituality, Religion, and Aging

Edited by
Vern L. Bengtson and Merril
Silverstein

Routledge
Taylor & Francis Group
NEW YORK AND LONDON

First published 2019
by Routledge
711 Third Avenue, New York, NY 10017

and by Routledge
2 Park Square, Milton Park, Abingdon, Oxon OX14 4RN

Routledge is an imprint of the Taylor & Francis Group, an informa business

Library of Congress Cataloging in Publication Data
A catalog record for this title has been requested

ISBN: 978-1-138-61480-2 (hbk)
ISBN: 978-1-138-61481-9 (pbk)
ISBN: 978-0-429-46389-1 (ebk)

Typeset in Bembo
by Taylor & Francis Books

Contents

Figures

Tables

Acknowledgements

This project was supported by grant #56497 from the John Templeton Foundation, "Religious transitions, transmission, and trajectories among baby boomers and their families." We want to acknowledge the encouragement and support throughout the project of Dr. Kimon Sergeant, Director of Research for the Foundation. We are grateful to Hannah Gruhn-Bengtson for editing the papers in this volume and managing the overall project. The book is the outcome of a conference held in Washington, DC, in October of 2017, in conjunction with the annual meeting of the Society for the Scientific Study of Religion.

This book is the product of many individuals' efforts. At the University of Southern California's Suzanne Dworak-Peck School of Social Work, we thank Dean Marilyn Flynn for her support. We are grateful to Mita Patel, Iris Aguilar, Dr. William Vega, and Dr. Maria Aranda of the USC Edward R. Roybal Institute on Aging, and Kamilah Mayfield and Sherin Samaan of the Hamovitch Research Center, for administrative and financial assistance. At Syracuse University, we are grateful to Debra Gamble for grant management. At the University of California Santa Barbara, Samantha Copping Kang assisted in implementation of the conference, and Camille Endacott and Gabrielle Gonzales provided useful comments on papers. We appreciate the help of Roman Williams, Executive Director of the Society for the Scientific Study of Religion, in setting up our conference in conjunction with the SSSR meetings.

Chapter 1

Emerging Developments in Spirituality, Religion, and Aging

Vern L. Bengtson

UNIVERSITY OF SOUTHERN CALIFORNIA

Samantha L. C. Kang, Camille G. Endacott, and Gabrielle G. Gonzales

UNIVERSITY OF CALIFORNIA SANTA BARBARA

Merril Silverstein

SYRACUSE UNIVERSITY

Interest in spirituality, religion, and aging is certainly not new, and litera-ture discussing their connections goes back thousands of years. In the Hebrew Bible we read "Gray hair is a crown of glory; it is gained in a righteous life" (Proverbs 16:31). An ancient Islamic text contains a similar passage: "Gray hair is the light of a Muslim. No one turns gray in Islam but for every gray hair he will receive one reward and his status will be raised by one degree" (in Silsilat al-Ahaadeeth al-Saheehah, 1242).

Today the interplay between spirituality and aging is emerging as the focus of a considerable body of research. Many thousands of research papers have been published in the past few decades about connections between age or aging and religious behavior, beliefs, and related issues. Indeed, a Google Scholar search resulted in 186,000 citations of materials published under these titles since 1980. The topics have ranged from religion and health to psychological well-being, the meaning of death and dying, and the role of churches in meeting the needs of older adults.

But the overwhelming number – perhaps 80 percent – of the recent empirical research has focused primarily on health, and on relationships between health, aging, and various aspects of religious practice. In a variety of ways, these studies have examined whether, and how, religiosity is related to health in later life. The

Acknowledgements This research was supported by the John Templeton Foun-dation, grant ID-56407. We gratefully acknowledge the assistance of Hannah Gruhn-Bengtson in editing numerous drafts of this manuscript, and also the 146 older adults and clergy who provided the interview data for our project.

answer from this vast body of research is that there is certainly a connection; but, as reviewed in the chapters by Krause, Idler, and George in this volume, it is complex, and the causal relationships are not entirely clear. Moreover, there are many more dimensions in addition to health status in which spiritual and religious expressions are involved with the process and outcomes of aging.

Examining the linkages among aging, religion, and spirituality may be particularly relevant today because of three worldwide developments – revolutions might be a more appropriate word – that have significant implications for the early decades of the 21st century. In this chapter, we first present an overview of these developments, which taken together constitute the changing context of aging and religion and which have many implications for churches and religious organizations as well as older individuals themselves. Next we summarize findings emerging from our own research program reflecting four issues: To what extent does religiosity change with age? What are the changes – trajectories – in religious and spiritual development in later life? Are churches – with their youth-centric focus – meeting the needs of their growing numbers of older members? And how do non-religious older adults look at their beliefs as they face the end of life?

Three Transforming Changes: Demographics, Denominations, and Doctrines

Examining the linkages among aging, religion, and spirituality has become perhaps more urgent than ever before because of three worldwide and revolutionary changes to the population structures and religious attachments in human societies. These involve the aging of societies, the increasing longevity of persons living within them, and the growing diversity of religious and spiritual expression among their inhabitants.

Societies Are Aging

Across the world societies are aging, and the shape of nations' populations by age has changed remarkably over the past century. For most of human history, a graph of the number of individuals in a group or society by age would result in a shape resembling a pyramid, with many individuals at the bottom (the very young and young, ages 0–10 and 11–19) and very few individuals at the top (above age 55). However, during the past century every industrialized society across the globe has experienced a radical re-shaping of its age distribution, with a growing number of individuals at the top of the population pyramid and a diminishing number at the bottom.

This can be seen very clearly in the United States (Figure 1.1) where the population age distribution changed in its shape from a regular pyramid to something like a pillar in less than a century, from 1900 to 1995. In addition, something interesting occurred around the mid-point of the century, starting in 1946: there was a boom in births, resulting in larger birth cohorts

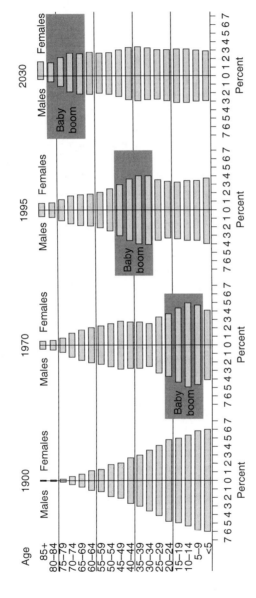

Figure 1.1 Age Structure of United States: Population Pyramid Showing Changes since 1990
Source: Baby Boom 1900, 1970, 1995, 2030 (est.). Adapted from Colby & Ortman, 2014. Retrieved from https://www.census.gov/prod/2014pubs/p25-1141.pdf. Adapted with permission.

than ever before. These "baby boomers" changed the age population distribution of society as they grew and now they are growing old. Every day 10,000 Americans turn age 65, one every 32 minutes (Erber, 2015). Keep these statistics in mind; we will return to them later to consider their implications for religion and aging.

Individuals Are Living Longer

The contributors to societal aging, and the reason that societies around the globe have been increasingly changing the shape of their age distributions from pyramids to pillars since the 1900s, can be traced to two main factors: decreased fertility and increased life expectancy. Families have been having fewer children at the same time that individuals have been living longer. Increased life expectancy has been accomplished by reducing childhood infectious diseases, granting survivors the chance to live to adulthood. In addition, life-sustaining medical techniques have prolonged lives much longer than ever before, benefiting heart disease, stroke, and cancer patients in their middle and later years.

The pattern of expanding life expectancy over the past century is striking (see Figure 1.2). In 1900, life expectancy for infants of both sexes born in the United States was 47 years. By 1940 this had climbed to 61 years, and by 1970 to 72 years. In 2000, life expectancy at birth was almost 76 years (Arias, 2010). Within the span of one century, the life expectancy of Americans increased by an astonishing 29 years of life. Put another way, American society had added the length of one generation to the average length of life.

Religious Attachments Are Changing

In the past three decades, a third remarkable trend has attracted attention: the changing religious landscape of societies around the world. This is more difficult to chart than the first two trends, since the evidence involves data from individuals responding to long surveys rather than data from census records. Nevertheless, these shifts have captured the attention of the mass media because of their suggestion of a profound cultural change. Nowhere has this been more evident than in American society.

For example, headlines appeared in May of 2014 saying, "Religion on the decline in the US" (Lauter & Branson-Potts, 2015). A CNN story proclaimed, "Millennials leaving church in droves, study finds…Americans considering themselves Christians drops 8%" (Burke, 2015). These stories – and there were thousands like them – were in response to the Pew Religion and Public Life report on the "America's Changing Religious Landscape" (Pew Research Center, 2015). This was based on nationwide surveys in 2007 and 2014 concerning how Americans identified themselves religiously. The comparisons were striking: In a very few years the proportion of those identifying themselves as Christian dropped from 78% to 71%, with each category of Christian

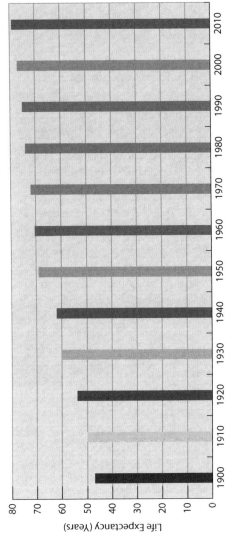

Figure 1.2 Changes in United States Life Expectancy at Birth, 1900–2010
Source: From Arias (2010), United States Life Tables 2006. Reprinted with permission.

faiths (Catholic, Mainline Protestant, Evangelical) losing members. Meanwhile those saying they were unaffiliated had increased from 16% to 23%. Moreover, these trends were very much age-, or cohort-, based: Declines in Christian faith identification were much higher in younger cohorts. Among Millennials, for example, the percentage of unaffiliated was higher than in other age groups (33%), having increased from 24% in 2007. But among those 65+ the unaffiliated represented 13% and 15%, respectively.

Changing U.S. Religious Landscape

Between 2007 and 2014, the Christian share of the population fell from 78.4% to 70.6%, driven mainly by declines among mainline Protestants and Catholics. The unaffiliated experienced the most growth, and the share of Americans who belong to non-Christian faiths also increased.

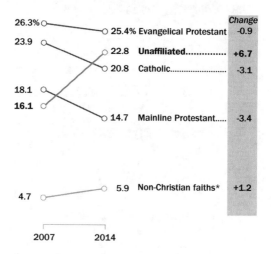

* Includes Jews, Muslims, Buddhists, Hindus, other world religions and other faiths. Those who did not answer the religious identity question, as well as groups whose share of the population did not change signicantly, including the historically black Protestant tradition, Mormons and others, are not shown.

Source: 2014 Religious Landscape Study, conducted June 4-sept, 30,2014

PEW RESEARCH CENTER

Figure 1.3 The Changing American Religious Landscape, 2007 to 2014
Source: Reprinted from the *Pew Research Center,* 2015. Retrieved from http://www.pewforum.org/2015/05/12/americas-changing-religious-landscape/. Copyright (2015) by the Pew Research Center. Reprinted with permission.

However, there are two important aspects of these data that have been primarily ignored and can lead to misinterpretation. First, the focus of data collection was on church membership and attendance, which was interpreted in these survey reports as "religiousness." However, there are many other aspects to religion than belonging to a church or attending its services, so a headline like "Religion on the Decline in the US" may be misleading if based only on church affiliation. Second, the focus of popular attention has been on the younger cohorts in these samples – religion is on the "decline" because a smaller percentage of young persons than in previous years indicate involvement in churches. Another look at these data, however, focusing on respondents who are beyond young adulthood, provides a different message: they are very, very much involved; and since these constitute an increasing majority of Americans, it is not accurate to proclaim that "religion is on the decline." At least not for the foreseeable future.

As can be seen in Figure 1.4, seniors represent the backbone of churches today, forming their most reliable constituency (Pew Research Center, 2015). Of respondents in the 50–64 age range, 38 percent attend religious services at least once a week, with an additional 34 percent once or twice a month or so. Of those 65 or older the number is even higher: 48 percent attend at least once a week, with an additional 25 percent twice a month or so. These are high rates of religious involvement. Religion does not seem to be "dying out" for these people, and they represent a majority of their age demographic group.

There is another factor that should be considered, one not mentioned by the Pew Report authors: maturation effects – change over time during the course of life in religious orientations and expressions. The data reported by the Pew pollsters are cross-sectional, comparing responses of those in one age group – 18 to 35 year olds, for example – to another, in surveys made ten or so years apart. But what if people change, in systematic ways as they grow up and grow older? What about possible trajectories in religiosity across the course of life? Only long-term longitudinal data following individuals through time, not cross-sectional poll data, can provide answers to this.

To sum up: Three worldwide developments are changing the configurations of religion, spirituality, and aging. First, nations today have higher percentages of older people, compared to other age groups, than ever before. Second, people are living longer, and with more years of healthier lives, than ever before. Third, seniors are the most religiously involved of all age groups. And if we take a perspective on religion that encompasses the entire life course, following the life development of individuals as they adapt over time, we may see a different picture than we do when we look at age cohorts in cross-section. What do we know about the religious and spiritual needs of older adults? What are churches and religious organizations doing to meet these needs? We next explore some new developments in this area with data from our own studies.

Attendance at religious services by age group

% of adults who attend religious services...

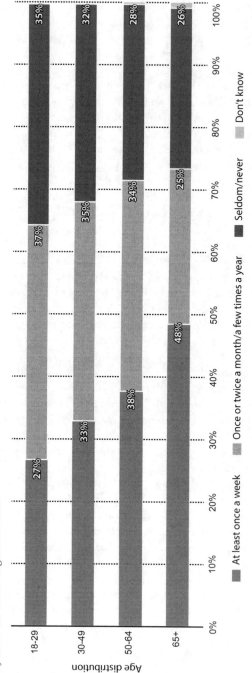

Figure 1.4 Attendance at Religious Services, by Age Group: Percentage of Adults who Attend, by frequency
Source: Reprinted from Pew Research Center, 2015. Retrieved from http://www.pewforum.org/religious-landscape-study/attendance-at-religious-services/. Reprinted with permission.

Religiosity and Cohort Differences Across the Course of Life

Does religiosity increase with age? To what extent does religiosity change after adolescence? Do those who left institutional religion at one time return?

With longitudinal data over a long period, we can see the career of religious expression over the course of life. The survey data by Pew and other studies reported earlier are based on cross-sectional assessments, which are good for showing age *differences*, such as between younger and older birth cohorts, but not age *changes*. In a previous analysis (Bengtson, Silverstein, Putney, & Harris, 2015) we examined the interplay among three time-related effects on religiosity: (1) individual aging and religious development over the life course; (2) cohort influences; and (3) effects of historical trends in religion. Data were from the 35-year Longitudinal Study of Generations (LSOG), which over eight survey waves involved over 3,400 individuals from an original 417 multigenerational families (for details about the design of the study see Bengtson, Putney, & Harris, 2013). These families were recruited in 1969 from a southern California health care plan that served primarily union members (Bengtson, 1975). The original sample was representative of the region's economically stable middle and working class families in the area, though minorities were under represented. Surveys were first mailed to the grandparents (G1s), their adult children (G2s), and then to grandchildren who were age 16 or older (G3s). Data were collected usually in three-year increments. Response rates averaged 80 percent between waves. Starting in 1991 the great-grandchildren (G4s) were recruited into the survey as they reached age 16. To assess changes in religiosity as individuals aged and across historical time we examined both objective and subjective aspects of religiosity: frequency of religious service attendance, self-described religious intensity, and beliefs about the Bible and the place of religion in public life. To assess changes in these three dimensions of religiosity over time we employed a three-level latent growth curve analysis using HLM (for details about procedures see Bengtson et al., 2015). To aid in the interpretation of statistically significant aging patterns by generational cohort we plotted the predicted values. Results are shown in Figures 1.5 and 1.6. (In these figures G1 refers to the oldest generation, those who had an average age of 67 in 1971 at the start of the study; G4 refers to the youngest generation, the Millennials, average age 17 who began entering the panel in 1991.)

The first thing we see in these figures is the complex interplay between age, cohort membership (history), and the different dimensions of religiosity that were measured. This itself is an important lesson from these data. When pollsters and headlines say, "Religion is on the decline!" it is important to ask, "What do you mean by religion? What *part* of religion?" Is it church attendance? Yes, church attendance declines with each succeeding cohort and decreases in later life (Figure 1.6). Intensity of feelings about the importance of religion? No; religious intensity appears in many cases to increase with advancing age (Figure 1.5). And what about Millennials? "Millennials are leaving churches in droves." That is true for their teens and early 20s; *but many are returning when they reach their 30s.* (Figure 1.5). In short, the pattern is varied as individuals grow up and grow old over the course of life.

Second, in each of these dimensions of religiosity we see cohort contrasts, though perhaps not as pronounced as we had anticipated. Younger cohorts had lower rates of religious intensity, religious service attendance, and orthodox religious beliefs than older cohorts. However, this was offset by what was the most surprising result in the study: that *within cohorts, there was a slight increase by age.*

An examination of Figure 1.5 illustrates the complex patterns of religious development and change across the life course. After age 18 there appears a sharp spike downward in religious intensity and religious participation until age 24. Then there is a slight curve upward at about age 28 (perhaps reflecting marriage). Following this there is a spike upward around 30–45 (kids baptized, start Sunday school, bar/bat mitzvah, involvement in church groups). A plateau appears throughout middle age (45–60), then a slight curve upward to about age 70. Finally, we see an increase in the later years of life, something that might be called a "retirement surge in religiosity" (Bengtson et al., 2015).

What does this suggest about the 75 million baby boomers who are steadily moving into their later years? We recently completed a ninth wave

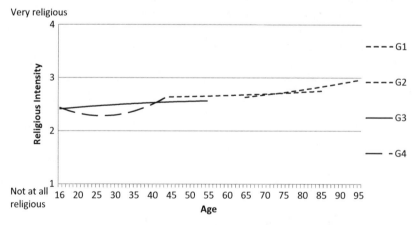

Figure 1.5 Religious Intensity: Trends by Age (Historical Period, Gender, and Education Controlled)
Source: Longitudinal Study of Generations, 1971–2005

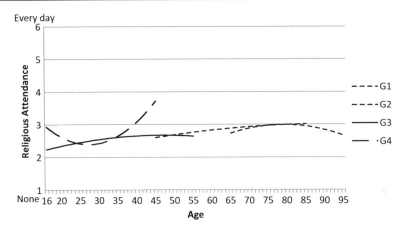

Figure 1.6 Religious Service Attendance: Trends by Age (Historical Period, Gender, Education Controlled)
Source: Longitudinal Study of Generations, 1971–2005

of surveys for the Longitudinal Study of Generations panel, allowing evaluations of religious continuity and change for individuals over 45 years (Silverstein & Bengtson, 2017). In examining the responses of 599 baby boomers in this sample, we found that more than one in five (21%) said they had become more religious during the last ten years. The majority (56%) indicated that their religiosity was stable over the period, while smaller proportions reported a decline in religiosity (11%), and 12% stated that they were never religious. There was a "return to religion" among a significant group of baby boomers.

In short, there are ups and downs in religious expression over the course of life. Religiosity changes after adolescence. Some people increase their religious involvement in the later years of life, many people switch from one religious form to another, and some people come back to religion after not being involved earlier in life.

That there are life-course trajectories of religious involvement and expression should be obvious from longitudinal studies that have followed individuals through the course of time (Dillon and Wink, 2005; Bengtson et al., 2015). Unfortunately, population-based religious research to date (e.g. Pew Research Center, 2015) has been based on cross-sectional surveys comparing younger birth cohorts to older ones, ignoring the fact the people do change with age.

Religious and Spiritual Trajectories in later Life

Several theories have been advanced to explain why later life is a fertile stage for spiritual and religious growth. In Erikson and Erikson's (1998) developmental theory, the last stages of life are characterized by attempts to resolve intrapsychic conflicts between generativity and stagnation, integrity and despair. Individuals who can reflect on their lives and come to terms with themselves attain what Erikson called *ego integrity* in old age. Tornstam (2005) calls the final stage of human development *gerotranscendence*, in which individuals redefine their relationships with themselves, others, and the natural world. These changing relationships lend themselves to activities that promote spiritual growth, such as self-examination and the development of personal credos, the disclosure of inner thoughts and confessions, the relaxation of defenses and concerns, and a more fully present experience of life (Loder, 1998).

In the context of these developmental theories, we wanted to explore how older adults capitalize on the opportunities for spiritual growth and what the role of religion and spirituality is in this development. Examining the varying trajectories of older adults' religious and spiritual development also sheds light on the diversity of individuals' experiences in later life. There have been a growing number of typologies of spirituality developed recently (Ammerman, 2013; Berghuijs, Pieper, & Bakker, 2013; Gall, Malette, & Guirguis-Younger, 2011; Hodge & McGrew, 2006) that suggest that spirituality and religion are not separate binary concepts but instead can be linked and related. These typologies, however, have been developed primarily with samples of young adults. How older adults experience spirituality and religion in later life has been less examined. While many older adults do tend to get more religious with age, as documented above, we know little about how religion and spirituality unfold in later life, and what the variations are. What are the trajectories of older adults' religious development following retirement, and how are religion and spirituality related in later life?

To explore the configuration of older adults' religious and spiritual trajectories, we utilized data from the Religious Development in Later Life study (RDLL) (see Bengtson, Endacott, & Kang, 2017, for details about the methods and procedures of the study). Four samples were involved in this study. First, we contacted clergy from a variety of faiths and interviewed them about aging, spirituality, and the place of older adults in their congregations. At the end of the interview we asked each to provide the names of several members of their congregations who might also be interviewed. This created a second sample, older individuals who were active members of congregations. Third, we also wanted to include older adults who were not affiliated with a religious organization, so we contacted some leaders of the local Humanist Society to obtain names of those who might be interviewed. A fourth group came from in-depth interviews with members of the Longitudinal Study of Generation panel who had responded to the wave-9 survey (Silverstein, & Bengtson, 2017). This resulted in a total sample of 112 older adults in the study, the characteristics of which are summarized in Table 1.1.

For the analysis of religious and spiritual trajectories among older adults, we examined data from only the older individuals who were members of congregations at this time (n = 67). Using the grounded theory method (Glaser & Strauss, 1967), we were able to identify six trajectories of older adults' spiritual and religious change that emerged from the data.

Increase in Both Religious Involvement and Spirituality

The most commonly seen type of religious and spiritual trajectory (n = 28/67) was an increase in both religious involvement (attending church, joining religious groups, or holding leadership positions in the congregation) as well as spiritual involvement (practices of meditation or prayer, for instance). Kevin (age 67, Evangelical) exemplified this trajectory. He said he has become more involved with his church's men's ministry since retirement and has also become more spiritually mature. He said, "I started slowly but surely getting more active and more involved... it wasn't like all at once, it sort of gradually stacked. But my heart was changed." Kevin and others who represented this trajectory discussed both outward changes in their religious behavior and inward changes in their spiritual life.

Increase in Religious Involvement, but Not in Spirituality

Another trajectory involved an increase in religious involvement but not in spiritual expression or practice. Some said that they had more time afforded by retirement and that they participated more frequently in religious activities (attending classes offered by their church or lectures

Table 1.1 Sample Characteristics of Older Adult Respondents

Religious Tradition	Age (Avg.)	Sex		Education (Years)	Marital Status				N
		M	F		S	W	M	D	
Black Protestant	76	5	8	15	1	3	8	1	13
Evangelical	75	9	13	15.7	1	0	16	5	22
Mainline Protestant	74.5	6	14	17	0	4	11	5	20
Jewish	84.5	3	6	17.1	1	2	6	0	9
Catholic	78.5	6	7	16	0	4	7	3	13
Unitarian/Other	77.4	6	7	18	1	0	11	0	13
Unaffiliated	69.8	8	14	17.2	1	1	13	7	22
Total	74.6	38	61	16.4	4	11	64	20	112

Table 1.2 Sample Characteristics of Clergy Respondents

Religious Tradition	Age (Avg.)	Sex		Education (Years)	Marital Status				N
		M	F		S	W	M	D	
Black Protestant	56.8	5	0	18.5	0	0	5	0	5
Evangelical	56.4	6	1	16.6	0	0	7	0	7
Mainline Protestant	54.3	5	2	20.7	0	0	6	1	7
Jewish	42	1	1	18	1	1	0	0	2
Catholic	66.7	6	0	18.8	6	0	0	0	6
Unitarian/Other	60	2	1	18.3	0	1	2	0	3
Total	57.43	25	5	18.2	7	2	20	1	30

sponsored by their temple) compared to earlier. When asked about changes in her religious involvement in later life, Shirley (72, Jewish Reform) said, "I'm learning more about Judaism now because I have the time." Shirley is highly involved in Jewish education classes and temple events, much more so than when she was younger. Unlike respondents who reported both an increase in religious involvement and an experience of spiritual growth, these respondents did not discuss an increase in spiritual practices.

Increase or an Evolving Sense of Spirituality, but Not in Religious Involvement

A third trajectory involved an increase in spiritual life and use of spiritual practices but without an increase in religious involvement in a congregation. Louise (76, Episcopalian) noticed a change in her spirituality as connected to her relationship with God. She said, "I feel my Lord is an experience now, not just something coming out of a book." Others discussed an increase in spiritual practices now that they had more time since retirement. James (74, Evangelical) said, "I now have a much more regular time for personal devotion because of the greater availability of time." These respondents cited the greater availability of time in later life to cultivate their personal spirituality and practice spiritual disciplines (meditation or Bible reading, for example), usually apart from their congregations.

Continuity, Little or No Change in Religious or Spiritual Engagement

The fourth trajectory was marked by continuity, in which no dramatic changes occurred in religious or spiritual engagement. Respondents said they had stayed the same or had slowly increased or grown "stronger" in their faith. For example, when asked about changes in his religious and spiritual involvement, Alexander (74, Catholic) said, "It's been steady."

Increase in Spirituality and Religious Involvement but in a Different Environment

These respondents discussed an increase in religious and spiritual connection, but discussed their involvement in denominations or religious traditions that were different from the tradition in which they were raised or where they practiced earlier in life. Almost all discussed being drawn to a more open and less dogmatic tradition where they felt more at ease. After attending Mainline Protestant churches, Roland (80, Unity) was drawn to the Unity churches at age 60. He said, "I was delighted that apparently, they did away with the Apostles' Creed and the Trinity. They've got a newer version that I can get into. It's much more accepting. Spirituality is much, much broader, and for some people it's just the recognition of marvelous life all around them."

Decrease, Reflecting a Turning Away or Decrease in Religiosity

Some older adults discussed a decrease in their religious and spiritual involvement, though this was discussed least frequently in our sample. While one respondent reported a clear decrease in interest in both religious and spiritual development, five other respondents discussed decreases but their trajectories were more complex. For example, some respondents said that they decreased in their religious attendance but that their spiritual involvement did not follow suit. For example, Susan (80, Unitarian) explained that she cannot participate in her congregation as much as she would like because of her health. She said, "I don't care to go out at night. I'm not as nimble as I was, I'm not as stable as I was, so I don't participate as much. But my heart will always be there, even if I can't go there." Others felt burnt-out from church involvement and stepped down from leadership positions, though they continued to attend services. Joseph (72, Evangelical) said that he and his wife would step back from leadership positions at church because "I think we've paid our dues." But for Morgan (81, Unitarian), religious participation in his local congregation was not his priority. He said, "I'd rather read the *New York Times* as much as I could on Sunday and try to do the crossword puzzle than go down there and stagger to my feet to sing hymns."

These typologies, based on extensive interviews, indicate first the varying ways that older adults arrive at their complex expressions of religion and spirituality. Second, they suggest that it is inappropriate to stereotype older individuals as being the same as they once were, as not changed from middle adulthood. Third, and equally important, older adults are not all alike in religious and spiritual expressions, and not as similar as others in their age cohort as large-scale surveys might suggest.

Furthermore, being aware of the varieties of religious and spiritual expression in later life may help churches and religious organizations to better minister to their senior members. To what extent are churches and religious organizations aware of the preferences and needs of their older members? What programs are they most likely to have that serve these older congregants, and how well are they serving them?

Clergy, Older Congregation Members, and Ageism in Churches

In the RDLL study we wanted to explore the perceptions of clergy regarding the roles of older individuals in their congregations and the programs or opportunities in place to serve them. We also wanted to get their thoughts about what changes congregations might make in order to best serve their growing senior populations. We recruited clergy from major Judeo-Christian faith traditions (Evangelical, Mainline Protestant, Black Protestant, Roman Catholic, Jewish, Unitarian, Quaker) sampled from areas in southern California. Table 1.2 summarizes characteristics of the clergy in our sample.

We collected data through semi-structured, in-depth interviews with these clergy. We asked questions that were like those in the older adults' interviews. This allowed us to compare answers between the two groups, which revealed many similarities as well as some striking disparities.

"Of Course We Have Programs for Seniors!" (But They Are for the Frail)

Clergy were asked whether their congregations provided any specific programs or activities for older adults, and if so, what kind. Most quickly responded that they had senior-related programs. But characteristic was the responses of Rev. Hammond (Episcopalian) "We have pastoral visitors who are commissioned to go and do visits with people who are sick or shut-in" and Rev. Ware (Episcopalian) "So, we do provide a parish nurse who primarily works with older people." In other words, the programs were for frail or homebound elders, such as transportation to and from services, meal deliveries, or medical assistance.

However, many clergy, as well as many congregants, responded that their congregations offered other kinds of services and activities involving seniors. Some were social programs, such as luncheons or organized outings; others were religious programs, such as Sunday school classes or Bible studies for seniors. There were also "de facto" groups that were comprised primarily of older adults but were not formally designated for seniors. It was striking that two-thirds of the clergy, and two-thirds of the congregants, responded that these current offerings were insufficient, and that churches and synagogues should be doing more for seniors.

Differences in Perceptions of Age and Aging

Perhaps the most significant difference between clergy and congregation members involved their perceptions of age and aging. From clergy we heard about ministries directed towards those who were ill, instead of those who were aging (blankets for cancer patients, matzo ball soup for the ill, and communion for the hospital-bound). We heard much less reflecting the fact that most older adults lead vibrant and active lives.

From the older adults themselves, however, we got a different perspective. While they also mentioned the need for services for homebound seniors, many decried the assumption that frailty always accompanies older age. They expressed frustration with this stereotype. Some expressed concern that healthy older adults were "invisible" in congregational life. Eleanor (79, Catholic) described feeling as though seniors were "overlooked" because church leadership assumed "they go to church already so we don't even have to approach them." Charlotte (65), a Methodist, gave the example of her mother, now in her 90s and still active, living by herself and driving to church where she still participates. Charlotte felt frustrated by the way her mother was "invisible" to the church because, though aged, she's not infirm:

> I wish they would pay more attention to her because she's not a shut-in. She falls in this category, well, she shows up… it would be great if somebody would just come by and visit a little. So, you know, there's provision for the infirmed or the perception of someone being shut off, but just for kind of regular people who… I don't know… pay more attention to them.

Other congregants felt that the spiritual challenges and developments of later life were similarly "invisible" or overlooked by churches and synagogues. They noted that support and guidance is provided for significant moments in adolescence and young adulthood (bar/bat mitzvahs, confirmations, marriages) but there is nothing equivalent offered for similar events in later life (retirement, widowhood). Marjorie (69, Mormon) explained, "We assume that you get to a certain age and you've just got it all figured out, and then we really just need to concentrate on those teenagers." Carol (77, Catholic) hoped her church would start offering programs designed to address the spiritual challenges of later life:

> It's all about the youth, you know, keep the youth, help the youth, they're the future of the church and everything. … But what about the elderly? What about all our experiences? Those of us that need help, you know, we can talk to each other about something. "Oh, my God! You mean you went through the same thing I did? How did you work through that?" Something like that.

Another contrast between clergy and older congregants had to do with recognition for the contributions of seniors. Vivian (83, Evangelical) said, "I think there's a failure to acknowledge old people as having wisdom or as still having a place." She said she planned to discuss ideas with her pastors for how her congregation could "better serve the old people." Few of the clergy we interviewed spontaneously mentioned the need for churches to capitalize on the wisdom and experience of older persons. Moreover, some older respondents described instances where they felt alienated by church leadership because of their age, sometimes as the result of more youth-oriented services.

Ageism in Congregations and Clergy

An explicit awareness of ageism was a troubling issue that surfaced in some of the interviews. By far the majority of these older members were intensely loyal to their clergy and to their congregations. Nevertheless, some said they had felt isolated and even alienated because of messages from the clergy themselves. Kevin (67, Evangelical) said that he switched churches when his former church replaced the older pastor with a younger one and began being more "youth-driven" in their ministry. He said, "We weren't the only ones in the church, but we sensed that we were no longer relevant." Anthony (78), Evangelical, said that his pastor made a sarcastic joke about the senior group when announcing church activities from the pulpit. Anthony said, "The mentality has to change in the administration of the church." His wife added, "And what's funny is we've been told that we are the most vibrant group in the church." Another congregant noted that the older age group represented the greatest financial supporters of the church but received no credit for this. Such experiences illustrate discrepancies between clergy and congregants. Though clergy members were sincere in expressing the desire to serve their older members, many members felt that church leadership ignored or was unaware of their needs.

If churches and synagogues hope to adequately meet the needs of the older adults in their congregations, both explicit and implicit forms of ageism will have to be addressed. Our research suggests that the first step might be to recognize that "senior" is not synonymous with "frail" and that the needs of a healthy and vibrant recent retiree are very different than those of a 96-year-old cancer patient; the one-adult-age-group-for-all model will not work.

Programs for Seniors that Seem to Work

One of the most successful alternative models of programming for active seniors was that in Rev. Kirby's (Presbyterian) church. Similar to what Knapp, Beaver, & Reed (2010) have recommended, this congregation offered multiple groups for older adults organized loosely around generational cohort and activity level. One group, "Presby Folks," was for active early retirees and offered evening socials once a month; a second, the "Adventurers," was for people in their 70s and 80s and offered a monthly luncheon and program. And finally, the church offered a Friday senior program for people in their 80s and 90s. These age cohort social groups have been together for a number of years and have grown old together. Having groups with innovative names (as opposed to simply a "seniors group") seems to have allowed older adults of all different activity levels and ages to find a meaningful place in the community – and made it clear that being retired is not equivalent to being frail.

Such programs would likely be more appealing to individuals 65+ who do not self-identify as "seniors" or "older adults" such as Nia (89, AME) or Marian (78, Episcopalian). Nia took offense at a question and exclaimed "I wouldn't call us old age!" and Marian informed her interviewer "I don't think I'm old." Choosing a neutral name without potential negative connotations would be an important step towards engaging such congregants. Congregations seeking to adopt such a model could form similar cohorts based groups when their members are at an earlier stage in adulthood. The specific programming offered by each group could then change as the needs of its associated cohort changed, providing members with meaningful support throughout the many stages of older adulthood.

Additionally, seniors who participated in mentorship programs were less likely to report feeling invisible or overlooked. While technically ministries *made up of* seniors rather than ministries *for* seniors, they provided older adults with a sense of purpose and value. In some cases, these programs were highly structured. Dean (77, Evangelical) found it incredibly meaningful to participate in a formal program that paired older adults with men in their 20s struggling with addiction. Other times, the mentoring was more informal and took place at intergenerational small groups or scriptural study classes. Both Pastor Turner and Pastor Carver's AME churches offered such small groups where older adults were valued for their experience and consulted by younger congregants. As Pastor Carver observed, the senior attendees "edify younger persons, just by sharing what they've been through and many of them have the gift of mentorship, in terms of working and grooming younger people."

Many of the older adults whose churches did not offer such opportunities for ministry explicitly requested them. Eleanor (79, Catholic) thought it would be wonderful if churches offered a "Little Grandmothers" program modeled after Big Brothers/Big Sisters where seniors would be paired up with younger adults to their mutual benefit. Marie (82, Presbyterian) wanted to see seniors paired specifically with small children to whom they could read stories after church. Nora (Evangelical) did not outline a specific program but urged clergy to start paying attention to seniors and "encouraging them, asking them if they don't want to mentor some younger people or to teach a Bible study or looking for ways to make them feel useful and to benefit from all that's been sown into their lives."

Regardless of what model of programming is chosen, our research makes it clear that congregations need to recognize that "senior" is not synonymous with "frail" and "retirement" is not synonymous with "stagnation." Aging is a dynamic process and older adults have a need for spiritual guidance and support – but they also have a great deal of wisdom and talent to share. If churches and synagogues are going to start recognizing that a "105-year-old person is just as important as that 15-year-old" as Joseph (72, Evangelical) hopes, they will need to be attentive to both what seniors need and what they have to offer.

Older Adults Who Are Nonreligious: Atheists, Humanists, and Others

Thus far we have focused on older adults who are religious and the clergy serving these congregants. But what about the growing number of individuals who do not identify themselves with any religion? Who are the unaffiliated older individuals, and how do they articulate their viewpoints and beliefs as they age and face the end of life?

The population of Americans who say they are of "no religion" has grown rapidly in the last decades. In 2017, 27% of all Americans identified themselves as non-religious. Of those above the age of 65 there were 17% who said they were nonreligious – an increase of 3% since 2012 (Pew Research Center, 2017). As the baby boomer generation continues to age it is important to research not only those who are religiously involved but also those who have dropped out or have never been involved in religion.

The analysis to follow is based on in-depth interviews with 20 non-affiliated older adults in our sample (see Table 1.1). Members of this group were varied in how they identified themselves: nine said they were Atheist, six Agnostic, and five "other" including two Humanists, a Pagan, a Materialist, and one "cultural but not religious" Jew. We focused our analysis on questions such as the following: How do these nonreligious seniors make meaning out of life in the absence of religious creeds and institutions? How have they coped with issues surrounding suffering and death? How have they dealt with the stigma of being nonreligious while living in one of the world's most religious countries?

Making Meaning

Science and rational thought are the means by which many nonreligious seniors made sense of their lives as well as the prospect of death. Many participants said they relied on scientific knowledge, notions of rationality, and ideas about the natural universe to explain death and dying. Mary, age 68, felt that "God is something that people who aren't science-oriented use to explain the world and to make themselves feel better with the whole life after death thing." When talking about death, Vincent, 73, said,

> When I die, that energy leaves the body. It's sort of like an electronic zap which becomes part of the buzzing universe. I believe in the principle of conservation of energy, so I think that after I'm dead there will be some energy there, but it will not have a personal identity. It's just goes in part of the energy pool, another electron in that great energy pool of the universe.

Sylvia, age 70, who grew up as a Mormon, reported, "I see death as the flower out there that died and its ashes help create nutrition for the rest of land. That's [death] just a natural thing. This planet, however old it is, all these things are born, and then die and are born, and then die. It's a natural cycle and ideally we do provide nutrition for the next living thing."

Several said they relied on science as their religion. As Sylvia put it, "That's my religion– science. It's something real, and while we may not get to the end of it, it's thrilling, [like] every time they create a bigger, larger telescope that they're sending out into the universe. So instead of making churches tax free I wish they would do that for science to promote more science." Some rejected ideas of religion that did not make sense to them in light of science, such as the notion of a God that intervened in the life of humans. Edward, 73, is a Humanist who said:

> I accept all the scientific notions of the behavior of the planetary system, behavior of the universe and the globular clusters and all that, all the way down to the behavior of you and I and tiny atoms. All that science works for me. Humanism has a wide variety of definitions, but one of them is, do you believe in rationality and science and the application of science to man's problems? That man is the only one that's going to solve his problem? God's not going to reach down.

Death and Suffering

In his research, Zuckerman (2012) noted how easily his non-religious respondents seemed to accept death and dying. In our study, we also found our non-religious seniors talking about death with easy acceptance. Marcie, age 69, said, "I think the thing that is meaning more and more to me now, as an older person, is an increasing acceptance of death being part of life. It's a sense of the inevitability that I will die, but it doesn't feel wrong anymore." Jane, 88 years old with a life-threatening disease, recounted a conversation with her social worker:

She [the social worker] said, "But, Jane, what are you going to do? You can't just die alone?" I said, "Why can't I die alone? Where does it say one must have company while you're dying?" She said, "But how will we know?" I said, "You won't know." She said, "What are you going to do when you need help?" I said, "The same thing I do any-time I need help. I call hospice."

Jane was asserting her independence in dying and her right to die alone.

Although accepting of death, some expressed fears about the pain and suffering that might accompany the dying process, and others mentioned concerns about loved ones during that process. Or as Naomi, age 63, put it, "I'm not afraid of the death. I'm more afraid being a burden on somebody." Vincent said:

I hope the dying process goes really fast. I'd like to put it off as long as I can, but I hope it goes fast. I just don't want to be a pain in the butt to people ...I'll become more dependent and it'll be a pain in the butt for my wife to take care of me and I hope that that period of time isn't too long. I'm not afraid to die. I love living. I certainly want to live, but I don't want to be a real burden.

Frank (85) shared these fears, saying, "I'm concerned about illness, you know? One of the problems of dying is how you die. It's nice to go quickly and not have time to say goodbye. I asked my doctor, 'If I ask for help in dying, medication of some kind, would you provide it?'"

Morality, Sense of Purpose, and Hypocrisy

A frequently voiced stereotype about those who are not part of a religion is that they have a questionable sense of morality. Many studies, however, have demonstrated that a system of morality and ethics is unrelated to a belief in God (Zuckerman, 2014). Several of our respondents made clear that they found moral standards and a sense of purpose in life in alternative systems. Naomi, age 63, used to be an observant Jew but dropped out later in life. She said, "I don't feel I need it. I feel God is inside me and I feel I'm a good person and I follow my own set of rules, and I don't feel I need organized religion." Frank (85) said he relied on science: "Personally, I find that Darwinism and science in general is a tremendously valuable belief system." In this instance, we see the theme of science as important in developing a moral belief system.

Several of our non-religious respondents suggested that it is those in religious institutions who are the ones with a questionable sense of morality. They saw religion and religious people as hypocritical (Putnam & Campbell, 2010; Baker & Smith, 2009; Baker, 2012; Zuckerman, 2012). Mary (68), who had been a church member previously, said both she and her husband "found the early life experience of religion to be oppressive and even more to be hypocritical, and so antithetical to religious ideas where behavior doesn't match ideals or principles or tenets."

Moreover, religion doesn't bring clarity to what is moral and ethical. Sheila, age 65, said:

> I have trouble reconciling the good and evil in the world, how that coexists, the light and darkness that don't go away. It's hard for me to feel like there's the karma or good acts or good thoughts or whatever lead to good results, they don't sometimes. People get put in concentration camps; they get killed; they get tortured for, I believe, no fault of their own. So, I don't get how it works. Children die young. That shouldn't happen.

Stigma, Persecution and Community

Some of the individuals in our sample grew up in religious homes (five of the 20) but chose to leave their religious upbringings. Many of them now often feel stigmatized for being non-religious, particularly those who identified themselves as Atheists, Pagans, or Humanists. Some atheists felt that they could not be open about being Atheist unless they were with like-minded people. When asked about her religion, Sylvia (70) said, "Depends on who asks me. If it's somebody I know well I'm an atheist. Somebody that I don't know well, that I've just met I just say I'm am a non-believer or agnostic, but I really am a committed Atheist." Frank, 85, said, "Atheist; but Atheism is a bad word. At least in America it's a bad word because it's associated with Communism."

For many Americans, churches provide needed community and social support, and this is beneficial to older congregants. Non-religious communities such as the Humanist Society also provide community and support for older adults, though they are much less visible than churches. They provide affirmation for non-traditional views. Pamela, 64, recalls, "When did I join the Humanists? '04, I think. Because prior to that it was like a dirty word. It was like saying you were a witch or something (laughs). Until I got into a club where I felt safe coming out." Mary, age 68, said, "Most of this group came together because they didn't feel comfortable sharing their beliefs or non-beliefs with other people without being ridiculed or looked down on or feeling odd, or not fitting. At least that was one of the reasons that I felt really comfortable in this group."

To sum up: The nonreligious older individuals in our study demonstrated many ways of making meaning out of life and death without a god or organized religion. Chief among these mechanisms was a confidence in science and in human rationality. None of these respondents evidenced any fear of death, though they were concerned by the prospect of burdening loved ones through the dying process. Most articulated a moral code that involved giving back and community involvement. Though some faced stigma and discrimination for their atheism, they found ways to cope with this by finding other like-minded individuals and communities.

Summary and Conclusion

How is aging related to religion and spirituality? Over the past century three worldwide developments – revolutions might be a more appropriate term – have changed previous configurations of age and religiosity. Individuals are living longer than ever before; societies have higher percentages of older people than ever before; and in the rapidly altering religious landscape around the world, seniors – including the huge baby boom cohorts as they age – represent the most religiously involved of all age groups.

In our research we have been examining questions emerging from these trends. Does religiosity increase with age? Data from our 45-year Longitudinal Study of Generations indicates that as religious intensity increases though church attendance does not. From intensive interviews with older members of churches and synagogues we identified six types of religious trajectories in later adulthood, from older individuals who reported an increase in both spirituality and religious involvement to those who have turned away from religion altogether.

To what extent are churches, with their youth-centric focus, meeting the needs of their growing numbers of older members? We compared responses of older congregation members with interviews from their pastors, priests, and rabbis. Most clergy equated seniors with frailty, while most of the older adults suggested the need for programs reflecting their more active interests and spiritual needs, and some identified ageism in their churches.

How do non-religious older adults create meaning in the absence of religious dogma? We interviewed nonaffiliated older adults, finding numerous examples of those who engage in non-theistic meaning-making. Many looked to science and rational thought instead of religious dogma in making sense out of death and suffering, morality and a sense of purpose, stigma and persecution.

These findings have important implications for researchers, leaders of religious organizations, and older individuals themselves. There are 75 million aging baby boomers in America today, many of whom say they are intensifying their religious and spiritual involvement (Silverstein & Bengtson, 2017). Yet in both congregations and religious research there has been a lack of sufficient attention to emerging developments in aging, religion, and spirituality. As individuals are living longer, their religious and spiritual lives are extending. Their religious careers change from youth into mid-life to later adulthood. After retirement, they have more time, more money, and often more passion than younger age groups. They are spiritually curious elders. They could be the source of revitalization for many congregations. But are congregations aware of this? Are churches paying any attention to the swell of aging boomers? All too often it appears that the answer is "no." And therein lies some peril for the churches of tomorrow.

References

Ammerman, N. (2013). Spiritual but not religious? Beyond binary choices in the study of religion. *Journal for the Scientific Study of Religion*, 52(2), 258–278.

Arias, E. (2010). United States life tables, 2006. *National Vital Statistics Reports*, 58 (21), 1–40.

Baker, J. (2012). Public perceptions of incompatibility between 'science and religion'. *Public Understanding of Science*, 21(3).

Baker, J., & Smith, B. G. (2009). The nones: social characteristics of the religiously unaffiliated. *Social Forces*, 87(3), 1251–1263.

Bengtson, V. L. (1975). Generation and family effects in value socialization. *American Sociological Review*, 40(3), 358–371.

Bengtson, V. L., Endacott, C., & Kang, S. L. C. (2017). Clergy and older adults: Contrasts in perceptions between seniors and their clergy. *Journal of Spirituality, Religion, and Aging.* doi:10.1080/15528030.2017.141427

Bengtson, V. L. (with Putney, N. S., & Harris, S. C.) (2013). *Families and Faith: How Religion is Passed Down Across Generations.* New York/London: Oxford University Press.

Bengtson, V. L., Silverstein, M. S., Putney, N. S., and Harris, S. C. (2015). Does religiosity increase with age? Age changes and age differences over 35 years. *Journal of the Scientific Study of Religion*, 54(2), 363–379.

Berghuijs, J., Pieper, J., & Bakker, C. (2013). Conceptions of spirituality among the Dutch population. *Archive for the Psychology of Religion*, 35, 369–397.

Burke, D. (2015, May 14). Millennials leaving church in droves, study finds. *CNN.* Retrieved from http://www.cnn.com/2015/05/12/living/pew-religion-study/index.html

Colby, S. L., & Ortman, J. M. (2014) Current Population Reports. *The Baby Boom Cohort in the United States: 2012 to 2060. Population Estimates and Projections.* US Department of Commerce, United States Census Bureau. Retrieved from http s://www.census.gov/prod/2014pubs/p25-1141.pdf

Dillon, M., & Wink, P. (2005) *In the Course of a Lifetime: Tracing Religious Belief, Practice, and Change.* Berkeley and Los Angeles: University of California Press.

Erber, J. P. (2015). *Aging and Older Adulthood* (3rd ed.). New York: Wiley.

Erikson, E. H., & Erikson, J. M. (1998). *The Life Cycle Completed: Extended Version.* New York, NY: W. W. Norton.

Gall, T. L., Malette, J., & Guirguis-Younger, M. (2011). Spirituality and religiousness: A diversity of definitions. *Journal of Spirituality in Mental Health*, 13, 158–181.

Glaser, B. G., & Strauss, A. L. (1967). *The Discovery of Grounded Theory: Strategies for Qualitative Research.* Chicago: Aldine de Gruyter.

Hodge, D. R., & McGrew, C. (2006). Spirituality, religion, and the interrelationship: A nationally representative study. *Journal of Social Work Education*, 42(3), 637–654.

Knapp, J. L., Beaver, L. M., & Reed, T. D. (2010). Perceptions of the elderly among ministers and ministry students: Implications for seminary curricula. *Educational Gerontology*, 28(4), 313–324. doi:10.1080/036012702753590424

Loder, J. E. (1998). *The Logic of the Spirit: Human Development in Theological Perspective*. San Francisco: Jossey-Bass.

Lauter, D. & Branson-Potts, H. (2015, May 12). U.S. has become notably less Christian, major study finds. *LA Times*. Retrieved from http://www.latimes.com/nation/la-na-us-religion-20150512-story.html

Pew Research Center (2015). America's changing religious landscape. Retrieved from http://www.pewforum.org/2015/05/12/americas-changing-religious-landscape/

Pew Research Center. (2017). More Americans now say they're spiritual but not religious. Retrieved from http://www.pewresearch.org/fact-tank/2017/09/06/more-americans-now-say-theyre-spiritual-but-not-religious/.

Putnam, D. & Campbell, D. (2010). *American Grace: How Religion Divides and United Us*. New York: Simon and Schuster.

TornstamL. (2005). *Gerotranscendence: A Developmental Theory of Positive Aging*. New York: Springer.

Silverstein, M., & Bengtson, V. L. (2017). Return to religion? Predictors of religious change among baby boomers in their transition to later life. *Journal of Population Ageing, 6*(3). doi:10.1007/s12062-017-9216-0

Zuckerman, P. (2012). *Faith No More: Why People Reject Religion*. New York: Oxford University Press.

Zuckerman, P. (2014). *Living the Secular Life*. New York: Penguin Press.

Chapter 2

The Current Landscape of American Religion
Diversity, Individuation, and the Implications for an Aging Population

Rhys H. Williams

LOYOLA UNIVERSITY, CHICAGO

Religion is a vast and vibrant part of American society, continually evolving as the American people change. This makes generalizations somewhat hazardous, as our society continues to expand and diversify, and religion does as well. However, one can identify a few overall trends in the religious field in the United States, some part of deep historical patterns and some more recent. These form the context in which any particular set of developments in religion, spirituality, and aging can occur.

This chapter will argue that the major development in contemporary American religion is the *intersection of "diversity" and "individuation."* Each of these two processes, and the two together, are producing ever more options for Americans in terms of: (1) organizational commitment; and (2) religious beliefs and practices. People have more religious options from which to choose, and more autonomy to make such choices in terms of their individual wants, needs, and preferences. And in turn, diversification and individuation are putting ever more pressure on Americans to understand and legitimate their religious involvement along those lines. More options are available, and there is more expectation that people will make choices for themselves.

In terms of religious traditions, there is more diversity within the United States than ever before, with substantial numbers of Muslims, Hindus, Buddhists, and religious "nones" now a part of the population in addition to ever more variations of Christianity and Judaism. Moreover, within each tradition there are more options based on more cultural varieties of religious practice; so, for example, Orthodox Christians can find Russian, and Greek, and Ukrainian Orthodox communities in many major cities, or there are congregations of Sunni, Shi'a, and Sufi Muslims. This expands the opportunities to tailor various aspects of the religious tradition in order to fit

Acknowledgements I thank Vern Bengtson and Merril Silverstein for comments on the first draft, and I thank Ryan Wong for invaluable research assistance.

commitment and practice to one's individual situation. Thus, there is more religious "hybridity," and more cultural pressures for individuals to fit traditions to themselves in the quest for religious and personal "authenticity." For new American immigrants of many religious backgrounds, this proliferation of options has often led to clear generational tensions between the first and second/third generations in terms of how they practice their faith.

But even native-born American Christians, who continue to be a majority in the country, are not immune to the processes of diversification and individuation. For example, there are increasingly fewer people in the pews of religious congregations, as even those who continue to identify with a denomination or tradition seem increasingly likely to believe that organizational involvement is optional (Chaves, 2017). In addition, less authority is being granted to denominational authority structures and religious traditions by people who are in the pews (Chaves, 2017). Increasing numbers of people consider themselves "spiritual but not religious;" while the numbers of such folks may be small overall, they are increasing and they come from demographics that once were the bulwark support populations for traditional congregations (Chaves, 2017). Finally, there are millions of regular congregational members who carefully sift their faith's religious teachings, incorporating some into their own belief system but paying little attention to others. All this is challenging the ways in which religious organizations work, and what it means to call oneself "religious."

Finally, in considering these trends and their effects on religion, spirituality, and aging, an important contextual factor is that American society has been experiencing increasing generational segregation (Hagestad & Uhlenberg, 2005; Uhlenberg & De Jong Gierveld, 2004). For over a century educational institutions have been sorted by age cohorts. Combined with ever-faster trends in pop culture, from music to slang, the age-range of peer cohort narrows. Also, family structures are decreasingly multi-generational (Bengtson, 2001), and even residential neighborhoods are not immune to this process. While there may be a recent surge in post-college twenty-somethings returning to their parents' homes for a few years, family groupings are nonetheless smaller than they once were. This is especially true as people age, as older Americans are increasingly likely to be living with age and generational peers rather than with extended multi-generational kin. Research has shown that age segregation has implications in terms of both belief and practice for young adult religiosity; this chapter will help set the stage for the essays in this volume that consider whether this is also true for those who are aging.

In sum, this chapter discusses the religious and cultural context for studying religion, aging, and spirituality by considering the dynamics of diversity, individuation, and their interaction in the religious landscape, reviewing recent sociological data to make the case.

Diversity

The increasing diversity in American religion is unmistakable. One consistent source of religious diversity is the increasing number of immigrants to the United States in the last 30–40 years, and the different religions represented in those groups of newcomers. As a number of scholars have documented (Portes & Rumbaut, 2014; Prothero, 2006; Warner & Wittner, 1998; Wuthnow, 2005) the changes in immigration policy in 1965 altered both the number of immigrants arriving legally and the regions from which those migrants originate. After a half-century of discouraging immigration from Eastern and Southern Europe, Africa, and even longer from Asia, the 1965 Hart-Cellers Act opened up those regions to legal immigration. And while the law placed some restrictions on Latin American immigration that had not been there previously (Zolberg, 2008), other aspects of the new policies, and the economic situation facing many Latin American countries, encouraged renewed immigration from Western Hemispheric nations.

The result, since the 1970s, has been numbers of immigrants from Asian nations unlike anything previously in American history. The increases have been notable for Chinese and Korean immigrants, people from Vietnam and Thailand, and South Asian immigrants from India and Pakistan. Not surprisingly, this has produced numbers of Muslims, Hindus, and Buddhists in the United States unlike ever before. Current estimates are that there are about 3.3 million Muslims (about 1% of the population), 3.8 million Buddhists (about 1.2%), and about 2.2 million Hindus (about 0.8%) in the US (Mohamed, 2016; Pew Research Center, 2014). Further, events in Eastern Europe that occurred shortly after the changes in immigration policy restrictions led to increased numbers of Polish and Russian Jewish immigrants. The Jewish community remains about 2% of the American population.

These numbers are difficult to state with precision, as the U.S. census does not ask about religion, and reports of numbers by religious groups themselves are notoriously unreliable, and also vary by the definition of religious "member." Some religious traditions include children, others do not. Some are more likely than others to include significant numbers of people who are nominally or "culturally" Jewish or Hindu or whatever, without being particularly religiously observant. Further, not all the non-Christian diversity comes through immigration. About 20–25% of American Muslims are African American, and Buddhism includes large numbers of American (usually white) converts.

This diversity is experienced differentially. It is more likely in urban places than rural or small towns, more likely on either coast than in the Mountain West or the South. Thus, for those native-born Christians who live around groups of Muslims, Hindus, or Buddhists, their overall small numbers in the population will probably seem surprising. And indeed the numbers are growing. But it will be a while until the numbers get large enough to be reflected in random national surveys without specific targeting or weighting of the samples. At present, we know that non-Christian religious diversity is growing, and culturally significant, but still numerically fairly small.

The first generation of these post-1965 non-Christian immigrant groups is aging, while many of the second generation are now starting their own families and producing a third generation. Soon, American Muslims, Hindus, and Buddhists will begin to face issues of aging that American Christians and Jews have for some time—how to understand and accommodate the ways in which religious practice changes with age, retirement, and eventual infirmity.

While the changes in American religious demographics since the 1970s are in many ways dramatic, it is important to recognize that religious diversity is in fact an old story in national life. The key is to recognize what becomes considered "diversity" in any given historical period. Many of the earliest groups of English and Western European settlers to the New World were fairly homogenous ethno-religious groups—and often determined to keep their new colonies that way. Thus, Puritan Massachusetts persecuted religious dissenters, and there were debates as to whether African slaves or Native Americans were even candidates for religious conversion (e.g., whether they actually had "souls" to save). But in a thinly settled land, with ever increasing numbers of new arrivals from Europe, enforcing such uniformity proved difficult. The first challenges to religious unity in Massachusetts were Baptists and Quakers in the early 18th century (Demerath & Williams, 1992), but religious minorities and the non-religious either migrated to more tolerant Rhode Island or Pennsylvania, or to the "frontier" of western Massachusetts, then New York.

The Scot-Irish groups that immigrated through the Carolinas and other mid-Atlantic regions in the early national period brought yet another type of Protestantism (Fischer, 1989; Hatch, 1989) to the country—one increasingly focused on personal experience and individual commitment rather than covenanted communities and doctrinal traditions. Communalist groups such as German Moravians (and later, Mennonites and Amish) moved into frontier areas so that they could preserve their distinctive religious cultures. Similarly, homegrown religious diversity began to flourish, as Mormons began in the "burn over" district of Western New York, and Disciples of Christ emerged out of Appalachia (Moore, 1986). Thus, while in 1790 the first census showed only about 1% of the nation to be non-Protestant, what these Protestants were varied significantly, from Congregational New England, through the multi-denominational Middle Atlantic, to the Anglican South and all along the frontier (Finke & Stark, 1992).

Finally, religious diversity has increased due to schisms among established Protestant groups. Whether over doctrinal matters, organizational policies, or particular religious practices, Protestantism was born in schism and has continued to fragment (or diversify, depending upon one's view) ever since. For example, in the United States the question of slavery ruptured every major Protestant denomination between 1840 and 1865, some of which have never re-merged. But issues such as the proper interpretation of the Bible, or the appropriate age for baptism, divided groups even absent national political issues. Due to definitional and counting issues, there is little agreement even on the basic number of Protestant denominations currently in the United States. The Pew Research Center, based on its 2004 survey, notes that American Protestantism encompasses "more than a dozen major denominational families—such as Baptists, Methodists, Lutherans and Pentecostals …[t]hese denominational families, in turn, are made up of a host of different denominations" (Pew Research Center, 2005). And this assessment of Protestant diversity does not count what have been called "new religious movements" that have emerged out of many different established religious traditions (such as the Jehovah's Witnesses, the Hare Krishnas, the Unification Church of the Rev. Sun Myung Moon, the Church of Scientology, just to name a few) (Melton, 2002; Lewis, 2003). In sum, the combination of immigration, schism, hybridity, and religious innovation means that the contemporary United States has an astounding diversity of religious options available.

Individuation

American culture and society are regularly analyzed for their high levels of "individualism" (Gans, 1991; Lasch, 1979). Indeed, that individuation is a cherished cultural value is central to my argument here. But importantly, individualism as a cultural value and presumption is reinforced and struc-tured by the legal system and the polity. The notion that rights—political, social, economic—append to individuals is central to U.S. law in almost every respect. It is as individuals, rather than as members of a social or cultural group, that we stand before the law. Even laws meant to redress centuries-old problems of discrimination and inequality, such as affirmative action policies, must be structured so that such redress does not imper-missibly violate the rights of any individual regardless of group status. The result of these structural arrangements, combined with cultural valoriza-tion, is a process of *individuation* that reaches both institutionally and in individuals' lives.

Cultural individualism has often come into conflict with the orientations of many religious groups (Williams, 2007). Many groups of believers see themselves first as a community, a group that stands in particular relation to the divine—this is particularly true among religious minorities, or among ethno-racial minorities. Thus, there is a tension in law and politics as related to religion: at what point can and should the state intervene on behalf of an individual, using an individualist conception of human or legal rights, when that individual is embedded in a community that judges certain actions as normative or religiously mandated? Balancing individual rights and the freedom of religion for religious groups, particularly minority religious groups, is the source of contention in many court cases (Williams 1995). In general, the courts have sought to protect children (thus, for example, Christian Scientist adults may forego standard medical care, but must provide it for their children) and protect others from physical abuse. But freedom of religion as a property of the community versus an inalienable right of the individual continues to trouble the American legal system.

The tension is embedded historically. The Puritan legacy is to understand the righteous society as a "community of saints" but it was a community of individually called saints, a "chosen people" of voluntary participants. And yet, the moral regulation of the community at the local level was severe (Shain, 1994). This mirrors a constant predicament facing religious groups—when the criterion for membership in the chosen community relies on an act of individualized piety, such as being "born again" or experiencing the personal reality of "being on fire for the Lord," can we accommodate the second and then the third generation? Of course, serious attempts are made to keep youth in the fold through education and socialization, but the results are not always what the parents would hope for. Are children then to be excluded? Over history, many religious groups developed compromise solutions, such as Puritan New England's "Half-way Covenant" (Hall, 2008) or the "Birthright" Quaker status prior to "complete convincement" (Levy, 1988).

As noted above, however, the tightly ordered religious communities of the early European settlers proved difficult to maintain in the United States, whatever the efforts to do so. The frontier offered a space where institutional control was more difficult and communal gatherings less frequent and more voluntary. The influx of new pietist Protestant groups and the fervor of the Second Great Awakening made individualized expressions of faith more normative. Some groups, such as the Amish or Moravians, and of course, the Mormons, managed to maintain themselves as tightly knit ethno-religious communities—there was social and geographical room to do that. But the impulse toward individualism in belief and practices became a deeply set cultural trend, facilitated by social, geographic, and legal features of the growing nation.

The embeddedness of individualism in American culture can be seen in some of the political and social trends of the late 19th to early 20th century, even when some of those trends were in putative opposition to each other. The period 1880 to 1920 spanned two eras that historians generally refer to as the "Gilded Age" (Cashman, 1993) and the "Progressive Era" (Pastorello, 2014). The former is noted as a period of rapidly increasing wealth and inequality (with the beginnings of an ideology of "Social Darwinism" to justify it), while the latter is notable for its attempts at increasing direct democracy (for example, through adding the "initiative" and "referendum" to many state constitutions, amending the Constitution to provide for the direct election of U.S. Senators, and attacks on urban political machines). The entire time period was one of rapid urbanization and industrialization and, not surprisingly, was also marked by movements resisting these trends (such as the Populism of the South and Midwest, often represented by William Jennings Bryan) (Kazin, 1998). Throughout the era immigrant numbers were high, particularly from Eastern and Southern Europe, and particularly people who were Catholic or Jewish. And again, not surprisingly, there was significant nativist backlash against such immigration, much of it couched in religious terms (Williams, 2016).

What is significant about this period for the purposes of this essay was assumptions about the value of individualism—often promoted by both sides of the political and social cleavages. The Protestant concern with Catholic immigrants often involved the latter's alleged failure to respect the individual, subordinating him or her to rigid church doctrine that discouraged independent thought and the free-will conversion experience Protestants thought essential for salvation. On the other hand, many Progressives were concerned about the capacities for poor Catholic and Jewish immigrants to succeed in American society and responded with outreach programs that encouraged "Americanization"—aspects of which included learning and speaking English, abandoning "old world" customs, and embracing Anglo-Saxon values (Pastorello, 2014). In all of this, the centrality of the individual to the American, and Protestant, worldview became even more salient as a crucial distinction between what made the United States "exceptional" compared to the "old" world. Thus was individuation furthered.

While it might give an historian heart palpitations to jump so quickly from the early national period, to the turn of the 20th century, to the 1960s, I do so here to illustrate both the continuity of individualism as a tendency in American religion, and to point to particular periods of accelerated social change (Roof, Chapter 8 in this volume). Thus, the explosion of cultural individualism in the era colloquially known as "the sixties" was not a revolution in the sense of introducing a completely new cultural landscape and meaning system to society, such as replacing the Orthodox Czarist regime with atheistic state socialism in 1917. Rather, the sixties in the United States took themes embedded deeply in American market capitalist ideology and applied them to middle-class social mores, promising a similar type of personal liberty, defined as freedom from external institutional constraint. The notion of "do your own thing"—and the presumption that such a dictum could and should be available to all, with little worry about the wellbeing of the collective—was nicely aligned with Adam Smith's contention that the pursuit of private interests would result in a public good. Like market capitalism, the cultural system assumed that moral individuals would engage in moral actions, with less theoretical attention to how such moral individuals were to be created.

I am not voicing a cultural conservative dismissal of 1960s politics. Groups of Americans who had been systematically excluded from full participation as citizens in socio-political life—from African Americans to women to Latina workers to gay and lesbian persons—challenged the institutional and cultural arrangements of their oppression. But one of the ways this manifested in longer term cultural change was emphasizing individual "rights" (Glendon, 1991; Skrentny, 2002), and, importantly, magnifying a deep distrust of established institutions and the "elites" who ran them. Political scientists Seymour Martin Lipset and William Schneider identified this as "the confidence gap" (Lipset & Schneider, 1983) and showed that the suspicion of elites had spread from government (where anti-war sentiment regarding Viet Nam amplified an existing wariness of "politicians") to institutions such as business and labor, creating a changed cultural climate. Mark Chaves (2017) brings this up-to-date in terms of the leadership of established religious institutions. Starting in the 1970s, but accelerated rapidly by the televangelist scandals of the late 1990s and the Catholic clerical abuse publicity of the early 2000s, trust in religious leaders had diminished considerably.

Declining trust in institutions, including religious institutions, is manifested in less direct ways as well. One significant trend, I argue, is the rise of people describing themselves as "spiritual but not religious" (SBNR). While the size and significance of this trend is a matter of some scholarly debate, the phrase itself is taken to mean that people are affirming a personal, individualized sense of the spiritual, of something beyond the material world, or even a type of personal relationship with some aspect of the transcendent or divine. But they are denying that they find this in "religion"—presumably organized religion and its institutionalized doctrines. An early example of this orientation in the sociology of religion literature is in Bellah, Madsen, Sullivan, Swidler, and Tipton's (1985) *Habits of the Heart*, in which one respondent distances herself from any religious tradition, but indicates she has a faith grounded in her own inner voice that both focuses on taking care of herself as well as guides her actions towards others; she calls it "Sheilaism" (1985). Bellah and his colleagues point to this as a self-centered "expressive individualism" run amok, cutting people off from "communities of memory" and meaningful social relationships. They also note, with displeasure, that in a 1978 Gallup Poll 80% of respondents thought it both possible and positive to develop one's moral sensibility and beliefs about life without the guidance of a religious institution (Bellah, et al., 1985). Bellah, et al. note quite rightly that one main purpose of these organizations is to help shape individuals' moral lives and frameworks; however, various strains of cultural individualism have convinced many Americans not only that they do not need such institutionalized guidance, but that it is somehow better, more virtuous, and more authentic to come to such understandings without the help of institutional authorities.

While Bellah, et al. did not use the phrase SBNR, other scholars have, and have often either implied or disputed its importance or magnitude. For example, Smith and Denton (2005) find little evidence of "spiritual but not religious" in their study of youth religiosity. Many of their respondents saw spirituality and religion as linked, and the idea of separating the two did not really resonate with them. However, while small numbers reported that SBNR was "very true" for them (8%), a significant number called it "somewhat true" (46%). And of the teens that described themselves as "non-religious" 13% said "very true" and 49% said "somewhat true" (Smith & Denton, 2005). Interestingly, what the authors did find wide-spread was an outlook and orientation they labelled "Moralistic Therapeutic Deism" (MTD). This was a generalized orientation to being a good person and treating others well, and included the assumption that connection to a deistic transcendent power was important for its therapeutic support to them—such as comforting and sustaining them in hard times (Smith & Denton, 2005). Smith and Denton despair over how widespread this orientation is; they would prefer that youth hold a theologically developed and clearly thought out set of religious beliefs, and are critical of religious institutions for not countering moralistic therapeutic deism, and its implied pop culture, self-help attributes, with more articulated and considered theological beliefs. That the MTD orientation might align with a formula-tion of "spiritual but not religious" in terms of emphasizing self-oriented needs and fulfillment is not considered in their dismissal of SBNR, nor do they engage interviewees' expressions of similar sentiments, even when the SBNR phrase itself is absent (e.g., Smith & Denton, 2005).

Other scholars, without employing the scolding tone used by Smith and Denton, also take issue with the SBNR formulation. Nancy Ammerman (2013) examines constructions of spirituality found in in-depth interviews with American adults. She found four "cultural packages" of meanings that conceptualize spirituality in different ways, with some fuzzy boundaries and overlapping among them. Many respondents understood spirituality as deeply connected to religion, and again, few used the phrase "spiritual but not religious," leading her to conclude that SBNR is more of a moral and political category than an empirical one. Nonetheless, a not-insignificant number of her respondents disconnected their spirituality from institutional authority. In a similar formulation, Warner (2014) wrote "in defense of religion" as a conceptual category and notes religion's analytic distinction from spirituality (religion being connected to community while spirituality connects individuals to sources of ultimate meaning); Warner argues sensibly that the two concepts need not be antithetical, nor can religion be totally absorbed by spirituality.

Scholarly doubts notwithstanding, Mark Chaves (2017) found the number of Americans willing to understand their own spirituality in ways aligned to SBNR to be increasing. His findings are drawn from General Social Survey (GSS) data, and involve responses to two different questions, asking whether the respondent considered themselves a religious person and whether they considered themselves a spiritual person. He found that the number of people who answered "not" or "slightly" to the first question was growing, but a portion of these same people did not answer that way to the question about whether they were spiritual—thus they were disclaiming a religious identity while claiming some spiritual connection. Chaves found the number of people with this array of answers to have risen from 9% in 1998 to 14% in 2006–08 to 16% in 2010–14. He notes that people are both less likely to call themselves "religious," but more likely to think of themselves as "spiritual" (Chaves, 2017). These finds are echoed, using analysis of the same pair of questions that Chaves examined, but with higher numbers and a more dramatic increase, in a recent Pew Research Center report. That report shows 19% fitting the SBNR category in 2012 and 27% doing so in 2017 (Lipka & Gecewicz, 2017).

These findings dovetail with the well-known trend in both GSS and Pew survey data that shows a significant increase in those people identifying as religious "nones" but without a concomitant rise in the number who are atheists. That is, many who answer "none" for affiliation still profess beliefs in God or a Higher Power, often believe in life after death, and engage in private religious practices such as prayer (Baker & Smith, 2009; Chaves, 2017). In sum, SBNR may be oversold in popular culture—and may be most apparent among well-educated middle-class whites who tend to score highly on many measures of individualism (though not solely there)—but it represents a real trend in the individuation of American belief and more evidence of general suspicion of institutional authority.

Other scholars writing in the late 1980s and early 1990s emphasized individualism in American religious practice. Philip Hammond (1992) called it the "third disestablishment"—the first was the legal separation of church and state in the Constitution, the second was the displacing of the Protestant cultural establishment after World War II, and the third was the abandoning of religious institutional authority after the 1960s. Religion became increasingly susceptible to the drive for "personal autonomy," at the cost of institutional authority and with increasing cultural hybridity.

Wade Clark Roof (1993; 1999; Chapter 8 in this volume) wrote similarly, but pegged these changes particularly to the rise and maturing of the "baby boom" generation. They became a "generation of seekers" who foregrounded personal fulfillment, reserved for themselves the right to adjudicate the appropriateness of religious-moral teachings offered by religious authorities, and had an in-and-out relationship to organizational belonging. Boomers feel free to move on, seeking the religious style and community that they felt (and feel) best fit their needs. At about this same time, Joseph Cardinal Ratzinger, who later became Pope Benedict XVI, became associated with the phrase "cafeteria Catholic" as a disparaging way to characterize those members of the faith who felt entitled to pick-and-choose among church teachings. D'Antonio, Davidson, Hoge, and Meyer (2001) did not use that normative language, but clearly found evidence for an increased sense of choice, particularly among younger generations of Catholics, as did Patrick McNamara (1992), who characterized young Catholics as following "conscience first, tradition second."

Extracting personal religious identity and sacred meaning-systems from institutional participation and authority can be found in other, more recent research as well. Jerome Baggett (2009) did interviews and a survey with parishioners from six Roman Catholic parishes in Northern California—generally the East Bay area. His survey found that solid majorities thought it possible to be a "good Catholic" without going to church every Sunday (61%), without their marriage being approved by the Church (61%), without obeying the teachings on divorce and remarriage (60%), and without believing in the infallibility of the pope (59%) (Baggett, 2009). Baggett notes that these percentages are lower than some other national surveys, but that they are significant because he was surveying people who were active in a parish. Further, only 38% of his respondents claimed that the "teaching authority" of the Vatican was "very important" to them, while 89% said that "spirituality and personal growth" was very important (Baggett, 2009). Clearly, even many active church-goers were finding meaning distinct from institutional authority, or at least they claimed to.

On occasion, I refer to Hammond, Roof, and colleagues as the "California School" in the sociology of religion—referring both to their institutional affiliations and the sites of much of their research. Their work may reflect the perhaps accentuated individualism of the Left Coast. However, historian Doug Rossinow (1998) reveals some similar dynamics in the "politics of authenticity" in 1960s "new left" in Texas. Rossinow demonstrated that liberal Christians developed a keen sense of "moral individualism" as a way of resisting the conformist conservative evangelical Protestantism on issues such as racial segregation, the Viet Nam War, and the women's movement. While many of these people worked to try to manage an individualism that was balanced with commitment to community (especially across racial lines) the touchstone of "authenticity" remained the individual conscience. The notion that religious authenticity emerges from individual reflection and choice remains a hallmark in many young people's thinking, especially white young adults (e.g., Williams, Irby, & Warner, 2016).

While the individuation of religious belief and commitment is a wide and deep cultural trend in American society and religion, it does not affect all racial, ethnic, or religious groups equally. It is more common among white, college-educated, middle-class people (where Gans, 1991, located "middle American individualism"). It is less common among religious groups who are religious and/or racial minorities in the United States (e.g., Williams, et al., 2016), in part because community cohesion is a good way to manage some of the precarity of societal life in those situations. Nonetheless, there is evidence (e.g., Min, 2010; Williams, 2011; Williams & Vashi, 2007) of second-generation members of immigrant families using the language of "choice" and individual decision-making when discussing their own religious commitments—community often matters deeply to them, but they negotiate that commitment within a framework that clearly values the individual conscience and volitional decision-making as integral to the authenticity of their religious identities.

Diversity and Individuation Intersect

Diversity need not be accompanied by individualism; multicultural pluralism can exist at the community level, and religion can remain a more or less ascribed characteristic even as the sheer varieties of religion within a society increase. And, as noted earlier, many groups of religious and/or ethno-racial minorities do not put as high a value on individualism and individual autonomy as do many native-born, white Americans. But a valuing of diversity, culturally as well as in legal frameworks, along with individualism together pose a significant challenge that can result in the fracturing of tra-ditional and corporatist forms of community. It can also lead to synthetic religious creations and a cultural hybridity that many would describe as creative and positive innovations.

However, there is no question that the two processes, in the context of declining confidence in institutional leaders, a generalized distrust of "elites," and work and family lives that are ever more speeded up and mobile, have resulted in declining connection to the most common form of American religious expression—the congregation. Robert Putnam (2000), among others, pointed to declining participation in voluntary associations—including religious congregations—as damaging to American civil society. Chaves (2017) has assembled 40 years of GSS data and three waves of the National Congregational Survey (NCS) and finds clear trends: fewer Americans belong to religious congregations, fewer Americans look to congregations as sites of religious and life authority, fewer Americans attend worship services regularly, and those who do are increasingly older. The patterns are distinct enough that he terms it a "decline" in the forms of "traditional" religiosity. The religious con-gregation is far from dead—or even dying—as it remains the most common form of voluntary association in the United States and is con-sistently shown to have positive effects on many aspects of life for participants. But participants are more irregular, more selective, and less fully committed over the life course than they once were.

Americans have more religious choices than ever. There are more different religions, and more congregations/temples/practitioners of each of the major world religions, than there ever were. It is increasingly acceptable to adopt and adapt practices from one tradition, even while not fully embracing that faith or abandoning one's received identity—the trajectory of Buddhism's "mindfulness" in American culture is evidence for that (Wilson, 2013), or the popular recognition of the concept of "JUBU"—Jewish *and* Buddhist (Kamenetz, 1994). Religious culture, in many ways, has been increasingly commodified, especially in popular culture industries, giving believers the opportunity to "consume" religion even more selectively. And the proliferation of media platforms, from talk radio to televangelism to web-based worship (Cowen, 2005) has also increased the numbers of ways in which religion can be experienced privately or selectively.

In the debates over "secularization" that have characterized sociology of religion for some time, too much of the debate had an "is not, is too" quality—that is, that religion was either declining and fading away, or was vibrant and dynamic. The possibility that *both* could be true, at least in part depending upon the changing forms and expressions of religious life, was too often ignored. That may well be the lesson here: the intersection of diversity and individuation, coupled with a clear decline in institutionalized religious authority, means that many Americans insist on carving out their own forms of spiritual and religious expression, and have many more forms and resources available with which to do so. The locus of religious authority has shifted to the individual, and experimentation and personalization are legitimate outcomes. Declaring oneself an atheist still arouses suspicion among many Americans (e.g., Edgell, Gerteis, & Hartmann, 2006; Edgell, Hartmann, Stewart, & Gerteis, 2016), but being a religious "none," calling oneself "spiritual but not religious," or maintaining a "cultural" connection to one's faith tradition, rather than an observant one, are increasingly common and acceptable.

What This May Mean for Religion, Spirituality, and Aging

The basic claim of this chapter is that increasing diversity of religious options in the United States combines with a deeply embedded cultural valuing of individual decision-making and self-fulfillment to produce a religious landscape that is ever more varied, and one in which people are able, and often expected, to tailor their belief and practice commitments to their own needs. Institutionalized religious authority has less sway than organizational images of hierarchy would imply and the legitimacy and acceptance of being without a faith, or without a religious community, is increasing. What do these institutional and cultural trends mean for religion, spirituality, and aging? This entire volume offers a set of well-researched answers to this question; I close here by only suggesting some things worth observing, in terms of belief systems, religious practices, and religious organizations and communities.

Regarding religious beliefs, it seems fairly safe to expect ever greater diversity and cultural hybridity, and having them legitimated by individual experience and needs. Combinations of traditions, such as JUBUs, or charismatic Catholics, should increase. Even one consistent negative reaction to cultural blending—that of renewed orthodoxy or fundamentalism—will be filtered through the worldviews and practices of a culture that is already non-traditional. There is substantial evidence that a satisfying spiritual life is helpful in promoting good health among the aging (Idler, Chapter 6 in this volume; Krause, Chapter 8 in this volume; George, Chapter 9 in this volume). Thus, the capacity to make that spiritual life personalized and individually salient would seem to have never been greater. Some scholars note that such religious innovations as "spiritual but not religious" are particularly acute among the Baby Boom generation—that is, the effects of the 1960s cultural trends are more salient for them than other generations (Roof, Chapter 10 in this volume). Since this is the current generation that is retiring and moving into old age, the availability of options and the valuing of individuation seems made for them.

However, another important dimension of the beneficial aspects of religion (on physical and mental health, life satisfaction, etc.) is the involvement in a community—basically, a congregation. Congregations can offer social and emotional support, networks that are both instrumentally useful (say, for example, for a ride to a doctor's appointment) and expressive opportunities, as well as doctrine and values that emphasize self-care and health. These are of great assistance to health and help people resist anxiety, depression, and loneliness. Thus, the decline in congregation involvement and attendance may be social factors that undercut the potential positive benefits of an agreeable spiritual life. There are a number of reasons that older people may not be particularly active in a religious congregation—whether they were raised in a non-religious household, or have health issues, or have competing life demands, or have relocated upon retirement and have difficulty connecting with a new community. But the general decline in congregational involvement may well have a potentially negative effect on the health and general well-being of the aging, and on congregations themselves.

Religious congregations in the United States overwhelmingly run on volunteer labor. As such, it is not surprising that American religious congregations flourished post-World War II—the widespread development of the suburban, one-income, nuclear family was an excellent source of that kind of effort. Volunteer labor from "stay-at-home" mothers became the backbone of much church programming (Edgell, 2005). Further, this arrangement also facilitated a clear shift in programming interest to children and young adults—thus, the "young family" became the symbol of a thriving congregation.

But the shifts in family structures, such as more women in full-time work force, or more single parenting, has left many congregations struggling to keep up. Focusing on young families has sometimes meant that senior congregational members are relatively neglected (Bengtson et al., Chapter 1 in this volume), but also differentiated programming can increase the age-segregation already in society. At least at this point, it would appear that the large numbers of retiring Baby Boomers are not going to result in a surge in volunteering for local religious congregations (Seaman, 2012). As noted above, Boomers have been less organizational in their religious commitments and less religious overall, and may have gotten used to the relative professionalization of congregational services that marked the flush periods of the late 1950s and 1960s. On the other hand, there is evidence that Boomers are more likely to volunteer generally than the generations before them (Einolf, 2009), so it may well continue into retirement—but that may not be in religious congregations specifically.

While all these trends portend potential challenges for religious congregations and their leadership as people approach retirement and old age, doomsday scenarios may be unwarranted. Robert Wuthnow (2002) engaged the literature on the organizational crisis in American civil society—represented by Putnam's (2000) analysis—and offered a slightly different take. Rather than a "decline" he saw a shift in the forms of association. That is, it may be true that older organizational forms were experiencing some decline, and this would include the religious congregation, but it was not true that associations were dead. New types of connections, more fluid, more episodic in life, were vibrant and growing. He called them "loose connections" but still acknowledged their importance.

In this way, religious organizational life may be transforming a bit like religious belief is. There is a decline in traditional beliefs, and in many traditional ways of belonging. But belief and belonging are not dead, they are being transformed into different forms and with changing dynamics. As American society moves into a period of a large generation retiring, and people living longer, the ways in which diversity and individuation affect spirituality and religion will no doubt change as well.

References

Ammerman, N. T. (2013). Spiritual but not religious? Beyond binary choices in the study of religion. *Journal for the Scientific Study of Religion*, 52(2), 258–278.

Baggett, J. P. (2009). *Sense of the faithful: How American Catholics live their faith*. New York: Oxford University Press.

Baker, J. O. & Smith, B. G. (2009). The nones: Social characteristics of the religiously unaffiliated. *Social Forces*, 87(3), 1251–1263.

Bellah, R. N., Madsen, R., Sullivan, W., Swidler, A., & Tipton, S. (1985). *Habits of the heart: Individualism and commitment in American life*. Berkeley: University of California Press.

Bengtson, V. L. (2001). Beyond the nuclear family: The increasing importance of multigenerational bonds. *Journal of Marriage and Family*, 63, 1–16.

Cashman, S. (1993). *America in the gilded age*, 3rd Ed. New York: New York University Press.

Chaves, M. (2017). *American religion: Contemporary trends*, 2nd Ed. Princeton, NJ: Princeton University Press.

Cowen, D. E. (2005). Online u-topia: Cyberspace and the mythology of placelessness. *Journal for the Scientific Study of Religion*, 445(3), 257–263.

D'Antonio, W. V., Davidson, J. D., Hoge, D. R., & Meyer, K. (2001). *American Catholics: Gender, generation, and commitment*. Walnut Creek, CA: Altamira Press.

Demerath, N. J. III & Williams, R. H. (1992). *A bridging of faiths: Religion and politics in a New England city*. Princeton, NJ: Princeton University Press.

Edgell, P. (2005). *Religion and family in a changing society*. Princeton, NJ: Princeton University Press.

Edgell, P., Gerteis, J., & Hartmann, D. (2006). Atheists as 'other': Moral boundaries and cultural membership in American society. *American Sociological Review*, 71, 211–234.

Edgell, P., Hartmann, D., Stewart, E., & Gerteis, J. (2016). Atheists and other cultural outsiders: Moral boundaries and the non-religious in the United States. *Social Forces*, 95(2), 607–638.

Einolf, C. J. (2009). Will the Boomers volunteer during retirement? Comparing the Baby Boom, Silent, and Long Civic cohorts. *Nonprofit and Voluntary Sector Quarterly*, 38(2), 181–199.

Finke, R. & Stark, R. (1992). *The churching of America*. New Brunswick, NJ: Rutgers University Press.

Fischer, D. H. (1989). *Albion's seed: Four British folkways in America*. New York: Oxford University Press.

Gans, H. J. (1991). *Middle American individualism: Political participation and liberal democracy*. New York: Oxford University Press.

Glendon, M. A. (1991). *Rights talk: The impoverishment of political discourse*. New York: The Free Press.

Hagestad, G. O. & Uhlenberg, P. (2005). The social separation of old and young: A root of ageism. *Journal of Social Issues*, 61(2), 343–360.

Hall, D. (2008). New England, 1660–1730. *The Cambridge Companion to Puritanism*, J. Coffey & P. Lim (Eds.). Cambridge: Cambridge University Press.

Hammond, P. E. (1992). *Religion and personal autonomy: The third disestablishment in America*. Columbia, SC: University of South Carolina Press.

Hatch, N. O. (1989). *The democratization of American Christianity*. New Haven, CT: Yale University Press.

Kamenetz, R. (1994). *The Jew in the Lotus*. New York: Harper Collins.

Kazin, M. (1998). *The populist persuasion: An American history*. Ithaca, NY: Cornell University Press.

Lasch, C. (1979). *Culture of Narcissism: American life in an age of diminishing expectations*. New York: W. W. Norton and Co.

Levy, B. (1988). *Quakers and the American family: British settlement in the Delaware Valley*. New York: Oxford University Press.

Lewis, J. R. (2003). *Legitimating new religions*. New Brunswick, NJ: Rutgers University Press.

Lipka, M. & Gecewicz, C. (2017). More Americans now say they're spiritual but not religious. http://www.pewresearch.org/fact-tank/2017/09/06/more-americans-now-say-theyre- spiritual-but-not-religious/

Lipset, S. M. & Schneider, W. (1983). *The confidence gap: Business, labor, and government in the public mind*. New York: Columbia University Press.

McNamara, P. H. (1992). *Conscience first, tradition second: A study of young American Catholics*. Albany: State University of New York Press.

Melton, J. G. (2002). *Encyclopedia of American religions*, 7th Ed. Detroit: Gale.

Min, P. G. (2010). *Preserving ethnicity through religion in America: Korean Protestants and Indian Hindus across generations*. New York: New York University Press.

Mohamed, B. (2016). A new estimate of the U.S. Muslim population. Pew Research Center. http://www.pewresearch.org/fact-tank/2016/01/06/a-new-estimate-of-the-u-s-muslim-population/

Moore, R. L. (1986). *Religious outsiders and the making of Americans*. New York: Oxford University Press.

Pastorello, K. (2014). *The Progressives: Activism and reform in American society, 1893–1927*. Malden, MA: Wiley-Blackwell.

Pew Research Center. (2005). The changing American religious composition of the US. http://www.pewforum.org/2015/05/12/chapter-1-the-changing-religious-composition-of-the-u-s/

Pew Research Center. (2014). Religious landscape study. http://www.pewforum.org/religious- landscape-study/

Portes, A. & Rumbaut, R. (2014). *Immigrant America*, 4th Ed. Berkeley: University of California Press.

Prothero, S. (Ed.). (2006). *A nation of religions: The politics of pluralism in multireligious America*. Raleigh: University of North Carolina Press.

Putnam, R. D. (2000). *Bowling alone: The collapse and revival of American community*. New York: Simon & Schuster.

Roof, W. C. (1993). *A generation of seekers: The spiritual journeys of the baby boom generation*. San Francisco: Harper Collins.

Roof, W. C. (1999). *Spiritual marketplace: Baby boomers and the remaking of American religion*. Princeton, NJ: Princeton University Press.

Rossinow, D. (1998). *The politics of authenticity: Liberalism, Christianity, and the new left in America*. New York: Columbia University Press.

Seaman, P. M. (2012). Time for my life now: Early Boomer women's anticipation of volunteering in retirement. *The Gerontologist*, 52(2), 245–254.

Shain, B. A. (1994). *The myth of American individualism: The Protestant origins of American political thought*. Princeton, NJ: Princeton University Press.

Skrentny, J. D. (2002). *The minority rights revolution*. Cambridge, MA: Belknap Press of Harvard University Press.

Smith, C. & Denton, M. L. (2005). *Soul searching*. New York: Oxford University Press.

Uhlenberg, P. & De Jong Gierveld, J. (2004). Age-segregation in later life: an examination of personal networks. *Ageing and Society*, 24(1), 5–28.

Warner, R. S. (2014). In defense of religion: The 2013 H. Paul Douglass lecture. *Review of Religious Research*, 56, 495–512.

Warner, R. S. & Wittner, J. G. (Eds.). (1998). *Gatherings in diaspora*. Philadelphia: Temple University Press.

Williams, R. H. (1995). Breaching the 'wall of separation': The balance between religious freedom and social order. In S. A. Editor (Ed.), *Armageddon in Waco: Critical perspectives on the Branch Davidian conflict*. Chicago: University of Chicago Press.

Williams, R. H. (2007). Liberalism, religion, and the dilemma of 'immigrant rights' in American political culture. In P. Hondagneu-Sotelo (Ed.), *Religion and social justice for immigrants*. New Brunswick, NJ: Rutgers University Press.

Williams, R. H. (2011). Creating an American Islam: Thoughts on religion, identity, and place. *Sociology of Religion*, 72(2), 127–153.

Williams, R. H. (2016). Preserving the Protestant nation: Religion and socio-political dimensions of immigration until 1920. In B. A. McGraw (Ed.), *The Wiley-Blackwell Companion to Religion & Politics in the U.S.* Malden, MA: Wiley-Blackwell.

Williams, R. H. & Vashi, G. (2007). Hijab and American Muslim women: Creating the space for autonomous selves. *Sociology of Religion*, 68(3), 269–287.

Williams, R. H., Irby, C. A., & Warner, R. S. (2016). 'Church' in black and white: The organizational lives of young adults. *Religions*, 7(7), 90. (doi:10.3390/rel7070090).

Wilson, J. (2013). *Mindful America: The mutual transformation of Buddhist meditation and American culture*. New York: Oxford University Press.

Wuthnow, R. (2002). *Loose connections: Joining together in America's fragmented communities*. Cambridge, MA: Harvard University Press.

Wuthnow, R. (2005). *America and the challenges of religious diversity*. Princeton, NJ: Princeton University Press.

Zolberg, A. (2008). *A nation by design: Immigration policy in the fashioning of America*. Cambridge, MA: Harvard University Press & the Russell Sage Foundation.

Chapter 3

Spiritual Journeys
Elders' Stories of Spiritual Development

Robert C. Atchley

MIAMI UNIVERSITY

This chapter examines the origins, makeup, and functions of spiritual journeys for elders. We look at what stimulates the development and presentation of spiritual journey narratives, how life stage influences the timing and content of spiritual journey statements, and how these statements compare with prominent theories of spiritual development.

As a topic of discussion, the inner experience of spirituality was called "private religion" in the early twentieth century (James, 1905). It was assumed that religion offered the major, if not the only, pathway to this type of experience. But by the 1970s it had become clear that many people have spiritual experiences without benefit of religion, so calling these experiences "religious" did not make sense.

During the 1960s there was a revival of the ancient idea that humans have an innate potential for spiritual experiences, a potential that can be developed into a capacity (Huxley, 1944). This idea, combined with the idea that we can exert influence over our own development, fueled an interest in spiritual development as a personal goal. Thus, people began to speak about their "spiritual journey" as an intentional direction for their spiritual development and to express a preference for a lifestyle that supported such a journey.

The concept of a spiritual journey refers to an individual's personal narrative about his or her spiritual life and its development. These narratives often include a chronology of experiences, actions, and insights connected with a search for spiritual connection and meaning (Manning, Chapter 4 in this volume).

Underlying the spiritual journey narrative is an intentional process of being open to and seeking spiritual experiences, using values and insights arising from spiritual experiences to make life choices, and learning from experience using this process. For most people who see themselves as being on a spiritual journey, bringing spirituality more completely into consciousness and learning to be consciously aware of spiritual experiences available in everyday life are important goals (Atchley, 2009).

Spiritual journeys also involve learning to persist and be content on a journey into imperfectly known territory, where insights are always limited, no matter how profound they may seem at the time. People who have been on a spiritual journey for decades usually develop a sense of humor about the contradictions and paradoxes they encounter, even as they use these enigmas as food for contemplation. Most have learned to be patient, to see waiting as an important spiritual practice—not "waiting for" but just waiting. Most spiritual journeys involve elements of commitment, self-discipline, and regular spiritual practice.

Spiritual Journeys

Data for this chapter come from survey analyses conducted by Wuthnow (1998, 2007) and Roof (1993, 1999), and my review and analysis of an archive of 160 spiritual journey presentations made by members and attenders of a large Quaker Meeting between 1995 and 2017.

In his insightful review of social change in spiritual thought and orientation in the last half of the twentieth century, Robert Wuthnow (1998) argued that spirituality in America shifted from a religion-centered "spirituality of dwelling" toward a person-centered "spirituality of seeking" and later toward a personal "spirituality of practice." For Wuthnow, spirituality of dwelling emphasized the comfort, security, and answers offered by a specific religious community. Spirituality of seeking emphasized finding one's own answers to important spiritual questions and an open approach to teachings and teachers. Spirituality of practice emphasized an ongoing commitment to practices such as meditation, prayer, or contemplative movement that nurture capacity for spiritual experience and sense of spiritual connection. Wuthnow concluded that in the twenty-first century many spiritual journeys attempt to balance dwelling, seeking, and practice.

Wade Clark Roof (1993, 1999, Chapter 8 in this volume) has studied spiritual experiences and narratives in a cohort of "pre-Baby-Boomers" and two cohorts of "Baby-Boomers." He followed several hundred respondents through the early part of middle age and found "there was a remarkable degree of clarity about themselves as engaged in a process-oriented spirituality and what that engagement may involve for them. Reflexive spirituality is not haphazard or left to chance; it seeks self-understanding and self-management" (Roof, 1999). He concluded that during the 1970s and 1980s, a large proportion of American adults suffered from what he called "wholeness hunger," which underlies much of today's spiritual malaise (Roof, 1999).

It is something felt by many people, something that underlies comments about "centering your life" and "finding connections" that are so frequently voiced. Once identified with New Age discourse, such terms now permeate the religious landscape in a more generic sense...modernity severs connections to place and community, alienates people from their natural environments, separates work and life, and dilutes ethical values—all of which makes the need for unifying experience so deeply felt.

Roof described spiritual journeys as "explorations—evolving, open-ended, and revisable" (1999). His respondents who were on a spiritual journey were likely to stick with it. The journey usually started with mysterious inner forces, but the individual made the decisions about which forks in the road to take and how to monitor results. Along the way, most people make choices that balance the need for openness and the need for group support and security.

Roof found three patterns or types of spiritual journey among his respondents. The first pattern involved assimilating and conforming to a religious culture and gradually integrating this culture into one's own personal constructs. Individuals who chose this pattern enjoyed the security of knowing what to expect and tolerated well the constraints their religion required. Even in this pattern, however, individuals usually saw themselves as responsible for the specific elements of the journey. The second pattern was an individualized journey within a religious context. It often involved clergy as personal counselors who helped the individual integrate religious beliefs and practices with personal constructs of meaning and purpose. The third pattern was the self-directed spiritual journey. Individuals following this pattern often used "spiritual directors," either freelance or clergy, to help them gain the self-awareness and make the decisions needed to fashion, maintain, and revise their spiritual journey.

Wuthnow (1998) found that most people on a spiritual journey created a narrative about it. "This story provides a way for them to understand their [spiritual] origins, how they have changed, and the role that crisis events or significant others have played in their lives, and where they think they are headed" (1998). He adds that the self-directed journey is both liberating and scary because it requires people to do more of the work needed to understand spirituality and put that understanding into practice (Wuthnow, 1998).

Wuthnow and Roof both emphasized the importance of seeking in explaining changes in spiritual orientation and behavior over the past 40 years. Seekers are actively pursuing and cultivating spiritual experience and integrating those experiences into their lives. Because Quaker Meetings often see themselves as "communities of seekers," the spiritual journey presentations of Friends seem particularly relevant. There is also a history among Friends of encouraging members and attenders to present their narrative spiritual journeys. A large majority does. The archive of 160 presentations represents 80 percent of members and regular attenders of the Meeting. Among presenters, women outnumbered men two to one in the archived presentations, which is close to the proportion of women to men in the Meeting.

What Stimulates People to Develop and Present their Spiritual Journeys?

"How did you come to be the spiritual being you are today?" This general question is the frame within which Quakers are asked to present their spiritual journeys. Having the question framed in this way is helpful in recruiting people to develop and present their narratives. It also helps that the community appreciates these presentations. Spiritual journeys are the most well-attended program presentations by far.

People are motivated to present their spiritual journeys when they realize that this narrative is an important part of their life story. It tells important things about them as people. It is also a useful type of life review. Spiritual journey narratives often deal with basic "meaning questions" about life, and coming to grips with these questions in order to present them can be a very daunting yet liberating experience. Most people come away from this experience with a sense of self-esteem and agency. They realize that they decided how their journey would go. Each journey is unique and although the underlying values may be similar, the playing out of them is highly individual.

> A journey of the spirit: How did I get to where I am now? Where am I now? It isn't just religious beliefs, but includes values, philosophy of life, and where one finds meaning. My spiritual journey has been molded by the social climate of the times and by people around me who turned out to be my guides.
>
> Woman, age 56

Social Contexts Shape Spiritual Journey Narratives

The social eras in which people experience their own spiritual development have profound impacts on the themes they present. Roof (1993) found that peace movement participation, social justice movement participation, the loosening up of culture in the 1960s, and participation in the 1960s counter-culture all had big impacts on the stories people told about their spiritual development. The importance of sociocultural context comes through in most of the spiritual journey presentations I reviewed.

> What did I gain from the Women's Movement? Everything. A couple of years of therapy in the 1970s opening me to finding myself. Not only did I have to figure out who I was without worrying about some man's approval, but I was able to make decisions I never would have made if attached to a man. Overcoming my upbringing of the 1950s was very hard work. I feel blessed to have had a passion. It was so energizing; it consumed my life. We wrote letters, we marched, I took my daughter to ERA rallies, we reviewed all the state laws and got all the he's and his's removed. The Women's Movement made huge changes to the fabric of American society. At this time, I feel like a modern-day feminist, only this time without the anger. I feel blessed that God has always existed for me.
>
> Woman, age 66

Ever since I declined the opportunity to be in ROTC during college, the issue of pacifism was worrying for me. Finally, during the Cold War arms race, I became a confirmed pacifist. During the Viet-Nam War, and the First Iraqi War, the Friends sponsored a silent vigil for peace on the Pearl Street Mall. There we were, standing in silence behind a big sign that said: We Stand for Peace. If people had questions, one of us was designated to give them a written handout on why we were protesting silently. If people needed to talk, we would take them aside and talk with them quietly. An important part of my journey was the weekly commitment to stand for something right, something in harmony with the divine as I saw it.

Man, age 70

Ideas have always been important "pointing fingers" for me. From the Bible I learned how Joseph was able to forgive the jealous brothers who so mistreated him. From Alan Watts, I learned that the nothing-ness of inner space could be Holy. From Aldous Huxley, Abraham Maslow, and Carl Rogers, I learned about the possibility of transcen-dent human potential. Although I was in my thirties in the 1960s, I was profoundly affected by the climate of ideas and the plethora of spiritual practices one could experience in that era.

Man, age 74

Life Stage Influences on Spiritual Journey Narratives

In my review of spiritual journey presentations, I found it was very rare for young adults to present. All but one of the 160 presentations in the archive I reviewed were made by individuals over the age of 40 and more than half of the presentations were made by individuals age 60 or older. This suggests that people need to do a lot of sorting and sifting (which Roof has termed "reflexive spirituality") before they are ready to formulate an overview of their spiritual journey. Thus, the creation of a spiritual journey narrative could be seen as a developmental task in its own right.

Regardless of the age at which spiritual journey presentations are created, most of them include childhood experiences. Early experiences of church and doctrine were sometimes negative, especially when youngsters were forced to attend services that did not speak to them.

Sundays were for me the worst day of the week. I had to dress up in an itchy wool suit, wear a tie, and sit through a totally meaningless church service. From my perspective, the church defined itself by what it was against—intellectual pursuits, cultural enjoyment, and all other reli-gions. I left as soon as I could, but the guilt of not believing was very strong.

Man, age 70

Other narratives included positive spiritual experiences that occurred in religious environments.

> The summer after first grade, I attended a vacation Bible school at a Baptist church across the street from our house. At the end of the week, the kids put on a program for the congregation. I was an enthusiastic singer and was given a solo to sing—Jesus Loves Me. As I sang, I realized that I was singing about something in me. I could feel Jesus's love. Fifty years later, that feeling is still there.
>
> Woman, age 58

Many profound spiritual experiences in childhood occurred in nature.

> When I was eight, I spent the summer on a cousin's remote farm in the mountains. One of my chores was to take the livestock down a steep path from the barnyard to a spring about a quarter of a mile away. The morning run began at first light. Our little caravan moved slowly over the mountainside and got to the spring about sunrise. I would sit on a rock and watch the sunrise beaming through the tall trees and be completely awestruck by the grandeur of nature.
>
> Man, age 68

> I grew up on a farm in western Kansas. Some of my earliest experiences of the awe of nature included looking across a huge wheat field what was swept into big amber waves by the wind and seemed to go on for miles, watching lightning flash across the prairie sky, and loving the feeling in my chest when the thunder struck.
>
> Woman, age 65

Sometimes spiritual journey narratives begin with character.

> Tradition seems to require that people describe their spiritual journeys chronologically and start with religious upbringing. For me, paradox, passions, and Grace are more relevant. Alternately flouting and bowing to tradition are probably among the most profound paradoxes in my life. I teach and write and speak about the importance of being respectful of others, and yet much of my life I have gotten into trouble because I always have had a profound tendency toward irreverence.
>
> Woman, age 41

Sometimes spiritual journeys are initiated by epiphanies.

> I'm going to share what I consider my first experience of the Holy Spirit. It happened during a very busy week of deadlines. I was

involved in several projects that had to be completed that week. I had been trying to allow a little time each day to have some quiet, meditative time. I couldn't see how to find meditative time in this busy week. I walked into my study and felt this overwhelming presence surrounding me. The room seemed much brighter than usual. In that presence, I knew it was OK not to meditate that week.

Woman, age 64

On Easter Sunday when I was 12, I felt a light envelope me, a current surge through my body in what Jean Shinoda Bolen calls a "sensory intuition," a "tuning fork phenomenon." In the Baptist tradition, this was a sign of a call to Christ, that it was time to be saved and join the church. I went to the front of the church crying, shaking, and laughing. I was sure of my experience and the divine presence.

Woman, age 62

The spiritual journey narratives in the Quaker archive fit well into the categories of life stage development created by Erikson, Erikson, and Kivnick (1986) and Tornstam (2005).

Erikson and his colleagues did not attach chronological definitions to their stages of psycho-social development. Instead they focused on what they saw as the developmental challenges that faced people in midlife, later life, and old age. Developmentally defined, middle age is about a choice between exercising generativity by nurturing the upcoming generations or remaining confined to one's habitual ruts. Instead of setting up the choice as either/or, Erikson et al. stressed balance between generativity and habituation, which they called care. The spiritual journey narratives in the archive showed many examples of care that began in middle age and extended into later life and old age.

I'm in my late sixties now, and some of my most satisfying experiences occur as I listen to, support, and encourage friends who are grappling with careers and friends entering retirement and later life. There are about a dozen people I meet with every few months, either in person, by e-mail or by phone.

Woman, age 68

Being a grandparent calls for all the wisdom I can muster. Having done a "top-down" approach to parenting, I feel somewhat chagrinned as I see myself being a very different kind of grandparent. I don't correct the grandkids, unless it's something highly egregious. I don't bear any weight of responsibility for training them or financing their educations. My job is to be present with them, accompany them, listen to them, and love them unconditionally. How liberating!

Man, age 76

Erikson's later life stage was about balancing integrity and despair to arrive at wisdom. Integrity is a quality of life that can balance and neutralize despair. Knowing that these two qualities co-exist in most later lives is wisdom. Integrity—fidelity to, and commitment to abide by, basic values—is a powerful force in Quaker narratives of spiritual journey in later life.

Quaker Testimonies are a great source of integrity for many Friends. Testimonies are actions taken individually or as a group that testify to the importance and value of Simplicity, Nonviolence, Integrity, Community, Equality, and Environmental Stewardship.

> I rarely measure value by money or its outward manifestations. I am not open prey for the propaganda of our society that urges buying and selling and spending and acquiring trophies—trophy children, trophy wives, trophy friends.
>
> Woman, age 58

> Nature feeds me tremendously. I've been struck by how much more strongly I experience connection to the Holy in the mountains or around wild animals than I felt in Notre Dame or St. Peter's. I feel a spiritual imperative to work to preserve the gift of our natural world at this time in history, when it is so seriously threatened.
>
> Woman, age 81

> Having spent the past 20 years of my life teaching people to use non-violent approaches to conflict resolution; I could easily have been discouraged by their resistance to doing the practice needed to make this approach work. But every time one of my students digs deep inside, touches the inner spirit and finds the strength to persist, my own spirit and resolve are strengthened.
>
> Man, age 68

According to Tornstam (2005), old age is a period of growing detachment from pre-occupations with outcomes and the manipulations required to produce them. One can hold values and at the same time be detached from any need for those values to be actualized in everyday life. Schachter-Shalomi and Miller (1995) called this "holding the field." A unique quality that elders in this stage have is a presence that is "being radiantly at peace."

In his mid-80s, William projects an air of robust good health. He attends Meeting regularly, but rarely speaks. Yet he constantly serves as a living example of what it means to be radiantly at peace. He is comfortable with his spiritual nature, and it shows in his clear voice, bright eyes, and ready smile. There is a serenity about William's being that many people in the group have remarked on. There is also a sense that the group is missing an important presence when William is not there. William never presented a spiritual journey, but the results of his journey were there for all to see.

James attends the same Meeting. He is in his early 90s and has numerous chronic conditions that cause him to move about slowly. He is nearly blind and in a great deal of chronic pain. When asked, he acknowledges that his physical existence is not very enjoyable at this stage of frailty. Yet, in meeting for worship, James will occasionally stand and ecstatically recite a Psalm from memory. At these times, he is completely transported by the Source of the Psalms, and these renderings invariably leave the group uplifted and in awe of this gentle man's direct connection with God.

Structuring Spiritual Journey Narratives

Moody and Carroll (1997) presented a "hero's journey," linear approach to spiritual development, and one Quaker presenter structured her spiritual journey specifically using Moody and Carroll's stages: Call, Search, Struggle, Breakthrough, and Return.

> The call is a request for attention from the divine. The search is an attempt to find the place, the teacher and teachings, and the practice that will guide our path. Often they are experienced separately, but for me they intertwine in many turns of the spiral. By high school, I was the only one in my family who still went to church. I would sit quietly in a back pew, reveling in the peace and blocking out the noisiness of the worship. I still felt centered by the singing.
>
> Many years passed. I moved away from my childhood home. I tried just about every type of church. I moved to Boulder and tried Buddhism. I needed something that aligned with the Christian tradition. In a women's dream group, I found my call in a dream. I was flying with a crone spirit, circling the earth. I despaired at the pollution, starvation and pain I saw. She held my hand and kept saying "Look for the Light, Look for the Light." Looking down on my beloved earth, I could see brilliant light sparkling from polluted rivers and from the souls of people everywhere.
>
> I began to read widely about women in Christian history, trying to find my reflection in the divine. I was incensed by the exclusion of the women's Biblical writings and writings of the women mystics of the Middle Ages. I read *The Complete Gospels* and discovered that Mary Magdalene was one of Jesus's cherished disciples, not the prostitute she was made out to be by the men who translated the early New Testament.
>
> My search culminated in a trip to Europe with four other women to visit the sites and study the teachings of Julian of Norwich, Clare of Assisi, and Catherine of Sienna. Our closure, my breakthrough, at the

end of the trip was reflective and full of fun. We talked of our own journeys during this pilgrimage…It occurred to me that my search had been for the sacred wisdom of the world—Sophia, not the levels of material, royal, and spiritual levels neatly separated.

The challenge of the return from any journey or insight is to come down from the mountain and live in the valley, day to day. My ongoing process is motivated not only by a vision of the divine that can guide my path but also by my work in conflict and social justice. I am convinced that women will never awaken to their full creativity and power until we incorporate our image into and are reflected by our images of the divine. Just as Julian knew, spirituality is not something we strive for…it is a gift from the spiritual gift shop. The dance is with the wholly (and holy) other, masculine and feminine, fancy and plain, striving and trusting, secular and sacred.

Woman, age 62

Ray and McFadden (2001) likened spiritual development to a "web or quilt" type of structure. A quilt has multiple layers and is crafted over time. Like the individual differences found in ways of being spiritual, so some people's quilts have an organizing structure immediately apparent to all; but others are of the "crazy-quilt" variety that, when viewed partially may make little sense, but can be quite beautiful when seen as a whole. Quilts, like spirituality, may have different functions at different times in the life span.

One result of honoring the images from the unconscious has been the development of one of my new healing passions—quilting. I have found the acts of designing, planning and creating a quilt merge at a deeper level to become a type of prayer. Appreciating the beauty of the colors and the feel of the fabric weave themselves with thoughts of loved ones for whom I am planning the gift. The spider's genius is to create from her own efforts and make the connections that sustain life.

Woman, age 48

Process

The data reviewed for this chapter support a concept of spiritual process that can involve a complex mixture of elements: early life spiritual experiences, family context, religious context, awakening to noumenous experience, disillusionment with organized religion, spiritual call, seeking, and finding, consolidating into a lifestyle, and tinkering (Wuthnow, 2007). Each of these elements offers a huge variety of options. All the spiritual journey narratives I reviewed reflected substantial individuation (Hillman, 1999). A self-directed spiritual journey appeals to a very large proportion of American adults.

However, there is always another large category of people: those who grew up with a specific religious plan and want to stick with it for life.

These two general patterns can be described as inside-out and outside-in. The inside-out conception assumes that we have an innate, accessible higher power and spirituality within us that we can experience, cultivate, and use as a guide for making life decisions. The outside-in conception assumes that the higher power is located outside ourselves. We can experience this higher power by surrender to its authority, revealed in scriptures and mediated by clergy. What happens to us is assumed to reflect "God's will."

Richard Rohr (2014) puts it this way:

> There are enough people going on solid inner journeys that it is not merely ideological or theoretical. For the first time, on a broad basis, this reformation can come from the inside, and in a positive, non-violent way. This reformation is not just from the top down, but much more from the bottom up. Not from outside in, but from inside out. Not from clergy to laity, but from a unified field.

It is tempting to see spiritual journeys as always having positive outcomes, but this is not the case. Coleman and Mills' chapter in this volume provides many examples of elders' being overcome by questioning related to contradictions and paradoxes that arose when their life experience did not match their expectations from their spiritual journey. This happened mainly to elders with an outside-in approach to their spiritual journey.

The spiritual journey narratives in the Quaker archive used an inside-out concept of their spiritual journeys. None of the presentations I reviewed revealed spiritual despair, even in the face of severe loss and infirmity. Many of the narratives cite spiritual crises in midlife and later, but by sticking with their inside-out process, these issues were resolved. When Quakers are struggling with their spiritual journey, they can ask for a "clearness committee" to meet with them and help them clarify what is troubling them and how to deal with it. The role of the clearness committee is to suggest questions that will help the individual come to a useful understanding.

Of course, these positive findings may be biased by the fact that people who are unhappy with how their spiritual journeys are turning out may be less motivated to present this to the group. But this is not common, since a large majority of the Meeting community made a spiritual journey presentation.

Conclusion

Spiritual journey narratives of young adults are often abbreviated versions designed to answer "what's your story" questions posed by friends and acquaintances. Fuller versions designed for self-assessment and lengthy presentation are primarily developed in midlife or later and relate to spiritual development motives such as generativity, integrity and gero-transcendence.

Wuthnow (2007) cites norms of civility as a factor that inhibits frank discussion of spirituality among young adults.

If spirituality is a matter of improvising, it goes without saying that people have to get along with those who are improvising in different ways. We may talk to our friends about spirituality and appreciate their opinions, but we are unlikely to appreciate our friends telling us what to do, and we are probably reluctant to offer our own opinions too strongly. It becomes incumbent on each of us to hedge our convictions in a language of opinion and feeling. Norms of civility and pluralism make young adults reluctant to formulate spiritual journey narratives and present them.

The patterns, observed by Roof and Wuthnow and illustrated by the archived presentations I reviewed, include the following stages: awakening to inner spirituality, disillusionment with doctrinal religion, dropping out of traditional churches, feeling drawn to spiritual seeking by inner spiritual experience, shopping for teachers, teachings, and spiritual communities, settling into a pattern of spiritual practice, and tinkering with this process in response to new spiritual experiences. This pattern does not appear just among Boomers; it fits the experience of many generations, mainly because most of us have spiritual needs, and our underlying social structure has persistent issues with religious belief and social policy that lead adults of all ages to an improvisational spiritual process.

Wuthnow (2007) concluded that spiritual tinkering is

> not just a form of restlessness that characterizes baby-boomers and then could be easily reversed among their offspring. Spiritual tinkering reflects the pluralistic religious society in which we live, the freedom we permit ourselves in making choices about faith, and the necessity of making those choices in the face of the uprootedness and change that most adults experience. It involves piecing together ideas from many sources, especially through conversations with one's friends.

Spiritual experience is a powerful magnet. When people have one, they want more. When they get more, they are led to develop a lifestyle that promotes having spiritual experience. A large proportion of adults finds their religion of origin an adequate resource for assimilating their spiritual experiences. But an even larger proportion choose a self-directed spiritual path, either within a religious context or on their own. Self-directed spirituality has caused much soul-searching within organized religion. It has been amazing to see highly structured religions such as Catholicism respond positively to those who wish to pursue a mystical path (Rohr, 2014). In many cases, the mystical path has been allowed to exist alongside the more traditional path. The result has been a "loosening" of religion in general.

The need for small groups within which to seek formation and nurturing of a self-directed spiritual life is strong. Such groups are stimulated and served by an explosion of books and online courses about spiritual journeying that have appeared in just the past ten years. The spiritual intimacy that develops within such groups can be strong glue that keeps the groups going.

The analysis of Quaker spiritual journey narratives revealed that most took a chronological approach, beginning with childhood spiritual experiences and experiences connected with organized religion. Nearly all presentations described a self-directed, and community-supported, spiritual journey. Most accounts described significant turning points, often related to life events such as crises of belief, spiritual epiphanies, geographic mobility, divorce, career crises, or illness. Most reflected a thoughtful life review and grappling with "meaning-of-life" questions. Most affirmed the importance of direct spiritual experiences in living a spiritually centered life. Many mentioned eras such as the 1960s, the Viet-Nam era, the Civil-Rights era, and the Women's-Movement era, and our current concerns about saving the planet as significant spiritual influences. There is an appreciation of spirituality as being and the importance of spirituality in action.

Common academic concepts of spiritual development appeared in these narratives, but only in one case did the existence of the concept shape the narrative. Erikson's concept of generativity showed up over and over in the many accounts of the spiritual significance of service in middle age and later life. The concepts of integrity and wisdom were common in discussions of self-esteem, the changing nature of service, and the value of relationships on the spiritual journey. The elements of Tornstam's concept of gero-transcendence appeared in the narratives of Friends in their 80s or older. They tended to stress "holding the field" rather than accumulating possessions or "making things happen."

Next Steps

Most of the chapters in this book deal with the relationship between aging and religion. Spirituality is often viewed as inseparable from religion. Yet a growing proportion of aging adults in western societies see themselves as being "spiritual but not religious." We continue to have trouble defining and measuring spirituality, mainly because it is essentially a qualitative, sensitizing concept rather than a quantitative, denotative concept (Herbert Blumer, cited in Turner, 1991). The same can be said for religion. Those aspects of religion that can be precisely measured do not say much about the experiences, beliefs, values, needs and motivations that lead to the numbers.

Much qualitative work remains to be done to more fully map what our stories, our narratives of spiritual journeying, can tell us about spirituality and its relation to religion and aging. The work in this book is a good step in that direction. A very large proportion of Americans see themselves as being on a spiritual journey, and this journey is important to them. Most elders on a spiritual journey have been on that journey for decades, and perceive that it has had profound effects on their capacity to cope with what life brings. The more we can understand these journeys, the better we can understand what is happening to religion in western countries and how the experience of aging is being influenced by spirituality and religion.

References

Atchley, R. C. (2009). *Spirituality and Aging*. Baltimore, MD: Johns Hopkins University Press.

Erikson, E. H., Erikson, J. M., & Kivnick, H. Q. (1986). *Vital Involvement in Old Age: The Experience of Old Age in Our Time*. New York: W. W. Norton & Co.

Hillman, J. (1999). *The Force of Character and the Lasting Life*. New York: Random House.

Huxley, A. (1944). *The Perennial Philosophy*. New York: Harper & Row.

James, W. (1905). *The Varieties of Religious Experience*. London: Longmans, Green, & Co.

Maslow, A. (1971). *The Further Reaches of Human Nature*. New York: Viking Press.

Moody, H. R., & Carroll, D. L. (1997). *The Five Stages of the Soul*. New York: Anchor Books.

Ray, Ruth E. and McFadden, Susan H. (2001) The web and the quilt: Alternatives to the heroic journey toward spiritual development. *Journal of Adult Development* 8 (4): 201–211.

Rohr, R. (2014). *Dancing Standing Still*. Mahwah, NJ: Paulist Press.

Roof, W. C. (1993). *A Generation of Seekers: The Spiritual Journeys of the Baby Boom Generation*. San Francisco: Harper.

Roof, W. C. (1999). *Spiritual Marketplace: Baby Boomers and the Remaking of American Religion*. Princeton, NJ: Princeton University Press.

Schachter-Shalomi, Z. S., & Miller, R. S. (1995). *From Age-ing to Sage-ing: A Profound New Vision of Growing Older*. New York: Warner Books.

Tornstam, L. (2005). *Gerotranscendence: A Developmental Theory of Positive Aging*. New York: Springer Publishing Co.

Turner, J. H. (1991). *The Structure of Sociological Theory*, 9th ed. Belmont, CA: Wadsworth.

Wuthnow, R. (1998). *After Heaven: Spirituality in America Since the 1950s*. Berkeley, CA: University of California Press.

Wuthnow, R. (2007). *After the Baby Boomers: How Twenty- and Thirty-Somethings Are Shaping the Future of American Religion*. Princeton, NJ: Princeton University Press.

Chapter 4

Meaning Making Narratives among Non-Religious Individuals Facing the End of Life

Christel Manning

SACRED HEART UNIVERSITY

This chapter begins with a story about my friend Vince. He was part of a group of about a dozen of us who gather monthly for dinner, wine, and conversation. A few years back I hosted a party for Vince to celebrate his 72nd birthday, which we suspected might be his last. He had stage four cancer.

We all ate and drank and later settled in on the sofas and chairs in the living room to have a toast for Vince. He thanked us and then asked to say a few words. "I'd like to talk about the elephant in the room" he said. "I am dying, and this is likely the last birthday I will celebrate with you." He then proceeded to reflect on his life and impending death. He talked about fear of what was happening to his body, fear of losing control, fear that we would not able to finish his project, his sadness at having to say goodbye to Judy and all of us. He also spoke of his gratitude for our friendship and for the richness of his life's adventures. And he expressed his curiosity about what dying might reveal in relation to his ongoing quest to define the nature of consciousness.

Fear of the unknown and sadness about goodbyes are natural reactions when you go into new territory, and Vince was no stranger to encountering it again and again as he sought answers to the many questions he had. Meaning of life to Vince was about seeking truth, both intellectually and experientially. He was at heart a scientist which caused him to reject religion, but which also caused him to be open to all kinds of experiences. Trained as an engineer, he quit his job at a large medical equipment corporation after ten years to move to Kenya to teach math to children. He traveled to Peru to take Iawaska with a Shaman. In his final years he became obsessed with creating a computer code that visualized the Mandelbrot set as a model of his ideas about consciousness and energy.

Vince was a committed atheist for as long as I knew him, over some 20 years, and some of us wondered if his impending death would soften that. Yet he refused what he saw as the false comfort of religion in the face of dying. Instead he seemed to face death as a final mystery to be probed, with fear yes but also with open eyes, as he had with all the other adventures in his life.

So why is this story important? Because Vince offers a contrast to how we normally think of religion and aging. Many people get more religious as they age (Bengtson, Chapter 1 in this volume), probably because religion offers an important toolkit for helping us make sense of the finality of life. Yet a growing number of people, like Vince, are not religious (Pew Research Center, 2012). This chapter reports on an on-going study of how atheist, agnostic, and secular individuals find meaning as they approach the end of life.

Religion and Meaning

There is a substantial body of literature examining the role of religion as people face the end of life. Much of this research examines religion's impact on the health, both physical and emotional, of older individuals, an impact that is often found to be positive (Woźniak, 2015). While some of that impact is linked to the social support older people find in their religious communities, it is also related to religion's role as a source of meaning (Krause, Chapter 8 in this volume). There are several schools of thought that explain why religion helps people find meaning.

One sees religion as an explanatory framework or schema that orders the events of our lives (Berger, 1967; Ellison, 1994; Pargament, 1997; Siegel, Anderman, & Schrimshaw, 2001). The end of life is frightening because it is a new experience and we do not know what comes after. For older people especially, the final years bring loss of partners, family and friends who would otherwise support them at this time. And for most people dying is a long drawn out process in which they gradually lose control of body and mind (Johnson, Chapter 11 in this volume). Religion can explain why we are in pain or why we had to lose somebody we love, for example, by framing suffering as redemptive or part of a divine plan. Religion also answers questions about what happens after death, for example by promising we will see loved ones again in heaven. Religion is like a grid onto which we can spread whatever is confusing or scary and thereby create order and certainty. Meaning, in this view, is about seeing order and purpose in what would otherwise be random events.

Another explanation is that religion offers action steps that give people a sense of control over their lives (Siegel et. al., 2001; Jenkins & Pargament, 1995; Cole & Pargament, 1999; Krause, 2007). Facing one's final years is often accompanied by losing the ability to engage in basic physical activities that we normally take for granted, such as getting out of bed, bathing and dressing, or feeding oneself. There is often a loss of mental acuity, like not being able to remember appointments, names, or places. Older people may also be caring for an ailing life partner and experience the stress of being powerless to alleviate their pain. Such loss of control makes people feel helpless and depressed, perceiving life as pointless. In this situation, religion offers people steps they can take to exert some influence over their lives. Reading scripture or meditation is something an individual can do for herself even with physical disability. When a person has run out of medical options, praying that God will heal is an action step he can still take on regular basis. And when a loved one dies, rituals like sitting Shiva or preparing for a funeral mass offer structured activities that give a sense of control and thus purpose to life. The benefit of religion comes from practice, a series of steps we can take that make us feel less helpless. Meaning here is about being able to take action to exert influence over our lives.

The two meaning making functions of religion, schemas and control, are of course related. Thus some define meaning as a sense of *coherence*, a feeling of confidence that events of one's life are ordered or purposeful, rather than random and chaotic, which in turn confers a sense of *control* over one's life, rather than helplessness (Woźniak, 2015). However we define meaning, the strong link between religion and meaning begs the question: how do people who are not religious find meaning as they near the end of life?

Meaning among the Non-religious

Surveys show a significant increase in the number of Americans who identify as non-religious. The "Nones", as they are commonly referred to, today comprise nearly a quarter of the U.S. population (up from around 8% for much of the 20th century). The turn away from religion is more pronounced among younger people: 36% of millennials are Nones compared to 11% of the silent generation, born 1928–45, and 17% of Baby Boomers, born 1946–64. But growth has increased in all age groups (Lipka, 2015). Although the None category comprises a wide variety of worldviews, some of which are not secular (Manning, 2015), a growing proportion of Nones are, in fact, non-religious. This trend, combined with the recent rise of an organized atheist movement (Cimino & Smith 2014), has led to increased scholarly attention to the non-religious. But that research has tended to focus on younger people, millennials in particular (Baker & Smith, 2015; Manning, 2015; Zuckerman, 2012).

Much less is known about older non-religious individuals, especially those facing the end of life. In my first database research session on the subject, I typed in "religion and aging" and got over a thousand results, compared to only two for "atheism and aging," and there were similar disparities for searches using related search terms such as "secular" or "non-religious" and "end of life" or "death and dying." It is sometimes thought that we can look to studies showing religion's health benefits to infer more negative outcomes for non-religious individuals, but such a conclusion is not warranted. Several recent reviews (Hwang, Hammer, & Cragun 2011; Weber, Pargament, & Kunik, 2012) show such studies typically compare more religious with less religious individuals and do not adequately sample atheists and agnostics. The few studies that engage in more rigorous comparisons suggest that non-religious people do just fine. Horning et. al. (2011) found secular individuals were less likely than religious individuals to see their lives as having some deeper meaning or purpose but still coped well with stress, albeit by using different coping methods (they are more likely to rely on humor while the religious use prayer). Wilkinson and Coleman (2010; Coleman, Chapter 5 in this volume) found that both atheism and religion can be a source of meaning for older people, and it is the strength of conviction, rather than being religious or non-religious, that enables effective coping. And Coleman suggests that while uncertainty is sometimes linked to depression, questioning also links to growth. In short, various studies challenge the perception that non-religion is bad for your health, but we still do not know much about how and where non-religious people find alternative sources of meaning.

At times, it seems the research on questions of meaning at the end of life is being held hostage to the debate over whether religion is good for your health, and therefore by implication secularity is less so. As a non-religious person it is rather obvious to me that people like Vince or I can be healthy and lead a meaningful life without religion. So I am more interested in exploring the process by which individuals (both religious or not) find meaning, and examining how that process might be similar or different.

Meaning Making as Story Telling

It is often assumed (even by the Templeton Foundation that is funding this study) that meaning comes from holding certain beliefs. But beliefs do not exist in a vacuum. To understand how people derive meaning from their beliefs we must pay attention to stories, because it is through the stories in which beliefs are embedded that human beings make sense of events in their lives (Day & Lee, 2014; Gockel, 2013). It is also widely assumed that religion provides meaning to life. But meaning is something we make; it is active rather than passive. Religion does not give us meaning, rather we draw on religion to create meaning. And different people do so in different ways. I suspect the same is true of secular meaning making.

In a helpful review of narrative research, Gockel (2013) asserts that if telling stories is the main way we make sense of events and thereby create meaning in our lives, then the analysis of such stories must attend to both the process and content of meaning making, exploring not only *what* is being said but *how*. While the methods of narrative research are diverse, they share some basic assumptions and interests.

First, stories create meaning (Atchley, Chapter 3 in this volume; Bruner, 2004). Language does not just capture and reflect experience but creates it. As we all know from watching the news these days, the same set of events can result in very different stories depending on who is telling the story. And even when the resulting story is similar in content, people use linguistic, rhetorical, structural devices to create different sets of meaning.

Second, stories are shaped by context. There are the broader social narratives that shape individual storytelling, what Swidler (1986) has called the cultural toolkit. Social narratives can come from religion, like Bible stories people grow up with. They can come from a particular family background, like being part of a Jewish family who survived the holocaust. Or they may come from popular culture, like media stories about what millennials are like. But social context is not like a mold that consistently forms stories into a particular shape. It is dynamic, a two-way street. Sometimes our stories push against social context, sometimes we adapt our stories to it. This is important to keep in mind as we do research on the non-religious individuals where both researchers and respondents will often frame their narratives in terms of or over against religious categories which dominate our social discourse.

There is also the interpersonal context, the relationship between the story teller and the listener. Stories are told differently in different settings and to different people. Gockel points out that "the same person may tell a different story about their battle with cancer to their partner, their oncologist and their cancer survivor group because of the nature of social relationships into which they are speaking and the power dynamics inherent in those relationships" (2013, p. 192). Interpersonal context, too, is not a one-way street. This can be both a benefit and a liability in research. Being relative strangers to our respondents can make them feel more comfortable to be open with us: we sign a consent form that promises anonymity, and they do not have to worry about revealing some family secret that might upset somebody closer to them. But it can also be a liability (Arvay, 2002). My respondents know I am a professor at a Catholic university, and they often make false assumptions about what that means, so I need to reassure them that I have no agenda. In short, both the what (content) and how (language use) of the story a person tells about her life is influenced by larger social narratives and by interpersonal relationships between teller and listener.

Finally, stories shape our identity. While some aspects of identity are rooted in social facts (such as gender, age, profession, or major life events like surviving cancer), how people think about who they are depends on the stories they tell themselves and others (Somers, 1994). Similar sets of circumstances may lead one person to identify as a survivor where another becomes a victim. The courts may suggest a man is a criminal but he perceives himself as an entrepreneur. A gifted painter who does her work on the side may never identify as an artist. One of my favorite films, *Big Fish*, focuses on the stories a dying father tells his son, the extent to which these stories are actually rooted in the social facts of the father's life, and what that tension reveals about who he actually is. The father, Edward Bloom, is objectively an ordinary man who grew up in small town Alabama, married, had children, and supported his family as a traveling salesman. But as Edward tells his life story, he is a hero who interacts with witches and giants, confronts monsters and saves lives. His son, Will, having heard these stories all this life, is estranged from his father because he believes them to be lies. When his father has a stroke Will attempts to mend their relationship and begins investigating the facts behind the tall tales (told in flashbacks in the film). Though the facts turn out to be less fantastical than Edward described, he is still remarkable man. And Will is astonished when all of the people from his father's stories attend the funeral service. He now understands how Edward's stories shaped who he became.

Who we are in life will, of course, affect how we see death. There is kind of a feedback loop operative in how stories make meaning. We tell stories to create meaning from events of the past and those stories in turn shape how we see our future. That loop makes the topic of meaning making both fascinating and complex.

Applying what we Know: Research in Progress

This chapter reports on an on-going project that applies what we know about religious meaning making narratives to help us understand how non-religious people create meaning at the end of life. A big reason why religion is such a powerful source of meaning is that it provides a readymade set of stories, a framework of meaning that people can adapt to explain what is happening to them in terms that provide coherence and control. Religious people usually learn in childhood stories such as the biblical story of Job and its message that suffering is a kind of test of one's faith, or the resurrection story with its promise that death really is not the end. These stories are then adapted to one's individual life situation: for example, a painful illness that a person knows will eventually kill her. She creates meaning by framing the illness as a test of her faith, she suffers as Christ did, so the illness is not random. She is not helpless. If she keeps her faith, she too will find life after death. In short, religion creates meaning at two levels: it provides *generic narratives* that function as a cultural tool for constructing meaning and are then adapted as needed in one's *personal narrative*.

What we do not yet understand well is how meaning-making works for non-religious people (Taves, 2016). While previous research (Heywood & Bering, 2013) has shown that the non-religious do, in fact, frame life events using purposive narratives, we know very little about the content, patterns and sources of these narratives. Are there generic stories that secular adults use to assign meaning, especially at the end of life? How do they rework these stories to create meaning of their personal experience? There is increasing recognition in the literature that there are different types of non-religious people (Lee, 2015; Manning, 2015), so we must also ask how narratives and their use vary by type of non-religious identity and by cultural background. The research on which I report here seeks to answer these questions.

The project, funded by a grant from the Templeton Foundation, is a qualitative study of U.S. elders (individuals over 70) that is being conducted over a period of two years. Phase 1, the basis for this chapter, is a pilot study of 30 elders that includes both non-religious and religious respondents for comparison. The purpose of the pilot is to test the research procedures and instruments and improve these as needed. Phase 2, to begin in spring 2018 and extend through summer 2019, will be a larger study of 100 additional respondents focusing specifically on non-religious individuals but including both European and African Americans for comparison.

Research activities for both phases include the following.

Recruitment of Respondents

Participants must be over 70 and suffer little to no cognitive impairment. The pilot study is being conducted in a medium sized city on the East Coast of the United States. Potential respondents for Phase 1 are identified and referred by a local elder care facility that provides both assisted living and nursing home care. Phase 2 will involve two additional care facilities. Respondents in the study may also suggest potential participants who reside elsewhere.

Screening and Selection

After receipt of consent, respondents complete a brief demographic questionnaire indicating their age, gender, education, race/ethnicity, and religious or non-religious identification. The main function of the survey is as a screening device to identify non-religious respondents. Previous research has demonstrated various problems with measures of identification, for example people who identify as Catholic but do not actually believe or practice that religion, or people who identify as non-religious but who hold conventional religious beliefs in God and engage in prayer and other spiritual practice. Thus, whatever identification they choose will be further probed during the interview.

Interviews

Interviews are conducted at the facility or respondent's home depending on respondent preference. Interviews are taped and take 30–90 minutes each.

Conversations are semi-structured with questions in three areas. An initial set of questions invites the respondent to look back and share some of their *life story* including their family, work, and interests. These open ended questions help to build comfort with the interviewer but also engage the respondent in what Johnson (Johnson, Chapter 11 in this volume) and Moody (Moody, Chapter 12 in this volume) call "life review" (reflection on what you have done with your life). A second set of questions focuses on the present and future, asking respondents to reflect on the *end of life*, including how respondents make sense of pain and illness, how they cope with loss of loved ones, and how they understand death and dying. A final set of questions seeks to unpack the respondents' *self-identification* (what the religious or non-religious preference they declared in the screening survey actually means) in order to facilitate more accurate coding. These questions are presented last in order to avoid framing the preceding discussion about death and dying as a religious one and thereby priming respondents to tell stories to fit their explicit identification.

Coding and Analysis

Interviews are transcribed by a professional transcribing company (https://www.rev.com/transcription). Transcripts will later be analyzed, using both software, such as Dedoose (http://www.dedoose.com) and manual review. Analysis proceeds along three dimensions. The first is thematic content, including narrative types and patterns, which are discussed in more detail below. Second, after both phases of the study are completed transcripts will be coded by culture/ethnicity (white/European American, black/African American) and by type of secularity (e.g., hard atheist, spiritual/agnostic, and indifferent). The final analysis will explore whether and how narrative types and patterns vary by types of cultural and secular identity.

What We Are Learning

This project has only just begun at this writing, and we are still in the midst of the pilot study. To date I have completed 25 interviews. The interviews have been transcribed but I have not yet completed coding or formal content analysis. Instead, the following section will reflect on how the process of doing this research is challenging how we think about meaning making as it relates to both religion and secularity.

Demographics

The pilot sample thus far includes 9 males and 16 females. The average age was 81, with 11 respondents in their seventies, 10 in their eighties, and 4 in their nineties. In terms of education, 10 had finished high school and 15 had at least some college. More than half of respondents (14) indicated they were in poor health, while the remainder (11) described themselves as healthy. When asked about race/ethnicity, all but 2 referred to themselves as "white," with half of them identifying with a particular ethnic tradition including Irish, Polish, Hungarian, Greek, Ukrainian, Italian. Several spoke English with a very heavy accent. When asked about religion, 10 identified with religion (either Catholic or Jewish) and 15 did not.

Most of these interviews were conducted at the elder care facility hosting the pilot study, and their demographics reflect that. The facility is located in a mixed income, historically immigrant neighborhood. Until the middle of the last century it was home to many Irish, Italians, Poles, and Jews; today it is mostly Puerto Rican and Ecuadorian, with a few African Americans in the mix. The population of the facility, the oldest in the city, reflects the older composition of the area, perhaps because many of the residents grew up nearby. There are two other major nursing homes in the area that were built more recently and serve a predominantly black population where we plan to go for the second phase of the study. As noted earlier, the larger study is designed to include African Americans which will also likely result in more respondents from a Protestant background.

Preliminary Patterns and Questions

The pilot project was designed to include both secular individuals and those who identify as religious. Since so much of previous research on meaning making at end of life has focused on religious rather than secular people, I wanted to make sure the types of questions I asked worked for both types. I was also interested in comparison. Though the pilot study is too small to make generalizations about religious or secular people, I was curious if I would find types of narratives unique to each group and if I might find overlap. Here are some preliminary patterns and questions that emerge from this data.

A Sampling: Five Stories

The research literature suggests that religion offers a framework through which individuals interpret their lives, including how they think about the end of life. I had expected Bible narratives to be a prominent pattern among religious respondents. But these rarely came up, and if so only in passing. This may be because the denominations represented in the pilot sample were Catholic and Jewish, traditions which have not historically emphasized Bible study as Protestants have. Here are some other generic narrative patterns that were utilized by religious respondents in the pilot study.

God has a plan

In this generic narrative respondents frame their life stories in terms of a divine plan: events, good or bad, unfold because God wants to challenge you or teach you or to help you out. God has a plan both for this life and what comes after. You may not always know where it leads, but that is why you must trust God.

An example of this type of narrative is Kamilla I.'s story. Kamilla is 86 years old and is a lifelong Catholic. She walks with a cane and her vision is poor, but is otherwise in good health. Widowed after 56 years of marriage, she has one daughter and no grandchildren. She lives in an assisted living facility.

Kamilla was born and raised in Hungary in an educated, middle class family. Her parents played piano, she sang and her brothers played cello and violin. She remembers fondly how they would play music together. But then the war came. "We left in 1944, in November and I was still in school and … I had three brothers and still, we were all in school." The family sought to immigrate to America. But "we had to wait for a sponsor, you know. And then they separated us." Her brothers went first to find jobs in Venezuela and she did not see them for several years. "It wasn't easy and kind of my mom was worried about it, you know. But thankfulness we made it" to America. They moved to Cleveland, Ohio. But Kamilla never finished high school. Her family lost everything, and they had to start from scratch in the United States. "And from one day to the other we didn't know what to … and my mom was going and going to a home and … begging for food because we didn't have nothing. We just go from one place to the other, we didn't even know if we gonna be a stay alive or dead." Kamilla concludes it was because "my parents had such a faith in God that we got help … we were safe and we were all six of us together." Others she knew did not make it, so the miracle of their survival could only be God's work.

They settled in the Hungarian section of Cleveland, Ohio, where her father opened a little store. "He fixed radios and TV… and people came. And then he made pictures when he went to the theater and take pictures for the people and if they want some pictures … for a few pennies or dollars, you can buy those pictures." She met her future husband in her father's store. "They were walking to my father's store and they were saying, you are from Venezuela and you know my sons. Come on, talk about it. So, my parents invited them. They were talking and then I fell in love with one of them, and we got married. So, I think that was another God send because I don't think I would find anybody like that, like him." She goes on to explain, "He was from Hungary too," and his father was educated and middle class. "We got quite along and interest. We like travel. He like interesting things, discover on this planet. I mean we had a lot of things in common. Of course the same language, right." Except he was Protestant. But Kamilla came to respect them. "They studied Bible. Which I read it once. It took me a year to read the whole Bible."

Kamilla married and went to work as a clerk for General Electric. They had a child, but it passed away in infancy. "God took it away for some reason." They had another daughter, and Kamilla stayed home to raise her. She had a happy marriage until her husband died suddenly. Then she fell into a depression. Her daughter, who had taken a job on the East Coast, moved her to the nursing home where she lives now. "My husband passed away. I was all by myself. I didn't feel like doing anything. I couldn't even cook for myself ... and I had no more friends. I didn't drive anymore. So my daughter said, 'Come on, Mom. I find a place for you, and we will be together, closer than, you know.'" Kamilla is very happy about this turn of events, which she again attributes to God.

> See this beautiful room I have? ... in the morning I had the kitchen sun come in and the people are nice and give the medication and take care of you and feed you and let you sit down and eat and don't have to do anything. And people come twice or three times a week. There's people come and play music and singing. I love it ... and there's a beautiful little garden, I don't know if you noticed? ...Because I love to be outdoors and you can sit down, you can walk. And even about three times a week, Monday, Wednesday and Friday, there's a guy who's bringing the C.D. and thing, music. And you can be outside and you can walk or you can just sit and listening or whatever. I say I couldn't be a better place, honestly. That's why I believe God led me here. To have this place and then I can be close to my daughter because she's the only one for me now.

Kamilla's trust in God's plan carries over to the future, even though she is uncertain about what the afterlife might mean. She admits she has all sorts of questions about this. "Well thank goodness I am pretty decent health. I am blessed with that. So, I don't have to worry about it. But I just wonder sometimes, 'If you pass away, what's gonna happen? Do I'm gonna see my parents or my husband or you know?'" She speculates about what will happen if people are cremated, or if they will be reincarnated: "They burn their body. How can you resurrect? So I said I wonder. Sometimes I heard something like you're gone into another person... I don't know. Nobody knows." But that uncertainty does not make her anxious because she trusts that God has good things in store for her. "I just let it go and let God take care of it so ... He created us so he will take care of it."

In Kamilla's narrative, everything that happened in her life – surviving the war and coming to America, meeting her husband, losing her child, finding a home to grow old – has meaning because "he had a plan for me or for us."

God gave us free will

For other religious respondents meaning is somewhat less predetermined. In this generic narrative, life events are random but God gives free will, so we shape our own destiny. Bad things happen but we can choose how to respond, and God can help us in the process. The soul will live on after the body dies, but we cannot know exactly what will happen to it. So we must use the time we have left wisely.

An example of this type of narrative is Pauline J. Now 80, Pauline is also Roman Catholic. A retired scientist, she suffered a series of seizures which eventually confined her to a wheelchair. She is divorced with two grown children and two grandchildren who live nearby.

Pauline was raised in Boston in a large Polish Catholic family. She had a happy but unremarkable childhood, did well in school, and got a master's degree in biochemistry. At a time when many women were home makers, she went to work for a pharmaceutical company, and continued working there after marrying and having children, a boy and a girl. She divorced shortly after the children were grown. "It was a very unhappy divorce and separation. He had an affair with a woman that lived next door … It was a matter of I was able to see him get up out of my bed and go to hers. I was really very … It was terrible. It was really terrible." She now feels that she should have seen it coming. "Marrying him was a bad decision."

Pauline loved her job, and she continued working into her sixties, with no plans to retire. But then, "I had a seizure… nobody ever tells you about these things, about getting older. I did a lot of reading and had nice, good doctors and was able to figure out what my limitations would be." Quitting work was a difficult decision. "I didn't enjoy retiring, but I knew that it wasn't safe for me to be in the laboratory. There were no desk jobs that I was interested in, so it was time to go." So she found other activities to keep her busy. "I volunteered a lot at the local libraries. I did a lot of adult education type teaching, I'm very much interested in quilting and patch-work. I had classes there and made quilts. Did a lot of that." But eventually she had to give up those things too. Pauline moved to a nursing home because a subsequent seizure made her unable to walk. She chose this facility because it was located near her adult children who visit her regularly.

Pauline is frustrated by her physical limitations and hates being dependent on others: "There's a sense of aggravation and a sense that you have to really work at accepting. The loss of independence, the loss of the ability to drive a car is incredibly, incredibly demeaning. I have to keep reminding myself, I'm older. I have to accept I can't do that anymore." But she tries to make the best of it: "I do a lot of reading, which keeps me very happy, very happy. There's some very fine ... I like a good mystery writer. This guy James Patterson ... Now I'm thinking about maybe I should try to spend some time writing. I'm thinking about a possible, two things: a book on patchwork quilting and a mystery story." Though she is physically disabled, she is proud to still have a good mind. "I haven't let myself be thrown into the idea of, Well, you're old. You're 80. Forget that. My God has seen fit to let me keep my mind. I'm gonna use it. ... Use it or lose it." This is the first time she has mentioned God in her story, and his role is quite different from what we saw in Kamilla's narrative.

God is present in Pauline's story but does not seem to be directing it. "Our lives are shaped by the choices we make. Okay? ... Up to a certain age people, our parents and friends, make choices for us. Okay? But at some point along the way, this is part of growing up that we are taught to make choices... . Hopefully we [learn] the difference between a good choice and a bad choice. My husband pops into mind. I made a bad choice." Her daughter was addicted to drugs for a while and is now recovered. While Kamilla might have framed this as a miracle, Pauline believes her daughter finally learned to make better choices. God gave us free will. Some things, like the place we are born into or the people we meet or having a seizure, are random but, "God has given me the ability to make choices and to choose." So we need to take responsibility for our own lives. "We have to accept [the consequences] and to learn to live with it. Or to try to make it better. I think that's part of growing up." God will be there to help us make good decisions. "If I need him, I call on him. I called on him this morning. I said, 'I'm gonna need some help. Gonna need some guidance.' ... I turn to a God to guide me, to show me, to put something in my life that will show me what it is I need to do. Not necessarily like a bolt of lightning, but just give me the awareness to see that there are things in my life already that can help me with whatever it is I'm trying to deal with." Pauline sees herself as the author of her life, for which she gets help from God when she needs it.

The framework of making right choices extends to the future. Pauline rejects the church's teaching about what happens after death. "I don't believe in an afterlife. I hear it talked about a lot. People write about it a lot". But that is just "so much speculation and perhaps hope" because people want to feel better. "It's just a big nothingness as far as I'm concerned. Yeah, whatever happens, happens. I don't want to waste my time thinking about it because it's something that we're not going to know." Instead, she focuses on making the best of the time she has left. "One day at a time. What comes, comes. I accept what comes. If I can see a way to make it better, I'll try." So she reads mysteries and collects quilting patterns and dreams about the mystery novel she may still write some day. Meaning in Pauline's story lies in self-determination, her freedom to choose for the better with God's help.

The stories of Kamilla and Pauline illustrate how religion can provide a generic narrative for creating meaning as we approach the end of life. That type of meaning system is something secular people reject. Here are three examples of alternative narrative types utilized by secular respondents in this study.

The laws of nature

Secular respondents often told stories that draw on the framework of natural science. In one version of this generic narrative, the notion that we are all part of a cycle of nature and humans are merely the most intelligent (or most ruthless) animal account for what happens in our lives. Though there is no divine plan, our life course is not random because genetics and the forces of socialization shape our ability to create a good life. Though the laws of nature are amoral, it is rational to do good because it improves life on the planet for everyone. Death is the natural end of life, so we should focus on living it well.

An example of this type of narrative is Sally N. Born into a culturally Jewish family, she has been an atheist since her early teens. A retired high school science teacher, she is now 84 and lives alone in a retirement condominium complex. She is twice divorced, most recently 25 years ago, has two children, and five grandkids.

Sally was raised in an upper middle class Jewish home in New York. Her mother was a published poet, her father a business man. "There was always enough money." But she had a conflicted relationship with her parents. Her father was not around much and her "mother was a very self-centered … She was not a very motherly mother, let's just put it that way. Luckily, when I was three-years-old, a maid entered the family, Addie. She was black, and she was really like my mother for several years. She was the huggable one. She was the one that really cared about me." Still, Sally recalls a mostly happy childhood and plenty of friends. "I was a tomboy. I liked to ride my bike. We had a bike club, and my mother actually, now this is what my mother was good at, she actually wrote a song for us that we could sing as a club member." Her teen years were more difficult. She lacked self confidence in school because she was not pretty enough, and then her parents split up when her mother came out as gay. "My father, considering that my parents were divorced, was as attentive as you could expect a separated father to be. I interacted with him quite a lot. I did not like his second wife. I liked his third wife better." But she hated living with her mother so much that "in my junior year of high school, I decided I wanted to leave home." She moved in with a family friend and later with her older sister to finish out high school in an elite private school. Through a teacher there, she became involved with Ethical Culture, a Jewish atheist organization, "which in effect promulgates all the ethical aspects of Judaism, without any of the religion."

Sally met her first husband in college. He was a communist and she became one too because "what you do when you're 18-years-old, and you're a girl, you immediately take on the colors and flavors of the person that you're going out with." They divorced after six years because "I discovered he was fooling around with somebody else." She went to graduate school, then traveled to Israel where she met her second husband. They lived there for nine years, though she returned temporarily to the United States when her husband was called to serve in the Six-day war. They had two children. But the second marriage did not last either. Once the children were grown, she divorced again. "He had been a good husband and a good father, but as two people living together it just didn't work." They were too different. "I mean we didn't have the same interests. He didn't have a sense of humor at all, to the point where if I made it a pun or something like that, he would kind of cast it aside. He couldn't take it." She thinks her children take after him, "which is a great sorrow to me, because there's nothing that keeps a relationship together better than good jokes between them."

Sally loved her work. "Teaching science is really a very special thing, especially with younger people, because it gives you the opportunity to be very creative... And I was very successful as a science teacher. So, you know, that gave me a lot of pleasure. It was my identity until I retired" [at age 67]. Since then, she has spent much of her time volunteering at a local science museum, being active in local politics, playing music, and caring for her grandchildren. "I have a very close relationship with those three grandchildren, especially the second one, who like me plays the guitar, and who was my inspiration for starting to play the guitar" about seven years ago.

As an atheist, Sally does not see her life in terms of divine direction nor does she emphasize making good choices. Looking back, "I don't believe I'm blessed. And I don't believe that [how life went] is anything of my doing either." Sometimes she "got lucky." Other times she did not but "the negative things, didn't impact me that much." She attributes this to innate personality traits. "There's a genetic connection in this ... your nature as a person. There's no question in my family that it's hereditary. My father had a very positive kind of outlook ... and we just are that way ... We all inherited kind of an upbeat personality ... it's just a characteristic of our being that we're basically optimistic people." She cites the example of "my daughter who has gone through a lot of trauma with her husband" when they divorced eight years ago. "And yet the way they have managed their lives ... mostly for the sake of their kids ... People can't believe that they're pulling it off. And that is only because of the strength of her personality and the 'upbeatness' of her nature, and that comes from my family, I know it. It is genetic." She thinks of her late brother, "Peter also exemplified it." Sally sees her atheism as a matter of genetics as well. She recalls listening to a program on NPR about how spirituality was "a hereditary characteristic. And I knew right away, that's not me ... I don't have an ounce of spirituality." She thinks spirituality is helpful to people because "it gives you a feeling of ... beyond yourself ... But I just don't have it." And that cannot be changed because "spiritual is not something that you can become." You are born with it – or not.

Now that she is older, Sally admits that she often thinks about death and dying. Though she feels generally happy and connected, she has lost her brother and several friends in recent years. "I mean this is something that everybody deals with, you come to a certain age and you suddenly realize, hey, when I die, the whole being of me is not going to be there anymore. How could that possibly be?" She feels religious concepts of afterlife developed to address that mental anguish. "It's hard to accept the idea that there must be some way of maintaining yourself, your mental self. It's hard to understand that [when your body dies] there's no more you." And yet the idea that your consciousness would exist beyond death is "so non-rational ... The whole idea [that] if you're still a thinking being, somehow, after you die, well that means that Socrates is still a thinking being, and George Washington is still a thinking being ... and that's just not possible." She concludes, "You have no choice; you have to accept the fact that you are passing out of existence." We cannot know what that will be like "until it happens." But she does know and "I definitely think often about the fact that I'm not gonna be here forever." And this realization is changing how she lives her life. "I'm beginning to see the need for less money in the bank, and to give more money to the kids ... I don't have a lot of money, but I contribute to my grandkids college funds every year ... and to spend more on myself. Like I bought that car; that's a new car. I was thinking this is gonna be my last car. I was gonna buy a cheap car. And then I thought to myself, wait a minute Sally. Why are you doing this? You're 84 years old? Get a really nice car. So ... I mean yes, your attitude does change. Because life is not forever. It is important to think about how you want to spend your time remaining."

Sally believes that one of the benefits of aging is becoming "more yourself ... you care a lot less about what other people think." But the downside of that is older people may "become more self-centered, and more egotistical." Not intentionally, "but just because your life relates less to what's going on outside, and more to yourself, and you have to fight the temptation to think about, and to talk about your illnesses all the time, you know?" So she tries hard to remain connected to the world around her. She shared a list she keeps in her kitchen of things that keep her life meaningful. "One of them is nature. One of them is beauty created by man like playing beautiful music and listening to beautiful music. One of them is good health. One of them is having a home that I love. One of them is having a family that I love and that loves me. And one of them is having good friends." Meaning in Sally's narrative is found in fulfilling her natural potential and staying connected to the world.

We are the sum of our choices

Sally's worldview is somewhat deterministic. Though there is no divine plan, evolution shapes nature, life and death. Joy and suffering, even whether or not we are spiritual, are the rational outcome of our genetic makeup. There are other variations of the scientific narrative that put more emphasis on free will. This pattern is similar to the religious version, except that the ability to choose well is not attributed to God. Events are random but you always have a choice for how to respond, so individuals feel they bear primary responsibility for what happened in their lives. Death is the end of life, so we should choose our actions carefully while we still can.

An example of this type of narrative is Agnes J. She was raised Catholic in a working class Polish American family but rejected her religion when she left for college. Like Sally, she is a retired high school science teacher with two grown children and two grandchildren. Now 71 and widowed, she lives in her own home in a modest immigrant neighborhood of a small city.

Agnes spent her childhood in "what was called the Polish ghetto of Buffalo, New York. So I was brought up in a very, very strict Catholic community." She loved the closeness of the neighborhood. "You could walk everywhere. I really enjoyed the city." But she came to reject the religion. "You *had* to believe, and there were dire consequences for not believing." Yet she recalls having doubts about it early on. "A lot of things didn't make sense to me even as a little tiny girl." Her family ran a bar, and there was violence and sexual abuse that was always kept a secret. "One of the mortal sins at that time was eating meat on Friday or not going to church. Then one of the venial sins was lying. As a six-year-old I was saying to myself that there are people in my family that lied, and it caused horrible things to happen. If I eat meat on Friday, I haven't done anything to anybody. If I don't go to church, I haven't done anything to anybody. That seems stupid." Yet it took over a decade for doubt to turn into rejection of her faith. "It had a grip on me for a number of years after, even though my head didn't really believe it. There was still that leftover fear because that's how you were indoctrinated into that faith." In college she took a course in comparative religion. "There was a point in that course where I was reading and all the things I struggled with ... All of a sudden it felt as if inside me a plug had been pulled like in a bathtub and all the belief drained out. It was like oh, this is just like every other religion, myth, etc., and that was that." She never went back.

Against her parents' wishes, Agnes decided "to leave the Buffalo area and I applied to graduate school." At the time, "there was money and more opportunity for women in science. I got a total fellowship to go to

University of Illinois." After finishing her degree, she got married and moved to California where she had met her first husband. The couple later moved to the East coast because he was offered a job there. They had two children, a boy and a girl. But her first marriage ended after she learned her husband was having an affair. Her kids were teenagers when she divorced him and moved to a different city where she continued working for another 20 years until retirement at 65.

Agnes believes that much of what happens in life is "random. Hurricanes, tornadoes, the family you are born into. All kinds of things are random and can wreak havoc with us, and we have absolutely no control over it. The only thing we control is our reaction. Every decision we make determines the consequences that happen to us. I don't think that there's anybody micromanaging anything." Rather, we "create our lives by our choices." When she chose to "apply to graduate schools, that set the course of my life very different than if I had decided not to do it." When she married her first husband, there were "other consequences that flow from that. Every time we say yes or no to an opportunity, there's certain things that happen and certain opportunities open up and certain doors close, and that's just the way I think life is." There is a moral component to this philosophy. "The choice that we make to treat someone good or bad has consequences that we don't even always see or understand or know. I think when they say what comes around goes around, to some extent that is true. People who are kind and generous, etc., it comes back to them." So choosing well is also about becoming a better person.

It was shortly after she retired that Agnes met her second husband, and they had seven happy years together. "He was an amazing man. It was an amazing relationship." Then he was diagnosed with advanced stage cancer. "When he died, it was like stunningly shocking to my system. I realized how quickly things can change on a dime, how what you have and enjoy really has to be enjoyed every minute because it might not be there tomorrow." Her husband's death affirmed her perception of life's random-ness. "It was like a door slamming. I had not expected to grow old alone. I was hoping, because he was generally a healthy man when I met him. I was hoping we would have time into our eighties. Losing that, that sort of pulls the rug out from under you." But it also strengthened her conviction that we create our own lives. "We are the sum of our choices."

Agnes too rejects the notion of afterlife. Humans, like the rest of nature, are composed of our "physicality and our energy ... like with anything on this planet that dies, our atoms and energy are recycled back into the uni-verse." Like Sally, she draws on the theory of evolution, but Agnes emphasizes that we have the power to effect its direction by the choices we make. "I'm here as a result of choices, of two people who decided to get married and so on and so forth ... but now we have overpopulated the world ... and we've done so many things that are so destructive. I think our

purpose now should be to try to make this world livable for future generations ... at this point in history, that's what our whole goal should be."
And that's what she tries to do with the time she has left. She is engaged in
her community, including a "women's group active in politics." She sees
her son and his wife regularly and watches their kids twice a week. She is
very physically active and does a lot of things that she enjoys outdoors ...
walking, bike riding. "I recently took up a new hobby, horseback riding,
and I go to the gym several times to a week. I have a lot of friends. We go
out to dinner. We go to plays. We go to music venues, to movies, dinner
at each other's houses, that kind of thing. I've been doing a lot more
reading since I retired." She appreciates having time to "stop what I am
doing when I hear a bird singing in my garden and just listen." The
meaning of life, to Agnes, lies in choosing to connect, not only to other
human beings but to nature.

Mystical connections

Both Agnes's and Sally's story convey meaning using the framework of
natural science which contrasts clearly with that of religion. Another generic
narrative utilized by non-religious individuals was less obviously secular. In
this type of story life events are understood in terms of impersonal opposing
forces or energies, and connections that create synchronicity. Death is seen
as entering into another kind of energetic connection.

An example of this generic narrative is Dan J.'s story. Dan was raised in a
liberal Protestant family in a small Midwestern town but drifted away from
religion in his youth. Deeply engaged in the civil rights activism of the
1960s and the environmental movement of the 1970s, he remains agnostic
and describes himself as a lifelong spiritual seeker. Now 76 and recovering
from a recent heart attack, he lives with his wife in a big house they share
with his son and daughter in law and their two young children.

As Dan tells it, his life story unfolds along seemingly random paths that
reveal deeper connections as he looks back. He remembers his childhood as
"mostly happy and uneventful." He always had friends to play with but "I
was also very shy and dyslexic" while his "little sister was very good at
school ... so I always felt bad about that." A first turning point came in high
school when he took advanced math courses and discovered "that was just
totally natural to me." He later took physics and chemistry and "suddenly ... before I was dumb and then I became one of the top students in
the school." Dan does not attribute this change to some exterior force such
as God or nature, nor to his ability to make good choices. Instead, he
describes his life as a process of discovering how everything is connected.

Dan went on to college to study mathematics but ended up majoring in
sociology "because those were the questions that interested me." He took a
year to work as a high school math teacher, then went on to graduate

school for a doctorate in sociology. It was there that he met his wife, Debra, another instance of synchronicity. He recalls how he knew of her even before they met. Debra came from a Jewish family deeply involved in the civil rights movement, and she and her sisters got arrested protesting against a local UPS office "that wouldn't hire any blacks... and they were in the paper." That spring, he read about "how this high school senior got arrested ... then over the summer, then there was even a bigger story about this girl who had just graduated from high school who got arrested and was in jail in Mississippi and so I knew that Debra existed. That fall, I started seeing signs about how they were starting a new civil rights group at [the university]. That sounded interesting and so I went to the first meeting and there she was." Their meeting was clearly meant to be.

Dan and Debra became a couple and worked together on civil rights issues and later "during the Vietnam War ...we got involved in the antiwar stuff." He recalls how much of the local leadership for the antiwar movement "came from the Quaker meeting" and how he later discovered that his mother comes from a long line of Quakers. He had been unaware of this until his mother showed him a genealogical record, "this amazing document that took my family history virtually back to the beginning of Quakerism in the 17th Century." His own interest in peace activism was thus not random but seemed connected to a larger web of connection.

When Dan finished graduate school, he signed up to volunteer with VISTA (an anti-poverty program billed as domestic version of the Peace Corps). They sent him to Oregon for training. Debra dropped out of grad school to follow him there, and they eventually married and spent the next few years cross crossing the United States working in various poverty stricken communities of the Southwest. They were living in South Texas and "needed to figure out where we were going next." Debra encouraged him to apply to teach "at one of the black colleges and so I sent a few letters off to them." He was offered a job at "a very small, little school in Memphis, Tennessee, and so we went there. That was the year of the garbage strike, so we got involved in the garbage strike." They became engaged in Martin Luther King's movement and were present when "he was killed. That whole thing was very traumatic. He wasn't the only one killed. There were a bunch of people that got killed. They threw one garbage worker into the back of a garbage truck and he got ground up, I remember." Dan feels that being there at that time was another instance of synchronicity, and he wonders if "maybe we should have stayed." Instead, they moved back to the Northeast where he worked with a non-profit teaching black kids who had dropped out of school while Debra got a doctorate.

Dan spent the rest of his career working in various experimental education programs and helping his wife, tenured at a major university, in her research on the health impacts of environmental pollution. "I got involved with the Sierra Club and then that inspired Debra and I to develop the research that we were doing." Along the way they raised two children: a daughter who now lives in California and a son who moved to Cambodia. About a decade ago, Dan found that "with federal money drying up" grant writing "got more and more difficult" so he retired. Yet he remains engaged in the same kinds of activities. He volunteers with Sierra Club and participates in a couple of local academic associations exploring alternative approaches to science. "It's not like there's this sharp divide. It all flows together. I still do a lot of things that I always did." He continues his path of discovery. "I am interested in things … and then things happen."

One of the ways Dan explores the connections in his life is by recording his dreams. "I started that probably, I don't know, 40 years ago." He feels that some of those dreams seemed to predict later life events, like when he dreamed of "an Asian woman changing my life." He joked that he initially wondered if maybe he had "unconscious desires to have an affair." But later that year his son married a Cambodian woman and returned to the United States. They moved in with Dan and Debra. The young woman did not speak English well, so Dan tutored her daily to prepare her to apply to community college. "I was spending a lot of my time either tutoring her or taking care of Miriam [their grandchild]. I was taking care of Miriam so she could go to school." In the process he became very close to his granddaughter. When his son and daughter-in-law moved back to Cambodia, Miriam, by then a teenager, remained with Dan and Debra.

Dan views his life as "surprising," and its unlikely turns signal to him a deeper meaning. He started his life "in a lumber mill town in the north woods of Wisconsin. I actually worked in the woods some when I was in high school … If anybody had told me back then that I'd marry Debra, that I'd get involved in the civil rights movement, that I'd find out about my Quaker heritage," work with Dr. King in Memphis and later the Black Panthers in New Haven, that he would "become a research scientist at [a major university] for a number of years, if anybody had told me any of that, I would have said, 'Are you out of your mind? How is anything like that going to happen? It would never happen.'" But the fact that it did happen leads Dan to think it is "more than random," and he thinks this is true "in a more general, wider sense." Though he does not believe in God or practice any particular religion, he is convinced "there's a connectedness … I assume that there's some intentionality behind reality." He would not "give a name to it like God or Allah" because we do "not know enough to say what exactly that's all about," but there are some fascinating leads in recent science. "The fact that this material stuff is all fluff. You get into quantum mechanics and its fluff. It stays here, but it's fluff. Is it spirit? What is it?" He wants to "understand that connectedness" because he thinks it relates to what happens when we die.

Death is a mystery. It must mean the end of consciousness because of "the brain. It's dead. It's gone." And yet Dan wonders "whether is possible there's some kind of greater spiritual connectedness" that links to the "intentionality" he sees behind his life. That intentionality is linked some-how to the good. "Martin Luther King was giving a lot of positive possi-bilities to the world, and so it was too bad that he was killed. But in order to rise above that, it seems like you have to accept some kind of con-nectedness between the fact of his taking a risk of being killed and these good things, the good possibilities for improving the world. It just seems like in order to go there, you have to have some kind of a spiritual sense of a connection." He experienced that connection years ago when he attended a Quaker meeting. They have "this expression of a 'gathered meeting,' meaning they're connected, that soulfully and spiritually the people are connected." He thinks that other practices "like mindfulness meditation … are probably a lot of the same territory." Those practices tap into another dimension of reality that we do not yet fully understand. Dan seems at peace with that mystery.

Secular or Religious

These five meaning making narratives are a subset of a larger pool of data that is yet to be analyzed. I chose these stories in part because they reflect distinctive patterns that recurred among self-identified religious or secular respondents (there were additional patterns but discussing them all is beyond the scope of this chapter). What initially strikes me about these stories is less the difference between religious and secular meaning themes (I expected that) than the similarities. All of these narratives offer a framework that imposes order on life, a schema that explains why life happened as it did – because God planned it that way, because we are genetically programmed, because we choose well, or because there are mysterious energetic connec-tions that science has yet to understand. The extent to which these narra-tives are linked to a sense of control over one's life is mixed. Both the religious and the secular version of the "Free Will" narratives place strong emphasis on individual responsibility (the choices we make), whereas both the "God has a plan" story and the "Law of Nature" story suggest that life is to some extent shaped by outside forces (God or evolution) bigger than we are. One might argue that relying on God to lead life in the right direction is delegating control to someone who is both trusted and competent, and that the kinds of people, like Kamilla, who employ this narrative typically engage in frequent prayer and other rituals that confer a sense of control over one's life. Neither is true of the genetic determinism that pervades Sally's story. Yet her inference that genetic gifts imply some moral respon-sibility to do good does just that. The mystical connections narrative does not imply control over life's direction unless linked to some kind of spiritual practice, like the Quaker gathering or mindfulness meditation Dan refers to – or perhaps that kind of scientific research that my friend Vince was so passionately devoted to. This narrative type also raises the question: is it secular or is it religious?

Prior to each interview, I ask respondents about their religious or secular identification, and then towards the end of the interview I invite them to further unpack that identity. The five narratives above were chosen in part because the story teller's identity was clear cut and matched up nicely with their meaning making framework. A devout Roman Catholic like Kamilla tells a story of divine guidance and looks forward to heaven. An atheist like Sally explains her life in terms of superior genetics and supportive family of origins and seeks to live what is left to the fullest because death just means the journey is over. And so on. More often, however, respondents' religious or secular preference obscures a fuzzier identity that expresses doubt, or draws on more than one meaning making framework, or articulates a meaning narrative that is not clearly religious or secular.

People who identify as non-religious are often interested in so called alternative spiritualities like meditation. We saw that Dan identifies as non-religious but he is deeply connected to and interested in spiritual connection. Religious respondents often identify this way for cultural reasons. At the beginning of one interview, I asked a respondent, "What is your ethnic identification?" Catholic. What is your religious affiliation? None. Turns out she was raised Catholic but does not go to church anymore and was not sure she believed in God. But growing up in an Irish family she could not quite shake the Catholic label. Another respondent identifies as Jewish, had both his sons bar mitzvahed, and he actively participates in his synagogue. But he explains his life in terms of free will, does not think God plays any role, and death means life is over. He proudly informed me that Judaism is the only religion that does not require you to believe in God or supernatural causes.

So what do we mean by religious and secular? This question comes up whenever we study the Nones or non-religious people. I spent many pages on it in my last book (Manning, 2015) and recent articles (Manning, 2016, 2017), and it has been a prominent theme in journal articles (for example, Kosmin & Keysar 2002; Lim, McGregor, & Putnam, 2010; Winchester 2016) and at conferences I attended. Perhaps it cannot be resolved. And yet we still need to grapple with the question.

What is Meaning, Anyway?

Perhaps the biggest challenge of this research is defining what we mean by meaning, and developing questions that get at the meaning of meaning. I alluded earlier to the fact that the scientific literature defines meaning in different ways, so we should not be surprised that there is a lack of consensus among the people we study. One striking example that emerges from this research is the difference between assigning meaning to the past and finding meaning in the present.

When people tell stories that link life events in some kind of purposive causal sequence, they are assigning meaning to things that already happened. Meaning in this sense is about explaining the past (and sometimes giving direction for the future). Events are seen as meaningful if an individual can see a purpose behind what happened. For example, a man may say he was miserable when his wife left him, but he learned something. Eventually he became a stronger person, so there was a purpose to his suffering. That purpose may or may not be religious. One person may believe God wanted a painful event to happen to him, while another thinks it was random or his own fault. Assigning such meaning in this way usually comes after the fact. Meaning making is a kind of intellectual exercise in which we apply a particular interpretive frame or schema, the first of religion's two meaning making functions reviewed earlier.

By contrast, when people talk about what makes their life meaningful *now*, it is less about explanation than about what they do and how they feel. Religion's second meaning making function, to offer practices like prayer or meditation that give people a sense of control over their lives, is relevant here. But such practices are not only about control, they are also about feelings of connection and love – to God or to universal energy or to the other people who are practicing with them. When I asked people what kinds of practices give meaning to life now that they are older, both religious and non-religious respondents gave similar answers: my family and friends give meaning to my life; life is meaningful when I can help others or the planet; I spend a lot of time in the garden just looking at things, like flowers and beetles, and it makes me feel connected. Meaning making here is more of an emotional experience.

For religious people that connection could be to God, as we saw with Pauline, but it might also be with family, as with Kamilla's daughter, or even with animals. In one interview I spoke for nearly two hours with Katerina M., a 92-year-old Ukrainian Catholic woman living in the nursing home. She had both legs amputated due to diabetes and is nearly blind. Never married, she has no children or grandchildren but spoke fondly of the nieces and nephews that occasionally visit her. She prays regularly and expects to see her deceased brother "on the other side." But what stood out was her connection to her dogs. Photos of various poodles she had over the course of her life were posted all over the walls of her room. She was heartbroken that Bonny, her most recent poodle, was not permitted to live in the nursing home with her, and she looked forward every week to the day when her niece brought the dog for a visit. Her answer to my question about what makes life most meaningful to you now, was "being with Bonny;" she has instructed her family to bury her dog next to her. For secular people, the connection might be to nature or the universe. Dan and Agnes talked about that in different ways. But as often connection is to other people. Recall how Sally, who sees death as simply the end of experience, thinks of a meaningful life as staying connected to the world, especially the people she loves. The questions used in the pilot study encourage respondents to think about meaning as it applies to both past and present, and I am still experimenting with what are the best types of questions to get at that.

Conclusion

This chapter has discussed the importance of attending to non-religious forms of meaning making when we do research on religion and aging. The term "meaning making" reflects the theory underlying this project. That meaning is something human beings create by drawing on various cultural resources that are available to us. Religion is one such resource, but it is not the only one. This chapter draws our attention to other resources that may compete with or complement religious ones. Preliminary patterns from this ongoing study suggest several directions for further exploration.

First, it appears that secular schema may provide an alternative framework through which people create meaning, and that framework can give a sense of order and purpose similar to the order and purpose religion gives. The findings also illustrate the complexity and diversity of meaning making schemas. While some Catholics and Jews draw on distinctively religious narratives (like God has a plan for my life) and some atheists draw on secular narratives (like evolution), there is frequent mixing, like secularists who tell mystical stories, or religious individuals whose stories are entirely framed by luck.

The messiness of meaning making stories points to a second important insight from this research: the inadequacy of our categories. Our measures of religion include belief, practice, and belonging, and we distinguish between many different varieties (e.g., Catholic, Jewish, etc.). But our understanding of secular worldviews is too often defined by the absence of religion, rather than to what non-religious people do believe or practice.

Finally, the patterns discussed here suggest we should pay more attention to the behavioral and emotional aspects of meaning making rather than just the intellectual ones. The notion that religion or some secular philosophy gives meaning by assigning purpose to the life we have lived is important, to be sure. But it overshadows another important source of meaning: emotional connection. Religion can provide this through structured activities like prayer or worship which people perceive gives them a connection to God. However, the preliminary findings of this study suggest that they, along with non-religious folk, often find it elsewhere. So one important avenue for future research on both religious and non-religious individuals will be to explore whether and how both find such connections.

This has been a deeply rewarding project, and I am truly grateful to the individuals who have shared a piece of their stories with me. I look forward to learning more about how non-religious individuals create meaning at the end of life. Not only are the non-religious a growing proportion of the aging population, but focusing on non-religious worldviews can offer new perspectives about how religion works.

References

Arvay, M. (2002). Doing reflexivity: a collaborative narrative approach. In L. Finlay & B. Gough (Eds.), *Doing Reflexivity: A Critical Guide for Qualitative Researchers in Health and Social Science* (pp. 257–276). London: Blackwell Press.

Berger, P. (1967). *The Sacred Canopy*. Garden City, NY: Doubleday.

Baker, J., & Smith, B. (2015). *American Secularism: Cultural Contours of Nonreligious Belief Systems*. New York University Press.

Bruner, J. (2004). Life as narrative. *Social Research*, 71(3), 691–710.

Cimino, R., & Smith, C. (2014). *Atheist Awakening: Secular Activism and Community in America*. Oxford University Press.

Cole, B. S., & Pargament, K. I. (1999). Spiritual surrender: A paradoxical path to control. In W. R. Miller (Ed.), *Integrating spirituality into treatment: Resources for practitioners* (179–198). Washington, DC: American Psychological Association.

Day, A., & Lee, L. (2014). Making sense of surveys and censuses: issues in religious self-identification. Introduction. *Religion*, 44(3), 345–356.

Ellison, C. (1994). Religion, the life stress paradigm, and the study of depression. In J. S. Levin (Ed.), *Religion in Aging and Health. Theoretical Foundations and Methodological Frontiers*, 1st ed. (pp. 78–124). Thousand Oaks, CA: SAGE Focus Edition.

Gockel, A. (2013). Telling the ultimate tale: the merits of narrative research in the Psychology of Religion. *Qualitative Research in Psychology*, 10, 189–203.

Heywood, B., & Bering, J. (2013). "Meant to be:" How religious beliefs and cultural religiosity affect the implicit bias to think teleologically. *Religion, Brain & Behavior*, 4(3), 183–201.

Horning, S., et. al., (2011). Atheistic, agnostic, and religious older adults on well-being and coping behaviors. *Journal of Aging Studies*, 25, 177–188.

Hwang, K., Hammer, J. H., & Cragun, R. T. (2011). Extending religion–health research to secular minorities: issues and concerns. *Journal of Religion and Health*, 50, 608–622.

Jenkins, R. A., & Pargament, K. I. (1995). Religion and spirituality as resources for coping with cancer. *Journal of Psychosocial Oncology*, 13, 51–74.

Krause, N. (2007). Social involvement in religious institutions and God-mediated control beliefs: a longitudinal investigation. *Journal for the Scientific Study of Religion*, 46, 519–537.

Kosmin, B. A., & Keysar, A. (Eds.) (2002). *Secularism & Secularity: Contemporary International Perspectives*. Hartford, CT: Institute for the Study of Secularism in Society and Culture.

Lim, C., McGregor, C. A., & Putnam, R. (2010). Secular and liminal: discovering heterogeneity among religious nones. *Journal for the Scientific Study of Religion*, 49 (4), 596–618.

Lee, L. (2015). *Recognizing the Non-Religious: Reimagining the Secular*. Oxford University Press.

Lipka, M. (2015). Religious 'nones' not only growing, they're becoming more secular. Retrieved from: http://www.pewresearch.org/fact-tank/2015/11/11/religious-nones-are-not-only-growing-theyre-becoming-more-secular/

Manning, C. (2015). *Losing our Religion: How Unaffiliated Parents Are Raising their Children*. New York University Press.

Manning, C. (2016). Secularity and Family Life. In P. Zuckerman (Ed.), *Beyond Religion* (Ch. 6). Farmington Hills, MI: Gale-Cengage.

Manning, C. (2017). The impact of Nones on the study and teaching of religion in America. In P. Goff, L. Schmidt, & Nate Wynne (Eds.), *Proceedings: Fifth Biennial Conference on Religion and American Culture* (pp. 13–15). Indianapolis: Center for the Study of Religion and American Culture.

Pargament, K. I. (1997). *The Psychology of Religion and Coping: Theory, Research, and Practice*. New York: Guilford Press.

Pew Research Center (2012). Nones on the rise. Retrieved from: http://www.pewforum.org/2012/10/09/nones-on-the-rise/

Siegel, K., Anderman, S. J., & Schrimshaw, E. W. (2001). Religion and coping with health-related stress. *Psychology and Health*, 16(6), 631–653.

Somers, M. (1994). The narrative constitution of identity: a relational and network approach. *Theory and Society*, 23(5), 605–649.

Swidler, A. (1986). Culture in action: symbols and strategies. *American Sociological Review*, 51(2), 273–286.

Taves, A. (2016). On the Virtues of a Meaning Systems Framework for Studying Nonreligious and Religious Worldviews in the Context of Everyday Life. Retrieved from: https://nsrn.net/2016/10/04/methods-series-on-the-virtues-of-a-meaning-systems-framework-for-studying-nonreligious-and-religious-worldviews-in-the-context-of-everyday-life/

Weber, S., Pargament, K. I., & Kunik, M. E. (2012). Psychological Distress among Religious Nonbelievers: A Systematic Review. *Journal of Religion & Health*, 51(1), 72–86.

Wilkinson, P. & Coleman, P. G. (2010). Strong beliefs and coping in old age: a case-based comparison of atheism and religious faith. *Ageing and Society*, 30(2), 337–361.

Winchester, D. (2016). Religion as theoretical case, lens, and resource for critique. *Sociology of Religion*, 77(3), 241–260.

Woźniak, B. (2015). Religiousness, well-being and ageing: selected explanations of positive relationships. *Anthropological Review*, 78(3), 259–268.

Zuckerman, P. (2012). *Faith no More: Why People Reject Religion*. Oxford University Press.

Chapter 5

Uncertain Faith in Later Life
Studies of the Last Religious Generations in England (UK)

Peter G. Coleman and Marie A. Mills

UNIVERSITY OF SOUTHAMPTON

Although considerable evidence has been collected on the health and other benefits of religious belief and practice, attention also needs to be given to the difficulties religiously shaped attitudes may produce in the course of people's lives (e.g. Strawbridge et al., 1998; Krause & Wulff, 2004; Exline & Rose, 2005; Gall, Charbonneau, & Florack, 2011).

Believers face challenges to their faith from external influences around them and rely on support from fellow believers as well as from their own inner resources. The nature of the challenge has varied across historical time and culture, from periods of active persecution and rejection of displays of religious faith to periods of relative religious stability and homogeneity of belief within a population.

This chapter examines the religious attitudes of older people living in England (UK) over the last half century. This has been a time of huge social change, marked by a gradual loss of Christianity's presence in English and British society (Brown, 2001; Voas & Crockett, 2005). This is evidenced by the rise of "no religion" to the majority category in UK survey data (51% in 2013), a dramatic decline in expressed allegiance to the Church of England (the major Christian denomination) from 70% to 20% of the total

Acknowledgements To our colleagues who conducted many of these interviews and who also contributed to their analyses: to Dr. Andrew McCulloch whose PhD on older people's adjustment to social change identified a neglected and important topic; to Dr. Christine Ivani-Chalian and Mrs. Maureen Robinson who conducted interviews on the Southampton longitudinal study of aging over many years; and to Dr. John Spreadbury who conducted follow-up interviews with our sample of bereaved spouses. Also to the many others who have made contributions to the studies reported, and commented on an initial draft: including Dr. Fionnuala McKiernan, Rev. Darline Joseph Marianathan, Rev. David Sillince, Rev. Dr. Peter Speck, and Dr. Peter Wilkinson. Lastly and most importantly to our older interviewees themselves who were prepared and patient enough to engage in discussion on sensitive and sometimes painful subjects and to seek to express answers to probing and difficult questions. Their real names have been replaced in the text by pseudonyms.

population, and correspondingly huge declines in infant baptisms and church marriages. Historical surveys support the view that significant post-WWII decline began in the 1960s; the 1950s were, in fact, a time of higher religiosity than the preceding decades (Brown, 2017). Although similar trends are observable in other western countries, only the Netherlands appears to have shown a more precipitous decline during the same time period. The religiously observant Dutch society of the immediate post-WWII years largely disappeared over the following half century (van Rooden, 2010).

Through this period of change and religious decline, older people have come to be the most religiously observant part of the British population. For many years, people over 50 and increasingly over 60 and 70 have constituted the largest age groups attending Christian services. Although they may draw some comfort and strength from their identification as a faithful generation, they also inevitably have to acknowledge their failure to transmit their faith to their children and grandchildren. This loss of intergenerational support in itself threatens older people's hold on their own faith.

In what follows, data are presented from interviews with older people conducted by the authors and their colleagues in each of the decades since the 1960s. It is based on studies with individuals from a predominantly Christian shaped background, conducted in the south of England, in London itself, and in counties to the south and south-west (Hampshire, Surrey, and Wiltshire). The studies are presented in four sections. The first briefly considers data on attitudes to social change collected in interviews with older people from the later 1960s to the early 1980s. The second examines the evidence from a large multi-disciplinary and longitudinal study of aging carried out in one city in the south of England for over 25 years (1977–2002). The third analysis looks more in depth at the findings from a follow-up study of bereavement of a spouse in later life conducted in the first decade of the 21st century. In the final section, besides drawing together the evidence on historical changes in older people's religious and spiritual attitudes over the last 50 years, we draw attention to some of the implications for future research on aging, religion and spirituality.

Throughout this account the emphasis is neither on those who demonstrated a strong religious faith in their later years nor on those who had abandoned or never acquired a religious understanding of life. Instead, the focus is on those of "uncertain faith" who have constituted a substantial and sometimes the largest part of the people interviewed. Those were participants who had been socialized into a religious faith, predominantly Christian, when young, and who were still expressing a spiritual view of life and engaging in private prayer. But at the same time they were raising questions about the meaning and value of the doctrines and practices of their faith.

In our interviews we invited them to elaborate on their questioning and also to consider what might be its psychological and social sources and consequences.

Before beginning our account, we acknowledge the many problems of definition such an account entails, including assessing the presence of a religious or spiritual faith, as well as the difficulty in judging when doubt and questioning lead to its loss rather than strengthening its faith. To provide a clearer point of reference for this analysis we decided to focus on a central element in the Judeo-Christian faith, the belief in a God who loves human beings who are created in His image and to whom we can address our personal prayers. Although doctrines on the nature and action of Jesus Christ, on the work of the Holy Spirit and the role of the Church, are also essential to the Christian faith, we focus on doubts and questioning about the existence and nature of the Judeo-Christian God.

The Impact of the 1960s/1970s on Older People's Beliefs

Adjusting to social change is one of the more difficult developmental tasks expected of older people. It is not a new issue as witnessed in the book of Ecclesiastes, 7:10: "Do not say, 'Why were the old days better than these?' For it is not wise to ask such questions." Nevertheless, the degree of challenge has clearly varied over historical time. In retrospect the 1960s and 1970s appear to have been a time of particularly disturbing social change for the oldest generations who were alive then. They often expressed dismay at the liberalizing and other changes occurring in British society. Their plight was caught by sensitive social commentators at the time.

> Many of the old grew up in a world where they had to be disciplined, frugal, stoical, self-denying, poor; and what this taught them, often in bitterness and pain, appears to be of no use to their children and grandchildren, who have been shaped for different purposes by changed circumstances.
>
> (Seabrook, 1980)

This impact of rapid social change on the experience of aging was also recognized as an important issue by American gerontologists in this period (e.g. Kalish, 1969; Guttmann, 1980).

In interviews with older people living in congregate housing in London and Southampton in this period, we captured some of the turmoil they were experiencing as a result of social change, including threats to their personal religious beliefs (Coleman, 1986; Coleman & McCulloch, 1985, 1990). In follow-up studies with participants originally interviewed in London in the late 1960s and early 1970s, it is possible to chart individual

decline in religious affiliation over a ten-year period. This decline is sometimes with loss of meaning in religious rituals (both Christian and Jewish)
following the breakdown of families after divorce and separation (Coleman,
1986).

In analysis of interviews conducted in Southampton in the late 1970s and
early 1980s Andrew McCulloch employed the term "questioning" to
characterize a set of related attitudes (identified by factor analysis) common
to a large number of his participants. These attitudes comprised a failure to
understand, both emotionally and intellectually, modern society and
modern values. These were associated with a tendency to doubt previously
held religious beliefs because of the way society has changed. In particular,
"Job's Question" ("If there is a loving God, why does He allow suffering?")
occurred to these people frequently in some shape or form. Many seemed
to make a link between their perception that society was falling apart and
their difficulties in maintaining their beliefs.

> I don't know what the world's going to become, what it's going to be
> like in a few years' time … It's getting beyond belief … there are times
> when I've wondered even if I was in the right direction … I think it's
> everything that's happening today you see. It makes you wonder … I
> sometimes wonder if there are such places (after death). That's recently,
> recently that's come into my brain … Things you read in the paper,
> certain things, it makes you wonder. You even wonder if there's a
> God … My people, they're horrified, they can't understand what's
> happened to me.
>
> (Mrs. Sowerby, 1979)

The other major grouping was given the name "moral siege." This group
was characterized by an insistence that older people were morally and
spiritually superior, coupled with an enhanced perception of the differences
between generations and the need to protect oneself from present influences. Individuals expressing such attitudes tended to contrast their strong
sense of belief and trust in God with the "disbelieving" outer world.

Only a small minority in both the London and Southampton studies
seemed to be able to be both critical and appreciative of aspects of past as
well as present society. Even fewer took the opposite stance, identifying
more with the attitudes and preferences of the younger generations, and
criticizing instead the "out of date" attitudes of their own generation.

Nevertheless, it is important not to exaggerate the religiousness of the
older generation of the 1970s. Many of the men interviewed had served in
WWI and were cynical about the churches' role in supporting and sustaining that conflict, and only a minority even of the women were attending
church services regularly. Mrs. Foster, a practicing Baptist widow aged 87
years, pondered the reasons for this.

My husband never stopped me going or anything like that, but he wouldn't go. I know when I was baptized I thought perhaps that would make him think more seriously, but it didn't. You see, you can't make people think unless they really believe and know God. Because there's nothing in it to them. They can't make out what you're talking about if they don't see God as you do. See, he's not living for them. It's up to their feelings. I didn't have any influence. My mother never talked to us about religion, but she did take me to church and Sunday school, so I got it there. And it appealed to me you see. But my sisters didn't take any notice of it. Out of all the people in these flats, there's only one person that I know that goes to church. Funny isn't it?

(Mrs. Foster, 1970)

Some of the women interviewed had distanced themselves from traditional Christian teaching. They were considering some of the "new age" thinking which was finding popular expression at the time. That interest was stimulated by the visits of an Indian guru to the UK and the Beatles' interest in him. To at least one of them this made more sense than traditional Christianity.

I can't think of God, as God. Now that seems funny I expect. As he's pictured to us. I know, mind you, that there's some powerful force at work, but I can't think of God as the Church teaches him. Do you see what I mean? I think there are different forces at work … Of all the millions in the world, millions and millions of people, and yet he knows, according to the church, God knows each one of us, but I can't think that. But I think when we pray, if we do pray earnestly enough, we can call something into our environment. Yes, that helps us. I do think that whether by praying we pick something up or we contact something, I don't know, but I do think that we do contact something when we pray very earnestly. It seems as if we have got to get into such a state of mind that we can reach whatever it is that God, or whatever it is, is this power.

(Mrs. Parsons, 1970)

Indicative of future trends was the preparedness of some to make up their own mind as to what to believe, often in contradiction of church teaching. For example, Mrs. Masters had cared for her sick child until he died when only a few weeks old. She had had him christened beforehand and her Church of England vicar had commented afterwards how important this was, otherwise he could never have entered the Kingdom of Heaven. This had startled her and led her to oppose such teaching. More recently she had come to reject her understanding of the church's doctrine on Christ's atonement for all human sin. Instead her view was that "whatever mistakes we make here, that at some future date and some future life, we should be given the opportunity to put them right."

Declining Allegiance to Churches

Quantitative evidence on changes over time in older people's religious attitudes were first provided in the UK in a longitudinal multidisciplinary study of persons over the age of 65 years, average age 74 years (Coleman, Ivani-Chalian, & Robinson, 2004). They were recruited from general medical practices in the city of Southampton in 1977–78. Unusual for such studies conducted in this period, the initial survey contained seven questions on religious attitudes, membership and practice, attendance at church services and watching/listening to religious broadcasts. Unfortunately, there was no question included on personal prayer. In retrospect, however, the most useful question appears to have been whether individuals regarded religious faith to be an important feature of their lives.

At the first interview point (1978) the majority of the sample of 342 participants (66%) considered themselves members of Christian churches or other faiths, and a slightly larger number (71%) said that religion was meaningful to them. Consistent with the findings of other studies, a significantly higher proportion of women than men regarded themselves as members of religious organizations (77% versus 57%), and attributed much importance to religion in their lives (82% versus 61%).

As the sample aged, however, religious allegiance declined. At the ten-year follow-up in 1988, with the average age of the sample over 80, the differences were large. Of the remaining sample of 101, a quarter (26%) said that religion no longer meant much to them, compared with only a very few (3%) who had moved in the opposite direction. As a result, less than half of the sample at that point considered religion an important feature of their lives. This finding attracted considerable media attention in the UK since it was commonly assumed persons became more religious rather than less religious with age.

A further surprising observation was that those who were widowed were more likely to say that religion meant less to them when they were younger (22%) compared to those who were still married (9%). They were also less likely to attend church services. This was one of the first hints that bereavement in later life might itself be a source of changing religious attitudes. It was also noted that a declining meaningfulness in religion was associated with an increase in depressive symptoms in the sample.

From 1990 we began to take a closer interest in the religious life of our remaining sample. We observed no further decline in the proportion expressing religious allegiance as the average age of our sample rose to their middle 80s and beyond. Indeed, the Christian faith remained an important aspect of the last years of individuals' lives for slightly under half of the sample. This was evidenced especially by the value they attributed to personal prayer (Coleman, Ivani–Chalian, & Robinson, 2015). Table 5.1 provides a classification of the religious histories of all 40 members (17 men, 23 women) of the final sample derived from longitudinal case analyses.

As can be seen in Table 5.1, however, a relatively large group of 15 persons (4 men and 11 women) comprising more than a third of the sample, had distanced themselves from religion in the course of aging. Understanding the process of questioning they had been through provides some evidence on the factors involved. Below are three accounts of women who had distanced themselves from the Christian faith over successive interviews.

Mrs. Shields was one of the participants in our study who appeared to enjoy reflecting on her past life in our interviews. Born in Scotland she had moved south as a young woman with her parents. This had been a huge culture shock for her. She regretted she had not been allowed to benefit from the university education to which she had aspired. In Southampton she met and married a policeman who had also been transplanted from his culture of origin, in his case a Northern Irish one. Brought up in the Episcopalian Church of Scotland, Mrs. Shields still attended and enjoyed the services when she went back to Scotland feeling less at home in an English church. She had been interested in religious matters from a young age. At age 13 she wanted to become a nun and later on had enjoyed the debates about the meaning of life when she and her friends attended at the Unitarian church. These she said had broadened her mind and led her to question whether there was "a God guiding the world."

Nevertheless, she had brought up her children to go to church, and one son had remained a regular attender.

Throughout her life Mrs. Shields had continued to study the world's religions, found them interesting, but also saw them as the causes of a lot of conflict. Animal species, she said, did not have religion and did not fight among themselves as humans did. She had direct experience of this in

Table 5.1 Role of Religious Faith in Final Members of Southampton Ageing Study (1977–2002)

Group A (n=2): Religious faith remained a major part of identity since young adulthood
Group B (n=2): Faith gained major importance in later life (although present throughout)
Group C (n=13): Faith provided consistent sustaining element in their lives since young adulthood
Group D (n=4): Faith became of importance in later life despite earlier disinterest
Group E (n=15): Faith became of no importance to the person in the course of later life
Group F (n=4): Faith remained of limited or no significance since young adulthood

Source: Adapted from Coleman, Ivani-Chalian, & Robinson (2015)

Northern Ireland. Her husband was a Protestant and had gone back every year for the parades on July 12. Mrs. Shields had accompanied him and described vividly the drumming: the sounds, different for each group, but like "jungle drums", and with whips beating time on the drums. Sectarianism was so ingrained in Northern Ireland, she said, and she had come to the conclusion that "they should be left to it."

Mrs. Shields was 80 years old at her husband's death in 1992. She said that her local minister was taken by surprise when after his visit to see her she asked him not to pray with her as she "would feel uncomfortable also for him." She had come she said to claiming no special philosophy or principle of life, "just making the best of it." But she remained curious and particularly interested in hearing other people's views about religion. Interviewed again at the age of 86 she continued to say that there was so much about traditional Christian beliefs that she could not accept, including belief in life after death. She also spoke in detail about a near death experience she had had after a first child was stillborn, and the afterbirth became lodged and septic. The experience had been most vivid, a feeling that she was "going towards the window," that there was "someone on the other side," a "tract of water between her and a woman." This woman "seeing her was coming towards her." Perhaps surprisingly, but consistent with her questioning and skeptical frame of mind, this experience, although highly memorable, had not changed Mrs. Shields's views. She had found it neither pleasant nor unpleasant and "could not understand what it was all about."

Mrs. Wright had a degree in chemistry and worked as a pharmacist both before and after her marriage. She had brought up her two sons alone after her husband left her for another woman he had met during WWII. Her life had been difficult she said, but she had been determined to succeed. She approached the problems of aging in the same spirit.

She described how she had regularly attended prayers in the cathedral at lunchtime when she worked in the nearby city of Winchester. At the time of our first interview in 1977 she had only recently retired and was missing work. Religious practice was still important to her.

Throughout her 70s Mrs. Wright enjoyed an active lifestyle, working part-time as a teacher and taking on a lot of volunteer work. When interviewed at the age of 76 she was no longer attending church and expressed an attitude of life that she said had been influenced by reading Rudolph Steiner's philosophy: "To be wise is to learn from the mistakes one makes in life." In her early 80s she reminisced more with us, reviewing the difficult aspects of her early adult life following her husband's departure. She acknowledged the health problems she was facing and was actively seeking ways around them. At our last interview with her at the age of 86, at which time she was physically frail but mentally alert and free from depression, she spoke again about her change in religious attitudes. She said that she had come to disapprove of the hierarchical side of the major Christian denominations, and now equated her own beliefs principally with helping others. But she still strongly expressed a belief in God. "God is in His Heaven and will give guidance if there is a wrong turning." She was not worried about what the future might hold and was certainly not intending "to give up."

Mrs. Willis had been 62 years old when her husband died of cancer. As with many of our sample she described it as the major turning point of her later years which had led to a prolonged depression. She was, in fact, to live another 34 years. She indicated by her statements over the years a more gradual separation from attachment to the religion of her upbringing than both Mrs. Shields and Mrs. Wright. She remained like the latter very active socially, taking up work again for a number of years. She then continued with responsibilities in various voluntary and political organizations, until she became more incapacitated as the result of a stroke and deteriorating eyesight which contributed to an increase in depressive symptoms. She recovered as she found ways of continuing living independently in her own home until death.

In her later years she liked reminiscing about the happy circumstances of her childhood in the early part of the 20th century, her work as a tailor before she married, her husband's work and the birth of her children. She spoke too about religion, about how religious life had changed in England. When she was young, she had attended church services three times a day on Sunday, morning, afternoon, and evening. After she married, she did not go any more. She still felt some shame about that. "What would God think, that we only pray when we are in trouble?" A difficulty for her was that she had always been a skeptical person, questioning the stories in the Bible, such as the account of creation in Genesis. She remembered once asking "And who made God?" and being disturbed by her own question. But at the same time she marveled at the detail and perfection of created organisms and could not accept Darwin's theory of evolution as the whole answer. She argued about these issues with her son with whom she had a very close relationship. He was well read in biology and was not religious. There appeared to be an element of sadness about her lack of faith.

But at our last interview as she was approaching her 95th birthday she expressed herself content with life. Although she was increasingly frail and accepting of her own pending death, she had come to see it as a natural progression. We raised the subject of religion again, but she no longer expressed any doubts about the matter. She explained that she had begun losing her religious beliefs after her husband died. She had started questioning things she had previously accepted and had concluded eventually that religious belief was pointless.

Bereavement of spouse, as well as other unexpected family deaths and loss of close relationships through divorce or separation, seemed to underlie a number of the other participants' trajectories of religious disillusion. For example, Mrs. Procter had been divorced at age 59, seven years before entering our study. She had neither children nor any other close relatives, and responded to the new situation by taking up a very active social life. Her life was a struggle against loneliness and in her later 70s against cancer. At this point she acknowledged to us the void she experienced due to the loss of her husband's companionship and affection. She described their divorce as "the biggest turning point" in her life. She had distanced herself from the religious faith of her childhood, and, as Mrs. Wright had done, come to pride herself on her own inner resources which had enabled her to fight against her problems and "to not give in."

Men in our sample elaborated less about their religious attitudes, but Mr. Woodley provided a very explicit account of the disappointment he experienced in his church after his wife died.

> I felt very let down with religion, because I was always brought up in the Church of England ... After the funeral the parson just said, "Cheerio, I'm off", and nobody even bothered whether I was all right or not ... I've nothing against the church, the teachings of the church, put it that way ... but it doesn't bother me that I don't go to church ... I try to do the best I can for everybody ... well if that's not enough it's just too bad.

We noted that his rejection of the church had not appeared in his answers at the first study point four years after his wife died, but in an interview more than 15 years later.

Questioning of Faith after Bereavement of Spouse

The suggestion of an association between the experience of spousal bereavement in later life and declining church attendance and allegiance was part of the motivation for seeking funding for an in-depth investigation of the subject of religious faith and adjustment to bereavement. The funding came from the UK's Economic and Social Research Council's Growing Older research program (1999–2003). We obtained permission to approach bereaved spouses over the age of 60 years from GP practices in the cities of Southampton and Salisbury from the first anniversary of a death. We then interviewed them three times over the course of the succeeding year. Survivors were also followed up six years later. In the course of these interviews we explored both the experience of bereavement and the role played by their religious, spiritual or philosophical attitudes toward life and death.

Although the sample we collected was small (n=26), analysis of the results produced a surprisingly strong impression of a curvilinear association between indices of well-being and strength of spiritual belief (Coleman et al., 2007). The latter was assessed by a five item measure of belief in a transcendent spiritual power which could influence their lives (King, Speck, & Thomas, 2001). Those who expressed weak to moderate belief were more likely to indicate low levels of expressed meaning in life and symptoms of depression than those who expressed secure religious beliefs or a securely held atheistic and humanistic understanding of life. Obtaining such security of attitude, whether religious or irreligious, appears to be far from common and liable to break down in the face of difficulties. Bereavement of a spouse appears to be an especially critical testing time for religious faith, and as a consequence it is one of the more revealing contexts for studying belief in action (Pargament, 1997; Tedeschi & Calhoun, 2006; Spreadbury & Coleman, 2011).

We have recently looked again at the factors that may lead to dissolution of faith by re-examining the interviews with those of our sample of bereaved spouses who displayed religious attitudes but also strong doubts about their faith. There were ten participants in the study who had been socialized into a religious tradition when young, were still continuing to practice their religion, at least by praying regularly, but at the same time were seriously questioning their faith during the first year of our study. Of these ten individuals, four could be interviewed at the follow-up eight years after their spouses' death (a further four had either died or moved away and two declined for reasons of illness and/or frailty). By this point all four appeared to have moved further away from their Christian faith of origin. Table 5.2 provides a summary of the religious difficulties and trajectories experienced by these ten Questioners.

The most common religious question in this study, reflecting inter-viewees' recent experience of bereavement, was the difficulty of accepting Christian teaching about a good and powerful God who also cares for each individual person. Mrs. Silverwood, a Catholic by upbringing, protested strongly against this notion of God. She had been overwhelmed by her husband's sudden death.

> I feel it's so unjust because I mean, after all Sam's already suffered and then he's the one who suddenly gets cancer. I mean, why does he have to get cancer. I mean, I just don't understand. I'm really very rebellious about God. I really am. I don't think he's controlling our lives at all. I mean what's he doing up there?

Over the years of our interviews Mrs. Silverwood's beliefs in the Christian God diminished. Two years after her husband's death her doubts had increased.

> I think there is a power outside ourselves but I really am not always sure that it does influence our lives. I suppose it influences our lives from our point of view because in moments of distress you sort of think about God, but I don't think that anything comes directly from

Table 5.2 Religious Difficulties and Resolutions Expressed by Subjects in the Spousal Bereavement Study (2000–07): interviewed after first, second and eighth year anniversary after bereavement

Mrs. Brown, 63 years old: her faith shaken by loss of husband; cannot understand how God allows cruelty, but still believes God is "stronger than world's wickedness." At eighth year after bereavement putting more emphasis on role of fate in life's events.

Mrs. Lockyer, 65 years old: not "at peace" with her beliefs. At second year after bereavement becoming more inclined to believe in a "cold fate" rather than in a good God.

Mr. Chivers, 65 years old: cannot believe in God as a person nor in Jesus as God; cannot accept authority of church ministers, but still finds belief in God helpful. At second year after bereavement feeling more peaceful and hopeful that he will "know truth" after death.

Mrs. Hammond, 66 years old: believes in God but does not see Him as having much role in her life. At eighth year after bereavement continuing to avoid thinking about what she really believes, but would like to believe in life after death.

Mrs. Allen, 69 years old: imagines God as "loving but imperfect"; believes more in action of an impersonal fate. At second year after bereavement acknowledges that belief in God had helped her in adjusting to bereavement.

Mrs. Silverwood, 72 years old: unable to see that God is controlling our lives at all as there is so much injustice; dislikes authority wielded by priests. At eighth year after bereavement signs of faith almost disappeared.

Mrs. Davies, 72 years old: feels anger at God for allowing her husband's suffering and has doubts about his role in creation; her common sense does not allow her to fully accept church teaching. At second year after bereavement still unable to trust in the certainty of a "loving father", but attending church services again.

Mrs. Thompson, 76 years old: feels that a good and powerful God could not allow such terrible things; sees God more as a life force. At eighth year after bereavement raising similar questions; her faith still weaker.

Mrs. Forbes, 79 years old: unhappy with her beliefs; unsure whether God is listening to her prayers; the Church is not helpful. No change in attitudes by end of second year after bereavement.

Mrs. Webb, 82 years old: thinks that God has to be imperfect, also Jesus and the teaching of the Bible. At second year after bereavement becoming more critical of and detached.

above to influence our lives ... I probably think there is something there, but not something which could relate to me.

Six years later Mrs. Silverwood remained very depressed and continued to have the highest grief score in the sample. Any belief in a spiritual power outside of herself had almost completely disappeared.

Mrs. Davies and Mrs. Brown also associated questioning of their faith with their husbands' suffering and death. Both had had a strong religious education, but Mrs. Davies had stopped attending church regularly as an adult because of the busy nature of her life. She described herself as having "fallen by the wayside." But she was now praying every day and going to church regularly again, encouraged by her children, and hoping that she was communicating with God. She wished that she had a stronger faith, however, as some of her friends had. She questioned how a loving God could have allowed her husband, who had been a very good man, to suffer as he did. As a child too she had asked questions of the church leaders and found their teachings very rigid. In her interviews she frequently referred to her "common sense" which did not allow her to fully accept Christian doctrine.

Mrs. Brown in contrast had been a regular church attender and expected she would obtain more comfort from her faith when her husband died. His suffering, however, had seemed unjust. But, over time she was able to recover her faith and had come to feel that she could not have coped without it. It had helped that for two years into the bereavement she had a visitor from her local Anglican church with whom she could talk. But, she still had some difficult questions. She could see how God could let bad things happen to produce good results, she still could not understand unnecessary cruelty like the murder of children.

Six years later, at the age of 70, as with some of the other members of the sample with only moderate levels of belief, Mrs. Brown had come to place more importance on the role of fate in matters of life and death. Perhaps, it might be argued, this is a way of protecting uncertain faith from being made even more uncertain. Mrs. Brown described the process she had undergone.

> When my husband died first you sort of think, "Why?" You know, "Is there a God if He's taken my …". There are so many bad people and so why does He take the good people? So it does what I call "shake your religion" for a bit, but then that doesn't last long because that is silly. You know we don't know the reasons why, but you can't start saying, "I blame God" … You can't blame other people or God or anything for what happens. It's perhaps destiny or what is meant to be. I don't know the reason why. I wish it hadn't happened, but it did … I just come to terms that it must have been fate, you know not, not something that … I think perhaps from the minute you are born your destiny, your fate, we don't know what controls it, but perhaps it was meant to be.

For others the focus of their questioning of God is related more to their own health. Mrs. Allen had been confined to an electric wheelchair already in her early 60s as a result of osteoporosis and a standing tremor. She had been brought up in a convent in India, where she had learned to appreciate traditional Catholic liturgy but she stopped attending when her husband's work took them around the world. She now regards herself as a "lapsed

Catholic." She has been supported by her children and appreciated the visits of the local Anglican vicar after her husband's death although she did not feel she would benefit from spiritual counselling. Her prayers, she said, now consisted of "arguing with God about most things." She saw Him as a loving but imperfect God:

> He's looked after me now and again ... He's still the good God, but He gets it wrong more now than He did ... mucking my life up. I can't get on with doing things with and for other people.

She debated within herself about God's action or lack of it. The state of the world rocked her faith. "There's such dreadful things happening, you wonder whether it's got any meaning sometimes." But, she was able to relativize the news she received. You hear more about the bad things than the good, so you hope the good is, really in the long run, better." She was inclined to believe in fate: "It's just going to happen. You can't change it ... my illness is just bad luck." But at the final interview a year later her attitudes had changed somewhat and she now felt that her personal beliefs in God had enabled her to cope, although she continued to emphasize the role of fate in people's lives.

Others too have more generalized questioning of God's actions or lack of actions in the world, and doubts in particular about whether prayer is meaningful. Mrs. Lockyer described herself as not at peace with her beliefs and attributed the beginnings of her difficulties to the problems she encountered with her first husband who was a gambler and did not pay any bills. After their divorce, life had been very hard for her. She also expressed ambivalence about the value of prayer and attending church: "I hope that someone's listening, but I am not sure whether they are or not. I feel hopeful that they are." She spoke of going to church services in hopes of receiving "some kind of sign" but at the same time did not seem to expect it.

> I go now and again and I hear the church bells ringing and I'm so near. Because I think now, if you don't go today you're never going to believe in any of it again, so you'd better go and see. See what happens.

But over time she said she had become inclined to believe more in a cold and uncaring fate rather than a God who looked after people both in life and beyond death.

We suggested to Mrs. Lockyer the possibility of spiritual counselling, which she considered, but she appeared to be distancing herself more from her religious beliefs. We wondered whether her ambivalence also reflected her conflicted religious upbringing. She had been closer to her mother, who had not been a believer, than her father, who did believe. Her father had come back severely traumatized by his war experience (he had been one of the few survivors of the sinking of the Lancastria evacuating British troops from the French port of St. Nazaire in 1940) and unrecognizable as her father. She said she had never been able to develop a close relationship with him.

Mrs. Thompson's parents had not been religious and her own religious education had been limited. But her daughter had gone to Sunday school and continued to go to church. She took her mother to church when she stayed with her. Mrs. Thompson was very unsure of her beliefs, even of the existence of God. However, it was important to her to pray the Lord's prayer every evening and thank "whoever's up there … as I say, I think it's 50/50." Her doubts too centered on the problem of evil:

> Sometimes I think there's a God above and then I think to myself, well, how can God let so terrible things happen. And yet then you read on the other side there's so many good things and everything … when you look at nature, it's how it comes in the spring. You all think it's down and it comes up in another life. So, I don't know.

Six years later at the age of 83 Mrs. Thompson expressed very similar attitudes.

> I'm not a firm believer but you've got to be a bit hopeful and believe a little … I say to myself He does miracles in one way and yet why does He let other young children suffer who have never done a thing wrong and that sort of thing.

Her depression score was raised, and her belief score had weakened further, but she still continued to pray every morning and evening.

For others in this sample of Questioners the difficulties they experienced centered more on how God had been presented to them. A number disliked the notion of a masculine God, represented in an authoritarian "male ordered" church. Mrs. Silverwood expressed herself strongly on this point. She had rebelled against her Catholic upbringing at the university and had negative memories of the absolute authority of the priest and the control he exercised over people's lives. She said that the church needed better prepared clergy and gave as an example a very old Jesuit friend she appreciated who called her from time to time. Prayer for her meant being quiet, and when she thought of "something above" it was "the Virgin (Mary) … because she takes the place of my mother." (She cried.)

As in the case of Mrs. Lockyer, we considered whether there might be a relationship between Mrs. Silverwood's difficulties with faith and her early upbringing. She described her parents as quite cold and distant, with a strict father who rarely praised her and a mother who rarely nurtured her. Her late husband had been the protective and loving parent she had never had. He had been Jewish, and it is interesting that it was to his rabbi that she turned for consolation after her husband's death.

Mrs. Webb and Mrs. Forbes are some of the oldest members of this sample of bereaved spouses. They were less affected by their bereavements than the younger women we have mentioned so far, perhaps because they were also more expected. Mrs. Webb had been brought up as a Methodist and remembered its homey warmth and contrasted it with the Church of England, which she regarded as "cold" and "scrounging." Although she no longer attended church services, she kept to regular prayers at night and morning. She said they helped keep her calm amidst the worries of life. God she said was her "purpose" in life, and she felt he answered her prayers. But from the doubts she expressed, it appeared that her beliefs were not as strong as she had first suggested. She had many questions about her faith, not all of which were easy to understand. For example, she queried the teachings to be found in the Bible.

> We weren't there … It's what other people have put in the Bible, their belief, so you're believing in somebody else. You're not believing in what God's put down.

She also queried whether Jesus was always correct in what he did and taught: "Nobody's perfect; you all have to do something wrong." It seemed a pity that she was no longer in contact with a faith community like her original Methodist church.

Mrs. Forbes had also enjoyed going to the Methodist church when she was young, and like Mrs. Webb "wouldn't miss praying every morning and evening."

> It means a lot. I pray because I am thankful … Haven't a clue who's listening to me. I imagine someone. I believe someone is …

She did not see God as a person but more as a "floating image." But her faith now appeared to be in decline. "As you get older, you wonder. You don't quite know." She described an emptiness in her daily life much of the time just waiting to go to bed. She was "wishing her life away." Yet she did not seem to want to accept help, and the church did not seem helpful. To her it was "boring" and simply did not meet her needs. She had gone with a neighbor to a special service for those who had lost somebody within the year.

> A lot of them started crying, and I didn't think the minister was very good. Whatever he said didn't seem to relate to anything that I felt. No, don't think going to church will do me any good.

She also appeared difficult to help, knowing more what she did not want rather than what she did.

Mr. Chivers was the only man in this sample, and he was very different in his style of questioning. He was not distressed by his doubts, but was rather determined to find the answers. At his first interview he was excitable and rather overwrought. His wife had died very suddenly of a heart attack in front of him, and it had been a shattering experience as they had been "doing everything together" right up to her death. It is possible that he was still suffering from some degree of mild post-traumatic disorder. However, he was also convinced that his wife had appeared to him since her death, and this experience had consoled him, convincing him of a continuing life. "I just know that there's something else there. I know we're going somewhere. It's as simple as that." In time his grief and depression scores, very high at the outset, dissipated. This could also have been helped by a developing relationship with another woman, a friend of his wife's.

Over the course of the study the strength of Mr. Chivers' spiritual beliefs increased as his sense of well-being improved. He had been brought up by his mother as a Methodist.

His demanding father did not go to church and never expressed his beliefs. Mr. Chivers thought that he did believe, however, but associated expression of belief with weakness: "There was no future in weakness." Mr. Chivers had also experienced a similar reluctance when young, but now that he was old, he could admit to it. His faith had become important to him: "I know which side I would rather be on, Christian. It's right or wrong – the ten commandments." Yet at the same time he expressed his antipathy towards ecclesiastical authority.

> I was in the Army. Everything was set out. I've always been in uniform. I was twenty odd years in the fire service. Everything I've been was ruled all the way through, governed. But, I can't take it with religion. I've got to feel separately and independently ... I've just got to believe what's inside of me.

He did not attend church services, but every Tuesday went into his local Anglican church to pray and to meditate. He was fortunate in having an understanding vicar who left him in peace perhaps sensing that it would do no good to press him to become more involved.

> Mr. Chivers prayed every day: "I feel I owe someone something. It just helps me pray to God. Like everyone else, it's nice to say thank you. I feel I could be critical. I'm not, but I ask a few questions.

One of his questions was, "Where have I got to get to?" Contrary to some of the other subjects he did not think life events were down to luck or chance: "There is an underlying purpose and it's up to you to find it."

At the same time, he could not accept that Jesus of Nazareth was God.

> There's got to be a God, there's no other way it could work in my view. Funny enough, I don't think Jesus Christ is God. Never have ... He might have been a very good prophet, but I think he was possibly put in a position to tell us or try to tell us the way to go, but I can't go along with the proposition that Jesus Christ and God are the same. I just can't. No way, never have been able to. I respect him for, I respect him for what he put up for us but ...

Interestingly despite the improvement in his mood and general well-being, Mr. Chivers continued at our last interview to score low on the sense of personal meaning scale. But this was compensated for by the assurity that one day he would have the answers to his questions. "I can never hate something I don't know the reason for. One day I shall be told."

Mrs. Hammond, the last member of this sample of bereaved spouses, received belief scores that were only moderate and did not appear at all troubled by her doubts, at least in the first year of interviews. She had a relatively high sense of personal meaning and was not depressed. She had a large and close family which allowed her to feel needed and useful as well as loved. She was not critical towards the Christian church. She simply expressed no great need for it. Her own parents and grandparents had not been religious. Although she had attended Sunday school as well as church services from the age of 7 until 13, and had even taught "the little ones" herself which she enjoyed, she did not see the need for attending.

Being religious for her was principally "being good and not doing harm".

Mrs. Hammond found it difficult to describe her view of God or answer other questions about her beliefs.

> I haven't really thought about that ... I've got such a really lovely family that just won't let me think about things to be honest.

When interviewed six years later she was still closely related to her family. However, she was now showing mild signs of depression and her sense of personal meaning had decreased. She was also expressing more doubt about her spiritual beliefs and spoke in particular about her uncertainty concerning whether there is life after death.

This sample of ten bereaved spouses of weak to moderate Christian faith group for the most part exhibited downward trajectories in well-being, except perhaps Mr. Chivers. He showed clear evidence of growth in spiritual belief (Tedeschi & Calhoun, 2006) in his struggles that followed the sudden death of his wife. This impression was reinforced by the further feedback we received on our initial results. A brief mention of our bereavement study in SAGA Magazine, a specialist magazine for older people, led to many readers writing to us with their comments. Over a period of seven months more than a hundred letters were sent to the research team, many long and detailed. A large proportion included narratives of disillusionment with the church and with the Christian faith, often as a result of lack of support especially following bereavement and watching close relatives suffer. They also commonly expressed the wish to be better consulted and their concerns taken more seriously by their religious ministers (Mills, Speck, & Coleman, 2011).

Believing and Disbelieving in the Last Stages of Life

Our studies have illustrated how many older people, despite their relatively strong early religious socialization, have also participated in the decline in religious allegiance within England over the last half century. More importantly, loss of faith has also been occurring as part of the aging process itself. This is a finding that may surprise some ministers of religion. But they need to know that older people's faith cannot be taken for granted. The expectation of the older secure believer is as much a stereotype as so many of the other false expectations society has held and continues to hold in regard to age. Churches and other religious bodies cannot expect to force beliefs on children let alone on those with so many years' experience with life. People of all ages appear to believe more on the basis of their own feelings, reasoning, and intuition. The later stages of life generally provide more time for reflection, so increased questioning of religious doctrine and authority is to be expected as persons seek to come to a greater ownership of what they really believe.

One important development between the earlier and later generations of British older people considered in these studies, is the cumulative decline in Christian faith and worship that has occurred over the last 50 years in Britain as well as many other Western European countries. Although older people still tend to be more religious than younger people, the difference between generations is becoming less marked. We have evidence of the attitudes of more recent generations of English church members from a comparative study conducted in 2010 of the religious practices of people 75 years of age and older (born 1915–35) in London and Southampton, together with counterparts in South Eastern Europe (Romania and Bulgaria) (Coleman et al., 2013). Whereas the latter had experienced a recovery of religious faith in their societies following long years of state sponsored persecution, the former were well aware of the declining hold of Christianity in an increasingly liberal and secularized society. Compared with church members in our earlier interviews, they showed a greater sensitivity to the huge challenge facing the clergy in ministering to church members who rarely attended services, let alone those wholly outside membership of the church. They were aware that religious authorities were often seen as "irrelevant" and spoke "over people's heads." Some admitted wistfully that even though the churches were giving of their best, it was clearly inadequate to the needs and problems people faced nowadays.

The British baby boom generation who grew to adulthood in the 1960s and were strongly influenced by the changing social attitudes of that time have now become the focus of studies on aging. Joanna Walker has been investigating spiritual development as a learning experience in later life (Walker, 2016) and is currently conducting interviews of older people in the south of England. As one might expect, this is a generation which gives primacy to personal expression. The newly retired tend to be more eclectic than previous cohorts in making choices between their own and other religious traditions. They think they have the right to decide themselves what to accept and what to reject. However, beliefs in transcendent spiritual powers and in the continued existence of soul or spirit after death have not decreased to the same extent as allegiance to traditional Christian doctrine. It is principally the authority of the major Christian churches and especially the Church of England which has weakened, despite its continuing presence in traditional state institutions such as the monarchy, parliament and the courts. As some commentators have pointed out, we have to go back a long time in the history of Western Europe, to the days of the later Roman Empire, to find a similar loss of cultural support for traditional religion.

Implications for Research

What are the implications of these observations for research on spirituality, religion and aging? We would like to emphasize three points. The first is that we need to pay closer attention to how people come to acquire, develop, and change their religious and spiritual beliefs throughout life. Philosophical and psychological analysis can contribute to the dilemmas of belief and unbelief which seem to trouble people so much in later life. As we indicated in the accounts of some of our bereaved spouses, it is possible to discern links between attitudes to God and the influence of earlier life experience, in particular the impact of insecure attachment with parents (Kirkpatrick, 2005). Some of our cases could also no doubt be subjected to psychoanalytic interpretations of failure to grow from an egocentric to a more mature faith (e.g. Genia, 1990). But for many older people the issues of spiritual doubt and questioning in later life appear to reflect the present day concerns of the aging person.

The following example from our SAGA study mentioned earlier (Mills, Speck, & Coleman, 2011) illustrates both the puzzle and pain for an older person whose religious belief is failing.

I have been a church member since I joined a choir at the age of eight and am now in my 70th year. For most of that time I have been a faithful and regular attender. I have held most of the offices open to lay persons and have been a member of numerous committees. I became Headmaster of a Church Primary School and was a governor, and for two years Chairman of Governors of a Church Secondary School. My week did not seem complete unless I had worshipped and worked for the faith I held. In 1992 I retired to another area ... I still attended, but some of the sparkle had gone, but I attributed this to the difference in attitude of the two churches and soldiered on.

In May of last year, I returned to live in my old area and anticipated a renewal of zeal when once again in my old haunts. It has not proved to be so. I can hardly believe how easily I can forego Sunday worship and have determined not to get involved in any of the groups available. I try to convince myself that it is not a lack of faith, but is due to disillusionment with the practices of the church and the behavior of some of the clergy. I am not sure that I have succeeded. I want to believe or a great deal of my life has been futile. But I cannot pretend that the situation is other than as it is.

The philosopher Charles Taylor (2002) has written about the continuing value of William James's (1902/2002) analysis of religious belief and disbelief. As he points out, James's insights may be especially valuable today because they deal with a very bare understanding of spiritual belief focused simply on the acknowledgement of a transcendent reality. It is rooted more in feeling than in reason, a "heart" based acknowledgement of the likelihood of there being a good God, rather than a complex theology centered in the "head." It is also helpful that James himself was on the negative side of the dichotomy he drew between the happy "once-born" believer, who experiences the goodness of the world God has made, and the troubled "twice-born," only too aware of the presence of evil in the world, the fear of falling into an abyss of meaningless, and the danger of despair. Religion was the answer to such terrors. Importantly, religious belief was not to be reached by detached consideration—the "scientific" stance—but by the insight, common to St. Augustine, Pascal and others, that God is to be reached by advancing towards Him, rather than standing back.

What is to be believed has to be, by definition, beyond our ability to create for ourselves. To believe in God therefore one has to be prepared to reach out to Him even though one cannot know that He is there.

But, as philosophers from both religious and atheistic backgrounds stress, religious belief and practice also have a fundamentally communal character. While admiring James's analysis for being prescient of the 20th century's turn to greater interest in personal spiritual experience, Taylor also criticizes him for underrating the shared communal element in religious belief. The social element is also key to a religious person's sense of identity. For example, we do not know what precisely lies behind the decline of faith in the case example given above, but it is likely to relate as much to a failure of sense of communal belonging as to loss of personal faith. Crane (2017) has also emphasized how the creation and maintenance of religion within a society are dependent on people working together towards a common end in their search of transcendent meaning. Because of these strong social linkages, atheists cannot expect religion to be removed from society without leaving a substantial gap in its character.

Our second point is that research on the benefits (as well as problems) associated with religious belief and practice needs to be based on more sensitive comparisons with non- religious ways of making meaning in life. The most widely shared theoretical explanations for the associations between religion and mental health emphasize influence via sense of meaning (Krause, Chapter 8 in this volume; George, Chapter 7 in this volume). It is not surprising that holding to a religious faith contributes to perceived meaning in life, but there are other ways of thinking about and experiencing life which may be effective providers of meaning. So far most of the research studies on the health benefits of religion have been conducted in the US where religious faith is more widely held than other parts of the Western world. The comparisons drawn are typically either between the majority who hold to a religious way of life and the minority who do not or between those of varying strengths and frequency of religious belief and practice. The more religious tend to perceive higher levels of meaning in their lives and to avoid depressive states of mind (Idler, Chapter 6 this volume).

But as Christel Manning (Chapter 4 in this volume) indicates there have been relatively few studies examining how non-religious persons create meaning in later life. Clearly meaningful lives can be constructed both in and out of difficult times without recourse to religious faith (e.g. Andrews, 1991). Although it may be demonstrable that persons of strong religious faith cope better than those with a weak religious faith, it does not follow that other systems of meaning do not provide equally good resources in dealing with life's difficulties. In a subsequent study in Southampton we began exploring this topic by conducting case studies on matched pairs of committed religious believers and members of the British Humanist Association who had been confronting similar challenges in late life such as bereavement, frailty and the prospect of impending death. Analyses suggested that both sides coped equally well with the challenges they faced. The study offered support to the hypothesis that it is the coherence of existential attitudes and the strength with which they are held, rather than the content of belief, which influence adjustment to the challenges of later life such as bereavement and declining health (Wilkinson & Coleman, 2010).

The Humanists included in this study all professed a purely material conceptualization of the universe and a scientific evidence-based approach to life's problems as the best way of seeking explanations. It therefore seemed appropriate to adopt atheist scientist Richard Dawkins's (2006) model of the meaning providing functions of belief systems. This proposes that a scientific and atheistic based set of beliefs can give rise to a "world view" that fulfils the same four basic functions in people's lives that religions traditionally fulfil: "explanation, exhortation, consolation and inspiration" (Dawkins, 2006). The evidence from our study supports this position (Wilkinson & Coleman, 2010). One could imagine a similar approach being taken with other types of non-religious world views, both spiritual and non-spiritual. What is needed is analysis of the meaning-providing characteristics of the world views in question and comparison with those holding equally strongly to religious views. Monika Ardelt's contribution to this volume also illustrates how "wisdom" characteristics have been shown to have somewhat different benefits to those associated with "religious spirituality" (Ardelt, Chapter 9 in this volume).

The need for such a broader approach to research on religion, spirituality and meaning will become more important if, as seems likely, religion based attitudes to life continue declining. Indeed, those concerned with older people's welfare should already begin considering how they might be given more opportunities to explore alternative non-religious ways of thinking and feeling about life, both spiritual (e.g. Atchley, 2009; Sherman, 2010; Harris, 2015) and non-spiritual (e.g. Dawkins, 2006; Barker, 2015).

Our third and final point concerns the need for the Christian churches and other religious organizations to become more closely involved themselves in studies on aging, religion, and spirituality. Researchers themselves also need to be better informed about religious teaching on the meaning of aging (Coleman, Schröder-Butterfill, & Spreadbury, 2016). In the following paragraphs we can only focus on the life of Christian churches, but acknowledge that much can also be learned from examining practices relating to aging in the contexts of other religious faiths.

The participants in our studies did appear to reflect more on religious and spiritual issues as they became older. Many became preoccupied with the theological problem of "theodicy," the challenge of believing both in an all-powerful God of love and the simultaneous existence of evil. But they showed little awareness of the many different approaches to this challenge within the Judeo-Christian tradition. The very ancient character of the book of Job and the centrality of the psalms of lament both within the Hebrew scriptures and the liturgies of the Christian churches (Brown & Miller, 2005), demonstrates the huge concern for this issue within the tradition. But what was understood and remembered of "answers" received when they were young may no longer satisfy persons later in life. Older people need to have the opportunity to reflect anew on the meanings provided by the religious tradition.

As most theologians and pastors would agree, Christianity does not in fact provide an "answer" to the problem of evil, rather a "response" in the life, death, and resurrection of Jesus, with its striking message that God shares completely in people's lives, their struggles as well as joys. The cross is central to the Christian faith, but the churches have sometimes failed to convey that sense of shared suffering in favor of an emphasis either on God's judgement on sin or on Jesus as a bringer of peace. Christianity is a complex religion and its various strands (including Catholic, Orthodox, Protestant) reflect somewhat different interpretations of its central teachings on the nature of Jesus, the Trinity, and the Church. But all possess a rich and continuing theological tradition in regard to the presence of God in suffering and doubt. The influences of Søren Kierkegaard, as well as the powerful witness of Dietrich Bonhoeffer, are strongly felt in the theology of protest, lament, and suffering. Contemporary voices include those of Walter Brueggemann ("From whom no secrets are hid") and Jamie Moran ("The wound of existence"). The problem again is the lack of the Churches' engagement with persons as they grow older. Catechesis is too often seen as an issue for youth not age.

In light of the neglect of ministry with and to older people in religious organizations today (Bengtson, Endacott, & Kang, 2017), churches in Britain have been accused of an ageism that has remained strong even as more secular forms of discrimination have been removed (Merchant, 2003; Hawley & Jewell, 2009). This has become more evident as church congregations have grown older and ministers perhaps more concerned with evangelizing and retaining younger people. But older people need attention particularly at the difficult turning points of late life. At the same time, they should not be perceived solely as recipients of pastoral care. They need to be encouraged to become more involved, listened to, and contribute from their life experience of witnessing to a Christian faith.

Research should be conducted on different ways of being vital members of churches in an aging society.

In our studies we noted a reluctance by our older respondents to turn to their religious ministers for help. Understandably, some of our participants had been disappointed in the past. Although there may not be sufficient ordained priests and ministers to respond to older people's doubts and questioning, there are plenty of church members, younger as well as older, who are in a position to do so. Lessons can be learned from the various forms of small groups that have grown up in recent years and which support older people in exploration of their past lives, their present concerns, and their spiritual exploration (e.g. Birren & Deutchman, 1991; Birren & Svensson, 2013). Small groups led appropriately would also be an effective means of dealing with religious doubts and uncertainties. Theological clarity of course remains important but teaching has also to be communicated effectively. For example, a number of our interviewees had attempted to resolve their problems in believing in a good God by seeing God as limited or imperfect but had apparently not sought help for their difficulties. Churches as communities of faith should become more welcoming to those who are wrestling with God, who feel hurt by God, or simply cannot understand His ways.

References

Andrews, M. (1991). *Lifetimes of commitment. Aging, politics, psychology.* Cambridge: Cambridge University Press.
Atchley, R.C. (2009). *Spirituality and aging.* Baltimore: John Hopkins.
Barker, D. (2015). *Life driven purpose: how an atheist finds meaning.* Durham, NC: Pitchstone Publishing.
Bengtson, V. L., Endacott, C., & Kang, S. E. (2017). Older adults in churches: Differences in perceptions of clergy and older congregation members. *Journal of Religion, Spirituality & Aging,* doi:10.1080/15528030.2017,1414727
Birren, J. E., & Deutchman, D. E. (1991). *Guiding autobiography groups for older adults: exploring the fabric of life.* Baltimore, MD: John Hopkins University Press.
Birren, J. E., & Svensson, C. (2013). Reminiscence, life review, and auto-biography: emergence of a new era. *International Journal of Reminiscence and Life Review,* 1, 1–16.
Brown, C. G. (2001). *The death of Christian Britain.* London: Routledge.
Brown, C. G. (2017). *Becoming atheist: humanism and the secular west.* London: Bloomsbury.
Brown, S. A., & Miller, P. D. (Eds.) (2005). *Lament. Reclaiming practices in pulpit, pew, and public square.* Louisville: Westminster John Knox Press.
Coleman, P. G. (1986). *Ageing and reminiscence processes: social and clinical implications.* Chichester: Wiley.
Coleman, P. G., Ivani-Chalian, C., & Robinson, M. (2004). Religious attitudes among British older people: stability and change in a 20-year longitudinal study. *Ageing and Society,* 24, 167–188.
Coleman, P. G., Ivani-Chalian, C., & Robinson, M. (2015). *Self and meaning in the lives of older people: case studies over twenty years.* Cambridge: Cambridge University Press.
Coleman, P. G., Koleva, D., & Bornat, J. (Eds.) (2013). *Ageing, ritual and social change: comparing the secular and religious in Eastern and Western Europe.* Farnham, Surrey: Ashgate.
Coleman, P. G., & McCulloch, A. W. (1985). The study of psychosocial change in late life: some conceptual and methodological issues. In J. M. A. Munnichs, P. Mussen, E. Olbrich (Eds.). *Life-span and change in a gerontological perspective* (pp. 239–255). New York: Academic Press.
Coleman, P. G., & McCulloch, A. W. (1990). Societal change, values, and social support: exploratory studies into adjustment in late life. *Journal of Aging Studies,* 4, 321–332.
Coleman, P. G., McKiernan, F., Mills, M., & Speck, P. (2007). In sure and uncertain faith: belief and coping with loss of spouse in later life. *Ageing and Society,* 27, 869–890.

Coleman, P. G., Schröder-Butterfill, E., & Spreadbury, J. H. (2016). Religion, spirituality and aging. In V. L. Bengtson & R. A. Settersten, Jr. (Eds.), *Handbook of theories of aging*, Third edition (pp. 577–598). New York: Springer Publishing Company.

Crane, T. (2017). *The meaning of belief. Religion from an atheist's point of view.* Cambridge, Boston: Harvard University Press.

Dawkins, R. (2006). *The God delusion*. London: Bantam Books.

Exline, J. J. & Rose, E. (2005). Religious and spiritual struggles. In R. F. Paloutzian & C. L. Park (Eds.), *Handbook of the psychology of religion* (pp. 315–330). New York: The Guilford Press.

Gall, T. L., Charbonneau, C., & Florack, P. (2011). The relationship between religious/spiritual factors and perceived growth following a diagnosis of breast cancer. *Psychology and Health*, 26, 287–305.

Genia, V. (1990). Religious development: a synthesis and reformulation. *Journal of Religion and Health*, 29, 85–99.

Guttmann, D. (1980). Observations on culture and mental health in later life. In J.E. Birren, & B. Sloane (Eds.). *Handbook of mental health and aging* (pp. 429–447). Englewood Cliffs: Prentice Hall.

Harris, S. (2015). *Waking up: searching for spirituality without religion.* New York: Simon & Schuster.

Hawley, G., & Jewell, A. (2009). *Crying in the wilderness: Giving voice to older people in the church.* Derby: MHA Care Group.

James, W. (1902). *Varieties of religious experience: a study in human nature.* New York: Longmans, Green, and Co. (2002). New York: Routledge.

Kalish, R. L. (1969). The old and new as generation gap allies. *The Gerontologist*, 9, 83–89.

King, M., Speck, P., & Thomas, A. (2001). The Royal Free interview for religious and spiritual beliefs: developments and standardization. *Psychological Medicine*, 25, 1125–1134.

Kirkpatrick, L. A. (2005). *Attachment, evolution, and the psychology of religion.* New York: The Guilford Press.

Krause, N., & Wulff, K. M. (2004). Religious doubt and health: exploring the potential dark side of religion. *Sociology of Religion*, 65, 35–56.

Merchant, R. (2003). *Pioneering the third age. The church in an ageing population.* Carlisle: Paternoster Press.

Mills, M. A., Speck, P., & Coleman, P. G. (2011). Listening and enabling the sharing of beliefs and values in later life. In P. G. Coleman, & Colleagues, *Belief and ageing: spiritual pathways in later life* (pp. 35–58). Bristol: The Policy Press.

Pargament, K. I. (1997). *The psychology of religion and coping: theory, research, practice.* New York: Guildford Press.

Seabrook, J. (1980). *The way we are.* Mitcham, Surrey: Age Concern England.

Sherman, E. (2010). *Contemplative aging. A way of being in later life.* New York: Gordian Knot Books.

Spreadbury, J. H., & Coleman, P. G. (2011). Religious responses in coping with spousal bereavement. In P. G. Coleman, et al., *Belief and ageing: spiritual pathways in later life* (pp. 79–96). Bristol: The Policy Press.

Strawbridge, W. J., Shema, S. J., Cohen, R. D., Roberts, R. E., & Kaplan, G. A. (1998). Religiosity buffers effects of some stressors on depression but exacerbates others. *Journal of Gerontology: Social Sciences*, 53B, S118–S126.

Taylor, C. (2002). *Varieties of religion today: William James revisited.* Cambridge, MA: Harvard University Press.

Tedeschi, R. G., & Calhoun, L. G. (2006). Time of change? The spiritual challenges of bereavement and loss. *Omega,* 53, 105–116.

Van Rooden, P. (2010). The strange death of Dutch Christendom. In C. G. Brown, & M. Snape (Eds.), *Secularization in the Christian World* (pp. 175–195). Farnham, Surrey: Ashgate.

Voas, D., & Crockett, A. (2005). Religion in Britain: neither believing nor belonging. *Sociology,* 39, 11–28. Firsthand York: The Guilford Press.

Walker, J. (2016). Spiritual development in later life: a learning experience? In: M. Johnson, & J. Walker (Eds.). *Spiritual dimensions of ageing* (pp. 249–269). Cambridge: Cambridge University Press.

Wilkinson, P. J., & Coleman, P. G. (2010). Strong beliefs and coping in old age: a case based comparison of atheism and religion. *Ageing & Society,* 30, 337–361.

Chapter 6

Religion and Health in the US Context of Secularization and Aging

Ellen Idler

EMORY UNIVERSITY

Patterns of religious involvement vary by age and cohort in the US. Levels of religious participation in youth are largely determined by family and region, and these can vary a great deal from one community to another. Over the life course, processes of social and health selection bring individuals to levels of religious participation in old age that may or may not differ from the patterns they had when they were younger. Overall, however, the religious participation of older Americans is unquestionably different from that of younger Americans. The decline in average religious attendance and other measures of religious practice and importance for younger persons is now a matter of consensus in the research. There is also some research consensus that religious participation has largely beneficial effects on both physical and mental health. In this chapter we ask, what implications do the trends in religious participation hold for research in the health effects of religious participation? The aging of the US population is critical to understanding this.

An Increasingly Secular America

The US has for a long time been considered an exception to the general trends of secularization that are characteristic of most European societies. In their 2008 book, the late Peter Berger and co-authors Grace Davie and Effie Fokas argued that the higher levels of religious participation in the US compared with Europe are strong evidence against the thesis that the modernization of societies inevitably brings with it secularization. Other critics of the secularization thesis called the US the theory's "fatal anomaly" because relatively high levels of religious belief and practice were maintained in an unquestionably modernized society (Gorski & Altinordu, 2008). These and other vigorous arguments for American exceptionalism in its religious patterns (Torpey, 2010; de Graaf, 2013) had to some extent even turned the tide against the secularization thesis in academic debates. New studies, however, are making the case that while the US has lagged behind Europe in the secularization process, the evidence is now incontrovertible that the US is, in fact, following the European path.

There are many ways of measuring "religiosity" but the trends are similar for all of them. Religious "Nones" – those who claim no religious affiliation when asked in a survey – made up just 3% of the U.S. population in 1957 (Voas & Chaves, 2016); today they are nearly 23% (Thiessen & Wilkins-Laflamme, 2017; Pew Research Center, 2015). In 1990 the number of Americans who said they "never" attended religious services was 13%; by 2014 it had doubled to 26%. Until 1993, half of the US population said they attended religious services once a month or more often, but since then the median response has been only "several times a year" (Voas & Chaves, 2016). In 1998 the proportion of people who said that religion "was very important to their life" was 61%; in 2017 it was 53%. Moreover, there is an increasingly negative view of religion in the US: in 1973, when asked how much confidence they had in "the church, or organized religion" 43% of respondents to the Gallup Poll said "a great deal" and just 7% said "very little." In 2017 those numbers had reversed to 23% most positive and 25% most negative (Gallup Polls, 2017).

The new research demonstrates clearly that the overall decline in religiosity is stratified by cohort, or generation. A Pew Research Center report (2015) indicates that between 2004 and 2014 every generation born since World War II has shown an increase in the number of "nonaffiliated" (those who claim not to belong to any religious group or denomination), even though the proportion that was affiliated to begin with in 2004 was fewer with each younger generation, so the fastest declines have been from the initially lowest bases. Putnam and Campbell (2010) find that respondents reaching adulthood in every decade of the 20th century report that they attended religious services less often than their parents, and this gap was growing even as overall attendance was declining. Along with race, age (or cohort) is the factor that most differentiates Americans' religiosity (Putnam & Campbell, 2010). The accumulating evidence is summed up by Voas and Chaves (2016) who conclude that religious involvement in America has been declining for decades, and that it is driven not primarily by changes in religiosity at the individual level. Rather, it is driven by generational change; with indicator after indicator, they find that each successive birth cohort starts and stays less religiously observant than the previous cohort. Voas and Chaves' long time series and decomposition analysis make a strong argument that this is a cohort, and not an aging or period effect.

This process has resulted in the consistent finding that the oldest Americans are the most religious by any measure, and this has been true as long as there has been polling on the issue. In the 1983 General Social Survey (GSS), almost 70% of Americans born before 1915 said they had a "strong" religious affiliation; in that year just 40% of those born between 1955 and 1964 said the same. By 2013 the oldest GSS respondents (1935–44 birth cohort) are at 56% "strong" affiliation, while the youngest (1985–94 birth cohort) are at 30%, with all in-between birth cohorts arrayed in sequence

(Voas & Chaves 2016). There is a similar picture for attendance at services monthly or more often, using an even longer time series. In 1973, 60% of the earliest cohort, born before 1915, said they regularly attended services, while just 42% of the youngest cohort in that year reported the same. By 2013, the oldest respondents, born 1935–44, were at 55% (almost identical to their proportion in 1973), and the youngest cohort was at 34%. The authors' graphs of over-time GSS data are striking in their visual similarity – wavy but essentially level parallel lines are ordered from most to least religiosity by oldest to youngest cohorts (Voas & Chaves 2016).

Age-related Health Declines and Religion

This US decline in religious involvement is interesting from a health researcher's perspective for several reasons. First, many if not most of the studies of religion as a predictor of health outcomes have been conducted with older adult populations. One reason for this is the relative rarity of population-based health research that has included any measures of religious involvement in its surveys. US government and some private funders have seen religion as a problematic area to study, but including questions about religious involvement in surveys has been justified more often for research in aging populations. Thus much of what we know about the health effects of religious involvement comes from data on older, more religiously observant cohorts. There are important exceptions, of course. Some examples of religion-mortality analyses based on younger adult populations include Hummer, et al. (1999) and Musick, House, & Williams (2004), but nevertheless much of our knowledge comes from studying older cohorts where more frequent attendance at religious services results in relatively plentiful religiously based social ties. Age-stratified analyses in adult populations are needed to know if the health effects of religion are moderated by age, or if they are similar for younger and older cohorts. I have not found any examples of these.

A second reason this issue is interesting is that older persons are more likely than younger persons to have chronic health conditions, and the health problems themselves may have an effect on one or more measures of religious involvement, thereby raising the issue of potential reverse causality in research aimed at finding the effects of religion on health. For example, poor physical health could prevent an older person from attending religious services and also increase his/her risk of future poor health or disability. Or a diagnosis of a new condition could spur an older person to seek consolation in their religion, or alternatively, to call into question their religious beliefs and values in a time of suffering. In all of these cases, religious participation or practice is the response to changes in health status rather than the influence on it. Recent research on religion as a predictor of mortality has attended closely to these issues; VanderWeele, et al. (2017) and

Li, Stampfer, Williams, & VanderWeele (2016) use sensitivity analyses and marginal structural models to assess the potential for reverse causation. Using data from the Harvard Nurses' Health Study, Li, et al. (2016) find that addressing potential feedback and reverse causation made little difference to the findings: frequent attendance at services was associated with a 33% reduction in the hazard of mortality from all causes (HR 0.67, 95% CI 0.62–0.71) after all confounders and mediators were included. The mean age of nurses in the sample was about 62 years of age. True to the patterns, but somewhat ironically, those who attended most frequently (for whom the adjusted mortality risk was the least) were older on average than those who attended less often. Sensitivity analyses were carried out for various groups but unfortunately not by age.

Third, the research on religion as a risk factor for mortality consistently shows that attendance at religious services is associated with longer survival. Thus the higher levels of religiosity of older persons in the survey data may be at least partially driven by the higher mortality rates of those who were less religious and who had higher rates of mortality. This would be a selection effect for old age among those who were most religiously observant earlier in life. New approaches such as decomposition analyses could be useful here, but very long panel data would be necessary to detect such effects.

In the present paper we begin an investigation of these questions with data from the University of Michigan's Health and Retirement Study by asking:

- Do we see the same age-based patterns of religious participation in the HRS that are seen in other surveys?
- Among the multiple dimensions of health and of religion, which health problems are associated with which measures of religious involvement and in which directions?
- Does the association of religion with health vary by age?

Examining Religion, Health, and Aging

Methods

To explore these questions, I used data from the Health and Retirement Study (HRS), a survey of non-institutionalized US adults representative of the population aged 41 and over. The HRS began in 1992 as a study of health and economic circumstances associated with aging among adults aged 51–61, and since then has expanded to include both older and younger adults. Details of the multistage sample design are available elsewhere (Sonnega, et al., 2014; Health and Retirement Study http://hrsonline.isr. umich.edu). African-American and Hispanic households are oversampled at about twice the rate of white households; most interviews are conducted face-to-face. I used the 2004 Wave because multiple questions about religious involvement were introduced for the first time in that year and also the sample first included early baby boomers (birth cohorts 1948–53). Spouses of respondents who were selected for the survey were also interviewed regardless of age, resulting in additional sample members younger than 41. The 2004 sample size is 20,192. All analyses are cross-sectional.

The HRS included three measures of religious involvement and these became our primary dependent or outcome variables. Respondents were asked their religious affiliation, which HRS combined into Mainline Protestants, Conservative Protestants, Roman Catholics, Jews, other religion, and no religion. HRS coded "How often have you attended religious services in the past year?" in five categories from never to more than once per week; I reduced these categories to four: "frequently" (more than once per week), "regularly" (2–4 times per month), "occasionally" (1–12 times per year) and "never." I retained the HRS coding of "How important is religion in your life?" in three categories from "not too important" to "very important".

Demographic characteristics include age (continuous); female gender; self-reported race (white, black, other); self-reported Hispanic/Latino ethnicity; and US native born.

The HRS has pioneered an "unfolding bracket" method of eliciting information on income, assets, and debt that assists respondents to derive a value, for instance, for the current amount of their home mortgage by asking "is the amount more than, less than, or about ____", repeating the question 2–4 more times to arrive at a closely estimated value (Servais, 2004). We used these HRS imputed values for household income and household net worth (sum of all assets and debts), dividing them into quartiles. Education is recorded in years (0–17).

Our health status measures included an unweighted count of chronic conditions that could be causes of death (diabetes, cancer, lung disease, heart disease, stroke) and an unweighted count of non-cause-of-death conditions (high blood pressure, arthritis, other conditions). Other health measures included days in bed in the last month, self-rated health (excellent to poor), a count of symptoms (e. g. incontinence, swelling, shortness of breath), pain, a count of Activities of Daily Living (ADLs, 0–9), a count of Instrumental Activities of Daily Living (IADLs, 0–14), and sensory (vision and/or hearing) impairment. Measures of mental health included the Center for Epidemiologic Studies' Depression scale (scored 0–1, 9 item-means summed), self-reported emotional/psychiatric problems, and self-reported memory problems.

Stata Version 14.2 was used for all analyses. I performed multivariable ordinary least squares regression and logistic regression to assess the association of all health conditions with the three measures of religious involvement, first for the full sample, and then stratified by respondent age (24–49, 50–64, 65–74, 90+). Results of the full sample analyses are reported in Table 6.2; stratified analyses are presented graphically.

Religious Involvement

Table 6.1 shows frequencies for the full sample, and males and females separately. Women showed higher levels of religious involvement than men, as expected. About 58% of women attended services regularly/ frequently, compared with 47% of men, and almost 30% of men never attended services. Over 75% of women said religion is "very important" to them, compared with fewer than 60% of men. Women were some- what more likely to identify themselves as Mainline Protestant, and less likely than men to say they have no religious affiliation. Proportions identifying as Conservative Protestant, Roman Catholic, Jewish, and Other religion were similar for men and women. Compared with US national data from the same time period, the HRS has fewer Non- affiliated and Other religions, and higher proportions for Protestants, Catholics, and Jews (Pew Research Center, 2015).

The mean age for the sample was 66.5 (range 24–107); women were slightly younger (65.1) due to the fact that the household-added spouses were likely to be female and younger. Overall, 58.5% of the sample were female. By race, 80.5% were white, 14.3% African-American, and 5.2% Other race. Latinos made up 9.6% of the sample and 90% of the sample were born in the US. Men were considerably more likely than women to be presently married, 76.3% compared with 54.1%; similar proportions of men and women were never married, but women were far more likely to be widowed (28.3% compared to 9.0%).

With respect to socioeconomic status, women reported slightly lower levels of education, and considerably lower levels of income, assets, and net worth than men. Women's mean household income was $52,940 while men's was $67,380. Overall net worth was even more different: $372,920 for women compared with $484,220 for men.

Health conditions showed inconsistent differences by gender. Of five possible cause-of-death conditions, women reported an average of 0.67 and men 0.77. Non-cause-of-death conditions (range 0–3) were 1.2 for women and 1.1 for men. Bed days per month were 0.8 for women and 0.6 for men. Self-rated health was on average "good" for both men and women, but women reported an average 1.3 symptoms compared with 0.9 for men. Pain reports were slightly higher for women, 0.7 compared with 0.6 for men. ADL and IADL scores were both higher for women: 1.5 compared to 1.1 for men (ADL) and 3.4 compared to 2.4 (IADL). Sensory impairment (vision and hearing) was poorer for men (0.5 compared to 0.4).

Mental health reports were all poorer for women. Their item–mean CESD scores were higher than men's: 0.24 compared to 0.18 on a mean scale of 0–1. Emotional/psychiatric problems were almost twice as common for women, 21.2% compared to 11.7%, and memory problems were similarly higher for women, 2.9% compared to 1.8%.

Table 6.1 Descriptive Statistics for Religion, Demographics, and Health Status, Health and Retirement Study 2004

Variable	*Full Sample* % / mean (se)	*Male* % / mean (se)	*Female* % / mean (se)
Religion			
Attends frequently	15.32	12.70	17.17
Attends regularly	38.10	34.65	40.55
Attends occasionally	21.50	23.16	20.33
Never attends	25.08	29.49	21.95
Religion is "very important"	68.14	58.26	75.14
Mainline Protestant	28.03	24.21	30.74
Conservative Protestant	38.04	37.89	38.16
Roman Catholic	27.07	27.18	26.98
Jewish	2.23	2.18	2.26
Other religion	1.36	1.40	1.33
No religion	7.65	10.32	5.76
Demographic characteristics			
Age in years at 2004 interview (range 24–107)	66.53 (.08)	66.58 (.12)	65.05 (.12)
Baby Boomer (born 1946–1980)	28.21	26.63	29.33
Gender (female)	58.51	–	100.00
Race			
White	80.47	86.09	85.10
African-American	14.31	8.74	10.13
Other race	5.19	5.18	4.76
Latino	9.58	7.34	7.27
US born	89.54	90.02	89.20
Marital status			
Married	63.28	76.32	54.10
Never married	3.60	3.72	3.52
Widowed	20.31	9.00	28.33
Divorced/separated	12.81	11.05	14.05
Socioeconomic characteristics			
Education in years (range 0–17)	12.31 (.02)	12.46 (.04)	12.21 (.03)
Household income in $ (range 0–3.66M)	58.93K (622.70)	67.38K (1.08K)	52.94K (736.27)

	Full Sample	Male	Female
Household assets in $ (range −499K − 76.6M)	271.36K (9.10K)	321.40K (17.35K)	235.87K (9.51K)
Household net worth in $ (range −499K − 77.2M)	419.10K (10.01K)	484.22K (18.78K)	372.92K (10.71K)
Chronic conditions			
Chronic conditions (cause of death) count (range 0–5)	0.70 (.01)	0.77 (.90)	0.67 (.87)
Chronic conditions (non–cause of death) count (range 0–3)	1.15 (.01)	1.07 (.01)	1.21 (.77)
Bed days (range 0–31)	0.73 (.02)	0.58 (3.13)	0.84 (3.69)
Self-rated health (range 1–5)	3.14 (.01)	3.13 (1.14)	3.11 (1.14)
Symptoms (range 0–7)	1.13 (.01)	0.91 (1.32)	1.33 (1.54)
Pain (range 0–2)	0.69 (.01)	0.63 (.78)	0.74 (.82)
Functional limitations			
ADL (range 0–9)	1.20 (.02)	1.08 (1.74)	1.47 (2.00)
IADL (range 0–14)	2.83 (.02)	2.44 (2.93)	3.40 (3.25)
Sensory impairment (range 0–2)	0.43 (.00)	0.50 (.68)	0.40 (.63)
Mental health			
CESD (range 0–3)	0.22 (.00)	0.18 (.00)	0.24 (.00)
Emotional problems	17.29	11.71	21.24
Memory problems	2.61	1.78	2.92
Observations	20,129	8,351	11,778

Note: ADL = Activities of Daily Living; IADL = Instrumental Activities of Daily Living; CESD = Centers for Epidemiologic Studies Depression scale

To see if religious involvement was patterned by age, I plotted the bivariate frequencies for the three religion measures by five age strata (24–49, N = 856; 50–64, N = 8,149; 65–74, N = 6,056; 75–89, N = 4,529; 90+, N = 503). The percent naming some religious affiliation was greater for each older age group, from a low of 86% for those 20–49 to a high of 96% for those 90 and older. The percentage saying religion was "very important" also increases steadily from 63.3% of the youngest respondents to 73.2% of the oldest. The pattern for attendance at services weekly or more often is similar, with the exception of those 90+ who attended less often than those aged 65–74 and 75–89, but more than those aged 24–49. Thus, as expected for this nationally representative sample of the US population in 2004, there are linear increases in religiosity across age strata for religious affiliation and importance, and also for attendance with an exception for the oldest group (see Bengtson et al., Chapter 1 in this volume, for similar results). In the data table (not shown) it can be seen that the 90+ group is much more likely than any other age group to "never" attend (36.2% compared to 23–25% for all other age groups).

I ran similar stratified frequencies for the physical health conditions. There are (mostly) similar linear patterns in the opposite direction, with each older age group showing a smaller proportion reporting no condition. For example, 80% of those 24–49 report no hearing or vision impairment, but less than 30% of those 90+ can say the same. An exception is the slightly higher proportion of those 90+ reporting no cause-of-death conditions compared with those 75–89, reversing the overall downward trend. A bigger exception is that reports of pain are very equivalent across age strata: a little over 50% in each group report no pain. Overall, however, the patterns are strong: the older a

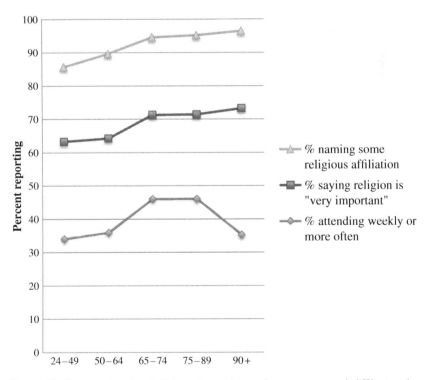

Figure 6.1 Frequencies for Religious Attendance, Importance, and Affiliation by Age, HRS 2004

respondent is, the more likely he or she is to be religious and the less likely he/she is to be healthy.

Health and Dimensions of Religiosity

A key aim of the analysis was to take a closer look at the cross-sectional associations between various dimensions of health and our three measures of religiosity. The arguments for reverse causality in health research uniformly consider poor health simply to be an impediment to religious participation (especially attendance at services) in a way that increases the risk of even poorer later health outcomes. But other associations (including no association) between religion and health are possible, depending on which measures of religion and which measures of health are being considered.

In Table 6.2 there are three models, two OLS and one logistic regression, for the three measures of religiosity regressed on the complete set of demographic, socioeconomic, and health variables available in the HRS. We examine attendance at services first. Positive coefficients show an association with higher levels of attendance. Not surprisingly, older respondents, women, married persons, African-Americans, other non-whites, Hispanics and the foreign born show higher attendance levels than younger, male, unmarried, white, non-Hispanic, native born respondents. Higher levels of education and assets but lower levels of income are associated with higher attendance.

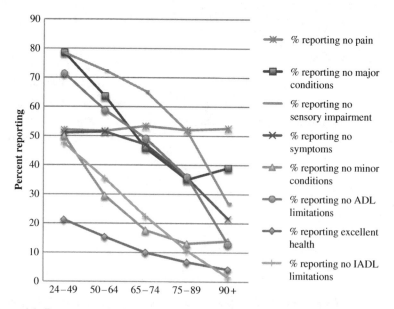

Figure 6.2 Frequencies for Various Health Indicators, by Age, HRS 2004

Attendance is significantly associated either positively or negatively with every one of the demographic and SES measures.

By contrast religious attendance has fewer associations with the health measures. Of twelve health measures, attendance has a significant association with only six, and these are not consistent in their direction. The count of chronic conditions that can be causes of death, for example, is not associated with attendance; in other words, respondents with serious illnesses such as heart disease, cancer, or diabetes are no more or less likely to attend than those who do not have such diagnoses. Perhaps even more surprising, respondents with a higher number of chronic conditions that do not cause death (arthritis, high blood pressure) report higher, not lower, levels of attendance. Other health measures, including the number of days in bed, number of symptoms, and amount of pain reported, have no association in either direction with attendance. Self-rated health is better for those who attend more often. Greater limitation in ADLs (but not IADLs) and more sensory impairment are associated with lower attendance levels. Finally, higher levels of CESD depressive symptoms and self-reported emotional problems (but not memory problems) are associated with lower attendance levels. Thus overall, there is some evidence that poor health, especially poor mental health, is associated with lower attendance levels but in many cases there is not any association one way or the other, and in one case poorer health is associated with higher, not lower, levels of attendance.

The second measure of religious involvement is the subjective feeling of the importance of religion. Its associations with the demographic factors are very similar to those seen in the previous model for attendance. It is also associated with all three SES characteristics, but while there was a mix of SES advantage and disadvantage in the associations with attendance, greater importance of religion is associated consistently with lower levels of education, income, and assets, or SES disadvantage. Even fewer health measures are associated with importance of religion than with attendance – just five of twelve. Three (CESD depressive symptoms, sensory impairment, and self-rated health) are associated in the direction of poorer health with less importance of religion, but higher numbers of symptoms, and more non-fatal chronic conditions are associated with greater importance of religion to the respondent.

Finally, I modeled the affiliation status of the respondents (none vs. any, so negative signs indicate some affiliation). Older respondents, African-Americans, Hispanics, the non-native born, and those who were married are more likely to be affiliated. There are no associations with being female, of other race, or any of the SES measures. Even fewer health measures were associated with affiliation than with importance or attendance, but interestingly, both fatal and non-fatal chronic conditions are positively associated with having some religious affiliation (negative signs for no affiliation). Respondents with higher levels of pain and CESD depressive symptoms are more likely to report having no affiliation.

Table 6.2 OLS/Logistic Regression for Frequency of Religious Attendance, Importance of Religion, and No Religious Affiliation, Health and Retirement Study 2004

Variable	Attendance	Importance	No Affiliation
Demographic characteristics			
Age in years at 2004 interview (range 24–107)	.011★★★	.007★★★	−.043★★★
Female	.401★★★	.478★★★	−.704
Race (white ref.)			
African-American	.850★★★	.700★★★	−.746★★★
Other race	.123★	.165★★	.045
Latino	.513★★★	.383★★★	−.965★★★
US born	−.029★★	−.070★★★	.072★
Marital status (married ref.)			
Widowed	−.239★★★	−.205★★★	.328★★
Divorced/separated	−.511★★★	−.416★★★	.696★★★
Never married	−.386★★★	−.448★★★	.688★★★
Socioeconomic characteristics			
Education in years (range 0–17)	.009★	−.025★★★	.018
Household income in $ (range 0–3.66M)	−.064★★★	−.090★★★	.056
Household assets in $ (range −499K – 76.6M)	.070★★★	−.044★★★	.018
Chronic conditions			
Chronic conditions (cause of death) count (range 0–5)	−.009	.009	−.092★
Chronic conditions (non–cause of death) count (range 0–3)	.094★★★	.049★★	−.151★★★
Bed days (range 0–31)	−.003	.003	.005
Self-rated health (range 1–5)	.080★★★	.052★★★	−.016
Symptoms (range 0–7)	.009	.031★★★	.023
Pain (range 0–2)	.008	.003	.161★★★
Functional limitations			
ADL (range 0–9)	−.023★	.006	−.027
IADL (range 0–14)	−.006	.007	−.024
Sensory impairment (range 0–2)	−.047★	−.036★	−.071
Mental health			
CESD (range 0–9)	−.499★★★	−.234★★★	.371★
Emotional problems	−.090★★	−.016	.139

	Attendance	Importance	No Affiliation
Memory problems	.014	.009	.058
Observations	17,733	17,723	17,750
R^2	.093	.103	.072

Note: ADL = Activities of Daily Living; IADL = Instrumental Activities of Daily Living; CESD = Centers for Epidemiologic Studies Depression scale

Together these three models show that some types of health conditions are associated with some measures of religiosity, but many are not associated at all, and those that are may be associated with better or with poorer health.

Associations among Health, Religion, and Aging

The final aim of the analysis was to see if these associations of health measures with religion measures varied by the age of the respondent. I ran the same OLS and logistic regression models as in Table 6.2 for each of the five age strata; to see if there were any patterns, I then graphed the regression coefficients (only for those measures that were significant in Table 6.2) by age.

Figure 6.3 shows the age-stratified patterns of regression coefficients for the six health measures that are associated with attendance at services; the scale of the y-axis spans 0.0, such that coefficients below the line are associated with lower attendance, and those above the line with higher attendance. The order of the measures in the legend corresponds with the order of the endpoints of the plotted lines, on the right. Two of the measures (self-rated health and ADLs) appear nearly level, suggesting that their association with attendance does not vary much by age. Non-fatal conditions have a downward trend toward the 0.0 line, suggesting that although it is (perhaps unexpectedly) associated with higher levels of attendance for the younger respondents, it is less of a factor for those aged 75–89 and 90+. Two measures (emotional problems and sensory impairment) show upward trends, and in fact cross the 0.0 line, going from an association with lower attendance levels for younger respondents to an association with higher levels for those who are older. Finally, the most notable pattern is for CESD depressive symptoms; all coefficients are strongly negative and increasingly so for those aged 50 and older.

I performed a similar set of analyses for reported importance of religion, graphed in Figure 6.4. Sensory impairment, self-rated health, and symptoms are essentially flat, indicating few differences between age groups in their association with importance of religion. Non-fatal conditions are consistently above the 0.0 line, associated with greater importance of religion, especially so for those aged 90+. CESD scores are consistently negative but

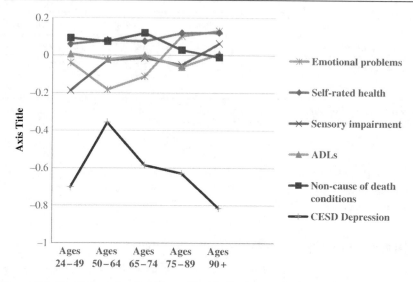

Figure 6.3 Coefficients for Significant Health Correlates of Attendance at Services, by Age Group, HRS 2004

vary in magnitude from one age stratum to another without a clear pattern by age.

Figure 6.5 shows the plotted coefficients for reporting no religious affiliation. Positive values above the 0.0 line indicate greater likelihood of reporting no affiliation. The age pattern for fatal conditions is flat; for non-fatal conditions and pain the coefficients are very similar for those aged from 24 to 89, but for those 90 and older, greater reports of pain and non-fatal conditions are associated with less likelihood of reporting no affiliation. And as in the other graphs, CESD depressive symptoms show a strong, and in this graph, increasing likelihood of reporting no affiliation for each older age group after 50.

Together these graphs show some age-related patterns in the association of health measures with three measures of religiosity, but they are not consistent in their direction with respect to their association with the three measures, or with age.

Thinking About Health and Religion: Age Matters

The purpose of this analysis was to examine the relationship between religiosity and health for Americans of different ages in the context of declining religious involvement in US society. Religion and health are multifaceted concepts, and their associations are multifaceted as well. The HRS data were ideal for examining these questions because of the data set's wide age range (respondents ages 24–107), its detailed measures of physical and

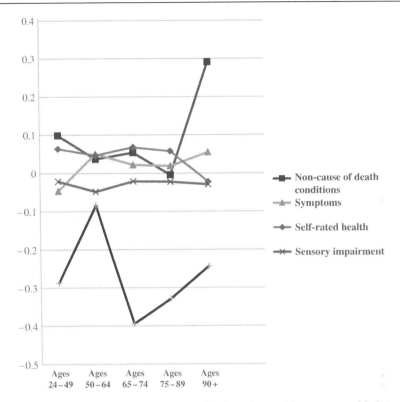

Figure 6.4 Coefficients for Significant Health Correlates of Importance of Religion, by Age Group, HRS 2004

mental health, and its three measures of religiosity. We found, as expected, that religious involvement was lower for each younger age stratum, with the exception of lower attendance levels for those 90+. The data also showed the expected association of increasing age with increasing poor health. Thus the HRS data strongly confirm the patterns from other US national data sets. To my knowledge, this is the first publication of data on religion from the HRS.

We also found that the association of religious involvement with health was quite inconsistent, contrary to the somewhat simplistic assumptions that have informed much research. For some health measures, religious involvement was associated with better health, sometimes it was associated with poorer health, and in many cases there was no association. And finally, we did not see strong age patterning in the association of religiosity with health. Sometimes the association seemed quite stable across age strata; in some cases, the association weakened, in others it strengthened. Overall, the association of religion with health depends on which measure of religion, and which measure of health, but not so much which age group is considered.

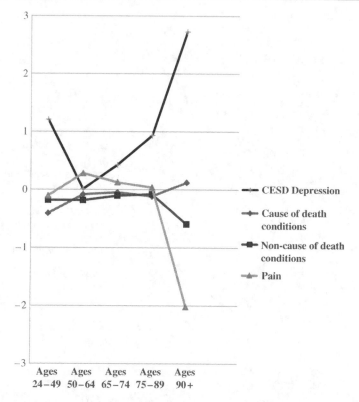

Figure 6.5 Coefficients for Significant Health Correlates of Having no Religious Affiliation, by Age Group, HRS 2004

There is one important exception where the association is strong, consistently negative across measures, and even to some extent stratified by age, and that is for the measure of CESD depressive symptoms. Alone among the health measures, symptoms of depression were significantly associated with all three measures of religiosity, and unlike the mostly flat or inconsistent age-stratified patterns for physical health, the association with depressive symptoms is to some extent stronger for the older age strata than it is for the younger strata. More than any other health condition, persons reporting more depressive symptoms have the lowest levels of religious engagement of any kind, and this seems to be particularly true for the oldest respondents.

An important limitation of this study is that the design is cross-sectional; all measures of health and measures of religiosity refer to the same time period. Despite new methods for addressing it (VanderWeele et al., 2017; Li et al., 2016), the potential for confounding due to reverse causation is real. And while it is of some concern for studies of mortality where the time order of predictors and outcome is clear, it is much more a concern for measures of mental health and well-being where the time order is not at all clear, and poor mental health could lead to reduced religious participation as plausibly as the reverse. Two recent US national studies have addressed this issue with respect to depression, and both found some evidence that prior diagnoses or episodes of depression led subsequently to lower levels of religious attendance, one in the Harvard Nurses' Health Study (Li et al., 2016) and one in the National Collaborative Perinatal Project (Maselko et al., 2012). In these studies, and in the present study with respect to depression, the negative correlation of religiosity with depression at a single time point could legitimately represent causal influence in either direction. This is unquestionably a concern with respect to overestimating the potential effect of religiosity on health. To say it in a different way, prior health problems may have pre-baseline negative effects on religiosity, which may bias its post-baseline association with health status, leading to a false picture of inflated effects of religiosity on health. Given that we have only cross-sectional analyses here, this issue cannot really be addressed, but there is an important implication: given the higher prevalence of measured and perhaps unmeasured health problems among older than younger persons, this issue of reverse causation is more of a concern for studies of older populations.

But there is another direction of reverse causation that should also be of concern because it leads to the opposite direction of bias. Health effects of religious involvement can alternatively take the form of an increased participation in religion following an onset of poor health. This phenomenon has long been noted in population-based samples (Ferraro & Koch, 1994; Ferraro & Kelley-Moore, 2000; Idler & Kasl, 1997a, 1997b) as well as in clinical or patient samples (Koenig, Pargament & Nielsen, 1998; Pargament et al., 1992). Persons experiencing the onset of serious illness and searching for meaning in that experience could understandably turn to religious interpretations of suffering, particularly when they are or have been exposed to such beliefs at earlier points in their life course. One review of studies of religion and coping with many forms of health-related stress finds that religion provides cognitive schema or frameworks for interpreting the experience, enhances the individual's coping resources, and promotes social support and integration (Siegel, Anderman, & Schrimshaw, 2001). The risk of underestimating the positive effect of religion on health will result if religious participation does not decrease, but actually increases as a response to poor health, thereby biasing baseline health downwards because those who were least healthy were more religious. From the perspective of this chapter this direction of bias is also likely to be a greater concern for research with older populations who have had greater exposure to religious language, rituals, and communities over their lifetime, and for whom turning to religion for consolation in a time of illness or suffering represents a perhaps more acceptable and normative means of coping.

Another important limitation of this study is that while three measures of religiosity is three more than many studies have, they by no means capture the many dimensions of religiosity that may have an impact on health (Idler et al., 2003). This is of particular importance if the traditional forms of religious participation that are measured in the HRS are declining historically and/or are being replaced by other forms in younger cohorts. The HRS asks about traditional measures of religion; it does not have a question about spirituality, for example, thus providing no representation for the 37% of (especially younger) Americans who say they are "spiritual but not religious" (Pew Research Center, 2012). It may be that the present analysis captures an increasingly less valid picture of the association of religion (and spirituality) for each younger age stratum. Note that this does not contradict our general finding that the cross-sectional association of these traditional religion measures with various measures of health status did not seem to vary much by age; the strength of the correlation does not depend on the size of the (sub)group in which it occurs.

Thus for some reasons we may have more confidence in the depiction of the association between religion and health for the older HRS cohorts. The questions about religion better represent the traditional forms of religiosity that today's 70- and olders practice and believe. And additionally this cohort has a greater lifetime exposure to religion. On the other hand, we may have more confidence in the findings for the younger cohorts because the possibility for bias due to confounding or reverse causality may be greater for the older cohorts because of their greater health problems.

In either case it is good to remind ourselves that the processes of health selection have been unquestionably maximized in these older cohorts; they are the survivors of their much larger cohorts. In the case of the oldest 2004 HRS respondent—who was 107 years old—they may be among the last dozen or fewer members of their birth cohort. If, as many studies have shown, attendance at religious services is a significant predictor of mortality, even in younger adult populations, then the most infrequent attenders have been at most risk over their lifetimes, and their numbers would have been reduced more quickly than those of frequent attenders. The oldest cohort, those 90 and older who were born between 1897 and 1914, were the most likely of any group to be affiliated with a religion and to say religion was important to them. A significant strength of the Health and Retirement Study is its low nonresponse rate, resulting in continuing follow-up of an extremely elderly sample; it is remarkable these were 503 HRS respondents aged 90 and older. And more than 30% of these 503 nonagenarians and centenarians were still attending religious services at least weekly, indicating either good health and/or quality caregiving. Survivorship is at least partly responsible for the higher religiosity of the oldest persons.

However stable the association between religion and health may be from one age stratum to the next, it is historically becoming a declining resource for the younger cohorts. A larger proportion of each younger cohort lacks exposure to religious practices and beliefs in childhood and young adulthood. This then reduces the likelihood that religion could even be a latent, if not activated, social resource. As it is with marriage, whose rates are also declining for each subsequent cohort, many more people in the US, as elsewhere in the world, will be reaching old age without the traditional social supports that have been there for previous generations. Although neither the social tie to religion nor the tie to a spouse may be easy to add in old age, religious congregations of all kinds are present in nearly every American community, and they welcome new members. Moreover, congregations frequently make great efforts to create accessible facilities for those with disabilities or impairments, and may even provide transportation for those without their own. All in all, religious resources may be easier to obtain if they are sought.

Conclusion

In this chapter I have tried to place current findings and issues in research on religion and health in the context of the inexorably changing patterns of religious engagement in the US. As reflected in the debates in the sociology of religion, it has taken scholars a long time to accept that the US is secularizing just as Western Europe has, albeit more slowly and with a later start. New access to longer spans of US data shows not a complete collapse of religiosity but a gradual drifting downward in frequency and intensity at the population level.

This is not to say that members of religious groups will not continue to teach and preach their beliefs to their younger generations, so that transmission will not stop suddenly, but it appears to continue to taper off. Some religious groups have been affected by the secularizing process more than others, so stratifying by religious affiliation would show quite different intercepts and slopes— declining more rapidly for Mainline Protestants for instance, and less rapidly but still declining for Conservative Protestants (Pew Research Center, 2015).

There are surely implications of these trends for the study of individuals and their well-being in old age. Cohort differences in social resources should be taken into account and researchers need to be alert to cultural changes. There are likely implications for social institutions as well—for religious congregations and for health care institutions, both with and without a faith-based component (Idler & Kellehear, 2017). These implications could best be mapped with a joint examination by sociologists of religion and health researchers; the results would have important potential implications for social care, health care, and social policy, as well as for religious institutions.

References

Berger, P., Davie, G., & Fokas, E. (2008). *Religious America, Secular Europe? A Theme and Variations*. Burlington, VT: Ashgate.

de Graaf, N. D. (2013). Secularization: Theoretical controversies generating empirical research. In R. Wittek, T. A. B. Snijders, & V. Nee (Eds.), *Handbook of Rational Choice Social Research*, 321–354. Stanford, CA: Stanford University Press.

Ferraro, K., & Kelley-Moore, J. (2000). Religious consolation among men and women: do health problems spur seeking? *Journal for the Scientific Study of Religion*, 39(2), 220–234.

Ferraro, K., & Koch, J. (1994). Religion and health among black and white adults: examining social support and consolation. *Journal for the Scientific Study of Religion*, 33(4), 362–375.

Gallup Polls (2017). (http://www.gallup.com/poll/1690/religion.aspx)

Gorski, P., & Altinordu, A. (2008). After secularization? *Annual Review of Sociology*, 34, 55–85.

Health and Retirement Study: A Longitudinal Study of Health, Retirement, and Aging. (http://hrsonline.isr.umich.edu)

Hummer, R. A., Rogers, R. G., Nam, C. B., et al., (1999). Religious involvement and US adult mortality. *Demography*, 36(2), 273–285.

Idler, E., & Kasl, S. (1997a). Religion among disabled and nondisabled persons I: cross-sectional patterns in health practices, social activities, and well-being. *Journal of Gerontology: Social Sciences*, 52B, S294–S305.

Idler, E., & Kasl, S. (1997b). Religion among disabled and nondisabled persons II: attendance at religious services as a predictor of the course of disability. *Journal of Gerontology: Social Sciences*, 52B, S306–S316.

Idler, E., & Kellehear, A. (2017). Religion in public health care institutions: US and UK perspectives. *Journal for the Scientific Study of Religion Symposium on Religion in Public Institutions in Cross-National Perspective*, 56(2), 234–240.

Idler, E., Musick, M., Ellison, C., George, L., Krause, N., Ory, M., Pargament, K., Powell, L., Underwood, L., & Williams, D. (2003). Measuring multiple dimensions of religion and spirituality for health research. *Research on Aging*, 25(4), 327–365.

Koenig, H., Pargament, K., & Nielsen, J. 1998. Religious coping and health status in medically ill hospitalized older patients. *Journal of Nervous and Mental Disease*, 9, 513–521.

Li, S., Okereke, O., Chang, S., Kawachi, I., & VanderWeele, T. (2016). Religious service attendance and lower depression among women – a prospective cohort study. *Annals of Behavioral Medicine*, 50, 876–884.

Li, S., Stampfer, M. J., Williams, D. R., & VanderWeele, T. J. (2016). Association of religious service attendance with mortality among women. *JAMA Internal Medicine*, 176(6), 777–785.

Maselko, J., Hayward, R. D., Hanlon, A., Buka, S., & Meador, K. (2012). Religious service attendance and major depression: a case of reverse causality? *American Journal of Epidemiology*, 175(6), 576–583.

Musick, M. A., House, J. S., & Williams, D. R. (2004). Attendance at religious services and mortality in a national sample. *Journal of Health and Social Behavior*, 45(2), 198–213.

Thiessen, J., & Wilkins-Laflamme, S. (2017). Becoming a religious none: irreligious socialization and disaffiliation. *Journal for the Scientific Study of Religion*, 56(1), 64–82.

Torpey, J. (2010). American exceptionalism? In B. S. Turner (Ed.), *The New Blackwell Companion to the Sociology of Religion*, 141–159. Chichester: Blackwell.

Pargament, K., Olsen, H., Reilly, B., Falgout, K., Ensing, D., & Van Haitsma, K. (1992). God help me: (II): the relationship of religious orientations to religious coping with negative life events. *Journal for the Scientific Study of Religion*, 31, 504–513.

Pew Research Center (2012). *"Nones" on the Rise: One-in-Five Adults Have No Religious Affiliation*. Washington, DC: Pew Research Center.

Pew Research Center (2015). *America's Changing Religious Landscape*. Washington, DC: Pew Research Center.

Putnam, R. D., & Campbell, D. E. (2010). *American Grace: How Religion Divides and Unites Us*. New York: Simon and Schuster.

Servais, M. (2004). *Overview of HRS Public Data Files for Cross-sectional and Longitudinal Analysis*. Ann Arbor: Institute for Social Research, University of Michigan.

Siegel, K., Anderman, S., & Schrimshaw, E. (2001). Religion and coping with health-related stress. *Psychology and Health*, 16, 631–653.

Sonnega, A., Faul, J., Ofstedal, M., Langa, K., Phillips, J., & Weir, D. (2014). Cohort profile: the health and retirement study. *International Journal of Epidemiology*, 43(2), 576–585.

VanderWeele, T. J., Yu, J., Cozler, Y. C., Wise, L., Argentieri, M. A., Rosenberg, L., Palmer, J. R., & Shields, A. E. (2017). Attendance at religious services, prayer, religious coping, and religious/spiritual identity as predictors of all-cause mortality in the black women's health study. *American Journal of Epidemiology*, 185(7), 515–522.

Voas, D., & Chaves, M. (2016). Is the United States a counterexample to the secularization thesis? *American Journal of Sociology*, 121(5), 1517–1556.

Chapter 7

Cognition and Culture
Implications for Understanding Religion/Spirituality

Linda K. George

DUKE UNIVERSITY

Over the past 15 years or so, social scientists have often used the metaphor of "getting under the skin" to refer to efforts to identify specific mechanisms by which social characteristics and conditions affect health. Stress researchers want to identify how traumas and challenges get under the skin to harm health. Social support scholars want to figure out how high-quality social relationships get under the skin to protect health. In the field of religion and health, investigators have attempted to find out how religion/spirituality get under the skin to foster well-being. The common denominator in these studies (other than use of the same under the skin metaphor) has been a focus on biomarkers or, less frequently, genetic factors as the likely mechanisms to explain this (e.g., Hybels, George, Blazer, et al., 2014). The purpose of this chapter is to focus on another way that religion and spirituality might get under the skin to affect individuals' lives; specifically, how the ways in which we think, and the conditions under which we think, might partially explain the frequently observed salubrious effects of religion/spirituality on health and well-being.

Two caveats are needed from the outset. First, this chapter focuses on cognition and culture—two topics about which I have no hands-on experience and about which I am far from expert. I focus on these topics as a relative novice because they seem promising avenues for better understanding the complex links between religion/spirituality and well-being. They also appear to address issues that have been nagging questions as I have ruminated about what we do and do not know about religion/spirituality, aging, and health. Second, very little research on culture and cognition has paid attention to age or aging, so the body of scientific knowledge is limited. I report the scarce empirical findings that link age and aging to culture and cognition. In addition, I point out aspects of this topic that seem to be especially promising targets for research on aging.

This chapter is organized in five parts. The first section describes my motivations in delving into the world of cognition and culture, those nagging questions about which I've ruminated. The next section provides an overview of the theoretical underpinnings of cognition and culture research.

I then turn to a specific subfield of cognition and culture research: moral worldviews. This section defines moral worldviews, examines how they are measured, and briefly reviews how they are distributed in modern societies. The next section drills down on what is known about the relationships among moral worldviews, religion, and behavior. I conclude with thoughts about how cognition and culture research can be applied more broadly to religion/spirituality research.

Why Cognition and Culture? Motivating Questions

As I struggle to keep abreast of the exponentially increasing volume of research examining the links between religion/spirituality and health, I found several issues that I view as unresolved which intrigued me. These ultimately led to my exploration of cognition and culture research, and my conviction that it has the potential to advance the field in new or under-studied directions.

First is the compelling research on relationships between religious coping and health. One attraction of this research is the distinction between positive and negative religious coping. This distinction has been critical in under-standing that religious practices can have either positive or negative associations with health. Another important finding in this research is evidence that religious coping is distinct from other forms of coping and makes unique contributions to health outcomes when non-religious coping is taken into account. Overall, substantial evidence supports the conclusion that religious coping is robustly related to health (cf., the review by Harrison, Koenig, Hays, et al., 2001; and the meta-analysis by Ano & Vasconcelles, 2005).

Much less attention, however, has been paid to the antecedents of religious coping. Is religious coping a direct consequence of religious socialization? Do some denominations promote religious coping to a greater extent than other denominations? Phrased simply, where does religious coping come from?

I know of only two papers that address these issues. One study examined the relationships between what the authors termed "general religious orientations," as measured by intrinsic, extrinsic, and quest religious orien-tations, and religious coping (Pargament, Olsen, Reilly, et al., 1992). Although the goal of this study was admirable, it also had methodological limitations in that the sample consisted of Christians who attended religious services regularly, and that the data were cross-sectional. The second study examined the social and situational antecedents of religious coping in a nationally representative sample of African Americans (Ellison & Taylor, 1996). The findings indicated significant relationships between specific stressful or negative experiences and specific forms of religious coping (e.g., prayer vs. reappraisal of the stressor). But these studies do not answer my question about the foundations of religious coping. It seems to me that religious coping fundamentally rests on a set of beliefs about the extent to which (and the ways in which) religion can help to either ameliorate stress or affect one's ability to get through it. It is this set of beliefs that I want to better understand.

Second, I have long been fascinated by the concept of sense of coherence, which was introduced by Aaron Antonovsky to explain why some people become sick under stressful conditions and others do not (Antonovsky, 1979). Antonovsky postulated that a sense of coherence (SOC) has three components. The first is comprehensibility, which is the belief that things happen in an orderly and predictable way and a sense that you can understand the events in your life. The second component is manageability, a belief that you have the skills, the support, and/or the resources necessary to take care of things—i.e., that things are largely in your control. The third component is meaningfulness, or the belief that life is worth living and that there are good reasons to care about what happens to you and to others. Antonovsky later developed a scale measuring these three dimensions of SOC (Antonovsky, 1993). That scale has been used in hundreds of studies across the globe and translated in 32 languages. There is compelling evidence that SOC is associated with better physical health, mental health, and subjective well-being (see Eriksson & Lindstrom, 2007 for a review).

In the vast majority of research, SOC is an independent variable, a predictor of outcomes of interest. Very little research has examined its antecedents. A few studies have examined the relationships between basic demographic variables and SOC. These report similar patterns are reported across US, European, and Pacific Rim populations: higher levels of SOC are reported by men than women, by middle-aged and older adults than by adolescents and young adults, and by persons with high levels of education and income (e.g., Eriksson & Lindstrom, 2007; Geyer, 1997). In addition, recent longitudinal research indicates that two opposing forces affect SOC in later life (Silverstein & Heap, 2015). Health declines and social resource losses are associated with decreases in SOC over time. Controlling on these losses, however, SOC increases consistently after age 65. Sense of Coherence is clearly a set of beliefs strongly related to health.

Although the research that led to the development of SOC was based on Israeli samples, many of whom were Holocaust survivors, Antonovsky (1979) did not address possible relationships between religion/spirituality and SOC. I would expect SOC to be higher among individuals strongly invested in religion/spirituality, but surprisingly few studies have investigated this hypothesis. The few relevant US studies are based on samples of chronically or terminally ill persons (e.g., Motzer & Stewart, 1996; Mullen, Smith, & Hill, 1994; Strang & Strang, 2001). In these studies, SOC is positively associated with religion/spirituality, as well as with less depression and higher perceived quality of life. And one study reports that SOC mediated a large proportion of the relationship between strength of religious faith and depressive symptoms (Mullen et al., 1994). Although evidence is scarce, a relationship between religion/spirituality and SOC is not universal. In a Swedish study, Larsson and Kallenberg (1996) report no relationship between religion and SOC, although they also caution that only 3% of their sample believes in God or a higher power.

Overall, strong evidence indicates that SOC is related to health and well-being. But as was the case for religious coping, I want to know where SOC "comes from." Sense of coherence appears to rest on—or perhaps be part of—a set of beliefs about the nature of the world and one's relationship to the world. But how does it develop? What characteristics and experiences determine whether one has a high or low sense of coherence? These are not purely rhetorical questions. If sense of coherence is a health-promoting psychosocial resource, how can it be fostered if we do not understand its foundations?

A third theme in previous research on religion/spirituality and health is the intriguing notion of religion/spirituality as placebo. The thesis that the placebo effect may partially explain the generally beneficial effects of religion/spirituality on health emerged in the late 1990s—a time that the placebo effect had reengaged the attention of philosophers, psychologists, and the medical sciences. As a result of this new scholarship, the placebo effect gained significant respect and is no longer viewed only as a methodological nuisance to be appropriately handled in clinical trials because humans are susceptible to illusion. An important theme in this scholarship was the contention that the placebo effect can be activated by stimuli far beyond the proverbial sugar pill (e.g., Lundh, 1987; Price, Finnis, & Benedetti, 2008). Many scholars now argue, for example, that multiple aspects of medical encounters (e.g., how physicians frame explanations of medical interventions and the optimism conveyed by health care providers) represent placebo effects (e.g., Price et al., 2008; Welch, 2003). Other scholars refute this conclusion, however, stating that these kinds of factors are true medical interventions rather than analogs to the "sugar pill" (e.g., Moerman & Jonas, 2002).

It is not surprising that the increased attention to the placebo effect in general spurred the idea that religious/spiritual faith might also activate a healing placebo effect (Harrington, 2011). No scholar promoted this viewpoint more consistently and ardently than Harvard cardiologist Herbert Benson, best known for discovering the relaxation response (Benson & Klipper, 2000). Benson contends that religion/spirituality has powerful health benefits. His research linked religious faith and practices to multiple health outcomes; he studied both Western and non-Western religions (primarily Buddhism), finding that practices in both (prayer in Western religions, meditation in Buddhism) foster health; and he has had some success in identifying the biological pathways by which religion/spirituality impacts health (Benson & Stark, 1997). Benson is not alone in interpreting findings in religion/spirituality and health research as possible evidence of the placebo effect (e.g., Harrington, 2011; Levin, 2009).

Despite increased attention, the placebo effect remains a difficult topic to research. Outside of clinical trials there are few analogs to the sugar pill. Unlike clinical trials, it is typically not possible to randomly assign individuals to stimuli assumed to represent "active ingredients" and placebos, including, of course, religious/spiritual faith and practices. What is non-controversial is the assumption that the placebo effect rests on the power of belief (Price et al., 2008; Stewart-Williams & Podd, 2004). The argument that belief may be a partial explanation for the links between religion/spirituality and health again leads me to question whether the ways we think and process information have received sufficient attention.

Searching for a Label

I believe there are important constellations of beliefs and values that undergird religious/spiritual practices that generate a sense of coherence or its absence and that make it possible for religion/spirituality to sometimes exert a placebo effect on health. Deciding what to call these constellations of beliefs and values has been more difficult.

I rejected two terms that were suggested to me by colleagues with whom I shared my musings. The term schema is not appropriate. A central concept in psychology and sociology, a schema is generally defined as a pattern of thought or mental representation that categorizes information and works virtually effortlessly to make the world comprehensible and guide behavior (e.g., Rumelhart, 1980). A voluminous amount of sophisticated theory and research is based on schemas, and they are vital in understanding a wide range of phenomena. But schema is not a match for the term I am seeking. Schemas are specific and the constellations of beliefs and values that I am trying to label are broader and more abstract. Indeed, these constellations incorporate multiple schemas.

Somewhat later I became intrigued by the concept of cognitive maps, which also is defined as a mental representation that organizes information and guides behavior. This concept also has generated a large body of research, especially in the neurosciences. But the term cognitive maps applies specifically to mental representations of locations and other spatial arrangements (e.g., McNaughton, Battaglia, Jensen, & Moser, 2006). Thus, it, too, is overly narrow.

Ultimately, I decided to use the term "worldview." There is broad consensus that worldview refers to the set of assumptions held by an individual or a society about physical and social reality. Worldviews are much broader and more abstract than schemas and exist at both individual and aggregate levels (Koltko-Rivera, 2004). Overall, more attention has been paid to worldviews shared by members of social aggregates than to individual differences in worldviews among members of aggregates, although both are recognized. Nonetheless, the ability to apply the term worldview at both levels is an advantage. The term worldviews has been used widely in previous scholarship, which is both an advantage and a disadvantage. The advantages are that worldview is a key concept in multiple disciplines and has been useful for understanding attitudes and behavior. The disadvantage is that the term has been conceptually and operationally defined many ways. As discussed below, I will use the term to refer to constellations of moral values—one of many ways it has been previously defined.

Theoretical Underpinnings of Cognition and Culture Research

Research on cognition and culture is based on a combination of dual-process theory, a long-respected conceptual framework from cognitive psychology, and newer conceptualizations of culture in sociology. Both components merit review.

Dual-process Theory

Although William James is generally credited with first proposing that the human brain uses two modes of processing, Jonathan Evans is widely acknowledged as the originator of formal dual-processing theory (Sloman, 1996). The theory's basic propositions are straightforward. Humans use two methods of thought and reasoning. The first method is fast, autonomous, and requires little, if any, conscious effort. The second method is conscious, deliberate, and analytical. Because it is efficient and effortless, most human thought is based on the fast, autonomous type. Deliberative thought is avoided if possible, but is activated in difficult situations or when one is called upon to provide a post-hoc explanation for behavior (e.g., Evans, 1984; 2007). Evans and other early dual-process scholars were cognitive psychologists. As a consequence, their applications focused on issues such as learning, decision-making, and reasoning. Approximately a decade later, social psychologists became enamored with dual-process theory, noting its importance for issues including persuasion, stereotypes, and attitude–behavior discrepancies (e.g., Devine, 1989; Smith & DeCoster, 2000). Dual-process theory remains an important part of these branches of psychology.

During the past 40 years, many refinements of the theory have been offered and the range of phenomena to which it has been applied exploded (e.g., Kahneman, 2011; Osman, 2004). Multiple labels have been used for these two modes of thought. For our purposes, I will refer to the fast, autonomous mode of thought as implicit or heuristic processing and to the deliberate, analytic mode of thought as explicit or systematic processing.

An extensive body of research has examined age differences in both heuristic and systematic processing. Much of this research focuses on highly specific decision-making tasks (e.g., how speed of task completion or memory demands affect accuracy). Thus, a comprehensive review of this research topic is beyond the scope of this chapter. General conclusions are possible, however. First, across a wide variety of decision-making contexts, older adults employ heuristic processing to a greater extent than young adults (Castel, Rossi, & McGillivray, 2012; Goodrich, 2013). When asked to justify their decisions, however, both older and younger persons primarily rely on systematic processing and no significant age differences are observed (Johnson, 1990; Kim, Goldstein, Hasher, & Zacko, 2005). Virtually all of this research is based on experimental designs and whether these differences reflect age changes or cohort effects is unknown, although they are generally interpreted as age changes.

Theories of Culture

Sociological conceptualizations of culture have had a more complicated history. Culture is generally defined as the total material and non-material achievements and resources of a society. Material culture consists of all the physical objects available in society. Non-material culture includes all the non-physical contents of culture, including ideas, norms, rules, values, belief systems, morals, language, organizations, and institutions. Throughout most of the 20th century, culture was viewed as relatively stable, universal, and coherent. The realities of modern societies, however, challenged and ultimately repudiated this view. Culture theory was modified in major ways. Temporally, culture is now viewed as dynamic, with various elements changing and being added at differing tempos. Rather than assumed to be universal, culture is now seen as varying substantially within societies—in short, as pluralistic. Nor is it now assumed that culture is coherent. Rather, its content is vast and complex with inherent contradictions and lacking an organized structure (c.f., DiMaggio, 1997 for a review).

Just as culture, as currently conceptualized, is less coherent than viewed earlier, so too are theories about how it works and what cultural content is most important for individuals and groups. With regard to cultural content, for example, some theorists argue that values are no longer meaningful foundations of individual attitudes and actions (Swidler, 1986); others believe that they are powerful motivators of individual behavior (Hitlin & Piliavin, 2004). As another example, there is general agreement that the major forms of cultural transmission are socialization and personal experience (the same mechanisms posited by earlier theories), but there is disagreement about their relative weights. Given the rise in individualism in the US, for example, some theorists suggest that culture is a "toolkit"—that individuals are relatively free to pick and choose the elements of culture that create and sustain their identities and behaviors (Swidler, 1986). As a result, these scholars see little potential for collective commitments and action. Other theorists argue that social groups exert sizeable power in shaping individuals' identities, behaviors, and actions. They acknowledge that societies are pluralistic, but groups are major forces of cultural transmission (e.g., Martin, 1992). In this view, groups also can forge bonds of commitment and collective action (Stryker, Serpe, & Hunt, 2005).

Cognition and Culture: Putting Them Together

In explaining how culture operates, culture theorists rely on another psychological concept: schemas. As noted previously, a schema is a mental representation of a concept; it contains knowledge about the concept, its meaning, and its relationship to other concepts (Rumelhart, 1980). Everyone has masses of schemas as a result of socialization and personal experience. Schemas allow us to live life as we know it and to believe and act as if we know how the world works. Schemas are continuously activated as we navigate the world and usually do so efficiently and without conscious effort. They are the fodder of heuristic processing. But schemas also can be deliberately and systematically processed. Because they are specific and distinct, individuals' schemas can be—and typically are—not internally consistent. As a result, for example, I can be highly competitive in one situation and non-competitive in situations governed by a different schema. If I am not forced to confront this contradiction, I will heuristically and comfortably behave in ways compatible with these contradictory schemas. If forced to face this discrepancy, however, I will use systematic processing to find a post-hoc explanation or a rationale for dismissing it as unimportant (Wilson, Dunn, Kraft, & Lisle, 1989).

If culture were stable, universal, and coherent, schemas for particular concepts would be relatively homogeneous across individuals. But culture is not stable, universal, and coherent. As a result, although there is usually some overlap in schemas for specific concepts across individuals, there also are substantial differences and, often, clear discrepancies. Much like inconsistencies among our own schemas, discrepancies across individuals can result in deliberate, systematic processing with the goal of making sense of those incongruities.

Cognition, Culture, and Morality

Research that combines dual-processing theory and recent conceptualizations of culture is quite young, spanning the last two decades. It is also fragmented, with the cultural content subjected to empirical scrutiny varying widely. Very little of this research explicitly examines religious cultural content. But substantial attention has been paid to how cognition and culture operate in the realm of morality. A brief review of this active research field can demonstrate its potential for advancing our understanding of how religion/spirituality affects many areas of life, including, perhaps, aging and health.

An initial challenge facing scholars in this field is defining morality. In their review of the field, Hitlin and Vaisey (2013) observe that morality has been implicitly defined in two primary ways. One conceptualization assumes that there are universal components of morality, all focused on distinguishing between good and bad. The goal of this approach is to understand what distinguishes between the moral and the immoral. The second more subtle and less common conceptualization focuses on the boundaries of morality. From this perspective the important distinction is between what is morally relevant and what is morally irrelevant. Both conceptualizations have been used to study the ways in which morality affects behavior.

As noted previously, cultural content is legion. Consequently, researchers focus on specific domains of cultural content. In the research reviewed here, the content is interchangeably referred to as the moral domain and moral worldviews. Even narrowing cultural content to a specific domain, the relevant array of specific schemas is vast. This has led to a tradition of creating within-domain typologies; in this case, moral typologies.

At least a dozen moral typologies have received significant scholarly attention. The numbers of categories in these typologies differ substantially. Hunter (1992), for example, who is credited with coining the term "culture wars," posited two overarching moral domains or worldviews: the orthodox and the progressive. These two categories can be paraphrased as conservative and liberal—ideologies that he views as permeating life far beyond the political arena and creating deep societal divisions. As another example, in their highly respected book, *Habits of the Heart* (1985), Robert Bellah and co-authors posit four moral worldviews that differ in degree and type of individualism. They postulate that over the previous century, individualistic moral worldviews became increasingly common and they question whether the social fabric can survive without increased commitment to the common good. Bellah et al. also argue that these four worldviews are strongly related to religion.

Two other taxonomies have been used in most recent research on moral worldviews. Both employ values as the basic unit of measurement. The Theory of Basic Human Values was developed by Shalom H. Schwartz in the early 1990s (Schwartz & Bilsky, 1990; Schwartz, 1992). Schwartz's goal was to develop a comprehensive set of values that is valid across societies and would, thus, be appropriate for cross-cultural research. After extensive research that ultimately included more than 60,000 adults in 64 nations (Schwartz, 2006), he concluded that ten basic value domains are valid across nations. The ten domains are stimulation, hedonism, self-direction, universalism, benevolence, conformity, tradition, security, power, and achievement. The ten domains also can be aggregated into four higher-order domains: openness to change, self-transcendence, conservatism, and self-enhancement. He developed the Schwartz Portrait Values Questionnaire (PVQ), which includes multi-item scales for each domain. Schwartz provides extensive documentation of the excellent reliability and validity of these ten value domains (Schwartz & Boehnke, 2004). Although Schwartz does not label the value domains as moral domains, they have been used in substantial research on morality.

Consistent age differences are observed for the PVQ across countries. With regard to the four higher-order domains, older adults (generally defined as those 60 or 65 and older) score higher on conservatism and self-transcendence than their younger counterparts (Schwartz, 2006; Schwarz & Bilsky, 1990). Conversely, older adults score lower than persons younger than age 60 on openness to change and self-enhancement. This same pattern is observed for individuals who score high or low on religion. That is, high levels of religious participation are positively associated with conservatism and self-transcendence and negatively related to openness to change and self-achievement (Schwartz, 1992; 2006). These associations are based on cross-sectional data, rendering it unclear whether they reflect age changes or cohort differences.

The second taxonomy of moral domains was developed by Jonathan Haidt and colleagues. Using data from a variety of sources ranging from political speeches to philosophical writings, Haidt and colleagues extracted statements that had clear moral or ethical content from these sources. They identified five moral principles within which all the statements seemed to fit (Graham, Haidt, & Nosek, 2009). The five moral domains, along with exemplars of content are:

- Harm/care: It is wrong to hurt people. It is good to relieve suffering.
- Fairness/reciprocity: Fairness is good. Individual rights should be protected.
- In-group/loyalty: Allegiance, loyalty, and patriotism are good.
- Authority/respect: Social order is necessary to human life and must be honored.
- Purity/sanctity: Certain aspects of life are sacred and should be kept pure.

Haidt et al. report that most Americans endorse all five moral principles, but weight their importance differently. A moral profile can be constructed for individuals based on the weights they assign to the five moral principles. These profiles can be aggregated and compared across groups. Extensive research on these moral principles led to the development of Moral Foundations Theory, in which Haidt argues that these principles are the foundations of morality in all cultures (Koleva, Graham, Iyer, Ditto, & Haidt,

2012). Haidt and colleagues also developed the Moral Foundations Questionnaire (MFQ) (Graham, Nosek, Haidt et al., 2011). The most recent version of the MFQ has 30 items and has received extensive psychometric assessment based on data from 32,607 persons.

Haidt and colleagues initially compared the moral profiles of political liberals and conservatives, based on their speeches and other materials. Not surprisingly, they found that liberals and conservatives differed greatly on the weights they attributed to these moral principles (Graham et al., 2009). Liberals highly weight harm/care and fairness/reciprocity, but give almost no weight to purity/sanctity. They are not morally offended if individuals burn American flags, express disdain for the military, or advocate overthrowing the government. Conservatives, in contrast, weigh the last three moral principles much more heavily than the first two. They value social order and its authorities, even at the expense of individual rights. They do not advocate wholesale trampling of individual rights, but they clearly prefer social order, even if some societal members suffer as a result. The bumper sticker that reads "Dissent is the highest form of patriotism" is sacrilege to right-wing politicians. For Haidt, the major problem in political debates is that neither liberals nor conservatives acknowledge that both sides are operating on moral grounds (Haidt, 2012; Haidt & Graham, 2007). Liberals typically view conservatives as out of touch with modern life at best, and ignorant at worst. Conservatives view liberals as ungrounded, reckless, and willing to dismantle order for chaos.

In addition to political orientation, the five moral domains are strongly related to other individual characteristics (Graham et al., 2011). Age differences similar to those reported by Schwartz are observed (Graham et al., 2011; Miles, 2014). Older adults weight in-group/loyalty, authority/respect, and purity/sanctity more heavily than younger adults do. Whether these are due to age changes or cohort differences is unclear. With regard to gender, women weight harm/care, authority/respect, and purity/sanctity more heavily than men. Gender is not related to fairness/reciprocity and in-group/loyalty. SES also is significantly related to the weights assigned to the five moral domains. Those with high education weight harm/care and fairness/reciprocity most heavily and generally assign low weights to the other three domains. Persons with low levels of education weight authority/respect, in-group/loyalty, and purity/sanctity more heavily than harm/care and fairness/reciprocity. Thus, the relationships between SES and the moral domains strongly resemble those observed for political orientation.

Linking Morality Worldviews to Religion and Behavior

Moral Worldviews and Religion

Scholars have documented robust relationships between specific moral domains and indicators of religious involvement. This literature is complex because of the variety of methods used to measure moral worldviews. Nonetheless, the pattern of results is remarkably similar regardless of how moral worldviews are measured, increasing confidence that the relationships are meaningful and valid.

In two studies, measures of worldview were based on Bellah et al.'s four-category typology (Bellah et al., 1985). Both studies were based on data from the National Study of Youth and Religion, a nationally representative study of adolescents age 13–17. In both, the four categories were observed, with one of them labeled theistic (Vaisey, 2009; Vaisey & Lizardo, 2010). Vaisey and Lizardo (2010) report that a theistic worldview was robustly associated with denomination and service attendance. Specifically, conservative Protestants were especially strong proponents of the theistic worldview and, for all denominations, more frequent religious service attendance was associated with a theistic worldview.

Other studies rely on measures that are moral worldviews, but are not based on established typologies. Victor, Miles, and Vaisey (2015), for example, applied factor analysis to a set of items that they believed reflected a wide range of values. Their analysis yielded a single factor that they concluded ranged from orthodox (religious) to progressive (individualistic). This study also was based on the National Study of Youth and Religion. Those who scored on the orthodox end of the scale reported more frequent attendance at religious services, higher levels of religious importance, and higher parental involvement in religion. Beyerlein and Vaisey (2013) examined moral domains using data from the Religion and Public Activism Survey, a representative sample of American adults. They categorized responses into three moral domains: person-centered/individualistic, society-centered/civic, and religious. Again, the religious worldview was associated with higher levels of religious service attendance.

Researchers increasingly rely on the Schwartz Portrait Values Questionnaire (PVQ) and Haidt's Moral Foundations Questionnaire (MFQ) to measure moral worldviews. Using data from two nationally representative web-surveys, Miles (2014) examined demographic and religious correlates of moral worldviews as measured using ten moral domains from the PVQ and Haidt's five moral domains. Religious affiliation was strongly associated with the PVQ value domains of tradition, conformity, and purity and Haidt's purity/sanctity domain. Miles and Vaisey (2015) compared the ability of four conceptualizations of moral worldviews to predict political orientation in a representative sample of American adults (the Measuring Morality Study). The four typologies of moral values included those of Schwartz and Haidt, as well as two simpler, dichotomous typologies (a total of 19 specific moral constructs). Factor analysis identified three underlying dimensions which the authors labeled Order-Focused (a focus on stability and tradition), Other-Focused, and Self-Focused. Religious affiliation, religious importance, and religious service attendance were significantly related to an Order-Focused worldview (and not to the other two moral dimensions). Haidt and colleagues have consistently found that religious participation, measured in a variety of ways, is significantly and positively associated with three of his five moral domains: authority/respect, in-group/loyalty, and, especially, purity/sanctity (Graham et al., 2011; Koleva et al., 2012).

In sum, specific dimensions of human values—dimensions that focus on tradition, in-group loyalty, conformity, and purity—are strongly related to multiple indicators of religious involvement. Importantly, the religious variables used in this research tradition do not include specific religious beliefs (e.g., belief in original sin or an afterlife), which might not be conceptually distinct from moral values. These depictions of religious worldviews have not been linked to health, although Graham and Haidt (2010; Graham et al., 2011) report that individuals who assign higher weights to the moral dimensions associated with religion are happier than those who assign higher weights to the harm/care and fairness/reciprocity domains.

Religious Priming

Linking religion to behavioral outcomes in a methodologically rigorous way has proven to be exceptionally difficult. A major complicating factor—which has not been resolved and which may not be resolvable—is religious priming. I will first attempt to succinctly summarize the messy and contentious research on religious priming. I will then describe my major concern that religious priming occurs in studies beyond those in which it is the topic of interest.

There is a voluminous literature on religious priming, the vast majority of which is based on experimental designs. In a typical experiment, research subjects are randomly assigned to receive or not receive a religious prime—an explicit statement about religious orthodoxy or exposure to a religious artifact such as the Koran or a cross. Participants then engage in a decision-making task after which it is determined whether exposure to the religious prime is associated with the decisions observed. Less frequently, there are three groups: a group exposed to a religious prime, a group exposed to a non-religious prime, and a control group that is not exposed to a prime. Dozens of studies are based on this basic experimental design.

Most studies have examined the relationships between religious primes and prosocial outcomes. In general, there are two forms of prosocial behavior. One form is donating a resource that benefits another person (i.e., the recipient) when (a) the recipient lacks or needs the resource, (b) donating the resource will reduce the donor's amount of that resource, and (c) the donor will remain anonymous. The other form of prosocial behavior consists of refraining from engaging in unethical acts such as cheating, lying, or stealing. A variety of specific tests exist for measuring prosocial outcomes. As documented in a recent meta-analysis based on 94 studies involving 11,653 study participants, a substantial majority of studies report that exposure to a religious prime increases both forms of prosocial behavior (Shariff, Willard, Andersen, & Norenzayan, 2016).

Research linking religious primes to other outcomes, however, paints a less rosy picture. Religious primes also have been associated with increased negative stereotypes of outgroups and racial prejudice (Johnson, Rowatt, & LaBouff, 2010; Yilmaz, Karadoller, & Sofuoglu, 2016), increased submissiveness to authoritarian persons (Saroglou, Corneille, & Van Cappellen, 2009; Van Pachtebeke, Freyer, & Sarglow, 2011), and more punitive assessments of non-normative or criminal behavior (McKay, Efferson, Whitehouse, & Fehr, 2011; Yelderman & Miller, 2017).

It is difficult to make sense of these starkly different portraits of the effects of religious primes. What can explain why religious primes promote prosocial behavior, but also promote prejudice, submissiveness, and punativeness? I do not know, of course. But I believe that one must carefully examine the research designs used in these studies. For example, the most recent study I found (Yelderman & Miller, 2017) concludes that religious primes increase guilty verdicts and severity of punishment in a mock insanity defense trial. But the religious prime used was fundamentalist Christian text and the sample consisted of fundamentalist Christians. In my view, this research design tells us almost nothing about the general relationship between religious primes and punitive assessments of criminal behavior.

Another relevant question about religious primes is whether they are moderated by research participants' personal characteristics. Are some people more susceptible to religious primes than other people? Substantial research suggests that religious people are more strongly influenced by religious primes than non-religious individuals. For example, in a recent study (Lang, Mitkidis, Kundt et al., 2016), research participants were randomly assigned to one of three conditions: hearing sacred music during the experiment, hearing non-sacred music, or being exposed to white noise. Study participants then participated in a procedure in which they had the opportunity to obtain monetary rewards. The procedure made it relatively easy for participants to cheat, thereby increasing the money they received at the end of the experiment. A simple comparison of the three groups revealed that study participants exposed to sacred music were less likely to cheat than those in the other two conditions. When study participants' self-reports of their religious involvement were taken into account, however, it was only those participants who described themselves as religious who were less likely to cheat when exposed to sacred music. Many other studies also report that religious primes are associated with higher levels of prosocial behavior only or primarily among religious persons. Indeed, in their meta-analysis, Shariff et al. (2016) state that although religious primes foster prosocial behavior among religious individuals, it remains unclear whether they do so for non-religious persons.

Despite decades of research, vexing questions about the influence of religious primes remain. As noted above, a substantial proportion of studies are based on samples that consist of individuals from a specific religious background (e.g., conservative Protestants, Muslims) and use religious primes targeted at that religion. This not only severely limits generalizability of results, but also appears to represent a "best case" opportunity to find evidence that religious primes affect outcomes of interest. I also am troubled by an issue that I have not seen considered in research on religious priming. What if simply being asked about one's religious participation acts as a religious prime? Imagine agreeing to participate in a study on decision-making and then being asked not only basic demographic questions, but also a battery of questions about one's religion. Would this not be a rather obvious cue that religion is somehow related to the purpose of the research? There may be ways of reducing this potential threat, such as asking questions about religion after the experimental procedure. But in the religious priming literature that I have read, that either has not been the case or the order of data collection is unclear. And I have seen no discussion of this issue and its potential implications.

A research tradition based almost exclusively on experiments also raises broader issues of external validity. Behavior is guided to a substantial degree by schemas and schemas are often situation-specific (e.g., different schemas are triggered in work environments than at a sporting event). Thus, outside the laboratory, it is unclear how, if, or when religious primes affect behavior. Does it make a difference whether a religious artifact or symbol is present in a work environment or at a cocktail party? Do religious primes in the "real world" affect only or primarily religious individuals as has been observed in laboratory studies? Does it matter how close the "match" is between the religious prime and the individual's religious tradition (e.g., do the Bible and the Koran affect behavior in similar ways for Muslims)?

In sum, although research on religious priming raises important issues about the relationships between religious involvement and behavior, I suggest that it provides little in the ways of answers. Fortunately, although small in volume, emerging research on moral worldviews and behavior offers tantalizing and methodologically superior insights about the links between religion and behavior.

Moral Worldviews and Behavior

Most research on moral worldviews has examined their relationships with political ideology and attitudes, as previously reviewed. A smaller line of research examined the associations between moral values and other behaviors. Much of this scholarship is the work of Stephen Vaisey and colleagues. Vaisey posits that moral worldviews affect behavior primarily through heuristic cognitive processing (Vaisey, 2009; Hitlin & Vaisey, 2013). As such, individuals are unaware of how, when, and to what extent their moral worldviews affect their actions. Moral values can be used in deliberate, systematic processing, but this occurs rarely, in situations where individuals either confront situations where heuristic processing is problematic or they are asked post-hoc to justify their actions. Vaisey and colleagues have tested this theory using multiple data sets, multiple methods, and for a variety of behavioral outcomes.

Vaisey first tested these propositions in a study of moral worldviews and behaviors using data from the National Study of Youth and Religion, a nationally representative sample of adolescents age 13–17 (Vaisey, 2009). Moral worldviews were measured using Bellah et al.'s four-category typology and all four worldviews were observed in the sample. Six behaviors comprised the dependent variables, including both helping others and refraining from non–normative/illegal behaviors. Adolescents who endorsed the theistic worldview reported higher levels of volunteering and spontaneously helping others and lower levels of alcohol use, illegal drug use, keeping secrets from parents, and cheating at school than adolescents who endorsed the other three categories of moral values. A subset of the sample were asked in interviews to explain what motivated their self-reported behaviors. These questions were intended to force sample members to use systematic processing in formulating their responses. Study participants found it difficult to explain their behaviors and their answers corresponded very little with their moral worldviews. Vaisey interpreted these findings as support for the conclusion that, as hypothesized, the adolescents used heuristic processing when answering the survey questions.

In a subsequent study, also using data from the National Study of Youth and Religion, Vaisey and Lizardo (2010) examined the relationships between moral world views and social network composition. Data were from baseline and a three-year follow-up. Worldviews were measured at baseline with items corresponding to Bellah et al.'s typology, but were coded into three categories: individualistic, community, and theistic. Among adolescents who endorsed theistic values at baseline, over the next three years, most new network members also reported theistic values. In addition, a theistic worldview was associated with lower levels of problem behaviors as reported by both adolescents and their parents. Importantly, this pattern of moral homophily was observed with denomination, parental religious involvement, and religious service attendance statistically controlled.

Victor, Miles, and Vaisey (2015) examined the association of moral worldviews and sexual behavior among adolescents entering young adulthood. Data were from the National Study of Youth and Religion. Moral worldview was assessed at baseline on a continuum ranging from orthodox (similar to theistic) to progressive (similar to individualistic). Sexual behavior was assessed on three occasions (baseline, and three and six years post-baseline). Although the moral continuum was not related to having experienced sexual intercourse, individuals reporting orthodox values reported significantly fewer sexual partners than those with more progressive values—but this pattern applied only to participants who also reported religious involvement.

Beyerlein and Vaisey (2013) investigated whether moral worldviews can help explain why certain people engage in different amounts and types of civic actions. Data were from a nationally representative survey of American adults (the Religion and Public Activism Survey). Survey items from multiple moral typologies were coded in three worldviews: person-centered/individualistic, society-centered/civic, and religious. Persons endorsing society-centered/civic worldviews reported the highest levels of volunteering. Both society-centered and religious worldviews, however, were associated with significantly higher levels of volunteering than the individualistic worldview. In addition, most volunteering by study participants endorsing the religious worldview was for religious organizations. In contrast, sample members reporting a civic worldview volunteered for a wider range of organizations.

A study by Miles (2015) provides the best evidence to date that relationships between moral worldviews and behavior are governed by heuristic cognitive processing. Data for this study were from an online experiment in which participants had the opportunity to donate or not donate some or all of their raffle tickets to a (presumed) other study participant who would otherwise have no raffle tickets. Thus, the dependent variable was prosocial behavior. Participants were randomly assigned to two conditions: high cognitive load or low cognitive load. Research subjects assigned to the high cognitive load condition were told to remember a complex eight-digit number; those in the low cognitive load condition were asked to memorize an easy eight-digit number (24601358 vs. 20002000). Participants were asked to repeat the memorized number at multiple points during the experiment. Previous research found that memorizing a complex number precludes systematic processing, but leaves heuristic processing unhindered. Moral values were measured using the Schwartz PVQ and coded into the four higher-order domains (openness to change, self-transcendence, conservation, and self-enhancement). Past research indicated that a self-transcendent worldview is most strongly associated with self-reports of prosocial behavior, so Miles focused on that worldview. As expected, results showed both main and interactive effects for self-transcendence. The main effect showed that study participants high on self-transcendence were more generous in donating raffle tickets to a needy recipient than participants who were low on this worldview. The interaction indicated that subjects who scored high on self-transcendence and high cognitive load were the most generous. Other scholars have reported results supporting the conclusion that moral worldviews affect attitudes and behavior via heuristic cognitive processing (e.g., Haidt, 2001; 2007; Vaisey, 2009), but I believe that this study provides the strongest evidence substantiating that conclusion.

Overall, although the number of studies is small, this research indicates that moral worldviews are robustly and strongly related to a variety of behavioral outcomes. These associations hold with religious variables taken into account (Vaisey, 2009). It also appears that moral values operate via automatic, heuristic cognitive processing. The extent to which the relationships between moral worldviews and behaviors differ by age, race/ethnicity, gender, and other social characteristics remains unknown. Clearly, more research is needed to determine whether this research has important implications for our understanding of religion/spirituality, aging, and, perhaps, health.

Future Prospects

Research on cognition and morality sets the stage for exciting research on religion/spirituality, life course development, and, perhaps, health. Most importantly, it provides a set of tools for advancing our knowledge of the constellations of beliefs and norms that may be related to a wide range of outcomes of interest. In this section, I briefly outline four research topics that hold promise for using cognition and culture research to inform our understanding of religion/spirituality.

Moral Worldviews as a Dimension of Religion

Based on research to date, it is clear that some moral worldviews are religious worldviews. And although extant research documents that religious worldviews are correlated with other dimensions of religious experience (e.g., service attendance, religious importance), a more thorough and systematic exploration is merited. For example, the associations of religious worldviews with religious coping, private religious practices, and intrinsic/extrinsic religious orientation should be examined. A better picture of where religious worldviews fit into the complex architecture of religion is needed.

The samples examining religious worldviews need to be expanded. To date, many studies have been based on adolescents/young adults. A couple of studies based on more age-heterogeneous samples report that age is positively associated with religious worldviews (Beyerlein & Vaisey, 2013; Miles, 2014), but this falls far short of an adequate portrait of the distribution of religious worldviews across the life course. The associations of gender, racial/ethnic, and socioeconomic status remain equally unexplored.

Longitudinal studies of religious (and other) worldviews also are a priority for future research. If age proves to be robustly related to religious worldviews, whether this pattern represents age changes, cohort differences, or both remains unresolved. The stability of worldviews remains unknown. To what extent, if any, do stressors or traumas alter religious worldviews? Does regular attendance at religious services strengthen religious worldviews? Or, conversely, do strong religious worldviews motivate high levels of service attendance? I perceive no interest in the dynamics of religious worldviews among current cognition and culture scholars. This is a prime topic for aging and life course scholars to explore.

Research to date also has largely pigeon-holed study participants into a single dominant worldview (i.e., person A has a religious worldview and person B has an individualistic worldview). This approach is useful for some research purposes. But individuals also vary in the extent to which they endorse their dominant worldviews. Some individuals represent the highest levels of their worldviews; others barely exceed the threshold. Do these differences matter? And, if so, for what outcomes?

Expanding the Outcomes Related to Religious Worldviews

To date, research on worldviews has focused on two outcomes: political ideology and prosocial behaviors. This research is fascinating and provocative, but barely scratches the surface of the range of possible outcomes that may be related to worldviews. A myriad of possible outcomes comes to mind, including marital stability and quality, social capital, social network composition and social support, and educational and occupational aspirations and achievements. Worldviews also may be related to psychosocial resources including sense of mastery or control, self-esteem, sense of coherence, and self-control.

Because of the generally robust relationships between religion/spirituality and health, I am particularly interested in the relationships between worldviews and health and well-being. Are religious worldviews associated with physical and mental health in the same ways that other dimensions of religious involvement are? Worldviews also may differ in their relationships to specific health outcomes. Is it possible, for example, that religious worldviews are more strongly associated with health behaviors than other worldviews while individualistic worldviews are most strongly related to health care utilization? Longitudinal data on large samples would be needed as would careful attention to the wide range of factors to be statistically controlled to isolate, to the extent possible, the role of worldviews in health.

The Implications of Dual-processing

Evidence that worldviews affect attitudes and behaviors largely via heuristic processing is, in my opinion, of momentous importance for research on the relationships between religion/spirituality and outcomes of interest. This research suggests that interviewing individuals about the ways that religion/spirituality affects their lives is unlikely to yield accurate—or at least full—information. Instead, this research suggests that the most fruitful approach is to assess worldviews and identify the ways in which and the extent to which they are related to outcomes.

As persuasive as I find extant studies, they are very small in number. Much more research is needed to establish the generalizability of the conclusion that heuristic processing trumps systematic processing with regard to the effects of worldviews on attitudes and behavior. It is not simply the number of replications that is important. As previously noted, both the samples and the outcomes examined need to be more diverse.

Dual-processing research also needs to confront the issue of environmental cues and demands. Decades of research on schemas demonstrate that different environments trigger different schemas and that, as a result of this, individual behavior often is (or appears) inconsistent across situations. Studies of dual-processing and worldviews to date fail to take situation-specific triggers and schemas into account. Survey-based studies relate worldviews to self-reports of behaviors (typically prosocial behavior) that are not linked to the environments within which those behaviors took place. Experimental studies of dual-processing occur within the confines of research settings (in-person or online), with their own situational cues and constraints. Investigating these persisting issues in dual-processing research will not be the primary responsibility of scholars of religion/spirituality, but to the extent that those issues can be addressed, the knowledge base will be advanced.

What About Spirituality?

Noticeably absent from research on moral or religious worldviews is any mention of spirituality. This is, of course, an issue that must be addressed. Significant numbers of individuals describe themselves as being both religious and spiritual and parsing out the extent to which their attitudes, behaviors, health, and psychosocial characteristics are related to religion vs. spirituality is not possible. The subgroup of individuals who describe themselves as spiritual, but not religious, however, is ideal for examining worldviews and spirituality.

Because the slate is blank with regard to worldviews and spirituality, a host of fundamental questions require attention. First and foremost are two questions. Do individuals who describe themselves as spiritual but not religious have a distinctive worldview that has not been identified in previous research? If not, what worldview (e.g., individualistic, civic), if any, best describes persons who state that they are spiritual but not religious? I hypothesize that this subgroup largely endorses an individualistic worldview. Several authors posit that the spirituality "movement" is a result of the historic cultural shift toward individualism in modern and post-modern societies (e.g., Wuthnow, 1998). If they are correct, an individualistic worldview seems most likely to characterize individuals who identify as spiritual, but not religious.

Alternatively, one could argue that the subgroup of individuals who describe themselves as spiritual but not religious do have a distinctive set of moral principles. Many of my friends and colleagues describe themselves as spiritual, but not religious. When asked, they deny that their values are strongly individualistic, although they also seem unable to neatly label their most important values (perhaps because I am asking them to systematically process!). This is an empirical question that merits attention in future research.

I also hypothesize some common ground between persons who describe themselves as religious and those who identify as spiritual, but not religious. I think that both groups will score high on self-transcendence. Research based on Schwartz's typology of human values documents that religious individuals score significantly higher on self-transcendence than non-religious individuals. I believe that spiritual practices also will be associated with self-transcendent values.

A focus on self-transcendence also fits well with Lars Tornstam's theory of gerotranscendence (2005). According to Tornstam, gerotranscendence occurs in the last years of life as individuals increasingly shed concerns about the self and focus on understanding and communing with cosmic issues that transcend the self, time, and place. He posits that this is a developmental process that results in a new level of maturation and wisdom and describes it as a spiritual journey. Reactions to gerotranscendence theory have been mixed (e.g., Jewell, 2014). The theory has been strongly criticized on methodological grounds and empirical studies fail to find evidence that it is a developmental phenomenon. Nonetheless, the theory has been the foundation of multiple interventions aimed at decreasing symptoms of depression and anxiety in later life, with studies documenting its effectiveness in reducing symptoms and enhancing quality of life (e.g., Wadensten & Carlsson, 2003).

Conclusion

In conclusion, the purpose of this review was to identify a research tradition that has the potential to advance our understanding of how religion/spirituality operates in human lives. Cognition and culture research provides a new set of theories about how fundamental constellations of beliefs and values influence attitudes and behaviors. The toolkit for measuring worldviews is established; research designs that can measure heuristic vs. systematic processing are available. Although the state-of-the-science leaves more questions than answers, cognition and culture research, applied to research on religion/spirituality, merits substantial scientific investment.

References

Ano, G. G., & Vasconcelles, E. B. (2005). Religious coping and psychological adjustment to stress: A meta-analysis. *Journal of Clinical Psychology*, 61, 461–480.

Antonovsky, A. (1979). *Health, stress and coping*. San Francisco: Jossey-Bass.

Antonovsky, A. (1993). The structure and properties of the sense of coherence scale. *Social Science & Medicine*, 36, 725–733.

Bellah, R. N., Madsen, R., Sullivan, W. M., Swidler, A., & Tipton, S. M. (1985). *Habits of the heart: Individualism and commitment in American life*. Berkeley: University of California Press.

Benson, H., & Klipper, M. Z. (2000). *The relaxation response*, 2nd edition. New York: William-Morrow.

Benson, H., & Stark, M. (1997). *Timeless healing: The power and biology of belief*. New York: Scribner.

Beyerlein, K., & Vaisey, S. (2013). Individualism revisited: Moral worldviews and civic engagement. *Poetics*, 41, 384–406.

Castel, A. D., Rossi, A. D., & McGillivray, S. (2012). Beliefs about the "hot hand" in basketball across the adult life span. *Psychology and Aging*, 27, 601–605.

Devine, P. (1989). Stereotypes and prejudice: Their automatic and controlled component. *Journal of Personality and Social Psychology*, 58, 5–18.

DiMaggio, P. (1997). Culture and cognition. *Annual Review of Sociology*, 23, 263–287.

Ellison, C. G., & Taylor, R. J. (1996). Turning to prayer: Social and situational antecedents of religious coping among African Americans. *Review of Religious Research*, 38, 111–131.

Eriksson, M., & Lindstrom, B. (2007). Antonovsky's sense of coherence scale and its relation with quality of life: A systematic review. *Journal of Epidemiology & Community Health*, 61, 929–939.

Evans, J. (1984). Heuristic and analytic processes in reasoning. *British Journal of Psychology*, 75, 451–468.

Evans, J. (2007). Dual-processing accounts of reasoning, judgment, and social cognition. *Annual Review of Psychology*, 59, 268–269.

Geyer, S. (1997). Some conceptual considerations on the sense of coherence. *Social Science & Medicine*, 44, 1771–1779.

Goodrich, K. (2013). Effects of age and time of day on internet advertising outcomes. *Journal of Marketing Communications*, 19, 229–244.

Graham, J., & Haidt, J. (2010). Beyond beliefs: Religions bind individuals into moral communities. *Personality and Social Psychology Review*, 14, 140–150.

Graham, J., Haidt, J., & Nosek, B. (2009). Liberals and conservatives rely on different sets of moral foundations. *Journal of Personality and Social Psychology*, 96, 1029–1046.

Graham, J., Nosek, B. A., Haidt, J., Iyer, R., Koleva, S., & Ditto, P. H. (2011). Mapping the moral domain. *Journal of Personality and Social Psychology*, 101, 366–385.

Haidt, J. (2001). The emotional dog and its rational tail: A social intuitionist approach to moral judgment. *Psychological Review*, 108, 814–834.

Haidt, J. (2007). The new synthesis in moral psychology. *Science*, 316, 998–1002.

Haidt, J. (2012). *The righteous mind: Why good people are divided by politics and religion*. New York: Pantheon.

Haidt, J., & Graham, J. (2007). When morality opposes justice: Conservatives have moral intuitions that liberals may not recognize. *Social Justice Research*, 20, 98–116.

Harrington, A. (2011). The placebo effect: What's interesting for scholars of religion? *Zygon*, 46, 265–280.

Harrison, M. O., Koenig, H. G., Hays, J. C., Eme-Akwari, A. G., & Pargament, K. I. (2001). The epidemiology of religious coping: A review of recent literature. *International Review of Psychiatry*, 13, 86–93.

Hitlin, S., & PiliavinJ. A. (2004). Values: Reviving a dormant concept. *Annual Review of Sociology*, 30, 359–393.

Hitlin, S., & Vaisey, S. (2013). The new sociology of morality. *Annual Review of Sociology*, 39, 51–68.

Hunter, J. D. (1992). *Culture wars: The struggle to define America*. New York: Basic Books.

Hybels, C. F., George, L. K., Blazer, D. G., Pieper, C. F., Cohen, H. J., & Koenig, H. G. (2014). Inflammation and coagulation as mediators in the relationships between religious attendance and functional limitations in older adults. *Journal of Aging and Health*, 26, 679–697.

Jewell, A. J. (2014). Tornstam's notion of gerotranscendence: Re-examining and questioning the theory. *Journal of Aging Studies*, 30, 112–120.

Johnson, M. K., Rowatt, W. C., & LaBouff, J. (2010). Priming Christian religious concepts increases racial prejudice. *Social Psychological and Personality Science*, 1, 119–126.

Johnson, M. M. S. (1990). Age differences in decision-making: A process methodology for examining strategic information processing. *Journal of Gerontology: Psychological Sciences*, 45, P75–P78.

Kahneman, D. (2011). *Thinking, fast and slow, 1st edition*. New York: Farrar, Straus and Giroux.

Kim, S., Goldstein, D., Hasher, L., & Zacko, R. T. (2005). Framing effects in younger and older adults. *Journal of Gerontology: Psychological Sciences*, 60, P215–P218.

Koleva, S. P., Graham, J., Iyer, R., Ditto, P. H., & Haidt, J. (2012). Tracing the threads: How five moral concerns (especially purity) help explain culture war attitudes. *Journal of Research on Personality*, 46, 184–194.

Koltko-Rivera, M. E. (2004). The psychology of worldviews. *Review of General Psychology*, 8, 3–58.

Lang, M., Mitkidis, P., Kundt, R., Nichols, A., Krajcikova, L., & Xygalatas, D. (2016). Music as a sacred cue? Effects of religious music on moral behavior. *Frontiers in Psychology*, 7, 814–825.

Larsson, G., & Kallenberg, K. O. (1996). Sense of coherence, socioeconomic conditions and health: Interrelationships in a nation-wide Swedish sample. *European Journal of Public Health*, 6, 175–180.

Levin, J. (2009). How faith heals: A theoretical model. *Explore*, 5, 77–96.

Lundh, L. (1987). Placebo, belief, and health: A cognitive-emotion model. *Scandinavian Journal of Psychology*, 18, 128–143.

McNaughton, B. L., Battaglia, F. P., Jensen, O., & Moser, M. (2006). Path integration and the neural basis of the 'cognitive map.' *Nature Reviews Neuroscience*, 7, 663–678.

Martin, J. (1992). *Cultures in organizations: Three perspectives*. New York: Oxford University Press.

McKay, R., Efferson, C., Whitehouse, H., & Fehr, E. (2011). Wrath of God: Religious primes and punishment. *Proceedings of the Royal Society B*, 278, 1858–1863.

Miles, A. (2014). Demographic correlates of moral differences in the contemporary United States. *Poetics*, 46, 75–88.

Miles, A. (2015). The (re)genesis of values: Examining the importance of values for action. *American Sociological Review*, 80, 680–704.

Miles, A., & Vaisey, S. (2015). Morality and politics: Comparing alternate theories. *Social Science Research*, 53, 252–269.

Moerman, D. E., & Jonas, W. B. (2002). Deconstructing the placebo effect and finding the meaning. *Annals of Internal Medicine*, 136, 471–476.

Motzer, S., & Stewart, B. J. (1996). Sense of coherence as a predictor of quality of life in persons with coronary heart disease surviving cardiac arrest. *Research in Nursing and Health*, 19, 287–298.

Mullen, P. M., Smith, R. M., & Hill, W. (1994). Sense of coherence as a mediator of stress for cancer patients and spouses. *Journal of Psychosocial Oncology*, 11, 23–46.

Osman, M. (2004). An evaluation of dual-process theories of reasoning. *Psychonomic Bulletin & Review*, 11, 988–1010.

Pargament, K. I., Olsen, H., Reilly, B., Falgout, K., Ensing, D. S., & Van Haitsma, K. (1992). God help me (II): The relationship of religious orientations to religious coping with negative life events. *Journal for the Scientific Study of Religion*, 31, 504–513.

Price, D. D., Finnis, D. G., & Benedetti, F. (2008). A comprehensive review of the placebo effect: Recent advances and current thought. *Annual Review of Psychology*, 59, 565–590.

Rumelhart, D. E. (1980). *Schemata: The building blocks of cognition*. Hillsdale, NJ: Erlbaum.

Saroglou, V., Corneille, O., & Van Cappellen, P. (2009). Wrath of God: Religious primes and punishment. *Psychology of Religion*, 19, 143–154.

Schwartz, S. H. (1992). Universals in the content and structure of values: Theory and empirical tests in 20 countries. In M. Zanna (Ed.), *Advances in experimental social psychology*, 25, 1–65. New York: Academic Press.

Schwartz, S. H. (2006). Value orientations: Measurement, antecedents and consequences across nations. In R. Jowell, C. Roberts, R. Fitzgerald, & G. Eva (Eds.), *Measuring attitudes cross-nationally—lessons from the European Social Survey*, 169–193. London: Sage.

Schwartz, S. H., & Bilsky, W. (1990). Toward a theory of the universal content and structure of values: Extensions and cross cultural replications. *Journal of Personality and Social Psychology*, 58, 878–891.

Schwartz, S. H., & Boehnke, K. (2004). Evaluating the structure of human values with confirmatory factor analysis. *Journal of Research in Personality*, 38, 230–255.

Shariff, A. F., Willard, A. K., Andersen, E., & Norenzayan, A. (2016). Religious priming: A meta-analysis with a focus on personality. *Personality and Social Psychology Review*, 20, 27–48.

Silverstein, M., & Heap, J. (2015). Sense of coherence changes with aging over the second half of life. *Advances in Life Course Research*, 23, 98–107.

Sloman, S. A. (1996). The empirical case for two systems of reasoning. *Psychological Bulletin*, 119, 3–22.

Smith, E. R., & DeCoster, J. (2000). Dual-process models in social and cognitive psychology: Conceptual integration and links to underlying memory systems. *Personality and Social Psychology Review*, 4, 108–131.

Stewart-Williams, S., & Podd, J. (2004). The placebo effect: Dissolving the expectancy versus conditioning debate. *Psychological Bulletin*, 130, 324–340.

Strang, S., & Strang, P. (2001). Spiritual thoughts, coping and 'sense of coherence' in brain tumor patients and their spouses. *Palliative Medicine*, 15, 127–134.

Stryker, S. S., Serpe, R. T., & Hunt, M. O. (2005), Making good on a promise: The impact of larger social structures on commitments. In S. R. Thye, & E. J. Lawler (Eds.), *Social identification in groups (Advances in Group Processes)*, 22, 93–123. Bingley, UK: Emerald Group Publishing Limited.

Swidler, A. (1986). Culture in action: Symbols and strategies. *American Sociological Review*, 51, 273–286.

Tornstam, L. (2005). *Gerotranscendence: A developmental theory of positive aging.* New York: Springer.

Vaisey, S. (2009). Motivation and justification: A dual-process model of culture in action. *American Journal of Sociology*, 114, 1675–1715.

Vaisey, S., & Lizardo, O. (2010). Can cultural worldviews influence network composition? *Social Forces*, 88, 1595–1618.

Van Pachtebeke, M., Freyer, C., & Sarglow, V. (2011). When authoritarianism meets religion: Sacrificing others in the name of abstract deontology. *European Journal of Social Psychology*, 41, 898–903.

Victor, E. C., Miles, A., & Vaisey, S. (2015). The role of moral worldviews in predicting sexual behavior from adolescence to emerging adulthood. *Journal of Adolescent Research*, 30, 779–799.

Wadensten, B., & Carlsson, M. (2003). Theory-driven guidelines for practical care of older people, based on the theory of gerotranscendence. *Journal of Advanced Nursing*, 41, 462–470.

Welch, J. S. (2003). Ritual in Western medicine and its role in placebo healing. *Journal of Religion and Health*, 42, 21–33.

Wilson, T. D., Dunn, D. S., Kraft, D., & Lisle, D. J. (1989). Introspection, attitude change, and attitude-behavior consistency: The disruptive effects of explaining why we feel the way we do. *Advances in Experimental Social Psychology*, 22, 287–343.

Wuthnow, R. (1998). *After Heaven: Spirituality in America since the 1950s.* Berkeley: University of California Press.

Yelderman, L.A. & Miller, M. K. (2017). Religious fundamentalism, religiosity, and priming: Effects on attitudes, perceptions, and mock jurors' decisions in an insanity defense case. *Psychology, Crime, & Law*, 23, 147–170.

Yilmaz, O., Karadoller, D. Z., & Sofuoglu, G. (2016). Analytic thinking, religion, and prejudice: An experimental test of the dual-process model of mind. *International Journal for the Psychology of Religion*, 26, 360–369.

Chapter 8

How Religion Affects Health
Views from Midway Through an Odyssey

Neal Krause

UNIVERSITY OF MICHIGAN

The literature on religion and health is vast (Koenig, King, & Carson, 2012). Findings from literally thousands of studies suggest that greater involvement in religion is associated with better physical and mental health. Just watching this literature grow and mature has been rewarding for those of us who have been working in the field for decades. The development of research on religion and health is even more gratifying for gerontologists because a substantial amount of this research has focused on older adults (Krause & Hayward, 2015a). This makes sense because, as I discuss later in this chapter, a number of researchers argue that people tend to become more involved in religion as they get older (Bengtson et al., Chapter 1 in this volume; Atchley, Chapter 3 in this volume; Johnson, Chapter 7, in this volume). Even though many researchers are aware of the potential health-related benefits of religiousness, work in the field is far from complete. The purpose of this chapter is to discuss two issues that, when fully addressed, will hopefully take the field to the next level.

The first issue has to do with the need to develop a comprehensive theory that explains how greater involvement in religious life is associated with better health and well-being. The need for this type of theoretical work is hardly a new idea. In 1997 I briefly reviewed research on religion and health and concluded that, "we do not have a well-developed and intuitively pleasing sense of why these relationships exist" (Krause, 1997). Three years later I elaborated on this theme in greater detail (Krause, 2010). Since that time, other researchers have also pointed to the lack of sound theoretical development in the field (e.g., Levin, Chatters, & Taylor, 2011; Riesebrodt, 2010). I think it is safe to say that since I raised the issue in 1997, little has been done in the ensuing 20 years to resolve this challenge. We still do not have a theoretical framework that weaves the thousands of studies on religion and health into a coherent conceptual whole.

Acknowledgements This research was supported by a grant from the John Templeton Foundation (Grant 40077).

At its base, there are two reasons why the field continues to languish in this state of theoretical underdevelopment. First, although I lack hard data to support this claim, I suspect that most researchers in the religion and health field have not received formal training in theory construction. Second, even if they had, texts on formal theory construction suffer from a significant problem. In my opinion, these texts are written at such a general and abstract level that it is difficult to see how they can be used to develop sound theories in specific substantive areas, such as religion and health (see, for example, Stinchcombe, 1968).

The first goal in the discussion that follows is to provide an overview of one way in which we might go about devising a unified theory of religion and health. As you will see, my thoughts have changed a good deal since I presented my initial thinking on this matter (Krause, 2010). My views have evolved after conducting three years of intense work on the Landmark Spirituality and Health Survey (LSHS). I shall have more to say about this study below. I hope to present my thinking on how to devise a more comprehensive theory in a way that is generic, yet practical. I will provide a series of steps that researchers in any number of fields can follow. More importantly, I hope other investigators will feel free to modify what I propose in order to reflect their own interests and experience.

The second main issue in this chapter builds from the first. I will present empirical findings from the LSHS to show how my views on theory construction can be operationalized in a specific research setting. However, I want to emphasize at the outset that my colleagues and I were not able to bring our empirical work with the LSHS to fruition because we ran out of grant money. Even so, I hope other investigators find merit in what we have done so far and will pick up where we left off. I suppose that in the end, this is the way science is supposed to operate.

After exploring the two main issues I will close with a brief discussion of age differences in the relationship between religion and health. Theoretical perspectives as well as empirical research will be examined in this context.

Thoughts on Theory Development

In the discussion that follows, I present my approach on how to develop a theory of religion and health. This strategy consists of nine steps.

Step One – Assembling a Good Team

The field of religion and health is too broad for any one investigator to grasp. Instead, we all have found our own niche among the vast array of concepts that have been bantered about. As a result, we have our own biases about what is important. As Goethe put it so long ago, "We only see what we know" (Goethe, 1980). This is why it is imperative to assemble a group of highly experienced investigators in the field who collectively possess a wide range of expertise and interests. My team for the LSHS consisted of Robert Emmons, Peter Hill, Gail Ironson, and Kenneth Pargament. I wanted to keep the group small because it has been my observation that the productivity of a group is inversely related to its size: the larger the group, the less the group is able to accomplish.

Step Two – Staking Out the Content Domain of Religion

I asked each of the members of the core research team to assemble a wish list of survey items they would like to see included in the final questionnaire. Initially, each person developed a wish list of indicators on their own. Far from being a mechanical exercise, this step is inherently theoretical in nature because it required each core team member to think deeply about the theoretical processes that lie at the heart of religious life. Consequently, the items that are selected are mere indicants of these theoretical processes.

I developed my own wish list based on decades of research on religion and health. I spent three years doing intense qualitative research in order to find out how the typical individual views and experiences religious life. I devised a number of short scales to capture their perspectives. Included among these scales were God-mediated control beliefs (i.e., the belief that people work collaboratively with God to eradicate problems and attain desired goals) as well as spiritual support (i.e., assistance that is provided by fellow church members with the explicit goal of increasing the religious beliefs and behaviors of the recipient). Other core team members contributed their own vast experiences in other domains of religiousness. For example, Ken Pargament brought his notions of religious coping, sanctification theory, and spiritual struggles to the group for their consideration, as well.

Step Three – Collating Wish List Items

After each core team member assembled their wish list of items, they sent them to me. I pulled them together in one large comprehensive list. The interviews for the LSHS survey were contracted to last 70 minutes. I used this time frame to estimate the total number of items that could be administered during this time. The total number of items had to include not only religion items, but measures of health, psychological distress, well-being, and stress, as well.

I sent the collated list of survey items back to each core team member. I asked them to develop a list of questions they felt could be cut from the final questionnaire. They performed this exercise individually without input from the other group members. Once again, it is worth emphasizing that figuring out what to cut was driven, in part, by theoretical considerations.

Step Four – Meeting of Core Team Members

Once the wish lists of items to include and items to cut were collated, we met as a group for an intense two-day meeting. Our goal was to hit the target number of items. The initial wish lists would easily have taken 140 minutes to administer (i.e., they were about twice the target length). The meeting was very difficult in some ways (i.e., we each had to give up "pet" or favored items), but very rewarding at the same time because the deep discussion that followed enriched the appreciation of all the group members for the richness and depth of the conceptual domain of religion. Based on these discussions, a lot was left on the cutting room floor as competing views and interests were negotiated.

Toward the end of the meeting we wrestled with question order effects. I developed a deck of index cards for each core team member. Each card had the name of a scale or conceptual domain on it. I asked each core team member to sort the deck of cards so that they reflected the order in which the questions would be asked. Initially, each person sorted the deck on their own. Once we were finished we worked through the decks as a group, discussed alternative orderings, and came up with a final order of items.

Step Five – Pilot Testing and the Administration of the Nationwide Survey

After the meeting, I created a draft of the final questionnaire. I circulated this draft to the group for their final approval. I then sent the draft to the National Opinion Research Center (NORC) so it could be pilot tested. Following the pilot test, the national survey went into the field. From this point forward, the theory construction process was dominated by empirical analyses.

Before I turn to these findings I would like to provide a little more detail on the survey. The Landmark Spirituality and Health Survey is a nation-wide random probability survey of people age 18 and older who live in the coterminous United States. The interviews, which were conducted face-to-face in 2014, were administered by NORC. The response rate was 50 percent. A total of 3,010 interviews were completed successfully.

Here is a brief demographic overview of the participants in this study. The average age of the study participants is 45.7 years ($SD = 17.7$ years); 43.1% are men; 45.2% were married at the time of the interview; and the study participants completed an average of 13.3 years ($SD = 3.1$ years) of schooling.

Step Six – Exploratory Analyses

Once the survey was complete and a clean data file had been created I set out to conduct a comprehensive series of exploratory analyses. There are two reasons why I pursued an exploratory approach.

First, and most important, the relationships between many of indicators in our questionnaire had never been evaluated empirically. Looking for linkages across conceptual domains is, in essence, a theory generating process.

My second reason for conducting exploratory analyses is difficult to articulate. I have been conducting large nationwide surveys for the better part of 35 years. I think that, in total, I have conducted six nationwide surveys. Most of these have been longitudinal. I want to convey a subjective impression that emerged from this work.

I think every data set has its own personality. By this I mean that every data set has its own quirks, its own unique feel, and its own relatively unique way in which variables are related. These quirks can arise from any number of factors such as the nature of the relationship between a particular interviewer and a specific respondent. But more importantly, these quirks also arise from the nature of the relationships among the variables themselves. When you have many different measures of religion in the same study they are likely to be correlated in varying degrees. So in the process of conducting exploratory analyses, you develop a feel for how the relationship between one measure of religion and health changes when a second measure of religion is added to the model. You have to work with a data set extensively in order to fully understand its personality. It has been my experience that the data do not give up their secrets easily.

Let me come at this issue from another way. We did not conduct an experiment where we had complete control over who gets the stimulus and who does not. Moreover, we could not randomize people to experimental and control groups, thereby eradicating any differences that might exist between them at the outset. Instead, an enormous amount of self-selection was going on in the data. For example, people decide on their own whether they wish to attend religious services. We obviously cannot assign them at random to church-going and non-church-going groups. To make matters even more challenging, any relationship we observe in survey research may be a spurious reflection of an excluded third variable. Many times there is no way to know this has happened.

To state the problem succinctly, we are simply working with too many unknowns to do anything other than exploratory work. As a result, we have to be up front about what we have. In essence, we have messy data. It is like listening to an old vinyl record that has been badly scratched. You can vaguely hear the tune because it has been nearly drowned out by what sounds like rain on a tin roof.

In conducting the exploratory analyses, my goal was to write a paper using each measure of religion in the data set. More times than not, I tried to pair each measure of religion with a different health-related outcome. Altogether, the core research team wrote 52 papers.

There is a subtle advantage in writing a large number of papers. When you write a paper for publication in a scholarly journal, you must obviously conduct a literature review. As you write a series of papers you have the opportunity to look across the literature reviews for each paper to see where they might capture common elements in a larger theoretical process.

Step Seven – Consolidating Exploratory Findings

In the process of conducting exploratory analyses, my goal was to derive a wider theoretical perspective based on inductive reasoning. Cast within the context of the LSHS, this meant that I would begin with a series of analyses that look at the interface between a limited number of manageable indicators. Once a broad set of analyses were completed, the goal was to look for ways in which they might be integrated into a more coherent whole.

I would like to provide some advice at this juncture. In the process of conducting exploratory work, we often assessed whether the relationship between a given facet of religion and health varied by age, sex, race, and social class. In a number of instances, we found there were significant variations along these social structural lines. But these variations introduce a layer of complexity into the theory building process that, in my opinion, can quickly create a conceptual morass. Juggling the relationships between multiple dimensions of religion and health is hard enough. Trying to do this while taking variations by age, sex, race, and social class into account inevitably leads to theories that are overly complex and unwieldy. Working with these data has made me appreciate that there is a constant tension between breadth and depth in the theory construction process. So if you hope to devise a theory of religion and health, then you must have a high level of tolerance for ambiguity.

Just as I was wrestling with consolidating the empirical findings we ran out of money. So what I will discuss from this point forward will deal more with what I hoped to do rather than what I was actually able to accomplish. As a result, I think it is quite likely that I would have changed the theory building process once I got more deeply into the thick of things.

At this juncture I planned to consolidate our research findings by distributing the abstracts of the 52 papers we wrote to the core team members. Since virtually every paper was written by two or more team members, they were often quite familiar with the full papers as well as the abstracts. My goal was to treat the abstracts as if they were qualitative data. I was going to ask each team member to review the abstracts on their own and identify three conceptual themes that cut across them. They would then send the themes to me. I would collate them and send them back out to each group member. Following this, we would meet as a group to discuss the themes that were proposed and resolve any differences between them. Then, at the close of the meeting, I thought we might compute a measure of group concordance, such as the kappa statistic.

Step Eight – Collect Longitudinal Data

At this point the group would hopefully have assembled a list of three main conceptual themes in the exploratory analyses. We might have proposed, for example, that people who encounter more spiritual struggles experience more symptoms of depression. I shall have more to say about spiritual struggles shortly. But for the moment I will simply define them as difficulties that people encounter with their faith. You could build a good case for why spiritual struggles create mental health problems. But you could just as easily argue that people who initially suffer from depression are more likely to subsequently encounter spiritual struggles because their mental health challenges cause problems with their faith. So once three core areas of research on religion and health have been identified, we need to confront thorny issues involving the direction of causality with measures of religion and health that have been gathered at two points in time. Although we can never be fully assured of causality with survey data, we can at least get a better handle on which way causal flows are likely to operate.

Step Nine – Searching for Higher-order Influences

At this point my goal was to have three areas in hand which reflect the ways in which religion may influence health. Moreover, I hoped to have greater confidence in these specifications because we addressed issues in the direction of causality. The next step involves thinking more abstractly about a higher-order construct that pulls the three lower-order facets of religion into a more tightly integrated whole. I wanted the group to determine if the three lower-order areas of religious life are related because they are being driven by a higher-order construct. I am going to defer discussing what I mean here until after I have presented some empirical findings from the LSHS.

Step Ten – Replication and Extension

This is the final step I envisioned for our theory construction process. Let me acknowledge in advance that this is a bit of a pipe dream because it is overly ambitious and it is likely to be cost prohibitive. Still, if you do not dream big then a comprehensive theory of religion and health is less likely to emerge.

My initial goal was to obtain a theory of religion and health that was based on the insights of five experts in the field. But if you took another group of five different experts and you ran them through the process I describe above, it is likely that you would identify different clusters of core processes to explain the relationship between religion and health. So imagine if you had two or even three groups that followed the outline I have devised above. Each group could derive a list of three core facets of religion on their own. Then they could subsequently meet to hash out the differences between groups. Following this, a truly landmark study on religion and health could be conducted. But as I said, this step would in all likelihood be prohibitively expensive.

Summary

These are, for the moment, my best thoughts on how to add some coherence to the deeply fractured literature on religion and health. You may not agree with what I have proposed. That is fine. Even so, I hope the thoughts I have presented and the process I outlined open a dialog about how to make sense of the vast number of studies we have been conducting.

Empirical Findings from the LSHS

I want to present my own personal view of the three most important health-related aspects of religion that have emerged from the LSHS analyses. But before doing this, I would like to emphasize two points that should be kept in mind as I proceed.

First, what I am about to present only represents my thinking on what emerged from the LSHS exploratory analyses. It does not take into account the thinking of the other group members because, as I indicated earlier, we never got to this point.

Second, after you read through my view on what is in the data, I suspect that many of you will ask whether this is all there is to the relationship between religion and health. I think it is important to emphasize from the outset that we will never be able to explain 100% of the variance in the religion and health relationship. Our ability to think, and therefore the models we devise, are simply too crude. I like the way Bradley and Schaefer (1998) put it:

> It is therefore likely that there is no single best model of any particular situation, none that will more accurately reflect and predict reality than all others. Reality is too complex and models too limited. It is more likely that several models each shed light on different facets of the real situation."
>
> (p. 29)

On my bad days I am tempted to say that everything we do is little more than an artless simplification.

There is, however, a deeper problem with model building that many researchers do not fully appreciate. Ahadi and Diener (1989) conducted a Monte Carlo simulation in order to identify constraints on the magnitude of the relationship between two constructs. They summarize their findings this way: "It is a simple property of effect sizes that as the number of independent determinants of some behavior increases, the magnitude of the correlations between any one of the determinants and the behavior must decrease" (Ahadi & Diener, 1989). They focused on the correlations between personality traits and behaviors in their study. A specific finding from their work helps bring their conclusions into sharper focus: "When a behavior had only three determinants, we found that there appeared to be an upper bound correlation of approximately .50 for the prediction of a specific behavior from a specific trait" (Ahadi & Diener, 1989). Think about a variable like depressive symptoms. Depression can be caused by a bewildering array of factors ranging from the weather, to gender, stress, low social support, economic factors, and on and on. So the correlation between any particular facet of religion and depression is bound to be far below .50. Let me summarize my point this way. Sometimes when I receive a review of one of my papers, a reviewer will say something like, "You only explained 15% of the variance." My response is always the same: "Ain't it great?"

Having acknowledged these issues, let me return to my main purpose. As far as I can tell, there are three core areas that lie at the very heart of the religion and health relationship. I shall list the three areas and then discuss each one in greater detail. The first has to do with the role that religion plays in offsetting the effects of stress on health. The second main facet of religion has to do with the role that is played by social relationships in the church. I am thinking here about the role that like-minded religious others at church play outside the stress process. The third and final area that emerged from our work on religion and health has to do with spiritual struggles. For the moment, I will define spiritual struggles as the difficulties that a person may encounter with their faith, such as having a troubled relationship with God, encountering interpersonal difficulties with religious others, and believing that demonic forces are responsible for the challenges that are encountered in life.

Religion and the Stress Process

I think it is fair to say that no one gets out of this life without being exposed to a healthy dose of stress. Stress is indeed ubiquitous. I think it is also fair to say that virtually every major society in history has had some form of religion. So if both stress and religion are ubiquitous, then it seems reasonable to ask whether the two might be related. Perhaps religion emerged, at least in part, to help people cope with the unwanted events in their lives.

When I began my research career, I was primarily interested in the relationship between stress and health. I did not consider religion in my work. In fact, I judiciously strove to avoid it. I conducted my first community survey of stress and health in 1984. It was a small survey of older adults who lived in Galveston, Texas. I did not have a single question about religion in this survey. My budget was extremely tight, so I had to run the whole operation out of my office. When the interviewers dropped off their completed surveys at the end of the day, it seemed like they would inevitably say that another one of their study participants volunteered that they relied on their faith to cope with stress. Talk about missing the boat. Here I was conducting a survey on stress and health and I had not even included a single question on religion.

We wrote more than ten papers on religion and the stress process with the data from the LSHS. I would like to highlight two aspects of the findings in this work. First, an important feature of the LSHS is that data were collected on a fairly wide range of biomarkers. As a result, we were able to write a number of papers on religion, stress, and outcomes like C-reactive protein (Krause, Ironson, & Pargament, 2016). There are several advantages in having this kind of data. To begin with, we did not have to rely solely on self-reported measures of health. In addition, having biomarker data eases (but by no means eliminates) issues involving the direction of causality. We found, for example, that praying for others offsets the effects of life-time trauma on C-reactive protein. I find it hard to believe that levels of C-reactive protein cause either praying for others or lifetime trauma. Moreover, by including biomarkers in our work I suspect we are able to reach a wider audience than we typically reach with studies on religion and self-reports of health.

The second point I would like to emphasize about the papers that were written with the LSHS data is that religion offsets the effects of stress on health in not one, but in a number of ways. This means that we found, for example, that praying for others, social support received from religious others, God-mediated control beliefs, and religious coping responses are all involved in the stress process. At first this broad array of religious coping mechanisms may seem to create confusion and make the stress-buffering aspects of religion harder to grasp. I make my peace with this issue in two ways. First, if you assume that religion offsets the effects of stress on health in only one way, it is like saying that there is only one way to get from there to New York City – by flying. But in reality, you can fly, take a train, take a bus, drive a car, walk, or hitchhike. This gets back to the theme I introduced earlier on the inherent tension between theoretical specificity and theoretical scope. Second, in order to deal with the inherent tension that arises from grappling with multiple coping mechanisms, let me ask you to imagine this. Suppose there are causal relationships among the various religious coping mechanisms themselves. This means, for example, that people may learn to identify, adopt, and implement religious coping responses through interaction with like-minded religious others. In fact, I wrote several papers which provide support for this view (e.g., Krause, Ellison, Shaw, Marcum, & Boardman, 2001). Viewed in this way, the various religious coping responses may be more tightly knit than they seem initially because they share common conceptual roots.

I think the study of religion and the stress process is especially relevant for older people. A number of researchers have argued that as people grow older, their own personal resources tend to decline (Baltes & Smith, 1999). If personal resources decline with age, then it seems reasonable to argue that older people must look to external sources for help in coping with unwanted life events. Perhaps this is one reason why some studies suggest that people tend to become more deeply involved in religion as they grow older (Krause & Hayward, 2015a).

So when I say that religion helps people cope with stress, I am suggesting a two-tiered theoretical scheme that is differentiated by the level of abstraction. First, at a higher and more abstract level, there is the general notion that religion helps people cope with stress. Second, and underneath this more general specification, is a less abstract and more specific series of models that estimate the various ways religion may moderate the effects of stress on health. Moreover, as I note above, other models can be devised at this juncture to weave the various coping resources into a more coherent whole by looking at the relationships among them. Denoting religious coping issues with this type of two-tiered scheme represents a different way of thinking about theory construction that I have not seen before in the literature. My view of this two-tiered system is captured in Figure 8.1. I

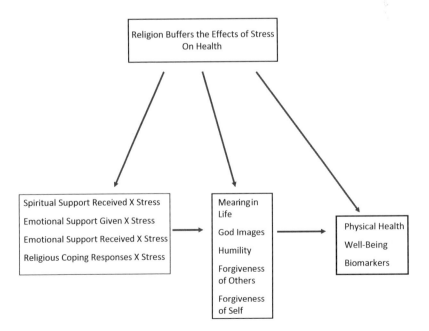

Figure 8.1 Religion, Stress, and Health

have included some variables that our research suggests might mediate the relationship between religion and stress on health, but I will not elaborate on them now.

Social Relationships in the Church and Health

My research with the LSHS and elsewhere consistently suggests that people turn to significant others at church when stressors arise in their lives. But I also strongly suspect that a good deal of the interaction with significant others is spent outside the stress process. For example, as I have written elsewhere, people form companion friendships, which involve the sharing and pursuit of common interests. Moreover, companion friends share pleasant activities together, like going out to dinner or going to a show (Krause, 2008). I am hardly the first to make this sort of observation.

The notion that social relationships alone lie at the core of religious life has been discussed numerous times over the last century or so. I shall illustrate this point by turning to the work of three giants in the social and behavioral sciences. Here is what one classic social theorist said over 100 years ago: "The faith that has come to be regarded as the essence and substance of religion is first of all a relationship *between human beings* ..." (Simmel, 1898/1997, emphasis in the original).

Writing at roughly the same time, here is what one of the early presidents of the American Psychological Association had to say. "[T]he fact is constantly recognized that religion is a social phenomenon. No man is religious by himself, nor does he choose his god, nor devise his offering, nor enjoy his blessings alone" (Baldwin, 1902). Finally, Josiah Royce was a leading philosopher in his time and a close friend of William James. He went as far as to maintain that salvation itself arises from the relationships that are formed among like-minded religious others: "our social experience is our primary source of religious insight. And the salvation that this insight brings to our knowledge is salvation through the fostering of human brotherhood. Such salvation accrues to the individual so far as he gives himself over to the service of man" (Royce, 1912/2001). Note that stress is never mentioned explicitly in any of these classic views.

Let us take a moment and reflect on how social relationships in the church might operate outside the stress process. Valuable insight into this issue is found in the Peter Berger's widely cited theory of religion. In essence, he argues that religion itself is a social product that people work out together when they interact with individuals who share a common faith. Berger maintains that religious worlds, "are socially constructed and socially maintained. Their continuing reality, both objective ... and subjective ... depends upon *specific* social processes, namely those processes that ongoingly reconstruct and maintain the particular worlds in question" (1967, emphasis in the original). Here is another take on the same issue. These insights come from Stark and Finke's (2000) theory on religion: "An individual's confidence in religious explanations is strengthened to the extent that others express their confidence in them." So in essence, these researchers are proposing that many basic religious teachings and principles are developed, exchanged, adopted, and maintained through social interaction among people who share a common faith.

We wrote over ten papers with the LSHS data that deal with social relationships in the church and health-related outcomes. None of these papers involves any kind of stressor yet each shows that social relationships in the church are associated with health, psychological well-being, or psychological distress. These papers show that social relationships in the church are associated with a wide range of religion measures including how people view God (God images), humility, whether people are willing to forgive others, compassion, whether people are willing to help others, and whether people are able to forgive themselves. In my view, religion is, to a large extent, about adopting rules in living, or virtues. The relationships that people form with like-minded religious others are a major conduit for the transmission of these virtues (Krause & Hayward, 2015b).

It is important to be a bit more specific about what I mean by social relationships in the church. At least four types of church-based social support are embedded in the studies listed above. More specifically, these papers focus on spiritual support that is provided to and received from others at church, emotional support that is both received from and given to fellow church members, and volunteering in formal programs to help those who are in need. I included volunteering in formal programs in this list because it represents a form of providing tangible support to others.

I think the study of social relationships in the church is especially important for those who work with older adults. Evidence in support of this view is found in Carstensen's (1992) Socioemotional Selectivity Theory. According to this perspective, as people grow older they tend to devote more energy and effort to maintaining social relationships that are valued more highly and that are especially close. In contrast, older people tend to disengage from social ties that are more peripheral in nature. It would be especially helpful to examine this process within the context of religion. More specifically, research is needed to see if social relationships that are formed in religious institutions are among the social ties that people strive to maintain as they grow older.

So once again, a two-tiered model has begun to emerge from our work. At the top there is the higher-order and more abstract notion that there are additive relationships between church-based social relationships and health. Below this general principle are more complex specifications which suggest that the four types of support I just discussed are associated with a range of specific aspects of religion, such as God images, forgiveness and virtues. Moreover, these specific aspects of religion are, in turn, associated with

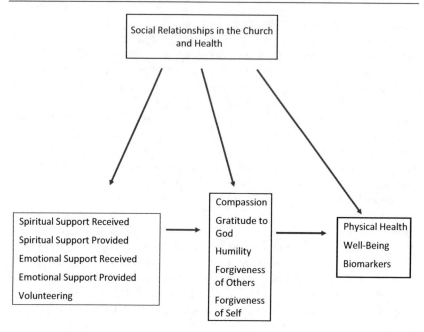

Figure 8.2 Social Relationships in the Church and Health

health. Figure 8.2 captures the two-tiered system of social relationships in the church and specific models that capture these relationships and health.

Spiritual Struggles and Health

Let me move on to the last of the three core components of religion – spiritual struggles. As I noted earlier, spiritual struggles refer to difficulties a person encounters with their faith, such as having a troubled relationship with God (e.g., feeling abandoned or punished by God), encountering difficulties with others over religion (e.g., feeling that others do not respect one's own religious beliefs), attributing unwanted stressful events to demonic sources, and having difficulty finding a sense of ultimate meaning in life (Exline, 2013). I think it is important to include spiritual struggles in studies of religion and health for the following reason. When studies on religion and health first began to emerge in the literature, the wide majority of researchers were concerned with the ways in which religion may benefit or enhance health. But as this literature began to evolve, researchers quickly became aware that greater involvement in religion is not always beneficial and that there may be a so-called "dark side" to religion. So focusing on spiritual struggles is important because it helps to create a more balanced perspective on the effects of being more deeply involved in religion: religion may convey certain health benefits, but it may also compromise health in ways that are often not anticipated.

Based on Erikson's (1959) widely cited theory of development over the life course, one might expect to find that spiritual struggles are more detrimental for older than for younger people. Erikson (1959) divides the life course into eight stages, each of which contains a special developmental challenge. The final stage is thought to arise later in life. The key developmental challenge is the crisis of integrity versus despair. This is a time of deep introspection where the individual reviews his or her life in an effort to weave the story of their life into a more coherent whole. If religion becomes more important with age (Krause & Hayward, 2015a) and people encounter significant spiritual struggles, then it is not difficult to see how spiritual struggles might be especially disruptive at this point in the life course. Support for this reasoning was reported in one of our recent papers (Krause, Pargament, Hill, Wong, & Ironson, 2017). We found that spiritual struggles exert a progressively stronger effect on health in successively older age groups.

We wrote more than ten papers with the LSHS data that examine the relationship between spiritual struggles and a range of health-related outcomes. These papers show that encountering more spiritual struggles is associated with a wide range of health outcomes such as self-rated health, problem drinking, psychological well-being, and psychological distress. Note also that spiritual struggles are also associated with some of the biomarkers, such as Interleukin-6 (Krause, Pargament, Ironson, & Hayward, 2017). Note further that the relationship between spiritual struggles and health is complex because we found a number of variations by age, race, and socioeconomic status.

There is an issue that I would like to pursue further. In all but one of the papers listed above, the data suggest that more spiritual struggles are associated with worse health. I think this is generally the case, but there is more to it than this. For hundreds of years, theologians and other scholars have argued that spiritual struggles are sometimes necessary in order for spiritual growth to take place. The essence of growth through spiritual struggles was captured centuries ago in the widely cited phrase, "dark night of the soul," that was coined by the Carmelite priest Saint John of the Cross (as quoted in Dura-Vila & Dein, 2009). A similar view was expressed more recently by Fowler (1996), who argued that the quest for a deeper faith frequently involves periods of disenchantment and disorientation that may bring about feelings of grief and loss. However, he went on to propose that sometimes these struggles can lead to deeper religious commitment and understanding, but other times they can promote feelings of despair (Fowler, 1981). Similar observations about the potential benefits of spiritual struggles may be found in the literature on religious doubt. For example, Tillich (1987) maintained that, "Many Christians, as well as members of other religious groups, feel anxiety, guilt and despair about what they call 'loss of faith' but serious doubt is confirmation of faith." Similarly, Allport (1950) argued that, "the mature religious sentiment is ordinarily fashioned in the workshop of doubt."

The fact that people may find that religious trials and tribulations may ultimately be a source of religious growth is not an isolated issue that only a few individuals experience. In work I have done elsewhere (Krause & Ellison, 2009), 65.3% of the study participants agreed (or strongly agreed) with the following statement: "Doubt is necessary for religious or spiritual growth." We found some evidence to support this view in our paper on spiritual struggles and IL-6. We planned to pursue it further by measuring growth through adversity explicitly.

So just like I have argued when I presented the other core dimensions of religion, it seems that the literature on spiritual struggles and health may best be viewed from a two-tiered perspective. At a higher and more abstract level is the notion that, in general, spiritual struggles are associated with worse health. But beneath this general observation is not one, but a series of specific models that reflect the ways in which spiritual struggles are associated with health and well-being, including the notion that spiritual struggles may be a source of religious growth and development. The two-tiered relationship that has been discussed in this section is reflected in Figure 8.3.

The finding that spiritual struggles are associated with health melds nicely with Atchley's discussion of spiritual journeys (Chapter 3 in this volume). Moreover, the discussion of religious doubt that was provided above is

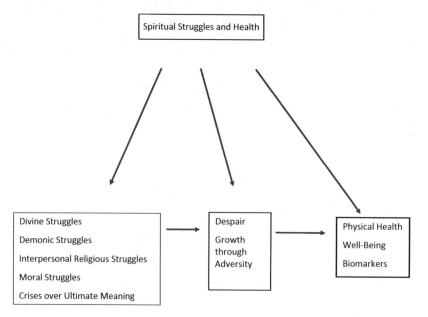

Figure 8.3 Spiritual Struggles and Health

complemented by discussion that Coleman and Mills provide in this volume (Chapter 5) on religious questioning.

Pulling It All Together

So far I have presented three clusters of studies on religion and health that include the stress-buffering role of religion, the additive effects of social relationships in the church, and spiritual struggles. But I think there is a way to weave these various facets of religion into a more coherent whole. There is one potentially important facet of religion that can help us reach this goal – a sense of meaning in life.

For decades, researchers from a number of academic disciplines have argued that deriving a sense of meaning is one of the fundamental goals not only of religion, but of life itself. For example, Victor Frankl (1946/1984), a widely cited psychiatrist, maintained that, "Man's search for meaning is the primary motivation in his life." Essentially, the same point is made by sociologist Peter Berger (1967), who argued that there is "a human craving for meaning that appears to have the force of instinct." And Abraham Maslow (1968), a past president of the American Psychological Association, captured the essence of this perspective when he observed that, "The human needs a framework of values, a philosophy of life … in about the same sense that he needs sunlight, calcium, and love." Although researchers have yet to agree on how to define meaning in life, many rely on the definition that was developed by Reker (2000). He defines meaning as "the cognizance of order, coherence, and purpose in one's existence, the pursuit and attainment of worthwhile goals, and an accompanying sense of fulfillment" (Reker, 2000).

I am certainly not the first researcher to argue that religion is associated with a greater sense of meaning in life. For example, this theoretical orientation was discussed several years ago by a number of investigators (e.g., Hood, Hill, & Spilka, 2014; Park, 2007). Moreover, the notion that religious involvement is associated with meaning in life has been observed in a number of empirical studies (e.g., Galek, Flannelly, Ellison, Silton, & Jankowski, 2015; Krause, Hayward, Bruce, & Woolever, 2013; Steger & Frazier, 2005). But I do not believe that researchers have viewed the relationship between religion and meaning in the same way that I am about to propose.

I would like to propose that a more comprehensive theory of religion and health is perhaps best captured by a three-tiered model. The top tier is comprised of meaning. The second tier is made up of the three general views I discuss above (i.e., the religious stress-buffering function of religion, social relationships in the church, and spiritual struggles). And the lowest tier contains the more specific models that I have discussed under each of these general functions. I think meaning unites the three aspects of religion that I have been discussing in the following way. When stressors in life arise, people often feel that their sense of meaning has been destroyed. Religion helps people rediscover and hold on to a sense of meaning in the midst of adversity. In addition to this, the rich social relationships that people maintain outside the stress process are a potent source of meaning. Meaning is not discovered individually. Instead, it is something that people jointly construct with significant others in the process of going through their daily lives. In addition to these factors, as I argued earlier, meaning may be a positive byproduct of spiritual struggles in that struggles, like religious doubt, are necessary for growth. This three-tiered system is reflected in Figure 8.4. In order to simplify this conceptual scheme, I have not included the intervening constructs or the health outcomes that were shown in the earlier models.

Whether the search for meaning serves the function I discuss above is an empirical question. Unfortunately, I have not had a chance to examine it fully because I have been deeply immersed in writing the 52 papers I identified earlier. So for the moment, let me provide some simple bivariate correlations. As I discussed earlier, spiritual support that is received from religious others is associated with a range of health outcomes outside the stress process. The LSHS data suggest that study participants who receive more spiritual support from fellow church members tend to have a greater sense of meaning in life ($r = .269$; $p < .001$). The simple correlations further reveal that people who encounter more spiritual struggles tend to have a diminished sense of meaning in life ($r = -.215$; $p < .001$). The first two-tiered model I presented involved the potential stress-buffering properties of religion. A more complex set of analyses was needed to see if religion offsets the effects of stress by bolstering a person's sense of meaning in life. I ran a set of OLS regression equations that were designed to see if God-mediated control offsets the negative effects of stressful events on meaning in life. You will recall that God-mediated control refers to the belief that God works together with people to overcome stressful events and to attain desired goals. I controlled for the effects of age, sex, education, the frequency of church attendance, and the frequency of private prayer in these models. Two findings emerged from these analyses. First, greater exposure to stress is associated with a diminished sense of meaning in life ($\beta = -.125$; $p < .001$). Second a statistically significant interaction is present in the data between a God-mediated control and stress on meaning in life ($p < .01$).

The notion that meaning in life is a "master" phenomena that helps weave a number of more specific dimensions of religion into a more tightly integrated whole is important because it stands at the juncture of three other chapters in this volume. More specifically, meaning in life is closely intertwined with Ardelt and Wingard's (Chapter 9 in this volume) discussion of wisdom and it is inextricably bound with George's insightful discussion of worldviews (Chapter 7 in this volume). Moreover, the parallels between my

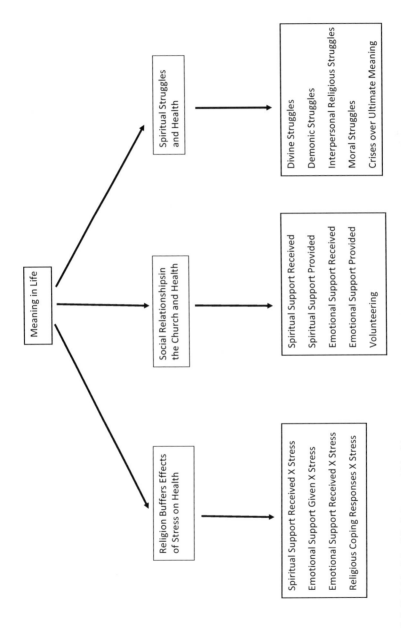

Figure 8.4 Full Model of Religion and Health

views on meaning that are provided above and Manning's discussion of meaning making among non-religious people (Chapter 4 in this volume) are quite evident.

Clearly a considerable amount of data analysis is needed to more firmly establish a relationship between the two-tiered models of religiousness and the higher-order meaning in life construct. Even so, I hope the preliminary findings I have presented help you agree that this is a fruitful issue to pursue in the future.

Exploring Variations by Age

Theoretical discussions of age differences in religiousness are fairly consistent in arguing that people tend to become more deeply involved in religion as they grow older. This perspective is captured in the work of Kohlberg (1973) and Tornstam (2005), which are briefly reviewed below.

Kohlberg (1973) is more widely known for his work on moral development during childhood, adolescence, and young adulthood. Even so, toward the end of his career, Kohlberg (1973) identified a final stage of development (i.e., Stage 7) that was encountered by most people during advanced adulthood. He maintained that people who attain the seventh stage of moral development adopt a religious or cosmic perspective that is concerned with issues involving the infinite and places an emphasis on seeing oneself as part of the larger unified whole of existence.

Tornstam (2005) devised the theory of gerotranscendence, which deals more with issues involving spirituality than with religion per se. Nevertheless, his views are useful because they are consistent with the work of Kohlberg (1973). Tornstam (2005) argues that as people approach late life, they experience a major shift in their world views. Instead of being concerned about material things, they become increasingly concerned with cosmic issues and wider existential concerns.

Although theoretical discussions of religion and aging are reasonably consistent, the same is not true with respect to empirical research on age differences in religiousness as reviewed by Krause (2008). For example, Argue and her colleagues analyzed data that were obtained over 12 years (Argue, Johnson, & White, 1999). They found that the importance of religion increases in a nonlinear fashion with age, and that the steepest increase occurs in the middle adult years. In contrast to the findings of Argue et al. (1999), Wink and Dillon (2001) examined changes in the importance of religion for people in their 30s through their 70s. Contrary to the results reported by Argue et al. (1999), Wink and Dillon (2001) report that the importance of religion decreased during the early 30s and 40s, but then increased in the 50s and early 60s.

We wrote five papers on age differences in religiousness with the data from the Landmark Spirituality and Health Survey. Two studies indicate that age differences in the relationship between various dimensions of religion and health are more pronounced in older than in younger age groups. But in contrast, our analyses also suggest that when different aspects of religion were evaluated, the findings appear to be more consequential for younger than for older people.

The disparities in our findings may be traced to at least two different factors. First, the results vary depending upon the dimension of religion that is being examined. For example, the data in one of our studies suggests that the negative relationship between spiritual struggles and self-rated health tends to become stronger in successively older age groups (Krause, Pargament, Hill, Wong, & Ironson, 2017). However, our data further reveal that religious transformations tend to offset the effects of lifetime trauma on happiness, but this relationship is more evident in younger than in older age groups (Krause, Pargament, & Ironson, 2017). Second, the relationship between religiousness and health outcomes appears to vary depending upon the health outcome that is examined. As I report above, the relationship between spiritual struggles and self-rated health is stronger in older than in younger age groups (Krause, Pargament, & Ironson, 2017). Even so, our data further indicate that the opposite holds true when problem drinking serves as the dependent variable (Krause, Pargament, Hill, & Ironson, 2017).

As the discussion that is provided above reveals, empirical research on age differences in religion and health is in its infancy. Moreover, the relationships among these constructs appears to be more complex than we may have anticipated initially because the results vary by the dimension of religion and the health outcome that is under consideration. Clearly, more definitive conclusions on the issue of age differences in religion and health await more rigorous and systematic analysis with data that have been collected over extended periods of time.

Conclusions

This chapter presents my best thinking on how to develop a unified theory of religion and health. But far from being an airtight final product, this is merely my thinking at midstream during a process that was far from complete. There are many loose ends. So why even bother to present something that is half-baked? I hope the work I have done so far opens up a dialogue on how to begin to unify our thinking about the work that all of us have been doing on religion and health. I hardly expect everyone to agree with what I proposed. But if I succeed in getting you to entertain the issue that we need to think about finding ways to integrate the results that have emerged out of our research, I will have accomplished my goal. I hope that other researchers either continue along the lines I have suggested or strike out in entirely new directions. Regardless of which way you go, I think it is time to step back and take stock of the findings from thousands of studies in order to see what we have really accomplished.

I shall close with a final observation. I will present this observation in the form of a question. Think back over all the research that has been done on religion during the past 100 years or so. Which specific types of research have endured the passage of time? I would argue that it is the theoretical pieces that last, not the empirical ones. Many argue that *Varieties of Religious Experience* by William James (1902/1997) and *Elementary Forms of Religious Life* by Durkheim (1915/1965) are the greatest social scientific studies of religion that have ever been conducted. I would be hard pressed to say that either of these classics are empirical pieces. In fact, on my bad days I wonder how many people really read the narrow little empirical papers we write and I cannot help but think that even if they are read, they are quickly forgotten. To the extent that this is true, I think it is time to circle the wagons and get about the business of engaging in some serious theory construction.

References

Ahadi, S., & Diener, E. (1989). Multiple determinants of effect size. *Journal of Personality and Social Psychology, 56,* 398–406.

Allport, G. W. (1950). *The individual and his religion.* New York: Macmillan.

Argue, A., Johnson, D. R., & White, L. K. (1999). Age and religiosity: Evidence from a three-wave panel analysis. *Journal for the Scientific Study of Religion, 38,* 423–435.

Baldwin, J. M. (1902). *Fragments in philosophy and science of being: Collected essays and addresses.* New York: Charles Scribner's Sons.

Baltes, P. B., & Smith, J. (1999). Multilevel and systemic analysis of old age: Theoretical and empirical evidence for a fourth age. In V. L. Bengtson & K. W. Schaie (Eds.), *Handbook of theories of aging,* 153–173. New York: Springer.

Berger, P. L. (1967). *The sacred sanopy: Elements of a sociological theory.* New York: Doubleday.

Bradley, W. J., & Schaefer, K. C. (1998). *The uses and misuses of data and models: The mathematization of the human sciences.* Thousand Oaks, CA: Sage.

Carstensen, L. L. (1992). Social and emotional patterns in adulthood: Support for socioemotional selectivity theory. *Psychology and Aging, 7,* 331–338.

Dura-Vila, G., & Dein, S. (2009). The Dark Night of the Soul: Spiritual distress and its psychiatric implications. *Mental Health, Religion & Culture, 12,* 543–559.

Durkheim, E. (1915/1965). *Elementary forms of religious life.* London: George, Allen Unwin, Ltd.

Erikson, E. (1959). *Identity and the life cycle.* New York: International University Press.

Exline, J. J. (2013). Religious and spiritual struggles. In K. I. Pargament (Ed.), *APA handbook of psychology, religion, and spirituality,* 1, 459–475. Washington DC: American Psychological Association.

Fowler, J. W. (1981). *Stages of faith: The psychology of human development and the quest for meaning.* New York: Harper & Row.

Fowler, J. W. (1996). *Faithful change: The personal and public challenges of postmodern life.* Nashville, Tennessee: Abingdon Press.

Frankl, V. E. (1946/1984). *Man's search for meaning*. New York: Washington Square Press.

Galek, K., Flannelly, K. J., Ellison, C. G., Silton, N. R., & Jankowski, K. R. (2015). Religion, meaning and purpose, and mental health. *Psychology of Religion and Spirituality*, 7, 1–12.

Goethe, J. W. (1980). *Goethe on art (Selected, edited, and translated by J. Cage)*. Berkeley, CA: University of California Press.

Hood, R. W., Hill, P. C., & Spilka, B. (2014). *The psychology of religion: An empirical approach*, 4th edition. New York: Guilford.

James, W. (1902/1997). *Selected writings – William James*. New York: Book-of-the-Month Club.

Koenig, H. G., King, D. E., & Carson, V. B. (2012). *Handbook of religion and health*, 2nd edition. New York: Oxford University Press.

Kohlberg, L. (1973). Stages and aging in moral development – some speculations. *The Gerontologist*, 13, 497–502.

Krause, N. (1997). Religion, aging, and health: Current status and future prospects. *Journal of Gerontology: Social Sciences*, 52B, S291–S293.

Krause, N. (2008). *Aging in the church: How social relationships affect health*. West Conshohocken, PA: Templeton Foundation Press.

Krause, N. (2010). Religion and health: Making sense of a disheveled literature. *Journal of Religion and Health*, 50, 20–35.

Krause, N., & Ellison, C. G. (2009). The doubting process: A longitudinal study of the precipitants and consequences of religious doubt. *Journal for the Scientific Study of Religion*, 48, 293–312.

Krause, N., & Hayward, R. D. (2015a). Religion, aging, and health. In L. K. George & K. F. Ferraro (Eds.), *Handbook of aging and the social sciences*, 8th edition, 251–269. San Diego, CA: Academic Press.

Krause, N., & Hayward, R. D. (2015b). Humility, compassion, and gratitude to God: Assessing the relationships among key religious virtues. *Psychology of Religion and Spirituality*, 7, 192–204.

Krause, N., Ironson, G., & Pargament, K. I. (2016). Lifetime trauma, praying for others, and C-reactive protein. *Biodemography and Social Biology*, 62, 249–261.

Krause, N., Pargament, K. I., & Ironson, G. (2017). Does a religious transformation buffer the effects of lifetime trauma on happiness? *International Journal for the Psychology of Religion*, 27, 104–115.

Krause, N., Pargament, K. I., Ironson, G., & Hayward, R. D. (2017). Spiritual struggles and interleukin-6: Assessing the potential costs and potential benefits. *Biodemography and Social Biology*. (In Press).

Krause, N., Hayward, R. D., Bruce, D., & Woolever, C. (2013). Church involvement, spiritual growth, meaning in life, and health. *Archive for the Psychology of Religion*, 35, 169–191.

Krause, N., Pargament, K. I., Hill, P. C., & Ironson, G. (2017). Spiritual struggles and problem drinking: Are younger adults at great risk than older adults? *Substance Use and Misuse*. (In Press).

Krause, N., Ellison, C. G., Shaw, B. A., Marcum, J. P., & Boardman, J. (2001). Church-based social support and religious coping. *Journal for the Scientific Study of Religion*, 40, 637–656.

Krause, N., Pargament, K. I., Hill, P. C., Wong, S., & Ironson, G. (2017). Exploring the relationships among age, spiritual struggles, and health. *Journal of Religion, Spirituality, and Aging*, 29, 266–285.

Levin, J., Chatters, L. M., & Taylor, R. J. (2011). Theory in religion, aging, and health: An overview. *Journal of Religion and Health*, 50, 389–406.

Maslow, A. H. (1968). *Toward a psychology of being*. New York: Van Nostrand.

Park, C. L. (2007). Religiousness/spirituality and health: A meaning systems perspective. *Journal of Behavioral Medicine*, 30, 319–328.

Reker, G. T. (2000). Theoretical perspectives, dimensions, and measurement of existential meaning. In G. T. Reker & K. Chamberlain (Eds.), *Exploring existential meaning: Optimizing human development across the life span*, 39–55. Thousand Oaks, CA: Sage.

Riesebrodt, M. (2010). *The promise of salvation: A theory of religion*. Chicago: University of Chicago Press.

Royce, J. (1912/2001). *The sources of religious insight*. Washington, DC: Catholic University of America Press.

Simmel, G. (1898/1997). A contribution to the sociology of religion. In H. J. Helle (Ed.), *Essays on religion – Georg Simmel*, 101–120. New Haven, CT: Yale University Press.

Stark, R., & Finke, R. (2000). *Acts of faith: Explaining the human side of religion*. Berkeley, CA: University of California Press.

Steger, M.F., & Frazier, P. (2005). Meaning in life: One link in the chain from religiousness to well-being. *Journal of Counseling Psychology*, 52, 574–582.

Stinchcombe, A. L. (1968). *Constructing social theories*. New York: Harcourt, Brace, & World.

Tillich, P. (1987). *The essential Tillich: An anthology of the writing of Paul Tillich*. Chicago: University of Chicago Press.

Tornstam, L. (2005). *Gerotranscendence: A developmental theory of positive aging*. New York: Springer.

Wink, P., & Dillon, M. (2001). Religious involvement and health outcomes in late adulthood: Findings from a longitudinal study of women and men. In T. G. Plante, & A. C. Sherman (Eds.), *Faith and health: Psychological perspectives*, 75–106. New York: Guilford.

Chapter 9

Spirituality and Wisdom
Their Differential Effects on Older Adults' Spiritual Behavior, Well-Being, and Attitudes Toward Death

Monika Ardelt and Kimberly Wingard

UNIVERSITY OF FLORIDA

Spirituality and Wisdom

Both spirituality and wisdom appear to be paths to aging well and dying well. Both try to understand the deeper meaning of life and death (Fischer, 2015; Walsh, 2014, 2015) and how to live a life that is "the perfect integration of mind and character for the greater good" (Staudinger & Glück, 2011, p. 221). Although contemporary research on wisdom initially focused more on cognitive conceptions of wisdom, such as expertise in wisdom-related knowledge about the fundamental pragmatics of life (Baltes & Staudinger, 2000), recent integration of more contemplative philosophies of wisdom highlight the overlapping qualities of spirituality and wisdom (Bangen, Meeks, & Jeste, 2013; Fischer, 2015; Jeste & Vahia, 2008; Walsh, 2015).

Yet, only few studies have analyzed the similarities and differences between spirituality and wisdom (Le, 2008; Wink & Dillon, 2003). Are spiritual people likely to be wise and wise people likely to be spiritual? Do spirituality and wisdom promote spiritual activities as well as aging well and dying well? Using a sample of 116 older community residents, 23 nursing home residents, and 19 hospice patients (age 56+), the purpose of our study was to investigate the differential effects of religious spirituality and wisdom on religious behavior, psychological and subjective well-being, and attitudes toward death, controlling for demographic characteristics and subjective health. Qualitative in-depth interviews with exemplars of high spirituality but relatively low wisdom, and relatively high wisdom but low spirituality

Acknowledgements The research was supported by a Brookdale National Fellowship, a grant from NIH/NIA (R03AG14855–01) and a Research Initiation Project Award from the College of Liberal Arts and Sciences at the University of Florida.

are used to illustrate some of the effects of spirituality and wisdom on aging well and dying well.

The Concept of Spirituality

Allport and Ross (1967) distinguished between an intrinsic religious orientation and an extrinsic religious orientation. Individuals who have an extrinsic religious orientation use their religion for self-serving extrinsic purposes, such as finding companionship and acceptance in the religious congregation, increasing one's standing in the community, or finding solace in times of hardship. The religious ideology itself is less important. By contrast, people with an intrinsic religious orientation live their religion by dedicating their life to God or a higher power. Physical, social, and other needs are addressed in terms prescribed by the religious doctrine, and internal tranquility comes from adherence to its practices.

Traditionally, spirituality was considered synonymous to an intrinsic religious orientation, characterized as "deeply religious people who have dedicated their lives to the service of their religion and to their fellow human, and whose lives exemplify the teachings of their faith tradition" (Koenig, 2008, p. 349). However, the modern understanding of spirituality has expanded to an existential form of spirituality to include those outside of faith traditions. Existential spirituality primarily refers to different forms of inner reflection. This type of spirituality has become increasingly popular as traditional religious behaviors are replaced by more secular attitudes (Wink & Dillon, 2003) and many people consider themselves spiritual but not religious (Koenig, 2008; Zinnbauer et al., 1997). By contrast, religious spirituality in this study is defined as a combination of an intrinsic religious orientation and spiritual beliefs that focus on attitudes and beliefs about faith, religion, and the sacred, and the relationship to a higher power rather than secular existential issues.

The Concept of Wisdom

Wisdom has been defined in a number of ways (Staudinger & Glück, 2011), ranging from cognitive wisdom conceptions, such as expert wisdom-related knowledge in the fundamental pragmatics of life, including life planning, management, and review (Baltes & Staudinger, 2000) or "explanatory knowledge of the fundamental truths in the domain of living well – an orienting knowledge about what is good and right" (Fischer, 2015, p. 73), to more integrative wisdom conceptions that combine cognitive and affective aspects of wisdom, such as "deep accurate insight and understanding of oneself and the central existential issues of life, plus skillful benevolent responsiveness" (Walsh, 2015, p. 282), and non-cognitive wisdom conceptions, such as the combination of critical life experiences, emotional regulation, reflectiveness/reminiscence, openness to experience, and humor (Webster, 2003) and self-transcendence (Levenson, Jennings, Aldwin, & Shiraishi, 2005).

We use the integrative Three-Dimensional Wisdom Model (3D-WM), which defines and operationalizes wisdom as the integration of cognitive, reflective, and compassionate (affective) personality characteristics (Ardelt, 1997, 2003, 2004), based on Clayton and Birren's (1980) earlier research on implicit wisdom theories of young, middle-aged, and older adults. The cognitive dimension reflects a person's desire to know a deeper truth and to understand the interpersonal and intrapersonal aspects of life. It requires knowledge and acceptance of the positive and negative sides of human nature, the inherent limits of knowledge, and life's unpredictability and uncertainties. The reflective dimension represents self-awareness and the ability to look at phenomena and events from different perspectives, including oneself. Unbiased and mindful reflection reduces ego-centeredness, enables one to overcome subjectivity and projections (which are the major obstacles in the discovery of a deeper and more objective truth), and increases insights into one's own and others' motives and behaviors. A reduced ego-centeredness and a better understanding of the complexities of human nature are likely to result in greater sympathy and compassion for others, which characterizes the compassionate wisdom dimension.

The Relation between Spirituality and Wisdom

While the goals of both spirituality and wisdom are to understand the deeper meaning of the human existence and death and to live a life that is good and right for the individual, the community, and society at large (Fischer, 2015; Staudinger & Glück, 2011; Walsh, 2014, 2015), the methods to achieve these goals might differ. Religious spirituality is a belief system that is assumed to be practiced and enacted within a faith community, including communal and private spiritual practices, such as regular attendance of communal religious ceremonies and individual or collective prayer (Monod et al., 2011). For example, studies have found that younger and older adults who are spiritually religious also tend to pray or meditate more frequently and to attend religious services more often than those who are less spiritually religious (Skarupski, Fitchett, Evans, & de Leon, 2010; Tsaousis, Karademas, & Kalatzi, 2013). Moreover, individuals who have dedicated their lives to their faith and a higher power are also likely to turn to their faith in times of troubles and hardship and, therefore, tend to engage in religious/spiritual coping (Ai, Park, Huang, Rodgers, & Tice, 2007; Ellison & Taylor, 1996; Jackson & Bergeman, 2011; Lee & Chan, 2009). Wisdom and wise coping skills, by contrast, might be found through more idiosyncratic and less institutionalized methods, such as philosophy (Curnow, 2011; Fischer, 2015), psychology (Helson & Srivastava, 2002;

Smith, Staudinger, & Baltes, 1994), and meditation (Williams, Mangelsdorf, Kontra, Nusbaum, & Hoeckner, 2016).

The evidence concerning whether religious spirituality and wisdom are related or independent from each other is mixed. Religiosity was positively related to wisdom in samples of Muslims from Pakistan and Jews from Canada, consisting of children, adolescents, and adults (Ferrari, Kahn, Benayon, & Nero, 2011). Among college students, religious/spiritual institutional and private practices were unrelated to wisdom. Yet, among primarily older adults, both belonging to a religious/spiritual community and the frequency of mystical experiences (e.g., loss of sense of self, feeling of oneness) were positively related to transcendent wisdom (self-knowledge, detachment, integration, and self-transcendence) but not wisdom-related knowledge (Le, 2008). Among older adults, church attendance was only weakly related to practical wisdom (Krause & Hayward, 2014). In a longitudinal study, Wink and Dillon (2003) found that institutionalized or tradition-centered religious beliefs and practices (religiousness) but not non-institutionalized or non-tradition-centered spiritual beliefs and practices (spirituality) in early adulthood (age 30s) were positively related to wisdom in late adulthood (late 60s or 70s). By contrast, spirituality but not religiousness in late middle adulthood (mid 50s or early 60s) and late adulthood was positively related to wisdom in late adulthood.

Because we assumed that religious older adults were not necessarily wise, and wise elders were not necessarily spiritual, we proposed the following hypotheses:

Hypothesis 1: Religious spirituality and wisdom are unrelated.
Hypothesis 2: If religious spirituality and wisdom are distinct, only spirituality is expected to be positively related to the frequency of spiritual behavior, consisting of shared spiritual activities, prayer, and spiritual coping.

Spirituality, Wisdom, and Aging Well

One of the most salient features of religion is that it gives meaning to one's life through the establishment of "an all-embracing sacred order" (Berger, 1969, p. 51) that includes meaning in the face of suffering, misfortune, illness, and death (Ardelt, Ai, & Eichenberger, 2008; Pargament, Magyar-Russell, & Murray-Swank, 2005; Wong, 2000). Religion also provides personal meaning if individuals follow their spiritual "calling," which gives meaning and importance to their life (Atchley, Chapter 3, this volume; Koenig, 2007). Similarly, one of the goals of wisdom is to find the deeper meaning of life and human existence (Ardelt, 2000; Ardelt, Achenbaum, & Oh, 2013). Through a deeper understanding of the interpersonal and intrapersonal universal aspects of life, wise older adults might be more likely to accept life's vicissitudes and preserve a sense of meaning and purpose even in adverse circumstances and when confronted with illness, disability, or death (Ardelt & Edwards, 2016; Erikson, 1982; Levenson, Aldwin, & Cupertino, 2001). Indeed, research has shown that among older adults, religiosity/spirituality (Bamonti, Lombardi, Duberstein, King, & Van Orden, 2016; Kim, Reed, Hayward, Kang, & Koenig, 2011) and wisdom (Ardelt, 2016; Etezadi & Pushkar, 2013) are positively related to a sense of purpose and meaning in life.

By contrast, the association between religious spirituality, mastery, and subjective well-being is less clear. Whereas some religious individuals might find a sense of control and well-being through their religion (Ardelt et al., 2008; Lee & Chan, 2009), others might turn to religion in times of helplessness and distress (Ai, Peterson, Bolling, & Rodgers, 2006; Caplan, Sawyer, Holt, & Brown, 2014; Ellison & Taylor, 1996; Idler, Chapter 6, this volume). Hence, the positive effect of religiosity on mastery and well-being and the reverse effect of helplessness and ill-being on greater religiosity might cancel each other out. In fact, the empirical evidence is mixed. In studies of elders in India and age-diverse adults in the United States, religiosity/spirituality was correlated only weakly with greater mastery but moderately with greater subjective well-being (Chokkanathan, 2013; Jackson & Bergeman, 2011). Yet, in a study in Greece, intrinsic religiosity was unrelated to subjective well-being among older adults and only weakly positively related among younger and middle-aged adults (Tsaousis et al., 2013). Similarly, an analysis of three large national probability surveys of older adults in the United States found no significant association between subjective religiosity and subjective well-being in two of the three samples and only a weak positive relationship in the third sample after controlling for demographic characteristics (Levin & Chatters, 1998). In an age-diverse nationally representative U.S. sample, religious identity was also only weakly related to happiness after controlling for life conditions and demographics (Green & Elliott, 2010).

By contrast, wisdom is expected to promote a sense of mastery and subjective well-being. Research has shown that wise individuals tend to learn from past experiences and mistakes and engage in active rather than passive coping when confronted with crises and obstacles in life (Ardelt, 2005), which is likely to provide a sense of mastery (Glück & Bluck, 2013) and enhance subjective well-being. Moreover, growing wiser might be accompanied by inner satisfaction and contentment due to a decrease in self-centered concerns and greater self-transcendence (Csikszentmihalyi & Nakamura, 2005). However, the empirical evidence is again mixed. Whereas many studies find a significant relation between wisdom and mastery (Ardelt, 2016; Etezadi & Pushkar, 2013) and wisdom and subjective well-being in old age (Ardelt, 1997, 2003; Grossmann, Na, Varnum, Kitayama, & Nisbett, 2013; Le, 2011; Takahashi & Overton, 2002), other studies report insignificant associations between wisdom and subjective well-being (Brugman, 2000; Mickler &

Staudinger, 2008; Wink & Helson, 1997), which might at least partly be due to the diverse operationalizations and measures of wisdom and well-being and the demographic compositions of the samples (Ardelt, 2011).

Based on the presumed similarities and differences between religious spirituality and wisdom, we proposed the following hypotheses:

Hypothesis 3: Both religious spirituality and wisdom are positively associated with a sense of purpose in life.
Hypothesis 4: Wisdom is positively related to mastery and subjective well-being. Religious spirituality is unrelated or only weakly positively related to mastery and subjective well-being.

Spirituality, Wisdom, and Dying Well

Carl Jung (1969, p. 408) remarked that religions might be considered "complicated systems of preparation for death." Hence, religious older adults should be less afraid and avoidant of death and more likely to accept death as a natural aspect of life and to look forward to life after death and a reunion with deceased loved ones. Moreover, compared to the vicissitudes on earth, heaven might be considered a celestial escape from a dreadful earthly existence. Wong, Reker, and Gesser (1994) named these attitudes neutral, approach, and escape acceptance of death, respectively. Indeed, some studies have found a negative association between religiosity and death anxiety among older adults (Falkenhain & Handal, 2003; Hui & Coleman, 2013; Thorson & Powell, 2000). Yet, in a meta-analysis of 49 studies of older adults, religiosity was unrelated to death anxiety (Fortner & Neimeyer, 1999). Similarly, in a sample of chronically ill older adults, religiosity was unrelated to fear of death but positively related to approach acceptance of death (Daaleman & Dobbs, 2010), and in a sample of hospice patients, intrinsic religiosity was unrelated to fear of death but negatively related to death avoidance and positively related to approach and escape acceptance of death, even after controlling for demographic characteristics, self-esteem, social support, and regret (Neimeyer, Currier, Coleman, Tomer, & Samuel, 2011).

Wink and Scott (2005) also did not find a significant linear association between religiousness and fear of death, but they discovered a non-linear relation: Older adults who either scored relatively high or relatively low on religiousness tended to fear death less than those who were moderately religious. Whereas intrinsically religious older adults might not be afraid of death because they are convinced that they will enter heaven after death, atheists who believe that death is the end of one's existence might also not fear death (Wilkinson & Coleman, 2010). Yet, individuals who believe in religious doctrine but are less committed to their religious faith might be worried whether they will end up in heaven or hell after death, which might explain their greater death anxiety.

Because wisdom is expected to provide greater insight into the meaning of life and death and to help individuals cope successfully with the vicissitudes of life to maintain subjective well-being even in times of adversity, wise older adults who can accept the limitations, uncertainty, and unpredictability of life are also likely to accept physical deterioration and death as a natural and inevitable part of the life cycle and, therefore, are expected to be less afraid and avoidant of death. As Erikson (1964, p. 133) remarked, "wisdom is detached concern with life itself in the face of death itself." However, whereas intrinsically religious older adults might look forward to a heavenly afterlife and a reunion with their loved ones after death, wise people might not necessarily believe in a life after death.

Based on these considerations, we formulated the following hypotheses:

Hypothesis 5: Greater religious spirituality and wisdom are inversely related to fear of death and death avoidance and positively related to neutral death acceptance. However, we hypothesized an inverse u-shaped association between religious spirituality and fear of death: older adults with either high or low religious spirituality scores are expected to be less afraid of death than those with moderate spirituality scores.

Hypothesis 6: Only religious spirituality is positively associated with approach and escape acceptance of death.

Although not hypothesized, we also explored whether the relation between religious spirituality and the other dependent variables might be curvilinear.

Studying the Differential Effects of Religious Spirituality and Wisdom on Spiritual Behavior, Well-Being, and Death Attitudes in Old Age

One hundred sixteen community residents, 23 nursing home residents, and 19 hospice patients who were diagnosed with a terminal illness and had a life expectancy of less than six months were recruited for this study between December 1997 and September 2001 (more detail about the recruitment process and the measures used in this study can be found in the Appendix). The 158 participants ranged in age from 56 to 98 years with a mean and median age of 74 years. Sixty-seven percent were women, 78% were white, 49% were married, 86% had at least a high school diploma, and 86% belonged to a religious group.

Quantitative Findings

Table 9.1 shows the means, standard deviations, and bivariate correlations between all variables used in this study. Religious spirituality was measured

Table 9.1 Bivariate Correlations; Pearson's r

	Spirituality	Wisdom	NH	Hospice	Female	Married	White	Age	SES	Health	M	SD	N
Spirituality	-	.04	.03	-.12	.27**	-.10	-.16*	-.07	-.12	.23**	3.93	.76	158
Wisdom	.04	-	-.25**	-.20**	.10	.17*	.06	-.32**	.38**	.28**	3.46	.46	158
Shared spiritual activities	.54**	.23**	-.21**	-.16*	.29**	.14	-.06	-.08	.05	.23**	2.63	1.36	147
Prayer frequency	.77**	.05	-.06	.00	.36**	-.07	-.17*	-.04	-.16*	.21**	3.84	1.32	147
Spiritual coping frequency	.58**	.14	.07	-.10	.10	-.06	-.17*	-.15	-.10	.24**	3.31	1.24	147
Purpose in life	.20**	.45**	-.35**	.04	.01	.14	-.06	-.02	.23**	.24**	4.23	.72	156
Mastery	-.07	.58**	-.31**	-.26**	-.02	.23**	.09	-.17*	.26**	.25**	3.54	.63	155
Subjective well-being	.25**	.54**	-.40**	-.26**	.09	.18*	.00	-.19*	.20*	.57**	3.66	.92	158
Fear of death	-.10	-.47**	.18*	.05	.05	-.09	-.18*	.07	-.21*	-.27**	2.45	.83	157
Death avoidance	-.01	-.40**	.24**	.10	-.06	-.17*	-.26**	.11	-.41**	-.00	2.45	.91	156
Neutral death acceptance	.03	.07	-.21**	-.01	-.05	.00	.14	.04	.24**	.12	4.32	.47	158

	Spirituality	Wisdom	NH	Hospice	Female	Married	White	Age	SES	Health	M	SD	N
Approach death acceptance	.77**	-.09	.11	-.04	.27**	-.12	-.16	-.08	-.32**	.16*	3.95	.94	157
Escape death acceptance	.21**	-.43**	.18*	.17*	.01	-.23**	-.21**	.21**	-.21**	-.11	3.67	.75	158
M	3.93	3.46	.15	.12	.67	.49	.78	74.24	5.42	3.03			
SD	.76	.46	.35	.33	.47	.50	.41	8.32	2.48	1.35			
N	158	158	158	158	158	158	158	158	158	158			

Notes: **p < .01; *p < .05; NH = nursing home resident; SES = socioeconomic status

by the average of the Intrinsic Religious Orientation Scale (Allport & Ross, 1967) and the Spiritual Beliefs Factor from the Spiritual Involvement and Beliefs Scale (Hatch, Burg, Naberhaus, & Hellmich, 1998). Three-dimensional wisdom was assessed by the Three-Dimensional Wisdom Scale (3D-WS), consisting of cognitive, reflective, and compassionate dimensions (Ardelt, 2003). As predicted in Hypothesis 1, religious spirituality and three-dimensional wisdom were not significantly correlated with each other. Spiritual elders tended to be female, African American, and freer from health worries and concerns than less spiritual older adults. Relatively wise elders were more likely to be community residents, married, younger, of higher socioeconomic status, and freer from health worries and concerns than those who scored lower on wisdom.

As hypothesized, religious spirituality was positively related to the frequency of shared spiritual activities, prayer, and spiritual coping (Hypothesis 2). Yet, wisdom was also positively correlated with the frequency of shared spiritual activities. Both spirituality and wisdom were associated with a greater sense of purpose in life (Hypothesis 3), measured by three items from Crumbaugh and Maholick's (1964) Purpose in Life Test. Wisdom, but not spirituality, was correlated with a feeling of greater mastery, assessed by Pearlin and Schooler's (1978) Mastery Scale. Wisdom also had a moderate association with greater subjective well-being, gauged by six items from the General Well-Being Schedule (Fazio, 1977), while the positive correlation between spirituality and subjective well-being was relatively weak (Hypothesis 4). Attitudes toward death were measured by the Death Attitude Profile–Revised (Wong et al., 1994). Contrary to Hypothesis 5, only wisdom, but not spirituality, was inversely correlated with fear of death and death avoidance, and neither spirituality nor wisdom was associated with a neutral acceptance of death. Yet as expected (Hypothesis 6), only spirituality, but not wisdom, was positively correlated with approach and escape acceptance of death. In fact, wisdom was even negatively related to escape acceptance of death.

Multivariate OLS regression analyses were conducted to test the relative contributions of religious spirituality and wisdom on variations in spiritual behavior, psychological and subjective well-being, and attitudes toward death after controlling for demographic variables and subjective health. In addition, we tested whether the associations between religious spirituality and the dependent variables were curvilinear.

As stated in Hypothesis 2, only religious spirituality, but not wisdom, predicted greater frequency of shared spiritual activities, frequency of prayer, and frequency of spiritual coping (see Table 9.2). Although results indicated that the association between spirituality and shared spiritual activities followed a u-curve, this did not mean that less spiritual older adults tended to engage more often in shared spiritual activities than those who were moderately spiritual. The minimum was at a spirituality score of 1.57, and as

Table 9.2 Effects of Religious Spirituality and Wisdom on Spiritual Behavior; Multivariate OLS Regression Analyses

Independent Variables	Frequency of Shared Spiritual Activities		Frequency of Prayer		Frequency of Spiritual Coping	
	b [95% CI]	β	b [95% CI]	β	b [95% CI]	β
Religious spirituality	1.14 [.79 – 1.48]	.65***	1.20 [1.01 – 1.38]	.70***	.88 [.65 – 1.11]	.55***
Religious spirituality squared	.24 [.02 – .46]	.22*	–	–	–	–
Wisdom	.35 [-.11 – .81]	.12	.16 [-.19 – .51]	.06	.34 [-.10 – .77]	.13
Controls						
Nursing home resident (0=no, 1=yes)	-.65 [-1.21 – .08]	-.17*	-.33 [-.77 – .10]	-.09	.18 [-.36 – .71]	.05
Hospice patient (0=no, 1=yes)	-.26 [-.84 – .32]	-.07	.46 [.02 – .90]	.12*	.04 [-.51 – .59]	.01
Gender (0=male,1=female)	.48 [.06 – .89]	.16*	.51 [.19 – .82]	.18**	-.27 [-.66 – .13]	-.10
Marital status (0=unmarried, 1=married)	.45 [.04 – .85]	.16*	.09 [-.21 – .40]	.04	-.13 [-.51 – .26]	-.05
Race (0=African American, 1=White)	-.15 [-.59 – .29]	-.05	-.26 [-.59 – .08]	-.09	-.17 [-.59 – .25]	-.06
Age	.02 [-.002 – .05]	.14	.01 [-.01 – .03]	.06	-.10 [-.03 – .01]	-.06
Socioeconomic status	-.01 [-.09 – .08]	-.01	-.06 [-.11 – .01]	-.10	-.03 [-.11 – .04]	-.07
Subjective health	.04 [-.10 – .18]	.04	.04 [-.06 – .15]	.05	.09 [-.04 – .22]	.10
Adjusted R2	.39		.62		.33	
N	147		147		147	

Notes: ***p < .001; **p < .01; *p < .05

shown in Figure 9.1a, older adults with very low spirituality scores (i.e., a score between 1 and 2) tended not to participate in shared spiritual activities at all. Starting at the midpoint of the spirituality scale, the positive association between spirituality and shared spiritual activities became more linear. Among the control variables, women and married older adults tended to engage in shared spiritual activities more often than men and unmarried elders, and nursing home residents tended to participate in shared spiritual activities less than community residents, probably due to a lack of opportunities for shared spiritual activities in the nursing home (Eisenhandler, 2003). Women and hospice patients tended to pray more often than men and community residents, but no demographic differences existed in regard to spiritual coping. The variables in the model explained 39%, 62%, and 33%, respectively, of the variation in the frequency of shared spiritual activities, prayer, and spiritual coping.

As expected and shown in Table 9.3, both religious spirituality and wisdom predicted a greater sense of purpose in life (Hypothesis 3), but only wisdom was moderately related to mastery and subjective well-being, whereas spirituality was

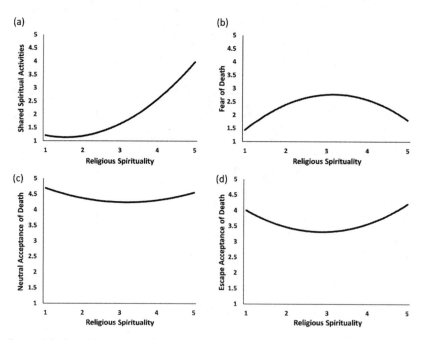

Figure 9.1 Curvilinear Associations between Religious Spirituality and Dependent Variables

Notes: (a) Association between Religious Spirituality and Predicted Frequency of Shared Spiritual Activities; (b) Association between Religious Spirituality and Predicted Fear of Death; (c) Association between Religious Spirituality and Predicted Neutral Acceptance of Death; (d) Association between Religious Spirituality and Predicted Escape Acceptance of Death

unrelated to mastery and only weakly related to subjective well-being (Hypothesis 4). Yet, as demonstrated by non-overlapping 95% confidence intervals, wisdom was not only more strongly related to subjective well-being than spirituality but also to purpose in life. Among the control variables, age was positively related to purpose in life, and nursing home residents and Whites tended to report less life purpose than community residents and African Americans. Not surprisingly, both disabled nursing home residents and terminally ill hospice patients tended to report a lower sense of mastery and subjective well-being in their lives than relatively healthy community residents. Consistent with prior research (George, 2010), subjective health was associated with greater subjective well-being. The variables in the model explained 31%, 39%, and 56%, respectively, of the variation in purpose in life, mastery, and subjective well-being.

Hypothesis 5 was only partially supported (see Table 9.4). As predicted, wisdom was related to less fear of death and death avoidance, and the association between religious spirituality and death fear followed an inverse u-curve, with the maximum at a spirituality score of 3.18, around the midpoint of the scale (see Figure 9.1b). Although predicted fear of death was relatively low in this sample, it was lowest among those older adults with either very high or very low spirituality scores. Yet contrary to expectations, spirituality was unrelated to death avoidance and had a curvilinear association with neutral acceptance of death, whereas wisdom was unrelated to neutral death acceptance. However, the curvilinear u-shaped association between spirituality and neutral acceptance of death was relatively flat, with the minimum at a spirituality score of 3.24 (see Figure 9.1c). None of the control variables were associated with death fear, but Whites and older adults of higher socioeconomic status tended to avoid thinking about death less than African Americans and elders of lower socioeconomic status. Nursing home residents and those of lower socioeconomic status tended to accept death less as a natural part of life than community residents and older adults with a higher socioeconomic status. The model variables explained 32%, 27%, and 7%, respectively, of the variation in fear of death, death avoidance, and neutral acceptance of death.

Hypothesis 6 that only spirituality, but not wisdom, would be positively related to greater approach and escape acceptance of death was partially confirmed (see Table 9.5). As predicted, spirituality was strongly related to greater approach acceptance of death, whereas wisdom was even negatively associated with escape acceptance of death. Yet, contrary to expectation, spirituality had a u-curve association with escape acceptance of death, with the minimum at a spirituality score of 2.89 (see Figure 9.1d) and greater predicted scores for escape acceptance of death for those older adults with either high or low religious spirituality scores. Among the control variables, socioeconomic status was associated with less approach acceptance of death. Compared to Whites, African Americans tended to accept death more as an escape from this worldly existence, a possible consequence of the effects of

Table 9.3 Effects of Religious Spirituality and Wisdom on Psychological and Subjective Well-Being; Multivariate OLS Regression Analyses

Independent Variables	Purpose in Life		Mastery		Subjective Well-Being	
	b [95% CI]	β	b [95% CI]	β	b [95% CI]	β
Religious spirituality	.19 [.05 – .32]	.20**	-.08 [-.19 – .03]	-.10	.17 [.03 – .31]	.14*
Wisdom	.64 [.39 – .89]	.41***	.67 [.47 – .88]	.49***	.71 [.46 – .96]	.35***
Controls						
Nursing home resident (0=no, 1=yes)	-.44 [-.75 – -.13]	-.22**	-.36 [-.62 – -.10]	-.20**	-.79 [-1.11 – -.47]	-.30***
Hospice patient (0=no, 1=yes)	.20 [-.12 – .52]	.09	-.42 [-.68 – -.15]	-.22**	-.51 [-.84 – -.18]	-.18**
Gender (0=male,1=female)	-.06 [-.29 – .16]	-.04	-.13 [-.32 – .06]	-.10	-.13 [-.36 – .09]	-.07
Marital status (0=unmarried, 1=married)	.12 [-.10 – .34]	.09	.05 [-.13 – .24]	.04	.04 [-.19 – .26]	.02
Race (0=African American, 1=White)	-.26 [-.51 – -.01]	-.15*	-.01 [-.22 – .20]	-.01	-.18 [-.43 – -.07]	-.08
Age	.02 [.002 – .03]	.18*	.00 [-.01 – .02]	.05	.01 [-.01 – .02]	.06
Socioeconomic status	.10 [-.04 – .05]	.03	-.01 [-.05 – .03]	-.03	-.02 [-.06 – .03]	-.04
Subjective health	.05 [-.03 – .13]	.10	.04 [-.02 – .11]	.09	.26 [.19 – .34]	.39***
Adjusted R²	.31		.39		.56	
N	156		155		158	

Notes: ***p < .001; **p < .01; *p < .05

Table 9.4 Effects of Religious Spirituality and Wisdom on Death Anxiety, Death Avoidance, and Neutral Acceptance of Death; Multivariate OLS Regression Analyses

Independent Variables	Fear of Death		Death Avoidance		Neutral Acceptance of Death	
	b [95% CI]	β	b [95% CI]	β	b [95% CI]	β
Religious spirituality	-.44 [-.66 - -.23]	-.41***	-.10 [-.27 - .08]	-.08	.14 [.004 - .28]	.23*
Religious spirituality squared	-.29 [-.42 - -.16]	-.42***	-	-	.10 [.01 - .18]	.24*
Wisdom	-.76 [-1.05 - -.48]	-.42***	-.51 [-.83 - -.18]	-.26**	-.09 [-.27 - .10]	-.08
Controls						
Nursing home resident (0=no, 1=yes)	.15 [-.21 - .51]	.06	.15 [-.26 - .56]	.06	-.26 [-.49 - -.02]	-.19*
Hospice patient (0=no, 1=yes)	-.07 [-.44 - .30]	-.03	.11 [-.32 - .53]	.04	-.05 [-.29 - .19]	-.04
Gender (0=male,1=female)	.20 [-.06 - .45]	.11	-.16 [-.45 - .13]	-.08	-.05 [-.22 - .11]	-.06
Marital status (0=unmarried, 1=married)	-.01 [-.26 - .24]	-.01	-.12 [-.41 - .17]	-.07	-.08 [-.25 - .08]	-.09
Race (0=African American, 1=White)	-.27 [-.55 - .01]	-.14	-.50 [-.82 - -.18]	-.23**	.11 [-.08 - .29]	.09
Age	-.01 [-.03 - .004]	-.11	.01 [-.01 - .02]	.04	.00 [-.01 - .01]	.03
Socioeconomic status	.01 [-.04 - .07]	.04	-.10 [-.16 - -.05]	-.28**	.03 [.001 - .07]	.18*
Subjective health	-.08 [-.17 - .01]	-.13	.10 [.004 - .20]	.16*	.03 [-.03 - .09]	.09
Adjusted R²	.32		.27		.07	
N	157		156		158	

Notes: ***p < .001; **p < .01; *p < .05

Table 9.5 Effects of Religious Spirituality and Wisdom on Approach and Escape Acceptance of Death; Multivariate OLS Regression Analyses

Independent Variables	Approach Acceptance of Death		Escape Acceptance of Death	
	b [95% CI]	β	b [95% CI]	β
Religious spirituality	.92 [.79 – 1.05]	.74***	.42 [.22 – .61]	.42***
Religious spirituality squared	–	–	.20 [.07 – .32]	.31**
Wisdom	-.10 [-.34 – .14]	-.05	-.64 [-.90 – -.37]	-.39***
Controls				
Nursing home resident (0=no, 1=yes)	.07 [-.23 – .37]	.03	.05 [-.28 – .38]	.02
Hospice patient (0=no, 1=yes)	.15 [-.16 – .46]	.05	.29 [-.06 – .63]	.12
Gender (0=male,1=female)	.08 [-.13 – .30]	.04	.04 [-.20 – .27]	.02
Marital status (0=unmarried, 1=married)	-.03 [-.24 – .19]	-.01	-.10 [-.34 – .13]	-.07
Race (0=African American, 1=White)	.01 [-.23 – .24]	.00	-.32 [-.58 – -.06]	-.18*
Age	-.01 [-.02 – .01]	-.05	.01 [-.004 – .02]	.11
Socioeconomic status	-.07 [-.12 – -.03]	-.19**	-.00 [-.05 – .04]	-.01
Subjective health	.01 [-.06 – .08]	.01	.01 [-.07 – .09]	.01
Adjusted R^2	.63		.29	
N	157		158	

Notes: ***p < .001; **p < .01; *p < .05

racism for these older adults. The model variables explained 63% and 29%, respectively, of the variation in approach and escape acceptance of death.

Qualitative Case Studies

Two case studies are used to illustrate the differences between religious spirituality and wisdom. The first case is Jerome (all names are pseudonyms), a 61-year old African American hospice patient who had a high religious spirituality score but the fourth lowest wisdom score. Jerome had metastatic cancer, had no high school degree, had been a farmer throughout life, was separated from his wife of 37 years, and lived at home. Jerome was a life-long Baptist. He stated that all of his present life was influenced by his religion. He said,

> I believe in the savior. I believe I'm in God's hands. ... I talk to Him daily. All through the day. I'm not going to take a chance. If something hits you, it hits you. You can't help it.

Jerome might have tried to stay in constant contact with God to keep the door to heaven open in case of a sudden death. To the question, "What does God mean to you?," Jerome answered,

> Everything. Without God we wouldn't be nothing. He is the one who created us. ... [God] never left me. He won't leave me. He promised that. He said, "I giveth and I will taketh, blessed be the name of the Lord." ... You see, I've got cancer. They gave me three or four months to live. But God hasn't killed me yet. ... God put me here and He isn't going to leave me. ... They gave me the diagnosis about a month and a half ago. But I know God has given me time.

Jerome is convinced that God is and always was with him, even during the times when he did not follow the teachings of his faith. He stated that his faith had become stronger due to his illness. He said, "I am more close in Spirit than I was. ... Some of it because I've got cancer." This kind of religious faith, however, might become problematic when the prophecy that God has given extra time fails. Although Jerome lived about three months longer than what the doctors expected, it is not clear if he was satisfied with the extra time that, in his mind, God had granted him or if he expected God to let him live a number of extra years. According to Jerome, "the devil does all the bad things, sickness and all" and God can stop the devil. Yet, what happens when sickness and misfortune continue? Does this mean that God is punishing the person for his or her sins? Without wise discernment and a mature religious and spiritual faith, viewing everything through a religious lens might set a person up for major disappointments and a spiritual crisis if God does not behave as one wishes.

Still, Jerome maintained that he was not afraid of death and that he was ready. He said, "Come and get me. ... It's just coming someday, why be afraid? ... when the time comes, take me out. In my sleep. – I pray for [it] every night." This sounds like a contradiction to his earlier statement about God having granted him extra time. It did not become clear from the interview whether Jerome was truly ready to die or if he hoped for the extra time that God had supposedly granted him.

For Jerome, the meaning of life consisted of living the right way or of choosing to do good rather than evil, but he acknowledged that it was not always easy to choose to do the right thing. He said,

> You've got a choice. I know you've got a choice. I can choose to drink, which I do drink. I can choose to smoke, which I do smoke. I can choose to quit, which I go through sometimes. ... I can do anything I want to do.

Jerome did not live an ethical life of service to others or a life that was dedicated to the greater good, which might explain his relatively low wisdom score. Although he married at age 24, he was intimately involved with two other women simultaneously for a number of years. He also had two children with other women, but none with his wife. He never met his daughter and left his son when he was seven years old. He did not know where his daughter and son currently were living, but knew that two years ago, his son had been in jail.

Jerome said his preparation for death consisted of asking for God's forgiveness: "Asked His forgiveness. That's all I can do for Him. Show me the right way, take me in His arms and love me to death." Jerome was aware that he had not always made the right choice in his life, but his belief in a loving and forgiving God made him ultimately unafraid of death.

By contrast, Mark, a 76- year old White hospice patient who lived at the hospice care center and suffered from the same metastatic cancer as Jerome, had a relatively high wisdom score but the lowest religious spirituality score in the sample. He had served in WWII, had a graduate degree, and had been an experimental psychologist in his professional life. He married at age 22, was widowed at age 54, after 32 years of marriage, and remarried three years later. He had been married to his second wife, who was about 16 years his junior, for 18 years. Mark was raised as a Catholic, he went to Catholic elementary school, had religious parents and siblings, and even had a sister who was a nun. Yet, he considered himself "a recovering Catholic." According to Mark, religion "was like a foreign language to me. ... my first recollection is that it was like utter madness to me." He explained,

I mean I never really went into religion. As far back as I can remember, probably in the first grade, I didn't know what they were talking about. Nothing has changed. ... I thought and still think it's a lot of crap. I don't buy any of it. I went along just to be sociable with the conventions of getting married in church and burying relatives through the church and all that sort of thing. ... [But religion] doesn't make any sense to me. It's like I sat down and wrote a story totally out of my imagination that somebody was performing miracles – totally outlandish, silly stuff that has no facts behind it. (Interviewer: It's not logical?) Yeah. You have to give yourself over like you turn your brains in.

Mark's scientific, rational mind just could not make sense of the logic-defying narrative of religious faith. Yet, he did not become an atheistic crusader, but granted others their religious beliefs and convictions. He said,

[Religion] didn't make sense, but most of the world thinks it makes sense so instead of arguing all my life I just go along with – if you want to go to church or want to do this – like, my first wife was pretty religious too. So my kids went to private Catholic schools.

Interestingly, Mark's second wife was also very religious and active in the Episcopalian church. She even studied her faith through an intensive four-year program. Mark tolerated his wife's faith without in any way supporting it, except for the occasional obligatory church visit with his wife.

Not surprisingly, Mark did not believe in God. To the question "In what do you believe?" he answered,

I don't know. Science. Logic. I don't [believe in] religion. I think it may be doing more harm than good. A lot of these people around the world killing each other because they're the wrong religion. I think we might be better off without any religion, but I think you have to have something. A lot of people need something. I wish I had it. I'm jealous of these people who go around smiling and happy like the world is wonderful and Christ is looking down on me. I wish I could do that but I just can't. ... I see happy people here dying. I think there's a lot more of us. Most of us are undercover. Really.

When the interviewer asked Mark if there was anything else he believed in or that was his guiding principle, he answered,

I believe in love. ... Caring about others, which I've often done. Not as much as I should have. ... when I was in the war part of my time I was a rifle man, which is the lowest you can be in the service. I found myself more helping wounded guys than trying to kill anybody. ... I've done what I could to help but ... I was oriented toward killing people (ironic laugh). I tried to keep them from bleeding to death, which wasn't always very successful.

To the question, "What do you think is the meaning of life?" Mark replied,

I guess, I've thought about it now and then, but I never came to any conclusion that there is any meaning. It's like people evolve or animals evolve. I wouldn't say they are a tribute to some superman. I don't know. It's just the way life is. ... (Interviewer: What do you think is the meaning of your life?) I don't know. Not much. I think if I had never been born the world would have continued on.

Although Mark believed in love and caring about others, his humanistic but non-spiritual perspective made it difficult for him to see a deeper meaning in life in general and also in his personal life more specifically. This, however, made him an exception among relatively wise elders who tended to score high on life meaning.

Mark declared that he was comfortable talking about death and dying, although he stated that he did not "think about it too much." He said,

Well, I think about it a little bit from a practical point of view, to straighten out things, financial stuff – but I'm not morbidly sitting around – I'm not thinking "what happens when I die?" because I've already done that scene – been there. (Interviewer: What do you think happens when you die?) I think you get eaten by worms.

Mark also remarked that he did not believe in life after death in any form and that this did not worry him "... because I don't think there's anything after death. It's not that there may not be, there is not, so why should I worry about something that doesn't exist?" In the same vein, Mark declared that he was not afraid of dying. He said, "I just accept it. There's no alternative to it. What should I do?"

Mark's scientific and rational mind told him that there was nothing beyond this earthly life and, hence, there was nothing to worry about. Consistent with the quantitative findings and other research (Manning, Chapter 4, this volume; Wink & Scott, 2005), those with a strong religious faith and those who are not religious at all are least afraid of death. Examples of spiritual struggle among those with moderate religious beliefs are given in chapters by Coleman and Mills (Chapter 5, in this volume) and Johnson (Chapter11, in this volume).

Discussion

This chapter has reported emerging research on the differential effects of religious spirituality and wisdom on aging well and attitudes toward death.

First, the study demonstrated that spirituality and wisdom are not the same. As predicted in Hypothesis 1, religious spirituality and wisdom were unrelated, indicating that spiritual older adults were not necessarily wise and wise older adults were not necessarily spiritual. Second, only religious spirituality but not wisdom was associated with greater frequency of spiritual behavior, consisting of shared spiritual activities, prayer, and spiritual coping, confirming Hypothesis 2. Although the association between spirituality and shared spiritual activities was u-shaped, Figure 9.1a shows a relatively flat and horizontal line between the lowest and the next lowest score on the religious spirituality scale followed by a gradual increase, which suggests that those with spirituality scores below the midpoint were unlikely to engage in shared spiritual activities at all. It should also be noted that compared to other spiritual activities scales, older adults who went to church once a week only received a score of 2 on the 1–5 point scale used in this study if no other shared spiritual activity occurred. Hence, it is not surprising that only those who scored 3.5 or higher on the 1–5 point religious spirituality scale had predicted shared spiritual activities scores above 2. By contrast, wisdom was unrelated to the frequency of spiritual behavior in this study, indicating that relatively wise elders were not more likely but also not less likely to engage in spiritual behavior than those lower on wisdom.

Third, as predicted in Hypotheses 3 and 4, wisdom was moderately related to a sense of greater purpose in life, mastery, and subjective well-being, whereas religious spirituality was unrelated to mastery and only weakly related to purpose in life and subjective well-being. Although the significantly weaker association between spirituality and subjective well-being was expected, the weaker relation with purpose in life was more surprising. As with mastery and subjective well-being, it is possible that an inverse association weakens this relationship if older adults who feel that their life has lost meaning and joy due to age-related losses and challenges turn to religion for solace. Relatively wise elders, by contrast, seem to understand the deeper meaning of life, are likely to have learned from their past life experiences, and know how to deal with life's vicissitudes, which gives them a sense of control over their lives rather than passively waiting for a divine intervention (Ardelt, 2005). A greater sense of purpose and mastery might at least partially explain why relatively wise older adults tend to express greater subjective well-being than those who score lower on wisdom (Ardelt & Edwards, 2016).

Fourth, Hypotheses 5 and 6 were partially supported. As predicted, religious spirituality had an inverse u-curve association with fear of death, whereas wisdom was associated with less death fear and death avoidance. Only spirituality, but not wisdom, was positively related to approach acceptance of death, while wisdom even had a negative association with escape acceptance of death. However, contrary to expectations, spirituality was unrelated to death avoidance, wisdom was unrelated to neutral acceptance of death, and spirituality had a u–curve association with neutral and escape acceptance of death.

While relatively wise elders tended to score higher on purpose in life, mastery, and subjective well-being, they also tended to be less afraid of death and were less likely to avoid thinking about death and to view death as an escape from an unpleasant earthly life than those who scored lower on wisdom, which confirms the paradox stated by Nicholson (1980, p. 251) that "it is the person who believes that his or her life has been most worthwhile who seems to have least qualms about the prospect of it coming to an end." The reason why wisdom was unrelated to neutral acceptance of death might be due to a ceiling effect. As seen in Figure 9.1c, average neutral acceptance of death was quite high, with only a slight dip for those with moderate spirituality scores, and all the variables in the model explained only 7% of the variation in neutral death acceptance.

However, results suggest that a little bit of religious spirituality can have a detrimental impact on dying well (Wink & Scott, 2005). Older adults who scored around the midpoint of the religious spirituality scale tended to be most afraid of death, least accepting of death as a natural aspect of life, and least convinced that death is an escape from a dreadful earthly existence. Although fear of death scores were generally low in this sample of older adults, those who were exposed to religious doctrine and attended religious activities occasionally might be more worried about their fate after death than those who were either convinced that they would enter heaven due to their strong spiritual faith or did not believe in spiritual judgment and a continued existence after death at all (Manning, Chapter 4, this volume; Wilkinson & Coleman, 2010). A greater fear of death might also explain why those with some religious spirituality tended to accept death slightly less as a natural aspect of life than those with either no or a very strong religious spirituality. Moreover, for older adults with moderate religious spirituality scores, death might not provide an escape from a dreadful earthly existence if the possibility of eternal hell or purgatory awaits. Hence, encouraging non–religious older adults to engage in spiritual activities at the end of life to boost their well-being and lessen their fear of death might actually be counter-productive if it raises the specter of eternal damnation for those who did not or cannot fully commit to a religious/spiritual faith. By contrast, older adults with either relatively high or relatively low spirituality scores were more likely than those with moderate spirituality scores to view death as an escape from a dreadful earthly existence, but probably for different reasons. Whereas those with high spirituality scores might compare their earthly existence with eternal life in heaven, those with low spirituality scores might just envision the end of all earthly struggles. However, the association between spirituality and greater approach acceptance of death was linear and relatively strong, supporting the assumption that those without spiritual beliefs were less likely to believe in a heavenly life after death. Given this strong relationship between spirituality and approach acceptance of death, it is not clear why spirituality did not lead to less death avoidance. One reason might be that older adults generally did not avoid death thoughts, as indicated by average death avoidance scores below the midpoint of the scale. Hence, neither spiritually religious older adults nor those that were less spiritually religious tended to avoid thinking about death.

The case analysis of Jerome, the exemplar of high religious spirituality and relatively low wisdom, indicated that a strong religious faith without wisdom does not necessarily prevent self-centered pursuits that are contrary to religious teachings. Jerome stated that the meaning of life was choosing to do good rather than evil, but he did not behave in this way, particularly not when he was younger. By contrast, for Mark, the relatively wise and low religious spirituality exemplar, religious faith was unnecessary to arrive at a humanistic and other-centered world view that placed love and caring at its center. Yet, his humanistic philosophy was not enough to provide Mark with a deeper sense of meaning in life, allowing him only to accept the material aspects of life. Neither Jerome nor Mark were afraid of death. Jerome had no fear of death, because he was convinced that God had forgiven his sins and loved him, whereas Mark did not worry about death because he was convinced that death was the end and there was no reason to "worry about something that doesn't exist," illustrating that both a strong religious faith and the absence of faith contribute to lower death anxiety (Manning, Chapter 4, this volume; Wink & Scott, 2005). Of course, it might be ideal to have both high spirituality and wisdom. A case analysis of three community residents who scored relatively high on religious spirituality and wisdom showed that all three elders were highly involved in their religious communities and expressed selflessness through gratitude and a commitment to serve, which transformed self-centered emotions and impulses into positive emotions, such as love and joy (Ardelt, 2008).

Study limitations include a relatively small sample size, the restriction of data collection to a narrow geographical area in the Southeast of the United States, and the cross-sectional nature of the data, which prohibits testing of the causal direction of the effect. Results might be different for older adults in other geographical areas and for different definitions and measurements of spirituality and wisdom. In this sample of older adults, who were born on average around 1925, religious spirituality and wisdom were unrelated, yet this association could become positive for older baby boomers, particularly if non-institutionalized spirituality is assessed (MacKinlay, 2014). Research with an updated, nationally representative sample is needed to test this hypothesis and longitudinal data are required to test the direction of the effects, particularly between spirituality, psychological well-being, and subjective well-being.

Conclusion

These findings suggest that wisdom and spirituality are not the same and have indeed differential effects. Yet, spiritual and wise elders, compared to other older adults in the sample, were most likely to report a greater sense of purpose in life and subjective well-being and less fear of death. Hence, spirituality and wisdom might indeed be two different pathways to aging well and dying well.

References

Ai, A. L., Park, C. L., Huang, B., Rodgers, W., & Tice, T. N. (2007). Psychosocial mediation of religious coping styles: A study of short-term psychological distress following cardiac surgery. *Personality and Social Psychology Bulletin, 33,* 867–882. doi:10.1177/0146167207301008.

Ai, A. L., Peterson, C., Bolling, S. F., & Rodgers, W. (2006). Depression, faith-based coping, and short-term postoperative global functioning in adult and older patients undergoing cardiac surgery. *Journal of Psychosomatic Research, 60,* 21–28.

Aiken, L. S., & West, S. G. (1991). *Multiple regression: Testing and interpreting interactions.* Thousand Oaks, CA: Sage.

Allport, G. W., & Ross, J. M. (1967). Personal religious orientation and prejudice. *Journal of Personality and Social Psychology, 5,* 432–443.

Ardelt, M. (1997). Wisdom and life satisfaction in old age. *Journal of Gerontology: Psychological Sciences, 52B,* P15–P27. doi:10.1093/geronb/52B.1.P15.

Ardelt, M. (2000). Intellectual versus wisdom-related knowledge: The case for a different kind of learning in the later years of life. *Educational Gerontology: An International Journal of Research and Practice, 26,* 771–789. doi:10.1080/036012700300001421.

Ardelt, M. (2003). Empirical assessment of a three-dimensional wisdom scale. *Research on Aging, 25,* 275–324. doi:10.1177/0164027503025003004.

Ardelt, M. (2004). Wisdom as expert knowledge system: A critical review of a contemporary operationalization of an ancient concept. *Human Development, 47,* 257–285. doi:10.1159/000079154.

Ardelt, M. (2005). How wise people cope with crises and obstacles in life. *ReVision: A Journal of Consciousness and Transformation, 28,* 7–19. doi:10.3200/REVN.28.1.7–19.

Ardelt, M. (2008). Self-development through selflessness: The paradoxical process of growing wiser. In H. A. Wayment & J. J. Bauer (Eds.), *Transcending self-interest: Psychological explorations of the quiet ego* (pp. 221–233). Washington, D.C.: American Psychological Association.

Ardelt, M. (2011). Wisdom, age, and well-being. In K. W. Schaie & S. L. Willis (Eds.), *Handbook of the psychology of aging* (7th ed., pp. 279–291). Amsterdam, The Netherlands: Elsevier.

Ardelt, M. (2016). Disentangling the relations between wisdom and different types of well-being in old age: Findings from a short-term longitudinal study. *Journal of Happiness Studies, 17,* 1963–1984. doi:10.1007/s10902-10015-9680-9682.

Ardelt, M., Achenbaum, W. A., & Oh, H. (2013). The paradoxical nature of personal wisdom and its relation to human development in the reflective, cognitive, and affective domains. In M. Ferrari & N. M. Weststrate (Eds.), *The scientific study of personal wisdom: From contemplative traditions to neuroscience* (pp. 265–295). New York, NY: Springer.

Ardelt, M., Ai, A. L., & Eichenberger, S. E. (2008). In search for meaning: The differential role of religion for middle-aged and older persons diagnosed with a life-threatening illness. *Journal of Religion, Spirituality and Aging*, 20, 288–312. doi:10.1080/15528030802232353.

Ardelt, M., & Edwards, C. A. (2016). Wisdom at the end of life: An analysis of mediating and moderating relations between wisdom and subjective well-being. *Journals of Gerontology, Series B: Psychological Sciences and Social Sciences*, 71, 502–513. doi:10.1093/geronb/gbv051.

Baltes, P. B., & Staudinger, U. M. (2000). Wisdom: A metaheuristic (pragmatic) to orchestrate mind and virtue toward excellence. *American Psychologist*, 55, 122–136. doi:10.1037/0003-066X.55.1.122.

Bamonti, P., Lombardi, S., Duberstein, P. R., King, D. A., & Van Orden, K. A. (2016). Spirituality attenuates the association between depression symptom severity and meaning in life. *Aging & Mental Health*, 20, 494–499. doi:10.1080/13607863.2015.1021752.

Bangen, K. J., Meeks, T. W., & Jeste, D. V. (2013). Defining and assessing wisdom: A review of the literature. *American Journal of Geriatric Psychiatry*, 21, 1254–1266. doi:10.1016/j.jagp.2012.11.020.

Berger, P. (1969). *The sacred canopy: Elements of a sociological theory of religion*. New York: Doubleday.

Brugman, G. M. (2000). *Wisdom: Source of narrative coherence and eudaimonia*. Delft, The Netherlands: Eburon.

Caplan, L., Sawyer, P., Holt, C., & Brown, C. J. (2014). Religiosity after a diagnosis of cancer among older adults. *Journal of Religion, Spirituality & Aging*, 26, 357–369. doi:10.1080/15528030.2014.928922.

Chokkanathan, S. (2013). Religiosity and well-being of older adults in Chennai, India. *Aging & Mental Health*, 17, 880–887. doi:10.1080/13607863.2013.790924.

Clayton, V. P., & Birren, J. E. (1980). The development of wisdom across the life-span: A reexamination of an ancient topic. In P. B. Baltes & O. G. Brim, Jr. (Eds.), *Life-span development and behavior* (Vol. 3, pp. 103–135). New York, N.Y.: Academic Press.

Crumbaugh, J. C., & Maholick, L. T. (1964). An experimental study in existentialism: The psychometric approach to Frankl's concept of noogenic neurosis. *Journal of Clinical Psychology*, 20, 200–207. doi:10.1002/1097-4679(196404)20:2<200: AID-JCLP2270200203>3.0.CO;2-U.

Csikszentmihalyi, M., & Nakamura, J. (2005). The role of emotions in the development of wisdom. In R. J. Sternberg & J. Jordan (Eds.), *A handbook of wisdom. Psychological perspectives* (pp. 220–242). New York, NY: Cambridge University Press.

Curnow, T. (2011). Sophia and phronesis: Past, present, and future. *Research in Human Development*, 8, 95–108. doi:10.1080/15427609.2011.568849.

Daaleman, T. P., & Dobbs, D. (2010). Religiosity, spirituality, and death attitudes in chronically ill older adults. *Research on Aging*, 32, 224–243. doi:10.1177/0164027509351476.

Eisenhandler, S. A. (2003). *Keeping the faith in late life*. New York: Springer.

Ellison, C. G., & Taylor, R. J. (1996). Turning to prayer: Social and situational antecedents of religious coping among African Americans. *Review of Religious Research*, 38, 111–131. doi:10.2307/3512336.

Erikson, E. H. (1964). *Insight and responsibility. Lectures on the ethical implications of psychoanalytic insight.* New York, NY: Norton.

Erikson, E. H. (1982). *The life cycle completed. A review.* New York, NY: Norton.

Etezadi, S., & Pushkar, D. (2013). Why are wise people happier? An explanatory model of wisdom and emotional well-being in older adults. *Journal of Happiness Studies*, 14, 929–950. doi:10.1007/s10902-10012-9362-9362.

Falkenhain, M., & Handal, P. J. (2003). Religion, death attitudes, and belief in afterlife in the elderly: Untangling the relationships. *Journal of Religion and Health*, 42, 67–76.

Fazio, A. F. (1977). *A concurrent validation study of the NCHS General Well-Being Schedule.* (Dept. of HEW Publ. No. HRA-78-1347). Hyattsville, MD: National Center for Health Statistics.

Ferrari, M., Kahn, A., Benayon, M., & Nero, J. (2011). Phronesis, sophia, and hochma: Developing wisdom in Islam and Judaism. *Research in Human Development*, 8, 128–148. doi:10.1080/15427609.2011.568869.

Fischer, A. (2015). Wisdom – The answer to all the questions really worth asking. *International Journal of Humanities and Social Science*, 5, 73–83.

Fortner, B. V., & Neimeyer, R. A. (1999). Death anxiety in older adults: A quantitative review. *Death Studies*, 23, 387–411.

George, L. K. (2010). Still happy after all these years: Research frontiers on subjective well-being in later life. *The Journals of Gerontology: Series B: Psychological Sciences and Social Sciences*, 65B, 331–339. doi:10.1093/geronb/gbq006.

Glück, J., & Bluck, S. (2013). The MORE life experience model: A theory of the development of wisdom. In M. Ferrari & N. Weststrate (Eds.), *The scientific study of personal wisdom: From contemplative traditions to neuroscience* (pp. 75–97). New York, NY: Springer.

Green, M., & Elliott, M. (2010). Religion, health, and psychological well-being. *Journal of Religion and Health*, 49, 149–163. doi:10.1007/s 10943-009-9242-1.

Grossmann, I., Na, J., Varnum, M. E. W., Kitayama, S., & Nisbett, R. E. (2013). A route to well-being: Intelligence versus wise reasoning. *Journal of Experimental Psychology: General*, 142, 944–953. doi:10.1037/a0029560.

Hatch, R. L., Burg, M. A., Naberhaus, D. S., & Hellmich, L. K. (1998). The Spiritual Involvement and Beliefs Scale. Development and testing of a new instrument. *The Journal of Family Practice*, 46, 476–486.

Helson, R., & Srivastava, S. (2002). Creative and wise people: Similarities, differences and how they develop. *Personality and Social Psychology Bulletin*, 28, 1430–1440. doi:10.1177/014616702236874

Hui, V. K.-Y., & Coleman, P. G. (2013). Afterlife beliefs and ego integrity as two mediators of the relationship between intrinsic religiosity and personal death anxiety among older adult British Christians. *Research on Aging*, 35, 144–162. doi:10.1177/0164027512436429.

Jackson, B. R., & Bergeman, C. S. (2011). How does religiosity enhance well-being? The role of perceived control. *Psychology of Religion and Spirituality*, 3, 149–161. doi:10.1037/a0021597.

Jeste, D. V., & Vahia, I. (2008). Comparison of the conceptualization of wisdom in ancient Indian literature with modern views: Focus on the Bhagavad Gita.

Psychiatry: Interpersonal and Biological Processes, 71, 197–209. doi:10.1521/psyc.2008.71.3.197.

Jung, C. G. (1969). *The soul and death: The collected works of C.G. Jung* (2nd ed., Vol. 8). Princeton, NJ: Princeton University Press.

Kim, S.-S., Reed, P. G., Hayward, R. D., Kang, Y., & Koenig, H. G. (2011). Spirituality and psychological well-being: Testing a theory of family interdependence among family caregivers and their elders. *Research in Nursing & Health*, 34, 103–115.

Koenig, H. G. (2007). Spirituality and pain: Finding purpose, meaning and hope in the midst of suffering. In P. T. P. Wong, L. C. J. Wong, M. J. McDonald & D. W. Klaassen (Eds.), *The positive psychology of meaning & spirituality. Selected papers from meaning conferences* (pp. 211–220). Abbortsford BC, Canada: INPM Press.

Koenig, H. G. (2008). Concerns about measuring 'spirituality' in research. *Journal of Nervous and Mental Disease*, 196, 349–355. doi:10.1097/NMD.0b013e31816ff796

Krause, N., & Hayward, R. D. (2014). Religious involvement, practical wisdom, and self-rated health. *Journal of Aging and Health*, 26, 540–558. doi:10.1177/0898264314524437.

Le, T. N. (2008). Age differences in spirituality, mystical experiences and wisdom. *Ageing & Society*, 28, 383–411. doi:10.1017/S0144686X0700685X.

Le, T. N. (2011). Life satisfaction, openness value, self-transcendence, and wisdom. *Journal of Happiness Studies*, 12, 171–182. doi:10.1007/s10902-10010-9182-9181.

Lee, E.-K. O., & Chan, K. (2009). Religious/spiritual and other adaptive coping strategies among Chinese American older immigrants. *Journal of Gerontological Social Work*, 52, 517–533. doi:10.1080/01634370902983203.

Levenson, M. R., Aldwin, C. M., & Cupertino, A. P. (2001). Transcending the self: Towards a liberative model of adult development. In A. L. Neri (Ed.), *Maturidade & Velhice: Um enfoque multidisciplinar* (pp. 99–116). Sao Paulo, BR: Papirus.

Levenson, M. R., Jennings, P. A., Aldwin, C. M., & Shiraishi, R. W. (2005). Self-transcendence: Conceptualization and measurement. *International Journal of Aging & Human Development*, 60, 127–143. doi:10.2190/XRXM-FYRA-7U0X-GRC0.

Levin, J. S., & Chatters, L. M. (1998). Religion, health, and psychological well-being in older adults: Findings from three national surveys. *Journal of Aging and Health*, 10, 504–531. doi:10.1177/089826439801000406.

MacKinlay, E. (2014). Baby boomers ageing well? Challenges in the search for meaning in later life. *Journal of Religion, Spirituality & Aging*, 26, 109–121. doi:10.1080/15528030.2013.811711.

Mickler, C., & Staudinger, U. M. (2008). Personal wisdom: Validation and age-related differences of a performance measure. *Psychology and Aging*, 23, 787–799. doi:10.1037/a0013928.

Monod, S., Brennan, M., Theologian, E. R., Martin, E., Rochat, S., & Bula, C. J. (2011). Instruments measuring spirituality in clinical research: A systematic review. *Journal of General Internal Medicine*, 26, 1345–1357. doi:10.1007/s11606-11011-1769-1767.

Neimeyer, R. A., Currier, J. M., Coleman, R., Tomer, A., & Samuel, E. (2011). Confronting suffering and death at the end of life: The impact of religiosity, psychosocial factors, and life regret among hospice patients. *Death Studies*, 35, 777–800. doi:10.1080/07481187.2011.583200.

Nicholson, J. (1980). *Seven ages. The truth about life crises – Does your age really matter?* Glasgow: William Collins Sons & Co.

O'Rand, A. M. (1982). Socioeconomic status and poverty. In D. J. Mangen & W. A. Peterson (Eds.), *Research Instruments in Social Gerontology* (Vol. 2. *Social Roles and Social Participation*, pp. 281–341). Minneapolis, MN: University of Minnesota Press.

Pargament, K. I., Magyar-Russell, G. M., & Murray-Swank, N. A. (2005). The sacred and the search for significance: Religion as a unique process. *Journal of Social Issues*, 61, 665–687.

Pearlin, L. I., & Schooler, C. (1978). The structure of coping. *Journal of Health and Social Behavior*, 19, 2–21. doi:10.2307/2136319.

Skarupski, K. A., Fitchett, G., Evans, D. A., & de Leon, C. F. M. (2010). Daily spiritual experiences in a biracial, community-based population of older adults. *Aging & Mental Health*, 14, 779–789. doi:10.1080/13607861003713265.

Smith, J., Staudinger, U. M., & Baltes, P. B. (1994). Occupational settings facilitating wisdom-related knowledge: The sample case of clinical psychologists. *Journal of Consulting and Clinical Psychology*, 62, 989–999. doi:10.1037/0022–006X.62.5.989.

Staudinger, U. M., & Glück, J. (2011). Psychological wisdom research: Commonalities and differences in a growing field. *Annual Review of Psychology*, 62, 215–241. doi:10.1146/annurev.psych.121208.131659.

Takahashi, M., & Overton, W. F. (2002). Wisdom: A culturally inclusive developmental perspective. *International Journal of Behavioral Development*, 26, 269–277. doi:10.1080/01650250143000139.

Thorson, J. A., & Powell, F. C. (2000). Developmental aspects of death anxiety and religion. In J. A. Thorson (Ed.), *Perspectives on spiritual well-being and aging* (pp. 142–158). Springfield, IL: Charles C. Thomas Publisher.

Tsaousis, I., Karademas, E., & Kalatzi, D. (2013). The role of core self-evaluations in the relationship between religious involvement and subjective well-being: A moderated mediation model. *Mental Health, Religion & Culture*, 16, 138–154. doi:10.1080/13674676.2011.651716.

Walsh, R. (2014). *The world's great wisdom: Timeless teachings from religions and philosophies*. Albany, N.Y.: University of New York Press.

Walsh, R. (2015). What is wisdom? Cross-cultural and cross-disciplinary syntheses. *Review of General Psychology*, 19, 278–293. doi:10.1037/gpr0000045.

Webster, J. D. (2003). An exploratory analysis of a self-assessed wisdom scale. *Journal of Adult Development*, 10, 13–22. doi:10.1023/A:1020782619051.

Wilkinson, P. J., & Coleman, P. G. (2010). Strong beliefs and coping in old age: A case-based comparison of atheism and religious faith. *Ageing & Society*, 30, 337–361. doi:10.1017/s0144686x09990353.

Williams, P. B., Mangelsdorf, H. H., Kontra, C., Nusbaum, H. C., & Hoeckner, B. (2016). The relationship between mental and somatic practices and wisdom. *PLoS ONE*, 11, e0149369. doi:10.1371/journal.pone.0149369.

Wink, P., & Dillon, M. (2003). Religiousness, spirituality, and psychosocial functioning in late adulthood: Findings from a longitudinal study. *Psychology and Aging*, 18, 916–924. doi:10.1037/0882–7974.18.4.916.

Wink, P., & Helson, R. (1997). Practical and transcendent wisdom: Their nature and some longitudinal findings. *Journal of Adult Development*, 4, 1–15. doi:10.1007/BF02511845.

Wink, P., & Scott, J. (2005). Does religiousness buffer against the fear of death and dying in late adulthood? Findings from a longitudinal study. *Journal of Gerontology: Psychological Sciences*, 60, P207–P214.

Wong, P. T. P. (2000). Meaning of life and meaning of death in successful aging. In A. Tomer (Ed.), *Death attitudes and the older adult. Theories, concepts, and applications* (pp. 23–35). Philadelphia, PA: Brunner-Routledge.

Wong, P. T. P., Reker, G. T., & Gesser, G. (1994). Death Attitude Profile-Revised: A multidimensional measure of attitudes toward death. In R. A. Neimeyer (Ed.), *Death anxiety handbook. Research, instrumentation, and application* (pp. 121–148). Washington, D.C.: Taylor & Francis.

Zinnbauer, B. J., Pargament, K. I., Cole, B., Rye, M. S., Butter, E. M., Belavich, T. G., et al. (1997). Religion and spirituality: Unfuzzying the fuzzy. *Journal for the Scientific Study of Religion, 36*, 549–564. doi: 10.2307/1387689.

Appendix: Study Methods

Data Collection

Data for this study were collected between December 1997 and September 2001 in North-Central Florida. The sample contained 116 community residents, 23 nursing home residents, and 19 hospice patients who were diagnosed with a terminal illness and had a life expectancy of less than six months. The community sample was recruited from 18 economically and racially diverse social groups of older adults, including church, social, and civil groups between December 1997 and June 1998 with a follow-up interview ten months later (see Ardelt, 2003). All of the data for the present study, with the exception of the demographics, come from the follow-up interview. The nursing home and hospice sample was recruited through local nursing homes and a local hospice organization between August 1999 and September 2001 with the intent to obtain equal representation by sex, race (white vs. minority), and socioeconomic status (high vs. low). Nine hospice patients lived in the community, seven were cared for in the hospice care center, and three resided in an assisted living facility. Community members completed a self-administered questionnaire delivered to their home and returned by mail in stamped, pre-addressed envelopes, whereas all nursing home residents and hospice patients were interviewed face-to-face. All respondents volunteered for the study and were mentally and physically able to answer the questionnaire.

Measures

Religious spirituality was assessed by the average of Allport and Ross' (1967) Intrinsic Religious Orientation Scale and the spiritual beliefs factor from the Spiritual Involvement and Beliefs Scale (Hatch et al., 1998). Intrinsic religious orientation consisted of nine items (e.g., I try hard to carry my religion over into all my other dealings in life) and spiritual beliefs of ten items (e.g., A spiritual force influences the events in my life). All items were assessed on 5-point scales (1 = strongly agree and 5 = strongly disagree) and scored in the direction of greater religious spirituality before the average of the items was computed. Cronbach's alpha was .89 for intrinsic religious orientation and .91 for spiritual beliefs, and the correlation between the two scales was r=.83 (p<.001). Religious spirituality was centered at the mean before squaring the variable to reduce the effect of multicollinearity (Aiken & West, 1991).

Wisdom was measured by the Three-Dimensional Wisdom Scale, consisting of cognitive, reflective, and compassionate dimensions (3D-WS; Ardelt, 2003) on one of two 5-point scales (1 = strongly agree or definitely true of myself and 5 = strongly disagree or not true of myself), scored in the direction of greater wisdom before the average of the items was computed. The cognitive dimension was the average of 14 items (e.g. Ignorance is bliss – reversed), which assessed an understanding of life or the desire to know the truth. The reflective dimension consisted of the average of 12 items (e.g., I always try to look at all sides of a problem) and measured the ability to look at phenomena and events from different perspectives and to avoid subjectivity and projections. The compassionate dimension was the average of 13 items (e.g., Sometimes I feel a real compassion for everyone) and captured the presence of sympathy and compassion, the motivation to nurture others' well-being, and the absence of indifferent or negative emotions and behavior toward others. Cronbach's alpha for the cognitive, reflective, and compassionate dimensions of wisdom was .87, .70, and .69, respectively. The average of the three dimensions was calculated to obtain a composite three-dimensional wisdom measure, resulting in a Cronbach's alpha of .70 for the three dimensions (.88 for the 39 items).

Spiritual behavior was measured by three single items from the Spiritual Involvement and Beliefs Scale (Hatch et al., 1998): Frequency of shared spiritual activities (During the last MONTH, how often did you participate in spiritual activities with at least one other person?; 1 = 0 times, 2 = 1–5 times, 3 = 6–10 times, 2 = 11–15 times, 5 = more than 15 times), frequency of prayer (During the last WEEK, how often did you pray?; 1 = 0 times, 2 = 1–3 times, 3 = 4–6 times, 2 = 7–9 times, 5 = 10 or more times), and frequency of spiritual coping (How often do you solve your problems without using spiritual resources?; 1 = never and 5 = always).

Psychological well-being was measured by purpose in life and mastery. Purpose in life was the average of three "pure" purpose and meaning items (e.g., I have discovered satisfying goals and a clear purpose in life) from Crumbaugh and Maholick's (1964) Purpose in Life Test. Mastery was the average of seven items (e.g., What happens to me in the future mostly depends on me) from Pearlin and Schooler's Mastery Scale (1978). All items were assessed on 5-point scales (1 = strongly agree and 5 = strongly disagree) and scored in the direction of greater psychological well-being. Cronbach's alpha was .57 for purpose in life and .72 for mastery.

Subjective well-being was assessed as the average of two items of the life satisfaction subscale (e.g., How happy, satisfied, or pleased have you been with your personal life during the past month?; 1 = very dissatisfied and 6 = extremely happy) and four items of the cheerfulness subscale (e.g., How have you been feeling in general during the past month?; 1 = in very low spirits and 6 = in excellent spirits) of the General Well-Being Schedule (Fazio, 1977). Cronbach's alpha was .88.

Attitudes toward death were measured by the Death Attitude Profile–Revised (Wong et al., 1994) on 5-point scales (1 = strongly disagree and 5 = strongly agree). Fear of death was the mean of seven items (e.g., I have an intense fear of death) with an alpha-value of .84. Death avoidance was the average of five items (e.g., I avoid death thoughts at all costs) with an alpha of .88. Neutral acceptance of death was the average of four items (e.g., Death is a natural aspect of life) with an alpha of .67. Approach acceptance of death was the mean of 10 items (e.g., I look forward to life after death) with an alpha of .97. Escape acceptance of death was the average of five items (e.g., Death provides an escape from this terrible world) with an alpha of .77.

Control variables were nursing home resident (0 = no, 1 = yes), hospice patient (0 = no, 1 = yes), gender (0 = male, 1 = female), marital status (0 = unmarried, 1 = married), race (0 = African American, 1 = white), age (in years), socioeconomic status, and subjective health. Socioeconomic status was the average of educational degree (0 = no high school and 4 = graduate degree) and occupation. Three independent judges rated the respondents' longest held occupation based on Hollingshead's Index of Occupations (O'Rand, 1982) on a 9-point scale (1 = farm laborers, mental service workers and 9 = higher executive, large business owner, major professional). At least two judges jointly decided occupations codes for those whose designation was not self-evident. Educational degree was transformed into a 9-point scale before the two scales were averaged. Life-long homemakers were assigned the score for their educational degree. Cronbach's alpha was .83. Subjective health was measured by two items of the General Well-Being Schedule (Fazio, 1977) that assessed health concern, worries, or distress (e.g., How concerned or worried about your health have you been?) on an 11-point scale (0 = not concerned at all and 10 = very concerned) and a 6-point scale (1 = all the time and 6 = none of the time). The scales were scored in the direction of greater subjective health and transformed into 0–5 scales before the mean was calculated. Cronbach's alpha was .76.

Chapter 10

Religion and Spirituality over the Life-Cycle

The Boomer Generation

Wade Clark Roof

UNIVERSITY OF CALIFORNIA SANTA BARBARA

From the time of their birth to the present, members of the post-war boomer generation have understood themselves, and have been understood by others, as distinctive—if for no other reason because of their huge numbers and influence on the culture. But they are also distinctive in another, far more critical way: theirs is the generation that collided with the 1960s, that radical decade of social, cultural, and political change that led to the remaking of American life when the older members of that generation were coming of age; and for the younger members growing up somewhat later "The Sixties" lived on if in no other way as a mythic reality. Boomers today are keenly aware that they are one of the most studied, analyzed, and watched over generations in the nation's history.

The generation came of age in what unquestionably was an "unsettled time," to use sociologist Ann Swidler's term (1986), a liminal moment when an older way of American life was collapsing and a new one emerging. Unlike in settled times when old, established ways of life largely go unchallenged, in unsettled times things are chaotic as new visions of a world arise and new social and cultural patterns are taking shape. Many young Americans put their lives on the line to make the world a better place— which generated strong passions and shaped memories they still carry with them. And importantly, generational theorizing suggests that it is during these early formative years that people's fundamental views of the world and how it operates are formed. In those confrontations boomers were rocked into existential awareness, I think, of the precariousness of social and religious realities—a shift in awareness which Peter Berger described in his book *The Precarious Vision* as arising out of an "experience or series of experiences revealing society to be something radically different from what had previously been taken for granted" (Berger, 1961, p. 10).

My view is that this 1960s encounter with the precariousness of social life and institutions led members of this generation to realize that they had the power not just to change American life, but also that they were capable of changing themselves. Put differently they became more reflexive in thinking about who they are—or perhaps could be. Rebellion against conventional 1950s-style religion probably helped open the way to a greater realization that in matters of personal faith and especially spirituality one should look within and ask questions like: Is there a sense of the sacred in my life? Am I not responsible for my own spiritual beliefs and practices? In effect, an engaging posture with oneself called for a contemplative act of stepping back from one's situation and assessing oneself. Self-examination of this sort likely encouraged a more consciously formed, truer sense of self for members of this generation as they moved out of their early era of social and political activism and approached major junctures in their life-cycle (Roof, 1999). In what follows I chart how the boomers' religious and spiritual views and practices have shifted at various times as they have aged, particularly so in midlife and now again as they approach retirement.

Early Description of the Generation

It is important at the outset that we recognize that members of this generation were far more divided on issues in their early years—and still are—than is often assumed. For sure, the widely held stereotype of "Sex, Drugs, and Rock-n-Roll" that early on characterized the generation was an over-generalization. That description arose out of a *Rolling Stone* survey of its readers which was hardly representative of American youth. Our own survey (N= 2620) of that generation in 1988–90 (Roof, 1999) revealed a generation that was actually slightly more traditional in outlook than countercultural. And in fact, Peter and Brigitte Berger in a *New York Times* Op Ed piece in the early 1970s portrayed the generation as even more divided ideologically than did our own survey, particularly along lines of education and social class. It is fair to say that the ideological polarization that emerged within the country in the post-1960s and still divides the country had its roots in the conflicts and tensions within this generation, i.e., between the "counter-culturalists" and "traditionalists" in that earlier period.

Interested in this generation's core meaning systems, we created an index of exposure to the counterculture in relation to four major perspectives—traditional theism, mysticism, individualism, and social scientific orientation. Theistic and mystical meaning-systems tap religious and/or spiritual affirmations whereas the items on individualism and social scientific perspective tap more secular views in American culture. Responses to these items are shown in Table 10.1 and fall out pretty much as would be expected. Respondents who were more highly exposed to the counterculture were also considerably more likely to be college students or graduates who defined themselves as leaning toward mystical or spiritual views and more accepting of social scientific interpretations. Alternatively, respondents who were less exposed to the counterculture and generally less educated were

Table 10.1 Views About Systems of Meaning by Baby Boomers' Exposure to Counterculture of the 1960s

Worldviews		*(Degree of Exposure to 1960s Counterculture)*			
		0	*1*	*2*	*3*
Theism					
	Picture God as Father	81%	74%	62%	54%
	Life is influenced by God	67	53	44	41
	Believe in eternal life	95	77	77	70
	Believe in Devil	79	65	61	37
	A child is born already guilty of sin	39	29	22	7
Mysticism					
	God is "within" us	22	27	34	54
	Life is influenced by new insights	51	51	57	63
	Prefer to be alone and meditate	6	13	14	34
	Believe in reincarnation	25	29	30	39
	All the great religions of the world are equally true and good	43	45	53	56
Individualism					
	Not succeeding is a person's own fault	67	70	66	55
	A person can control what happens in life	75	72	67	69
	Hard work always pays off	75	63	58	48
Social Science					
	Life is influenced by people in power	70	78	80	84
	Believe in scientific view of Creation	15	15	20	41
	Science may yet find answers to questions that religion now deals with	55	62	64	69

more inclined toward traditional theistic views, including reference to God as Father, more likely to hold a belief in the Devil, and to affirm the importance of individual initiative. The point in all of this is that one should be careful in generalizing about the boomer generation: early on it was, and still remains, far more diverse in its lifestyles, values, and core belief-systems generally than easy generalizations would suggest.

Turning Inward

The 1950s had been shaped by post-World War II affluence, rising expectations, belief that the country was returning to normalcy, strong family values, record religious attendance and church membership, as well as by a white middle-class seemingly quite happy with the prevailing conformist culture. Yet the country was in the throes of a cold war with the Soviet Union, envisioned by many Americans as a cosmic drama in which a God who loved the country was embattled with atheists over who would get to the moon first. As Reinhold Niebuhr (1958, p. 13) pointed out at the time, it was a culture that was simultaneously pious and secular, one full of cultural contradictions in racial and gender views waiting to explode. And explode it did, with the older boomers leading the protests.

It was also an era of disillusionments. Aside from the tragic events of the 1960s and that horrible year—1968—the 1970s followed with recessions, environmental disasters, long gas lines, corruption in high places, and young boomers having to scale down their aspirations for the future. All of this tempered that generation's optimism, forced many of them to grow up quickly, and led still others to question their belief in the American Dream in which they had been indoctrinated as children in the 1950s.

But relatively soon some new and important cultural shifts began shaping a new mood within the country. These included the increased exposure to non-Western religious traditions and the importance of spiritual practice, especially among those exposed to college; trends toward greater expressive individualism; the human potential and self-help movements; popular psychology with its attention to the self and its needs; liberation theologies and especially the feminist and early gay and lesbian movements; and the democratizing of divine presence emphasizing the presence of a God who was within rather than a God who was distant and impersonal. These many influences coalesced in shaping a diverse set of spiritual sensitivities that reinforced their reflexive posture and the quest for greater self-discovery.

This emerging new mood called for less attention to social roles as prescribed by others and more on a person's own exploration, which came to be described as "the search for self-fulfillment." Yet for many of the boomers the search often proved to be rather superficial—focused largely around a quest for new experiences, travel to exciting places, exploring new relationships, finding new hobbies, and the like—as pollster Daniel Yankelovitch (1981) critically observed. But there was the potential for finding deeper insights into life of the sort one of our interviewees described in 1988: "My life changed when my first baby was born. Then I realized the wonder and beauty of a new birth—this little thing and those first cries and smiles. I was part of the creation process. That's when I first encountered anything in my life I'd call sacred." Many others we talked to told stories of one or another experience that deeply touched their lives. Sixties-style protest was softening; caring and compassion were emerging as important. Looking at the cultural trends at the time, psychologist John F. Roschen (1990) commented that boomers in a fairly short period had gone on two quite differing journeys into the self, one being rather superficial as described above, but for others a second journey was born out of a deeper yearning to find meaning in life, to find stable anchors especially in close relationships, work and vocation; and to encounter and experience the sacred. For Roschen this amounted to a quest for a more "balanced care for self and others," which if discovered he thought would:

> bring out the virtues of connectedness, intimacy, love, fairness, a sense of justice, and commitment to duty which yearns to be reclaimed in the lives of many in the baby-boom generation. Fulfillment versus responsibility, and individual ambition versus the needs of others are at the crux of the baby-boomers' midlife dilemma.

Finding a more balanced life was of critical importance to many members of this generation. It amounted to an extended reflexive moment of sorting out life's basics, coming at a time that was soon to emerge into a new phase in their life-cycle when many of them were establishing more serious personal relationships, marrying, and many beginning to form families.

The Spiritual and the Religious

It was about this time as well that the distinction between the religious and the spiritual became more visibly drawn within the country. Historically the two—the religious and the spiritual—were fairly closely aligned within conventional religious life; indeed, in his analysis of the General Social Survey data during the 1980s, 1990s, and the 2000s, Mark Chaves (2011) found that approximately 80% of Americans described themselves as both religious and spiritual. But a more recent, more refined survey finds that Americans who can identify themselves religiously and/or spiritually sort themselves out largely as follows (see Public Religion Research Institute, November 6, 2017):

- Religious and Spiritual: 29%
- "Spiritual but Not Religious:" 18%
- Neither spiritual nor religious: 31%

But the importance of the distinction between "religious" and "spiritual" had become widely accepted within the popular culture, and was reinforced in the media and by the fact that so many young members of the boomer generation had earlier dropped out of religious institutions to explore spiritual alternatives.

The value of practice-oriented meditation became apparent to many in this generation as well as others established in religious communities. It was a spirituality that was more active than passive, self-cultivated and monitored, involving not just the mind but also the body. Moreover, it was a spiritual discipline that was neither contained within nor controlled by the established religious institutions, a point especially important to those of a generation eager to exert more agency and control over their own lives, beliefs, and values. Spiritual practices of this sort in their many diverse forms are now described as a "spirituality of seeking" with emphasis upon life as a journey, one always unfolding and with opportunities for engaging the sacred that was thought of as fluid and arising out of life-experiences, as opposed to a "spirituality of dwelling" that is more settled and involving a fairly stable universe of sacred beliefs and teachings plus historic practices and rituals for sustaining them—these were described by sociologist Robert Wuthnow (1998). If the first is likened to, say, the Jewish tabernacle which is portable and adaptable to varying social settings and experiences, the second is akin to the more stable and established temple.

Given their background, an emphasis upon "spirituality of seeking" was of considerable psychological importance to the boomers. It was empowering with its emphasis upon human agency; it encouraged a quest for unity and wholeness in life that was deeply personal; it emphasized life as involving feelings and not just the more cerebral or believing aspects of commitment. It also encouraged a sense that one could possibly "become" what they were actually "seeking"—that is, a more spiritually minded, openly exploratory life. Moreover, such experience was deemed to be uplifting and liberating, an old self in progression to a new, and presumably more enlightened self. As one of our interviewees said in 1988:

> Religion, I feel, is doctrine and tradition, and you have to do things a certain way. But spirituality is an inner feeling, however you perceive it in your world, in your mind, and however it feels is okay. There's not the parameters on it, that you have to believe in this way and only in this way. Spirituality, I think, is what enters you and lifts you up and moves you to be a better person, a more open person. I don't think religion does that. It tells you what to do and when to do it, when to kneel, when to stand up, all that stuff.

Aside from distancing members of the boomer generation from what many thought to be the country's largely bland religiosity, this new spirituality in its many and quite differing versions was a major step toward creating a more distinctive and expressive way of relating to the sacred. Indeed,

Canadian philosopher Charles Taylor (2007) in his epic volume *A Secular Age* argues that it marks the advent of a new "Age of Authenticity" in engaging the transcendent.

Institutional Religious Patterns

But the inward turn was occurring about the time boomers were facing midlife, and with all this inner spiritual-work going on, the question arises: what was the possibility of a return to the established religious institutions after so many of them had dropped out of them earlier, in the 1960s and 1970s? Whereas the parents of the boomer generation accounted for the postwar increase in religiosity, scholars wondered if their children were likely to remain much less observant than their parents had been at equivalent ages. Yet, some commentators predicted that with age many of them were likely to become more involved religiously. Both *Time* and *Newsweek* magazines carried cover stories in the late 1980s speculating about a possible return by the "generation who had dropped out" to churches, which prompted renewed interest in the boomers as they were reaching midlife. Fortunately, the timing of our large survey in 1988–89 (Roof, 1999) allowed us to examine these trends at the time of this speculation—thus allowing us to explore both the extent of their reported defections from the churches as well as whether or not there was any significant return to religious involvement.

We categorized them into three group: Dropouts, Returnees, and Loyalists.

- Fifty-eight percent of our boomer interviewees reported having dropped out of religious involvement in churches or religious communities for two years or more in their early adult years. We do not know how old they were at the time they dropped out.
- Thirty-eight percent of the Dropouts reported having returned to a church, synagogue, mosque, or some other such community in the intervening years. Returnees had been more exposed to countercultural values than the Loyalists who had not as yet dropped out, but were presumably less exposed than those who had not dropped out by the time of our interviews. Even so, returnees were less likely to actually join a church and/or hold to a strong denominational commitment. Having been exposed to countercultural values, returnees often brought with them some continued interest in New Age spiritual values and practices and were often inclined toward somewhat eclectic mixes of traditional and alternative beliefs and practices. They were more reflexive in their thinking, as evident in their more nuanced views of holding to a more mixed conventional religious as well as deepened spiritual perspectives, or what some commentators at the time dubbed "religion à la carte."

- This led some congregations to greater efforts at making their worship services more engaging spiritually, especially so for those who had earlier dropped out and later returned.

- Church-going members of this generation, and Returnees particularly, preferred to view religious involvement as "something you do if it meets your needs" rather than as a "duty and obligation." For boomers, notions of "duty" and "obligation" did not resonate with church-going.

- Conservative Protestants stood out among the major religious families as having the highest proportion of Loyalists (46% having never dropped out), the lowest proportion of Dropouts (30%), and the highest proportion of Returnees (24%). Traditional Christian teachings had a strong attraction in holding their members as well as attracting new attendees once they had left to return.

- Roman Catholics were relatively well-positioned, with 43% Loyalists, 21% Returnees, and 36% Dropouts. Their strong social justice teachings combined with many family-based rituals relating to life's transitions were often cited in our interviews as a reason for maintaining institutional ties.

- Mainline Protestants had a weaker profile among Christian groups, with 39% Loyalists, 21% Returnees, and 39% Dropouts. Roughly half of their attendees had left congregations and not returned by the time of our survey.

- Jews had the weakest profile overall with respect to holding on to their most committed religious believers: Loyalists, 16%; Dropouts, 70%; Returnee, 14%.

- Much was said about boomers during the countercultural years as having been exposed to, if not increasingly interested in, non-Western spiritualties. But based upon our data these interests did not lead to a discernible shift in religious affiliations as Muslim, Buddhist, Hindu, Sikh, or other such constituencies during this period.

Importantly, this categorization provides a portrait of a generation that was reaching midlife—after marrying, having children, settling down. It was also a generation in flux religiously and spiritually.

Two decades later there was also the huge 2015 Pew Changing Religious Landscape Survey on American religious affiliations which described nationwide (as well as boomer generation) religious preferences (Pew Research Center, 2015). These patterns (see Table 10.2) were as follows:

- For evangelical Protestant boomers, the numbers in this 2015 survey are fairly consistent with what we had found in our 1988–89 study 22 years earlier. Boomers were proportionately more evangelical than were Americans generally. As Putnam and Campbell (2010) observed, what was important was not as much how often people went to church but

Table 10.2 Dropouts, Returnees, and Loyalists, by Religious Tradition

Group		Mainline Protestant	Conservative Protestant	Catholic	Jewish	Other	Total
Percentage ever dropping out		60	54	57	84	50	58
Of these: percentage who have returned		34	44	37	17	23	38
Current profile							
	Loyalist	39	46	43	16	50	42
	Returnee	21	24	14	12	—	22
	Dropout	39	30	36	70	38	36
	N =	(369)	(460)	(542)	(161)	(81)	(1448)

rather which church they went to. Americans of all ages were troubled by the moral and religious developments arising out of the 1960s, and for the next two decades, young people who were conservative in both religion and politics swelled the ranks of evangelical Protestant denominations, and especially the mega-churches that disavowed denominational labels and termed themselves generically as "Christian." While working-class youth had long been drawn to these churches, they were supplanted in sizable numbers in the 1970s and 1980s by conservative-leaning middle-class college youth or recent graduates.

- The proportions of Mainline Protestant and Catholic boomers are also somewhat higher than those observed for the nation as a whole. These patterns suggest that between the time we interviewed the boomer population in 1989–90 and 2015 they had continued to re-affiliate with religious institutions. A lesser proportion of previously liberal members of this generation had also become more conservative, if for no other reason than by now many of them had children or even grandchildren.

- By this time sizable numbers of Americans, and especially the young, were leaving organized religion. As Putnam and Campbell (2010) observe, if the "First Shock" following the 1960s was the return of many young people to conservative churches, a "Second Shock" in the

Table 10.3 Religious Preferences of Boomers Compared to Total Population, 2017

Religious Tradition		Religious Preferences (%)	
		Boomers	Nationwide
Christian			
	Evangelical Protestant	28	25.4
	Mainline Protestant	17	14.7
	Historic Black Protestant	7	6.5
	Catholic	23	20.8
	Mormon	1	1.6
	Orthodox Christian	<1	0.5
	Jehovah's Witness	1	0.8
	Other Christian	1	0.4
Non-Christian			
	Jewish	2	1.9
	Muslim	<1	0.9
	Buddhist	1	0.7
	Hindu	<1	0.7
	Other World Religions	<1	0.3
	Other Faiths	1	1.5
None			
	Atheist	2	3.1
	Agnostic	2	4.0
	Nothing in particular	12	15.8

Source: Adapted from Pew Research Center (2015) America's Changing Religious Landscape. Retrieved from www.pewforum.org/2015/05/12/americas-changing-religious-landscape

1990s and early 2000s marked an increasing defection that was fueled partly by their displeasure with the conservative politics of evangelical and fundamentalist churches (Hout & Fischer, 2002). By this time 17% of boomers identified themselves as "None," though for the country as a whole the percentage was 22.8%. More boomers were leaving religious communities and becoming Nones than was true for those belonging to the older Silent and Greatest generations; but less was the case for the younger Generation Xers and millennials.

New Configurations of Spirituality and Religion

Boomers are remembered for twice having significantly shifted the religious and spiritual mood within the country. Early on, they were blamed for having greatly disrupted the country's religious establishment when so many of them dropped out of the churches in the 1960s and 1970s; and later they were hailed for bringing about greater public attention to spirituality and the experiential aspects of faith, a trend appreciated by many within religious communities who themselves were beginning to appreciate these aspects in worship. But as already noted, people's religious and spiritual identities became more diverse. And as the decades passed and the political mood within the country became more conservative, new and strikingly different configurations of religion, spirituality, belief, and practice that began to emerge were quite different from the older patterns. Indeed, in some respects the new configurations reflected a degree of protest against the previous, earlier and simpler, religious-versus-spiritual patterns of the earlier period.

In what follows we look at two new configurations of spirituality and religion in which boomers play an important role. One is the "Spiritual but Not Religious" (SBNR) population, and a second is the large religiously unaffiliated sector—the so-called "Nones." The first is of course a subset of the second, but the spiritual dynamics within the two constituencies differ considerably and thus are examined here separately. Interestingly, boomers account for almost a third (31%) within each of the two populations both SBNRs and Nones.

The "Spiritual but Not Religious"

This constituency is a mix of people reporting having grown up in various religious traditions, though of course mainly Christian. Those claiming to be evangelical Christians are in some ways the most interesting among the several configurations. Evangelical Christians are generally known for their stronger-than-average religious commitment, but according to Barna Research 10% of evangelicals do not attend church services, and indeed often make a point of emphasizing that they do not attend (Barna, 1995). Hence the defining label of "Spiritual but Not Religious," although some prefer to identify themselves simply as "Christ Followers," and still others say they belong to the "Jesus Yes, Church No" movement. Many say they meditate, pray and explore nature; claim to believe in God or a God-spirit as revealed in Jesus; and revere teachings found in various religious traditions; but they disdain the institutional church, believing that it corrupts the spirit of religion, particularly within Christianity. A majority of the SBNR are single, many of them partnered; they are overwhelmingly white and tend to be liberal politically, many advocating for gay and transgender rights. While the pattern of evangelicals turning their backs on churches—even evangelical churches—is not a new phenomenon historically within the American evangelical tradition, the Barna Research people worry that this trend might be on the rise today and could signal that evangelicals are losing their commitment to communally shared affirmations of Christian belief and practice (Barna, 1995).

So what is really going on here? One can only speculate, but as the SBNR identity suggests the door was opened for them to "come out," so to speak, as radically individualistic spiritual followers of Jesus who sought to break with organized religion. Some appear to be driven by a concern that institutions corrupt the spirit, as many of them say. Others are put off by evangelical churches because of the alliance with conservative politics. A third of this constituency are boomers with their long-standing interest in spiritual quests, personal meditation and practice. Thus, the question arises: Is this yet another working out of an anti-institutional, highly privatized style of spirituality, one which in this instance is focused upon what they believe to be a more authentic Jesus stripped of historical, institutionally defined imageries? If indeed this is the case, Jesus emerges as a spiritual figure for devotion not unlike the gurus in Eastern religious traditions who came to America in the 1960s and to whom some boomers at the time were attracted, e.g., Meher Baba and Maharaji. Testimonies we heard in our research from some of the earlier devotees confirmed that they looked upon Jesus in ways that were similar ("Jesus Freaks?" especially) to ways that they had once looked upon the Eastern religious teachers.

Alternatively, it may be that "following Jesus" in their deeply personal style is a prelude to an even larger question that perhaps is evolving—that is, "Who is a Good Christian?"—a topic evangelicals at various times in the past have passionately debated with other Christians. Plus, boomers have at times become enmeshed in other, quite similar religious controversies. Two decades or so ago Catholic boomers were involved within the larger Catholic debate over who is a "Good Catholic" with regard to doctrinal belief and commitment to social justice (Roof, 1999); thus it is possible that a similar controversy could occur on the part of boomer evangelicals within the SBNR constituency. A controversy could arise within the broad evangelical constituency of boomers, or possibly even within the larger Christian community led perhaps by passionate members of the SBNR. Of course these are just speculations in the absence of clearer, evolving patterns based on evidence.

The Nones

Second, there is the huge constituency of Nones, those identifying as neither religious nor spiritual in the Public Religion Research Institute survey. They are estimated to constitute 22% of Americans (Pew Research Center,

2015). They are known for their eclectic mix of religious and non-religious beliefs; their spiritual experiences, even if some are reluctant to define themselves as spiritual; and agnosticism and atheism espousing "believing in nothing in particular," as many reported to the Pew Research pollsters. So diverse are they that it is difficult, perhaps impossible, to describe them generally. What binds them is the view that the term "religious" is far too confining a label in an age of expanding possibilities for tailoring one's meaning-systems, spiritual views and practices. Life is fluid and ever-evolving, and thus their beliefs, practices, and affirmations of meaning in life are themselves similarly liquid, as Elizabeth Drescher (2016) points out in her recent book *Choosing Our Religion*.

To claim to be a None amounts to a declaration of spiritual independence, a rebellion against the larger and normative American religious culture, a point also emphasized by Christel Manning (2015) in her research on this constituency. Nones are *bricoleurs* (see Wuthnow, 1998) who piece together ideas, practices, bits of wisdom from one source or another, selecting religious teachings from all the major religions as well as generalized teachings such as the Golden Rule which does not predispose belief in God. In addition, they glean insights from their own everyday life-experiences; relations with family members and friends; what they have learned from nature and especially from pets; inspirations arising from art, dance, and music; and whatever they might intuit from the dynamics of mind, body, and spirit. Out of this huge and eclectic mix they craft rich personal stories about what is insightful and important to them, frequently re-configuring their constellations of belief and practice as they gain new insights or their life-situations change. If there is one overwhelming feature about their systems of belief and practice, perhaps it is their malleability. As Drescher (2016, p. 31) writes, "None seems to open to spiritual possibility, flexibility, fluidity, porousness, and variations over time for an increasing number of people."

Summing Up

In describing these two constituencies that are attracting so much attention today, my point is to underscore how members of the boomer generation are still shaping new spiritual styles—and in both the SBNRs and the Nones, this reflects an expanded freedom of exploration and meshing of spiritual themes for many, especially those who had unhappy conventional religious experiences in the past. Boomers make up the largest of the three older generations represented in both the SBNR and None constituencies, and for this reason they are likely to play something of an elder role within them. The SBNR boomer evangelicals take Jesus out of the traditional religious context and personalize a relationship with him; similarly, boomer Nones distance themselves from a 1950s religious past that was too conforming, too full of contradictions, and not very adaptable and/or insightful to many of the God-tangles that pop up in today's more complex lives. The greater freedom of individual choice in lifestyles, religion, spirituality, and meaning-system, along with the rise of a consumer marketplace of resources catering to expanding spiritual and meaning-making choices, now churn the culture offering new and different ways of imagining meaningful connections between the self and the sacred.

No one has summarized these broad religious shifts that came with the Sixties better than Michele Dillon and Paul Wink (2007) in their book *In the Course of a Lifetime*. They point to three fundamental cultural shifts that have redefined people's relationships to religion and spirituality. One is that both religion and spirituality today are less constrained by the imposed authority of a particular faith tradition and this, in turn, has opened the way to greater individual autonomy and the alignment of faith and spirituality with their particular wants and preferences. Second, this new freedom has contributed to the possibility that individuals could adhere to religious and/or spiritual beliefs and practices without necessarily affiliating with either a religious or a spiritual community. Third, religious and non-religious people alike have increasingly come to describe religious and spiritual teachings, as well as moral and ethical principles, in more non-sectarian and non-theological terms, a good example being the Golden Rule which does not presuppose an affirmation of belief in God or even a transcendent frame of reference.

The Current Scene

But what about contemporary religious and spiritual patterns for the baby boomer generation? How are we to describe these trends now, as boomers have begun to retire? As members of an aging population, chances are they would be more religiously inclined now than at an earlier time in their lives. A pattern of aging and increasing religious commitment is generally documented (Bengtson, Putney, & Harris, 2015); but less attention has been given to trends in spirituality, except the observation that from midlife on there is generally a growing interest in spiritual concerns.

With regard to aging and religiousness, Table 10.4 shows the Boomer responses to several major religious indicators of commitment that were used in the Pew Religious Landscape Survey of 2015 such as "importance of religion," "attending religious services," "certainty of belief in God," and "praying." Shown are patterns of responses for boomers as well as other generations close in age for comparison.

As seen in Table 10.4, levels of religious commitment generally increase with the aging of individuals within generations. But none of these generations has a high level of attendance at worship services, yet they score much higher on the other types of religious commitment.

Table 10.4 Indicators of Religious Activity and Beliefs by Generation of Respondent

Religious Commitment

	Religion is very important	Attend religious services weekly	Belief in God absolutely certain	Pray daily or more	
Generation Xers	53%	34%	66%	69%	
Baby Boomers	59	38	69	61	
Silent Generation	67	51	71	67	
Greatest Generation	72	51	66	69	

Frequency Reading Scripture

	At least once a week	Once/ twice a month	Several times a year	Seldom/ never	DK
Generation Xers	36%	11%	9%	44%	1%
Baby Boomers	38	9	8	44	1
Silent Generation	44	9	7	38	2
Greatest Generation	45	9	6	38	2

Interpreting Scripture as Word of God

	Literally True	Not all Literal	Not the Word of God	DK	
Generation Xers	32	21	33	13	
Baby Boomers	35	26	29	10	
Silent Generation	39	26	23	12	

Greatest Generation	44	20	19	17

Source of Guidance: Right vs. Wrong

	Religion	Reason	Common Sense	Science	
Generation Xers	33	10	45	10	
Baby Boomers	38	9	44	7	
Silent Generation	41	7	42	6	
Greatest Generation	40	6	43	6	

Basis of Moral and Ethical Decisions

	Absolute Standards	Situation	Neither/Both	DK	
Generation Xers	35	63	1	1	
Baby Boomers	38	59	2	1	
Silent Generation	37	59	2	2	
Greatest Generation	31	62	1	5	

Source: Adapted from Pew Research Center (2015) America's Changing Religious Landscape. Retrieved from http://www.pewforum.org/2015/05/12/americas-changing-religious-landscape/

With respect to the survey item on reading Scripture, 38% of boomers report doing so at least once a week, which is higher than for Generation Xers but less than either the Silent or the Greatest generations. Thirty-eight to 44 percent across the generations report they seldom or never read Scripture. More than a third of the boomer generation view Scripture as literally true, but 29% say just the opposite—that it is not the Word of God. Twenty-six percent of Boomers and similar proportions in the other generations opted for the middle and safer option in responses—the Scriptures are "Not All Literal."

Another item concerns the source of guidance when considering right-versus-wrong. More boomers as well as the other generations opt for "common sense" over "religion" as providing the best basis for judgment. Neither reason nor science were cited as important as a source of guidance. Finally, there is the question about what would be the proper basis for making moral and ethical decisions— "absolute standards" versus the "situation in question." Fifty-nine percent of boomers chose the "situation" alternative over "absolute standards," and the other generations showed much the same pattern. Given the importance Americans place on context in decision-making on ethical judgments, plus their inclination not to think in absolute terms, this finding is not surprising.

Thus across all the religious items in this survey we observe a pattern of increasing religious commitment as the generations age, a finding consistent with the 34-year longitudinal data of Bengtson et al. (2015). We look next at spiritual indicators as shown in Table 10.5. Here we find a similar pattern in relation to the aging of the generations drawing upon the same Pew survey data.

With respect to meditation, boomers say they engage in it more frequently than Generation Xers although somewhat less than those in the older Silent and Greatest Generations. On the two other items—feeling a "sense of spiritual peace and well-being" and having a "sense of wonder about the universe"—we observe roughly similar patterns. So, looking at both religious and spiritual indicators, we find a congruence of the two, which suggests that members of this generation are not as inclined today to draw as great a divide between the religious and the spiritual as was once the case in their younger years. The popularity of solitary spiritual quests premised on an explicit rejection of organized religion had waned considerably over time for boomers. As members of this generation aged, particularly in the period from midlife to retirement, they matured and became more settled—and perhaps were also more likely to be drawn to a "spirituality of dwelling," one that is more enriched experientially as a result of the inclusion of spiritual elements in worship services than in the past.

A more "enriched" spirituality of dwelling was now possible because over time many churches had absorbed a great number of spiritual practices into their religious services and activities. They retrieved spiritual and meditative exercises from various traditions, such as "centering prayer," medieval chants, mindfulness meditation, African American spiritual music, and the like, weaving them into their liturgies; in effect, modifying the people's religious experiences by enhancing spiritual sensitivities. Native American spirituality, ancient wisdom, plus some New Age practices are celebrated as well and often practiced in some depth especially in small groups within traditional faith communities. Some churches host recovery groups addressing a variety of personal addictions, or offer discussions on balancing personal and spiritual needs, on helping to reach out to others and thus cultivating a social consciousness. Mega-churches especially have contributed to overcoming the divide between the religious and the spiritual by

Table 10.5 Spiritual Practices and Beliefs by Generation of Respondents

		Weekly or more (%)
Meditation		
	Generation X	39
	Baby Boomers	45
	Silent Generation	56
	Greatest Generation	60
Feel strong sense of spiritual peace and well-being		
	Generation X	58
	Baby Boomers	62
	Silent Generation	66
	Greatest Generation	70
Feel strong sense of wonder about the Universe		
	Generation X	43
	Baby Boomers	48
	Silent Generation	45
	Greatest Generation	44

Source: Adapted from Pew Research Center (2015) America's Changing Religious Landscape. Retrieved from http://www.pewforum.org/2015/05/12/americas-changing-religious-landscape/

offering within the same institution a large, unifying worship service bringing the community together while also offering a wide array of small-group discussions and social activities. These have included such practical spiritual regimens as exercising to lose weight while moving to the beat of inspiring music—sometimes called "Jazzercise"—as found in some evangelical churches, as well as lectures and book discussions on various topics offering opportunities for aging boomers to engage in conversations about health issues, death and dying, and other aspects of aging. And there are the vast resources of the religious and spiritual book stores, retreat centers, plus the increased opportunity today for surfing and networking the Internet—all enhanced opportunities for learning about, and indeed participating in, lively discussions and engaging religious and spiritual issues in ways hitherto impossible. Note also that while the SBNR constituency is moderate to liberal politically, and thus likely open to new and shifting styles of spirituality, the larger population of boomers today is either traditional evangelical or Catholic, both likely to be more conservative politically and thus more likely to be drawn to more conventional religious styles and communities.

But this does not mean that there are not individualized spiritual seekers still around today. And many of them for sure are aging boomers—the quest continues! Over the years one after another American new spiritual movement has emerged attractive to seekers, and surely this will continue; one can expect as well that the spiritual marketplace will offer new meditative and spiritual exercises for loners as well as a means for incorporating them into small groups. Given the autonomy and freedom that Americans—particularly boomers—enjoy in defining who they are, using terms like religious, spiritual, religious and spiritual, spiritual but not religious, free-thinker, humanistic, agnostic, None, or whatever, as they age they will undoubtedly continue to sort themselves out in an expanding menu of religious and/or spiritual possibilities. Having asserted such freedom, indeed redefining that freedom during the 1960s, boomers will certainly continue to celebrate the opportunity for choice. As with "church-hopping" in conventional religious life, we can expect boomers to enjoy the freedom of shifting from one particular religious and/or spiritual style, or new sort of configuration combining the two as their preferences and life-circumstances change in the years that lie ahead. Shifts of this sort do not signal a lack of commitment but just the opposite: people who switch from one style of religiousness or spirituality to another are usually more committed to their new choice than they were to an earlier preference.

The Importance of Aging

As should be apparent, the perspective I have advanced in this chapter emphasizes a developmental perspective. Religious and spiritual views change as people age. For boomers as well as other generations, aging is related to increased religiousness and spirituality. Obviously there are exceptions—committed atheists and humanists, people who feel they were mistreated by clergy and have turned against organized religion, or possibly even children who have grown up in families that did not care enough about them, and hence they cannot imagine a loving God. But on the whole, as people age they are likely to become both more religious and spiritual as has been observed in previous research (Bengtson, Silverstein, Putney, & Harris, 2015).

More specific to the boomer generation, the heightened level of social and political unrest in the 1960s encouraged many boomers to try to build a better America. And in so doing many of them adopted a more reflexive view of life which encouraged them to take charge also of their own lives, question their deepest beliefs, practices, moral and ethical values, and perhaps to reform them as their opportunities and challenges have arisen as they aged. Assuming this to be the case, their aging process had the added benefits of considerable reflection about life's basic values— particularly concerning social obligations as they moved into new stages in life with regard to family, work and vocation. It may be that this reflexive stance on life has enhanced their sense of responsibility as they have aged. Other factors are involved as well: declining interest in worldly things, concern for their children's religious development, grand-parenting, the loss of a relative, and greater free time (Silverstein & Bengtson, 2017).

New Challenges of Retirement

As happens with all generations, boomers are now beginning to face new challenges as they transition into retirement. But given increasing patterns of longevity (Bengtson et al., Chapter 1 in this volume; Johnson, Chapter 11 in this volume), members of this generation on average will have an extended period of time to embrace life while still in their active phases of life, more so than for previous generations. And this sets the generation somewhat apart from other generations: It means that they will need to keep themselves active physically, mentally, and spiritually as best they can in anticipation of extended years. What follows are several comments about boomers keeping themselves active.

Staying involved

Retirement should not necessarily imply giving up older commitments. It may call for some reassessment of the number of commitments and evaluation of their relative importance. But it is important that as boomers retire they remain actively involved in important social and community activities—be that with family, religious, civic, special-purpose groups, or whatever, even if there is some lessening of their earlier commitments. Extension of the self in activities deepens one's sense of continuity and belonging. And for a generation once so involved in remaking the country, its members will likely want to continue being involved in civic matters in one degree or another. Plus, there is considerable research showing that volunteering, reaching out to helping others, and involvement in social causes reduces stress, combats depression, keeps one mentally stimulated, provides a sense of purpose, and makes people happier (according to the London School of Economics Research in Social Science and Medicine, 2015). The Positive Aging Movement, which has drawn many supporters in recent years, similarly encourages a more conscious view of aging, i.e. to increase awareness of one's needs and opportunities at every stage in the life-cycle, and to look forward to new opportunities, indeed to claim and savor every new phase of life that lies ahead—which is appropriate for a generation expected to have the greatest longevity of any generation ever (Pevny, 2014). Erikson, Erikson and Kivnick (1986) argued that successful aging in the latter phases of life rests upon maintaining a "vital involvement" in life as a means of confronting the challenges that come with increasing age. He also spoke of "generativity," of showing concern for others and particularly for one's descendants and future generations. Such concern is positively associated with religious and spiritual involvement, according to Dillon and Wink (2003).

Grandparenting

According to the U.S. Census, 10% of grandparents live with at least one grandchild. Given the high levels of divorce, many single mothers working, plus an increase in multi-family households often for financial reasons, the need for grandparents to assist with grandchildren is especially important at present. As Bengtson (2001) points out, grandparents are playing an increasingly significant role in their grandchildren's lives, perhaps more than ever before in American history. This extends beyond financial help to include the importance of intergenerational contact. And in situations where families are separated by distance, online skyping and cell phones now allow for maintaining those connections. Plus, there is the critical importance of transmitting values of caring and love, religious and spiritual values, and of course cultivating intergenerational solidarity. Speaking of generativity, or investing in one's descendants, here is a rich opportunity for boomer grandparents.

Meditation and spiritual inquiry are still important

Boomers hardly have to be convinced of the importance of yoga and meditation (plus other spiritual practices), but when social scientific research confirms the positive effects of such activity on the brain it is worth noting. Peter Hall (2017), a co-author in a recent research project on meditation in *The Week* reports that:

> Daily sessions of either practice can have dramatic effects on brain function. Mental tasks completed before and after each session found that yoga and meditation led to greater improvements in the participants' energy level, mood, executive function, and ability to control thoughts and emotions. Hatha yoga and mindfulness meditation both focus the brain's conscious processing power on a limited number of targets, like breathing and posing, and also reduce processing of non-essential information.

Mental training, Hall says, can enable people to focus more easily on what they choose to attend to in everyday life. Such training is obviously desirable as people age—probably good advice for boomers at this point in their lives. They may be increasingly drawn to spiritual interests that are new existentially to them, including concerns about death and dying but also on the importance of aging and brain functions, palliative care, the rights of the living to terminate their lives, and the renewed interest in so-called "near-death experiences" on the part of aging boomers who earlier in their lives were drawn to New Age spirituality and the paranormal, as Michael Kinsella's (2017) recent research suggests. The rapidly growing End-of-Life Movement is inspiring new research on brain functioning, that will likely be of interest to many boomers.

Keep on going

Sister Joan Chittister, O.S.B., in her book *The Gift of Years* writes:

> The answer to old age, Leon Edel once wrote, is to keep one's mind busy and to go on with one's life as if it is interminable. I always admired Chekov for building a new house when he was dying of Tuberculosis. To insist on living until we die may be one of life's greatest virtues. It is easy at any age simply to stop, to be satisfied with what is, to refuse to do more. But when we go on working—at something, for some reason, for someone, for something greater than ourselves—when we go on giving ourselves away right to the end, we have lived a full life...For some people it means watering the flowers every day of their lives. For others, it means continuing to write, to practice the piano, to prepare to make the world a better place before we go because we have been here.
>
> (Chittister, 2008, p. 11)

References

Barna, G. (1995). *Generation Next: What you Need to Know about Today's Youth.* Ventura, CA: Regal Books.

Bengtson, V. L. (2001). Beyond the nuclear family: The increasing importance of multigenerational relationships in American society. The 1998 Burgess Award Lecture. *Journal of Marriage and the Family*, 63(1), 1–16.

Bengtson, V. L. (with Putney, N. P., & Harris, S. C.) (2013). *Families and Faith: How Religion is Passed Down Across Generations.* New York: Oxford University Press.

Bengtson, V. L., Silverstein, M. S., Putney, N. P., & Harris, S. C. (2015). Does religiousness increase with age? Age changes and age differences over 35 years. *Journal of the Scientific Study of Religion*, 54(2), 363–379.

Berger, P. L. (1961). *The Sacred Canopy.* Garden City: Doubleday and Company, Inc.

Berger, P. L. & Berger, D. B. (1971, February 15). The bluing of America. *New York Times.*

Chaves, M. (2011). *American Religion: Contemporary Trends.* Princeton: Princeton University Press.

Chittister, J. (2008). *The Gift of Years.* New York: Blue Ridge.

Dillon, M. & Wink, P. (2003). Religiousness and spirituality: trajectories and vital involvement in late adulthood. In M. Dillon (Ed.), *Handbook of the Sociology of Religion* (pp. 179–189). Cambridge: Cambridge University Press.

Dillon, M. & Wink, P. (2007) *In the Course of a Lifetime: Tracing Religious Belief, Practice, and Change.* Berkeley: University of California Press.

Drescher, E. (2016). *Choosing Our Religion.* Oxford: Oxford University Press.

Erikson, E., Erikson, J. M., & Kivnick, H. Q. (1986). *Vital Involvement in Old Age.* New York: W.W. Norton.

Hall, P. (2017, September). Meditation and its beneficial effects. *The Week.*

Hout, M., & Fischer, C. (2003). Why more Americans have no religious preference: Politics and generations. *American Sociological Review,* 67(2) (April), 165–190.

Kinsella, M. (2017). The aging new age: Baby boomers, near-death experiences, and the emergence of the afterlife movement (Doctoral Dissertation). Department of Religious Studies, University of California, Santa Barbara.

London School of Economics Research in Social Science and Medicine (2015). Volunteering and its surprising benefits. http://helpguide.org/articles/healthy-living/volunteering-and-its-surprising-benefits.htm

Manning, C. (2015). *Losing Our Religion: How Unaffiliated Parents Are Raising their Children.* New York: New York University Press.

Niebuhr, R. (1958). *Pious and Secular America.* New York: Scribner's.

Pevny, R. (2014). *Conscious Living, Conscious Aging.* New York: Atria.

Pew Research Center. (2015) America's Changing Religious Landscape. Retrieved from http://www.pewforum.org/2015/05/12/americas-changing-religious-landscape/

Public Religion Research Institute. (2017, November 6). www.prri.org/

Putnam, R. D. & Campbell, D. E. (2010). *American Grace: How Religion Divides Us and Unites Us.* New York: Simon & Schuster.

Roof, W. C. (1999). *Spiritual Marketplace: Baby Boomers and the Remaking of American Religion.* Princeton: Princeton University Press.

Roschen, J. H. (1990). The baby-booms' second journey into self: Finding faith at mid-life. (Unpublished manuscript).

Silverstein, M., & Bengtson, V. L. (2017). Return to religion? Predictors of religious change among baby boomers in their transition to later life. *Journal of Population Ageing,* 6(3), doi:10.1007/s12062-12017-9216-0

Swidler, A. (1986). Culture in action: Symbols and strategies. *American Sociological Review,* 51, 273–286.

Taylor, C. (2007). *A Secular Age.* Cambridge: The Belknap Press of Harvard University Press.

Wuthnow, Robert (1998). *After Heaven: Spirituality in America since the 1950s.* Berkeley: University of California Press, 1998.

Yankelovitch, D. (1981). *New Rules: Searching for Self-Fulfillment in a World Turned Upside Down.* New York: Random House.

Chapter 11

Spirituality and Life Review at the End of Life in Old Age

Malcolm Johnson

UNIVERSITIES OF BATH AND BRISTOL, UK

The Human Spirit

The human spirit is capable of responding to the whole range of emotions and experiences that form the lifespan of an individual. It is the agency that registers emotions across the whole spectrum, from the elation of joy at wondrous experiences, events, achievements and relationships, to the despair and degradation of profound pain and loss. While most of us are treated to great pleasures and exquisitely lofty emotional highs, some live lives of endless oppression and cruel misuse. It is within this inescapable ordinariness of a spiritual void which grows out of the experience of so many that my preoccupation lies. The case for taking it so seriously is magnified by the doubling of the lifespan over the past 150 years, the welcome facility of retirement and the often daunting experiences of the Fourth Age.

Living to be old is still considered to be a great benefit. But dying slowly and painfully, with too much time to reflect and with little or no prospect of redressing the harms, the deficits, and the emotional pain, has few redeeming features. So my focus is on spirituality in late life, when finitude and the end of life are pressing. This exploration leads me to combine the latest UK data on the health profiles of the oldest old and to use them as a backdrop when considering the influence that the loss of health and autonomy has on life review and spiritual reflection.

Life review and spiritual reflection are commonplace activities throughout the adult lifespan. Some find that cues, experiences, overheard conversations, chance hearing of music or radio, items in newspapers, images or references in social media provoke recollections of incidents or times past. These mental notes, whether pleasurable or painful, are likely to be momentary and transient. Sometimes they will be worthy of re-telling to others. Sometimes they will provoke deep concerns, causing the recollection to continue. In our busy lives we tend to submerge the unpleasant fragments of past experience under a blanket of activity and pre-occupation. The unwelcome thoughts are driven back, deep inside ourselves, covered over by protective defensive layers.

As we move beyond retirement and into a likely slower pace of life, biographical reflection becomes a more predominant occupation. Recognition that most of our life has already been lived gives way to greater self-evaluation. Tornstam (2005) discusses this Third Age reflexivity, and has depicted it as one characterised by replacing the competitiveness and acquisitiveness of mainstream adulthood with an increased recognition of the needs and aspiration of people younger than ourselves. However, as we enter the Fourth Age and become faced with the impact of the chronic diseases which steal our capacity to function as independent persons, the focus turns inwards, on a fusion of survival activities and a more pressing attention to life review.

Personal reflection also includes exploration of the bigger questions of human existence. These include those that focus on the nature and existence of God, our beliefs and our track record of living. As will be discussed later, remembering the past is both a journey in self-assessment and a spiritual enterprise, enabled and often inescapably prompted by the lack of other stimuli and diversion. The Fourth Age is a period of over-abundance of time. In this context, the circumstances of the ill-health of people on their "last lap," where finitude looms ever larger, are directly relevant. The connection between the two is rarely mentioned and even less researched. So, in what follows I try to explore the triangular relationship between the predominant patterns of illness, the absence of meaningful stimulation and the unseen iceberg of "biographical pain" in late old age.

Ageing, Religion, and Spirituality

Within the long running debates about the decline of organised (principally Christian) religion in American society and across Europe, the central discourses have been about the shift from established religious traditions, practices and church attendance to more individualised patterns of beliefs and practices. Social scientists, Wuthnow (2005) and Putnam and Campbell (2010) significant among them, have approached the subject within a cultural analytical framework. They see the reduction in collective religious engagement as an artifact of political and social liberalism, from the 1960s onwards. The phrase "spiritual but not religious" is an increasingly used notation. Rhys Williams (Chapter 2 in this volume) provides a succinct summary of the current state of the debate, and Wade Clark Roof (Chapter 10 in this volume) plots the course of the baby boomers as the standard bearers of change through this period of re-formulation.

Ageing has been only a secondary feature in most of the research and literature. In the larger surveys age is seen predominantly as an analytical variable – with the baby boomers as a special category depicted as a convoy of de-religionisers, surging their way through the lifespan, changing all in their ambit. The monumental surveys of religion and public life conducted by the Pew Research Center use very broad age groupings. For example, in the 2015 *Changing Religious Landscape* Study the application of age as a variable, as a means to categorize findings, involved the following broad groupings: 18–29; 30–49; 50–64; 65 and older. On all of the dimensions of religiosity and spirituality surveyed, the results show a consistent age gradient, with the over 65s being the most observant. Putnam and Campbell (2010) used modified versions of the same Pew age breaks, and they also significantly lump the older population into the 65+ category. In *Sacred Stories, Spiritual Tribes* (2014) Nancy Tatom Ammerman, in her compelling examination of 95 narrative accounts, with the intent of "telling a more complicated story about modern religious lives," delivers sophisticated interpretations of personal stories. She concludes that "our modern preoccupation with identifying a distinctly religious domain has blinded us to the way the everyday world remains enchanted." Yet all her older subjects were depicted simply as "over 65s."

As gerontologists have been slow to look seriously at religion and spirituality, we have relatively few studies of any scale (though many qualitative studies) on this topic. Here we can turn to the stream of research and publications led by Neil Krause (Haywood & Krause, 2013a; Haywood & Krause, 2013b; Chapter 8 in this volume) and to the later work on the 40 years of the Longitudinal Study of Generations led by Vern Bengtson along with Merril Silverstein (Chapter 1 in this volume). These bodies of data and interpretation reveal – as might be expected – more nuanced experiences of retired people as they progress through the ensuing decades. In *Families and Faith* (2013) Bengtson and his colleagues revealed patterns of faith transmission down the generations which earlier research had not observed. The book also cast light on the varied dynamics of family interactions that promoted faith transmission and those that did not. Subsequent further analysis of the data (Bengtson, Silverstein, Putney, & Harris, 2015) showed that while older people tend to be more religious than younger adults "It is only near to the end of their lives when they become frail that religious participation declines." In a parallel way Peter Coleman's UK longitudinal study of equal duration (Chapter 5 in this volume), and his more recent investigations of later life in Eastern Europe, provide evidence that there are many older "questioners" who express increased doubts about the meaning and value of the doctrines and practices of their faith. In sum, old age can bring increasing unease with organised religion, which for some leads to exploration and refinement of belief. For some the final stage of life leaves them profoundly uncertain and in the end disconnected from their faith community.

Dying and Death in the Province of Old Age

For the first time in human history the overwhelming majority of deaths in our society are of "older people." Since the beginnings of the Public Heath

Movement, led by Edwin Chadwick from the mid nineteenth century, premature deaths have declined. Improvements in diet, personal and collective hygiene, followed by developments in more effective childbirth and control of infectious diseases in children and adults, better housing, plus the introduction of antibiotics, were major components in the systematic reduction of deaths.

The gain in life years has been remarkably consistent over a very long period. In a now classic paper Oeppen and Vaupel (2002) demonstrated that there has been an annual gain in expectation of life in northern Europe of three months per year over the last 160 years. If the trend was coming to an end, the increments would show signs of trailing off. But the trend has so far remained as strong and consistent as ever. So regardless of any scientific breakthrough which might lead to further reduction in the causes of death, our collective age will continue to rise.

Premature deaths are so greatly reduced, to the point where:

- 84% of deaths in England in 2013 were people over 65.
- 67% of all deaths were of people over 75.
- 39% were over 85.

All too many of those individuals (48%) end their lives, unsatisfactorily and at considerable public cost, in hospitals. Almost 25% of non-accidental deaths occur in care homes. A further 22% die at home and 6% in hospice care.

- In 2014 the period life expectancy at birth in the UK was 79.3 for males and 83.0 for females.
- By 2059 the period of life expectancy at birth is projected to reach 84.1 years for males and 86.9 years for females, an increase of around four years since 2014.
- By 2039 the cohort life expectancy at birth is projected to reach 93.9 for males and 96.5 for females, almost 10 years longer than period life expectancy.
- The period of life expectancy at birth is projected to rise by eight years for males and seven years for females over the 50 years to 2064.
- By 2064, cohort life expectancy at birth for females in England is projected to reach 100 years, 99 in the UK, Wales, and Northern Ireland and 98 in Scotland

(Ruth & Verne, 2010; Office for National Statistics, 2016)

The Fourth Age: Dying Slowly in Frail Old Age

Ages and stages of human life have been a feature of the writings of moralists, theologians and novelists since the late Middle Ages. During these centuries the calibrations of what were perceived as a good life varied from age to age and from world view to world view. Thomas Cole (1992) maps the history of such ideologies of how life should be lived and the virtues that were essential to each stage. Wonderful images of the life cycle, presented as models of the good and Christian life, became popular inspirational pictures mounted in the houses of the devout and successful. Some were depicted as circles of life and others as bridges, where those who journeyed through life became more disfigured and sick as they encountered the vicissitudes of living. Bunyan's *Pilgrim's Progress* is the best known of the moral literary form, where he separates the progress of spiritual development from physical ageing.

Yet for all the theological models, the one image which persisted in the public mind throughout the twentieth century was Shakespeare's seven ages of man as depicted at the end of the monologue "All the world's a stage …." in *As You Like It*:

> That ends this strange eventful history,
> Is second childishness and mere oblivion,
> Sans teeth, sans eyes, sans taste, sans everything.

This graphic representation of old age was formative in creating the deeply negative conception of late life which survives to some degree in contemporary thinking.

The identification of a definable new stage in the life course was articulated by the Cambridge historian, philosopher and demographer Peter Laslett (1989), a co-founder of the University of the Third Age in Britain, who fully formulated the new four stage pattern of the lifespan in his volume *A Fresh Map of Life*. There he draws the Third Age out of the history of population change and the emergence of retirement. Following a lengthy analysis, Laslett defines the latter stages of old age as follows:

The Third Age of Personal Achievement
The Fourth Age of Dependence and Decrepitude (Laslett, 1989)

Today we would see Laslett's use of the term decrepitude as archaic and an inappropriate description. Neither of these stages is a chronological age. The Third Age is defined by the exit of the individual from the workforce, into a period freed for personal fulfilment. So, some will never reach the Third Age because necessity requires them to continue in economic labour. Others, by ill health, early retirement, redundancy or simply by choice for those with enough resources, will enter it in their fifties or even earlier. Even less appreciated than the Third Age are the years of very late life. The Fourth Age presents even the most resilient with challenges of chronic illnesses which make their lives and those who care and support them arduous, undignified, painful and all too often disregarded.

Parameters of the Fourth Age

In England about 470,000 people die each year. As noted earlier, 80% of all deaths are people over 65. Two thirds of deaths are people over 75; one third are 85+. In simple terms this means that in any one year there is an annual cohort of some 315,000 people over 75, plus another group of 65,000 65–75s, who are "on the final lap" of life. These 380,000+ are destined to die, each year, from degenerative diseases that make their health frail for a long period before death. Heart disease, cancers, organ system failures (liver, kidney, heart, respiration) along with strokes and dementia account for the overwhelming majority of these deaths – around 90%. What we know about the living circumstances of these increasingly frail older people is that two thirds of those over 75 are women (more in the higher age groups as we saw earlier) and that two thirds of that group of women live alone, are widowed or never married.

As an overlay to the cluster of chronic illnesses that will bring their lives to an end they will typically suffer severe visual impairment. Of the 1 million blind people in the UK, 90% are late onset sufferers, principally of the unremediable condition macular degeneration. Similar proportions are severely hard of hearing.

Dementia is essentially a condition of old age, the incidence of which rises steeply with age and affects women more than men. Among those over 80, around 30% (Peters, 2001) suffer from dementia. With or without a diagnosis of dementia, the Berlin Ageing Study demonstrated that there is a high probability that intelligence and cognitive functioning will show decline during old age (Baltes, Staudinger, & Lindberger, 1999). As Margaret Baltes put it:

> even though the onset time and regulation of decline may differ across psychological domains, all domains will eventually exhibit some type of dysfunctionality and this may take the form of a cascade of decline. The Fourth Age would thus be characterised by a functional breakdown of the psychological system and less desirable psychological profiles (e.g., loss of positive wellbeing, psychological dependence on others, poor memory and impaired reasoning).
>
> (Baltes, 1998)

Depression is the epidemic condition of old age, although only 15–20% receive any treatment (Anderson & Krishnamoorty, 2012). It affects women twice as frequently as men and multiplies the impact of co–morbid conditions like angina, asthma, diabetes and dementia.

The prevalence of incontinence is less well documented, but studies show it affects levels of over one third of older people in the later stages of life (Chrome et al., 2001). It increases with age and most rapidly in the eighth decade. As well as being distressing and uncomfortable, incontinence is frequently precipitated by other medical conditions, such as stroke and diabetes (Harari, 2012).

As these debilitating conditions come in clusters, rather than on their own, they produce patterns of illness which make everyday life for the very old a struggle and a challenge for their careers (Johnson, 2013). As a consequence, the colloquial term "Frailty" has been adopted by the British Geriatrics Society as a technical diagnostic descriptor.

Trajectories of Dying

Lynn and Adamson (2003), having analysed huge Medicare datasets in the US, concluded that "One useful way of envisioning care for elderly people who are sick enough to die, follows from classifying them into three groups, using the trajectory of decline over time that is characteristic of each major type of disease or disability. Each trajectory corresponds to a different rhythm and set of priorities in care" (Lynn & Adamson, 2003, p. 142).

The three categories are depicted as follows.

Trajectory One: Short period of evident decline – typical of cancer.

Most patients with malignancies maintain comfort and functioning for a substantial period. However, once the illness becomes overwhelming, the patient's status usually declines quite rapidly in the final weeks and days preceding death.

Trajectory Two: Long-term limitations with intermittent exacerbations and sudden dying – typical of organ system failure.

Individuals in this category often live for a relatively long time and may have only minor limitations in everyday life. From time to time, some physiological stress overwhelms the body's reserves and leads to a worsening of serious symptoms. Patients survive a few such episodes but then die from a complication or exacerbation, often rather suddenly. For such patients, say Lynn and Adamson (2003), "on-going disease management, advance care planning, and [the provision of] services to the home are key to optimal care." *Trajectory Three: Prolonged dwindling – typical of dementia, disabling stroke, and frailty.*

Those who escape cancer and organ system failure are likely to die at older ages of either neurological failure (such as Alzheimer's or other dementia) or generalized frailty of multiple body systems. This large group of patients require supportive services at home, like meals on wheels, home help, regular nursing and then skilled palliative nursing. For many, care homes become the best option where round-the-clock care, every day, is standard and necessary.

Analyses of Medicare claims in the US, showed that about one fifth of those who die have a course consistent with the first trajectory (mostly cancer patients); another fifth share the course of the second group (mostly organ system failure patients); and two-fifths follow the third course (frailty/dementia). The last one-fifth of those who die are largely those whose deaths are sudden.

The group that needs the greatest attention currently receives the least. Those whom Lynn and Adamson tellingly, though inelegantly, label as experiencing "prolonged dwindling" are the ones whose last lap is often painful and depressing for the individual and exhausting for their (often elderly) care-givers. It goes on for too long. Confined to the house, and

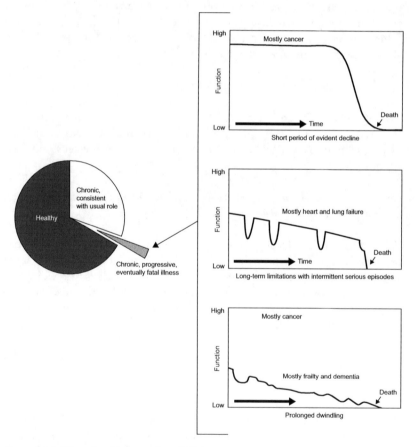

Figure 11.1 Changing Trajectories of Dying
Source: Adapted from Lynn &Adamson (2003)

with little to stimulate them, these older people deserve spiritual as well as functional care. This greatly disabled group are given detailed attention in Lynn, et al. (2008).

In a recent study of Care Homes in southern England, Ennis (2015) presents his findings in a manner which reflects the dwindling trajectory and its growing presence. Out of thirty-eight nursing care homes which took part in the study, (comprising 2444 individual residents) half of all residents fell into this category.

Spirituality in Late Life

So much of the consideration about the end of life relates to the essentials of personal humane care, maintenance of the body in ways which are known to be good practice and the management of physical pain. It has long been part of these conversations and writings to speak of care of the whole person and to stress the need for spiritual care. In practice the spiritual elements remain at the bottom of the list. Perhaps this is because the concept of spirituality remains difficult to encapsulate. In addition, it is also pushed down the priority list because of the dominance of instrumental tasks. Also because there is a lack of training. Where there are chaplains, as there are in hospitals and hospices and some care homes, the deeper questions of life and death are mostly left to them. Chaplains fulfil an important role in health and social care settings. But spiritual care also requires a culture of non-judgemental listening which includes all staff (Albans & Johnson, 2013).

Research and thinking about spirituality in later old age is under developed, though there has been an upsurge of interest in recent years. A recent volume titled *Spiritual Dimensions of Ageing* (Johnson & Walker, 2016) provides a range of approaches across several disciplines and nations. It demonstrates serious inquiry into the character of an intensified concern with inner meaning and life review as spiritual quests, among those who face the ending of their long lives. In the opening chapter, the leading American writer and gerontologist Robert Atchley writes:

> The essence of spirituality is the capability to experience pure being, an intense sense of presence, unadulterated by concepts, language, and other elements of culture. Pure being is often experienced as inner space, silence, stillness, or peace. It is through the experience of pure being that people report being most likely to experience union with the ground of being. The experience of pure being is a vantage point from which we can see the spiritual aspects of all other experiences.
>
> The existential aspect of ageing brings an increased awareness of the finitude of each human life and invites reflection on the deeper meaning of our existence. Not only are people aware of their own ageing

and death, but also they observe the ageing and deaths of older generations in their families. Perhaps more than any other stimulus, encounters with the reality and inevitability of death invite grappling with the great meaning questions that have confronted and confounded philosophers and theologians for thousands of years. Who are we really, and why are we here? Why do we have this life and consciousness? How are we related to the universe? For a large majority of ageing people throughout the world, these questions are invitations to begin, or dig deeper into a spiritual journey (Atchley, 2016)

Elizabeth MacKinlay's Australian based research has produced as series of universal spiritual tasks. In explaining them she writes:

> The task of finding final life meaning is only likely to occur as people become aware of their own mortality, whether it is through the process of increased awareness of growing older, through some major relational loss or through a life-threatening illness. Through the life journey, until this occurs, often people pay little attention to life's meaning. Viktor Frankl describes this search and finding of final life meanings by saying that as we journey through life, we lay down provisional meanings of events, but it is only as we become aware of our own mortality that we begin to process the events of our lives, to come to final meaning. (MacKinlay, 2016)

Some of these biographical reflections, self-evaluations set against models of good and righteous living, are set in questions like "What would my parents think of me?" and "How will God judge my life?" They may be causes of deep troubling anxieties. The author of this chapter has identified from his own research what he has called *Biographical Pain* (Johnson, 2009). This is defined as *the irremediable anguish which results from profoundly painful recollection of experienced wrongs which can now never be righted* when finitude or impairment terminates the possibility of cherished self-promises to redress deeply regretted actions.

> The presence of serious biographical pain is characterised by the surfacing of deeply buried fractures in the life biographies of individuals who always intended to 'put things right', but have now run out of capability to bring about that resolution. They will no longer be able to apologise, seek or give forgiveness, deliver restitution, deliver a good to balance out the bad for an evil act. The opportunity to redress wrongs has passed by and the individual is left with an overwhelming sense of guilt. (Johnson, 2016)

The point is to draw attention to the fact that pain at the end of life may well be the intolerable result of unheard and unassisted life review.

Addressing Spiritual Concerns as Finitude Presses

Coming to Terms With Who We Are

One important dimension of spirituality is the process of coming to terms with who you are, and what you have done in your life, as it comes to a close. This process of life review, given focus by Robert Butler (1963) over fifty years ago, is essentially a spiritual enterprise. Gerontologist and spirituality scholar Harry Moody in his book *The Five Stages of the Soul: Charting the Spiritual Passages That Shape Our Lives*, writes of "standing at the crossroads," the first of the Five Stages of the Soul:

> Wasn't life supposed to get better as the years pass? Didn't I do what I was supposed to: go to school, join the team, work hard, pay my dues? Now we are 34 years old. Or 40 years old. Or 59. And the years have given us neither the pleasure we assumed we'd get, nor the big payoffs we always dreamed about. Rewards and laurels may come from time to time, it's true, but the happiness they bring doesn't last long. There are peak moments, of course, and the stretches of sunshine. But why do they always seem over-shadowed by the gnawing sense of unfulfilment, the sameness of days? (Moody & Carroll, 1997)

Such experiences can bring to the fore all those unanswered questions about what you believe – or no longer believe.

The "Have I Been Good Enough?" Questions

Throughout our lives things go wrong. Other people treat us badly, dishonestly, cheatingly, violently, unlovingly. Their actions blemish and distort our lives. Can we and are we ready to forgive them?

Then there are the shameful things we have done. They live in our memories and tarnish our sense of wholeness. We feel guilt and sometimes anger. Can we put right those wrongs? Can we find absolution? Can we do some good to mitigate our past ill-deeds?

Can we forgive ourselves?

Trajectories of Life and Spirituality – Ages and Stages

Mention was made earlier of the preoccupation of reflective practitioners, researchers and writers to depict our progress through a set of problems, illnesses, pathologies or portions of life as a set of demarcated stages, each with its own characteristics, timescales and signals of recovery or of decline. Researchers of ageing and theologians who have written about spirituality have contributed to this body of literature. Over many years, maps of the journey, signalling the significant landmarks, have captured the professional and the popular imagination. For some conditions the patterns and sequences of symptoms are well evidenced as are the timescales. So monitoring and identifying significant changes is clearly good practice. It is a universal human need to have a sense of where we are going and to be able to tick off the markers of our passage, either to restoration of health or unwanted pathways towards death.

Indeed, Elizabeth Kubler-Ross's Five Stages of Dying, set out in her best-selling book *On Death and Dying* (1969), served not only to make it possible to talk more openly about the end of life, it instituted a sequence of stages which even today are – utterly inappropriately – taught as the appropriate way to die. Kubler-Ross's book was a most important publication: humane, full of insight and guidance for professionals and individuals. Yet its lessons were long misused by unthinking health professionals.

There is a huge appetite for recipes and formularies. In the field of spirituality there is no shortage of route maps. Some simply address the two halves of life, rough and ready demarcations, but others offer more elaborate schema. All of those noted below have been highly successful in making their mark on thinking and practice.

Carl Jung: The two halves of life: "The stages of life" in *The structure and dynamics of the psyche* (1970).
James Fowler: *Stages of faith: The psychology of human development and the quest for meaning* (1978).
Erik Erikson: Stages of psychosocial development in *Identity & the life cycle* (1959); *The life cycle completed* (1982)
Dan Levinson (et al.): *The Seasons of a Man's Life* (1978)
Harry Moody & David Carroll: *The Five Stages of the Soul* (1997)
Lars Tornstam: *Gerotranscendence: A developmental theory of positive aging* (2005)
Richard Rohr: Spirituality for the two halves of life in *Falling upward: A Spirituality of the two halves of life* (2011).

What remains in question is which of these imaginative approaches offers the most valuable guidance to personal explorers of their own inner lives and as frameworks for those who offer to assist others on their journeys. In the next section I present selected accounts drawn from the Spiritual Development in Later Life Study, along with some observations about how individuals appear to go about the serious business of distilling what they believe and how they match up to their templates of worthy living. These personal statements are from people in the Third Age, and not from the oldest old as earlier parts of this chapter have focused on. But they offer a picture of the spiritual work many have already done before finitude and the imminent prospect of death has settled on their lives.

Templeton:
Spiritual Trajectories of Older Congregants

Merril Silverstein and Vern Bengtson as principal investigators on the Templeton funded Spiritual Development and Aging Study have concluded:

Religiosity in later life is characterized more by stability than by change among baby boomers in their transition to later life.

Increased religiosity is motivated by personal growth, a desire for spirituality, challenges and losses, and societal concerns (Silverstein & Bengtson, 2017).

Across the survey data from their 585 respondents questioned over 45 years, these findings are instructive because they contribute to the ongoing debate about whether religious identity and affiliation grow or decline in later life. But the greater detail that derives from their over 100 extended interviews with congregants of faith communities and the clergy that lead them (Bengtson et al., Chapter 1 in this volume) about beliefs and spirituality are more telling. They tell stories which reveal a diversity of ways in which the majority who sustain their identity as believers, adopt a range of re-formulations of what they were taught and accepted earlier in life.

My interpretation from reading many of these transcripts is that there is certainly a sustained engagement with religious beliefs, but they have been put though the filter of life experience. On the one hand they have been refined to exclude what were previously clergy-declared belief requirements that have lost theological salience or social disapprobation, eg. divorce, contraception, same sex relationships, notions of the devil as the embodiment of evil and hell as a post death punishment for sinful living. On the other hand, there is an enduring engagement with basic ideas of living a good life that will be acceptable "when I meet God." There is affirmation of Coleman's (2009) observation that that religion is the bulwark of many older people, providing a framework for life.

There is extensive literature examining such themes as the quest for meaning and purpose, grappling with the inner self, how spirituality is conceived and operates, grappling with the inner self and more. These themes are extensively addressed in Johnson and Walker (2016). In that volume Joanna Walker (2016) adopts a characterization of *adult spiritual learners,* a modified version of which is employed below.

Adult Learners

This group includes those who are interested in spirituality as an aspect of self-development and conscious ageing. It also includes those who are reflecting deeply as a result of trauma or loss or other challenging life circumstances as well as those whose capacity for active learning has become limited through greater old age or disability. It also includes those who have left faith communities to pursue their own path

Non-engaged Learners

These are individuals who are not specifically aware of spiritual learning but, if asked, could identify understanding or behaviours that served a spiritual purpose for them (e.g. appreciation of nature, music, art, service to others, sense of personal quest etc.). This includes those who may hold more or less coherent views about the meaning of life but who take no evident actions to gain further information or insight. They may hold untested views influenced by mass media, parental or family mythologies, cultural or sub-cultural cosmologies, or based on positions learned at school, church or faith community, often in earlier life.

Active Learners:

In this group are those who have entered the 'spiritual learning pathway.' actively pursuing spiritual understanding or practices through formal studies; attendance at courses (with or without resulting credentials/qualifications), study days, summer schools, theological classes and engagement in spiritual movements. A notable sub-set of people in membership of faith communities fall into this category, but there are many others seeking beliefs, or holding none, who are also serious explorers.

Self-directed Learners

These learners are interested in and think about spiritual matters but do it in self-directed ways and not necessarily with others. They may develop their understanding of spirituality by focused reading of specialist literature in the form of books, magazines, blogs, websites or through broadcast media such as radio, television and films. Increasingly, there are interactive and lifestyle-based e-communities, which may offer communication with others, but essentially still enable individual control of the learning journey.

What these categories do not offer is anything which identifies the disposition of interviewees to examine the inner meaning of their lives, either based on their experiences as churchgoers or in terms of life review. The following are examples drawn from the Spiritual Development in Later Life Study (Chapters 1 in this volume). Some individuals, like James L., age 74, are "active learners," serious explorers of their own beliefs, in intensive reading and discussion in groups and in regular prayer.

James L. attends church services weekly. He attends a Bible study at church in addition. He's a part of a men's Bible study in Hartford, a city 1,500 away, even though he lives in Santa Barbara. He Skypes with the other members who are in Hartford. They Skype once a week. He also uses his computer for the Logos software, a Bible study program that he does every morning. He's also a part of a once-a-week book study group at his retirement community that reads books related to the spiritual realm. *Finding Calcutta* is an example of one of the books they have read. He takes some leadership roles, notably in the group Skype Bible study.

Over time James L. feels that his religious involvement has increased, largely because he has more time now that he is cutting back on his working hours. The most notable change in his religious practices has been his daily devotions using the computer software called Logos. It's a Bible study program that has a lot of support materials including translations from Greek, etc. It also has books that are recommended reading. James gets up every morning, about 6:15, and spends an hour studying on the computer and praying,

Another example is Allen G. (age 93). At a lower level Allan increased his involvement in church after his wife died and has found himself enwrapped in the life of the church. As this includes choir and other activities, he has become more reflexive in ways that are shaped by the church community in which he is engaged but not in a way that could be called deeply spiritual. We might call it "Religious Acculturation." The atmosphere of discussion draws him in and gives him a sense of better knowing who he is as a faith based person. But nothing too deep.

Still a different pattern is exemplified by Susan G. (age 80). Susan has a long history of being in the church, singing in the choir for 30 years. But when asked about spirituality, says she doesn't "buckle down." She talks about her own private reflections and concerns about what there might be after death. She doesn't give a high estimation of this thinking and demurs about whether it is properly spiritual. Susan is typical of many members of faith communities who give regular thought to the meanings of life, death and personhood, but find it hard to distil their beliefs. As a consequence, they avoid "heavy" theological discussions for fear of being "found out."

These are the "Quiet Strugglers," who can be found in the active membership of all churches. Because they remain unsure when they think others have got their beliefs sorted out, they remain stuck with ideas that may have rattled round in their heads for years. Lynn B. (age 74), for example, described God as "the source of everything – energy – a changeless thing. Acting in everything." She said she feels the presence of God "when something unexpected or undeserved comes about. Tears start running down my cheeks. I have a sense of fullness, of possibility, of protection that things have meaning." What does spiritual mean to her? "I am a seeker after God." What does religious mean? "Serving the outward forms, ideas about God." She had a conversion experience as she describes it, when she was three years old, and her mother asked her, "Do you want to ask Jesus to come into your heart?" She says that she has increased her spiritual involvement since retirement, but that she would have to separate spiritual from religious. She is losing patience with religious things. She has become less active in a leadership role than she was earlier. In terms of other changes that she's noticed, "I'm more patient with other people spiritually, knowing what a long road I have taken." She has been highly active in her church, but she has decreased her activity. Her spiritual life, however, has remained high and perhaps has increased.

Others take themselves off to other churches to find a set of beliefs and ecclesiologies that are closer to their pattern of uncertainties. Unitarianism sometimes fills this space, because its theology is less doctrinal and less demanding of supernatural belief. In a way these individuals are "Trading Down" to a level of faith and belief which is more secular and less expectant. There is a parallel with Orthodox Jews who move to Liberal Synagogues. There they find a place to be religious and explore their faith, but where the bar is not set so high.

Death in Old Age is Different

These circumstances are new experiences in the collective sense, and society is ill prepared for them. Reminiscence in the face of finitude is not new, but those who encounter death without the vocabulary of spirituality or the rituals of faith communities (including forgiveness and absolution) are less well equipped than were earlier generations. Profound anguish on the last lap of life could leave many in deep depression and unshared biographical pain. The sort of accompanying by non-judgemental "chaplains" or counsellors (trained or instructed laypersons), along with formal learning opportunities to prepare them, will become increasingly required, if epidemics of silently distraught older people are to be avoided. Learning how to know and resolve your past life may well become a new zone of engagement for older people.

Conclusions

Life review and biographical reflection intensify in late old age, often prompted by awareness of finitude. Dying predominantly occurs at later ages than ever before. There is increasing evidence of the significance of spiritual preoccupation and re-assessment of religious engagement. Changing patterns of co-morbidities in the Fourth Age have altered the trajectories of dying, making painful and undignified "long dwindling" the predominant end of life pathway.

The spiritual and religious dimensions of late life deserve more attention from researchers as well as health care practitioners. The inner lives of old people are just as important as maintaining their physical wellbeing.

As Atul Gawande observes: "The waning days of our lives are given over to treatments that addle our brains and sap our bodies for a sliver's chance of benefit .... And what if there are better approaches, right in front of our eyes, waiting to be recognized?" (Gawande, 2014).

References

Albans, K., & Johnson, M. L. (Eds.) (2013). *God, Me and the Very Old: Stories and Spirituality.* London: SCM Press.

Ammerman, N. T. (2014). *Sacred Stories, Spiritual Tribes: Finding Religion in Everyday Life.* Oxford: Oxford University Press.

Anderson, J. & Krishnamoorty, D. (2012). Depression. In M. Gosney, A. Harper, & S. Conroy. (Eds.). *Oxford Desk Reference: Geriatric Medicine.* Oxford: Oxford University Press. pp. 272–274.

Atchley, R. C. (2016). Spirituality and aging: Yesterday, today, and tomorrow. In M. Johnson and J. Walker (Eds.). *Spiritual Dimensions of Ageing.* Cambridge: Cambridge University Press, 13–31.

Baltes, M. M. (1998). The psychology of the oldest old: the fourth age. *Current Opinion in Psychiatry,* 11, 411–415.

Baltes, P., Staudinger, U. & Lindberger, H. (1999). Lifespan psychology: Theory and application to intellectual functioning. *Annual Review of Psychology,* 50: 471–507.

Bengtson, V. L., with Putney, N. M., & Harris, S. C. (2013). *Families and Faith: How Religion is Passed down the Generations.* Oxford: Oxford University Press.

Bengtson, V. L., Silverstein, M., Putney, N. M. & Harris, S. C. (2015). Does religiousness increase with age? Age changes and generational differences over time. *Journal for the Scientific Study of Religion,* 34(2), 363–379.

Butler, R. N. (1963). The life review. *Psychiatry,* 26, 655–676.

Chrome, P., Smith, A. E., Withnall, A., & Lyons, R. A., (2001). Urinary and faecal incontinence: Prevalence and status. *Reviews in Clinical Gerontology,* 11(2), 109–113.

Cole, T. (1992). *The journey of Life: A Cultural History of Aging in America.* Cambridge: Cambridge University Press.

Coleman, P. (2009). Ageing and personhood in twenty-first century Europe; a challenge to religion. *International Journal of Public Theology,* 3(1), 63–77.

Ennis, L., (2015). The cost of providing end of life care for nursing care home residents: a retrospective cohort study. *Health Services Management Research,* 28(1–2), 16.

Erikson, E. H. (1959). *Identity and the Life Cycle: Selected Papers.* New York: International Universities Press.

Erikson, E. H. (1982). *The Life Cycle Completed.* New York: Norton.

Fowler, J. (1981). *Stages of Faith: The Psychology of Human Development and the Quest for Meaning.* London: Harper & Row.

Gawande, A. (2014). *Being Mortal: Illness, Medicine, and What Matters at the End.* London: Profile Books.

Harari, H. (2012). Faecal incontinence in older people. In M. Gosney, A. Harper, & S. Conroy (Eds.), *Oxford Desk Reference: Geriatric Medicine* (pp. 318–322). Oxford: Oxford University Press.

Haywood, D. R., & Krause, N. (2013a). Changes in church-based social support relationships during older adulthood. *Journal of Gerontology: Social Sciences,* 68b, 1, January, 85–96.

Haywood, D. R., & Krause, N. (2013b). Trajectories of late-life change in God-mediated control. *Journal of Gerontology: Psychological Sciences,* 68b, 1, January, 49–58.

Johnson, M. L. (2009). Spirituality, finitude and theories of the lifespan. In V. L. Bengtson, D. Gans, N. M. Putney & M. Silverstein (Eds.), *Handbook of Theories of Aging* (pp. 659–674). New York: Springer, 2nd ed.

Johnson, M. L. (2013). The changing face of ageing and old age. In K. Albans, & M. Johnson (Eds.), *God, Me and Being Very Old*. London: SCM Press, 3–19.

Johnson, M. L. (2016). Spirituality, biographical review and biographical pain at the end of life in old age. In M. Johnson and J. Walker (Eds.). *Spiritual Dimensions of Ageing* (pp. 198–214). Cambridge: Cambridge University Press.

Johnson, M. L., & Walker, J. (Eds.) (2016). *Spiritual Dimensions of Ageing*. Cambridge: Cambridge University Press.

Jung, C. (1970). The stages of life. In *The Structure and Dynamics of the Psyche*: Volume 8, *The Collected Works of C. G. Jung* (pp. 387–403). Princeton, NJ: Princeton University Press, 2nd ed.

Kubler-Ross, E. (1969). *On Death and Dying*. New York: Simon & Schuster/ Touchstone.

Laslett, P. (1989). *A Fresh Map of Life: The Emergence of the Third Age*. London: Weidenfeld and Nicolson.

Levinson, D. J. with Darrow, N. D., Klein, E. B., Levinson, M. H., & McKee, B. (1978). *The Seasons of a Man's Life*. New York: Ballantine Books.

Lynn, J., & Adamson, D. M. (2003). *Living Well at the End of Life: Adapting Health Care to Serious Chronic Illness in Old Age*. Santa Monica: Rand, available online at https://goo.gl/ap5gZi

Lynn, J., Lynch Schuster, J., Wilkinson, A., & Noyes Simon, L., (2008). *Improving Care for the End of Life: A Sourcebook for Healthcare Managers and Clinicians*, 2nd ed.

MacKinlay, E. (2016). Ageing and spirituality across faiths. In M. Johnson and J. Walker (Eds.). *Spiritual Dimensions of Ageing* (pp. 32–50). Cambridge: Cambridge University Press.

Moody, H. R., & Carroll, D. (1997). *The Five Stages of the Soul: Charting the Spiritual Passages that Shape our Lives*. New York: Doubleday.

Oeppen, J., & Vaupel, J. W. (2002). Broken limits of life expectancy. *Science*, 296 (5570), 1029–1031.

Office for National Statistics. (2015). *Death Registrations in England and Wales, Summary Tables*, available at: https://goo.gl/murcrr

Office for National Statistics. (2016). *Mortality, 2014-based National Population Projections Reference Volume*. (March, 2016). London: Office for National Statistics.

Pew Research Center. (2015). *Religious Landscape Study*. www.pewresearch.org

Peters, R., (2001). The prevention of dementia. *Journal of Cardiovascular Risk*, 8, 253–256.

Putnam, R. D., & Campbell, D. E. (2010). *American Grace: How Religion Divides and Unites Us*. New York: Simon & Schuster.

Rohr, R. (2011). *Falling Upward: A Spirituality of the Two Halves of Life*. San Francisco: Jossey-Bass.

Ruth, K., & Verne, J. (2010). *Deaths in Older Adults in England*. National End of Life Intelligence Network, London: Public Health England.

Silverstein, M. & Bengtson, V. L. (2017). Return to religion? Predictors of religious change among baby boomers in their transition to later life. *Journal of Population Ageing*, 6(3), doi:10.1007/s12062-12017-9216-0.

Tornstam, L. (2005). *Gerotranscendence: A Developmental Theory of Positive Aging*. New York: Springer.

Walker, J. (2016). Spiritual development in later life: a learning experience. In M. L. Johnson, & J. Walker (Eds.). *Spiritual Dimensions of Ageing* (pp. 249–269). Cambridge: Cambridge University Press.

Wuthnow, R. (2005). *America and the Challenges of Religious Diversity*. Princeton: Princeton University Press.

Chapter 12

Stages on Life's Way
Life Review Through Dreams

Harry R. Moody

FIELDING GRADUATE UNIVERSITY

> We live life forwards, but understand it backwards.
>
> (Kierkegaard)

> Your young shall see visions and your old ones shall dream dreams.
>
> (Joel 2:28)

Our nightly dreams can be a powerful vehicle for life-review, but we have largely failed to look at dreams in this way. From its initial formulation by Robert Butler (1963) the concept of life-review has been focused on reminiscence as conscious activity: for example, in autobiography, memoir, story-telling, or reverie (Coleman, 1989; Webster & Haight, 2002).

Guided autobiography has become an important and recognized practice in aging (Birren & Cochran, 2001). With few exceptions (Magee, 2008), life-review has not been applied to night dreams. Yet there is reason to believe that later-life dreams involve the same dynamics described by theorists about life-review.

Dreams of life-review can involve a spiritual or existential dimension – for example addressing the question, what is the ultimate meaning of my life (Moody, 2005)? This search for meaning is the great task of later life, especially in our dreams, as the poet W.B. Yeats put it so well: "I lie awake night after night, and never get the answers right." (written three months before he died, in "The Man and the Echo") (Yeats, 1939/1969). We are now at a point where questions of spirituality and aging can be considered in ways that go beyond prevailing treatments of religion and aging, which are, namely, behavior or belief (Atchley, 2009). Considering the role of life-review and spirituality in dreams can open up new ways of understanding the search for meaning in the last stage of life.

In his pivotal article on life review, Robert Butler (1963), writing against prevailing views at the time, insisted that reminiscence in later life was not just a "sentimental journey" or an omen of senility. On the contrary, reminiscence, Butler argued, is a way of reviewing the events of our lives and finding meaning in them. While Butler never pushed his work in the direction of spiritual concerns or of dreams, we need to appreciate the possible spiritual dimensions of life-review, which can be traced to the origins of autobiographical consciousness itself (Olney, 1981; Eakin, 2008). Autobiography itself can be recognized as a form of spiritual practice in later life (Staude, 2005). Indeed, the first great work of autobiography was St. Augustine's *Confessions*, itself a spiritual life-review, carried out not in old age but in midlife. The book was completed around 400 CE, when Augustine was 46 years old (Conybeare, 2016).

Dreams of life-review are those dreams when, as Butler put it, we try to come to terms with everything that has happened to us and to make sense of our lives. In the process, we may discover a past that was never lost. Existential psychiatrist Medard Boss (1958) put it this way: "This repetition of the entire past of the dreamer could never have happened, even in the dream if any detail of the real past, however small, were ever truly lost. In fact, no action, no experience, no event is ever lost." Boss advocated a phenomenological approach to dreams, an approach that owes much to the father of modern phenomenology, philosopher Edmund Husserl, who was the teacher of Martin Heidegger. Boss distrusted any clear-cut separation between so-called manifest and latent dream meanings, such as Freud and Jung might advocate. Instead, he favored probing dream imagery in such a way that dreamers could discover for themselves the authentic meaning of their dreams. As my colleague Velva Lee Heraty (2014) put it so well: "The dream belongs to the dreamer."

Life-Review Dreams in Films

Before turning to some actual dreams of life-review, I want to put forward two fictional examples that illustrate some key points as a paradigm case. I begin with two widely known examples of life-review in late life dreams: the novel (and film) of Charles Dickens' *A Christmas Carol* and Swedish Director Ingmar Bergman's *Wild Strawberries*. Both have as their central feature a hero whose entire life is reshaped by dreams of life-review with a spiritual or existential dimension.

The case of Ebenezer Scrooge in Dickens' novel is the story of an old man whose sleep is disturbed by the ghosts of Jacob Marley warning that Scrooge that night will be visited by three ghostly messengers: the ghost of Christmas past, present, and future. In these three dream episodes, Scrooge engages in a life-review where he confronts his own past, along with all the guilt and regret that he feels. In the present time, Christmas present, Scrooge sees the lives of people around him, lives otherwise invisible to him. The ghost of Christmas future gives him a glimpse of his own tombstone: a message of mortality, which prompts Scrooge's painful question: "Is it too late for me?" Dickens' answer is, no, it is not too late, and he portrays Scrooge waking up a changed man. We should note here that it is the awareness of mortality that proves to be the critical trigger for life-review, as Butler himself recognized (Butler, 2002).

Geriatric psychiatrist Gene Cohen wrote a powerful treatment of the Scrooge story in which he analyzes Scrooge as a case of later-life depression (Cohen, 1993). Joseph Clarke (2009), working along similar lines, sees the story in terms of spiritual transformation, or what he regards as the metapsychology of character change. From a spiritual point of view, we might also note that during his night dreams of life-review, Scrooge moves through what I have called the *Five Stages of the Soul* (Moody, 1997): namely, *Call, Search, Struggle, Breakthrough* and *Return* (Moody, 2015).

My second example is the landmark film of 1957 *Wild Strawberries* (Archer, 1959), arguably the greatest film ever made about life-review. It has been hailed as the masterpiece of Swedish Director Ingmar Bergman, and is repeatedly cited on critics' lists of the ten greatest films ever made (French & French, 1995). Dreams have often appeared in film (Halpern, 2003). The message and meaning about life-review in *Wild Strawberries* is conveyed by powerful dreams experienced by the hero of the film, Prof. Isak Borg, played by silent film director Victor Sjöström. In the film Prof. Borg is an academic physician who experiences a deep reminiscence through dreams during a single day's drive with his daughter-in-law as they travel to the city of Lund, where the doctor is to receive an honorary degree, celebrating his 50 years of medical practice.

As he travels on the journey, Prof. Borg is accompanied by his daughter-in-law and the by various passengers picked up along the way. The day's journey becomes a mirror of "the journey of life" as Prof. Borg has a series of dreams in which he reviews pivotal moments of his life. A moment of climax in the very first of Prof. Borg's dreams comes when he is grabbed by a hand extending from a coffin and then sees that the face of the body is actually his own. This image is not unprecedented in the literature of depth psychology. For example, dream researcher E. Hartmann reports that one of his subjects, a Vietnam veteran who had the traumatic experience of identifying dead soldiers in one instance unexpectedly discovered a close friend in one of the body bags. He later had recurrent nightmares, reflecting post-traumatic stress disorder (Hartmann, 1998).

Ingmar Bergman claimed that he created the dream sequence in *Wild Strawberries* exactly as he had experienced it in his own dreams. About his own dreams, Bergman (Bjorkman et al., 1970) said "Yes, now and again, when they come in handy. Sometimes while I'm dreaming I think: 'I'll remember this, I'll make a film of it' — it's a sort of occupational disease." Interestingly enough, *Wild Strawberries* was made when Bergman was in his thirties. It is in essence, a mid-life product, anticipating the life-review of old age (Cohen-Shalev, 1992).

Erikson (2017) in "A Life History: Revisitation and Reinvolvement," has provided his own synopsis of Bergman's film, drawing closely on the screenplay for the film (Malmstrom & Kushner, 1960). Erikson has interpreted that film in terms of his stages of the human life cycle (Erikson, 1978). As in other modes of life-review, *Wild Strawberries* involves a "return of the repressed," as Freud would put it. Some of these reach back to childhood; others to Prof. Borg's marriage; and still others are intergenerational conflicts visible in Prof. Borg's son and daughter-in-law. But by the end of the film the conflicts are resolved in wonderful images of childhood recalled by the doctor as he falls asleep – a happy ending unusual in Bergman's films and a memorable visual image of ego-integrity in the last stage of life (Richter, 1986; Kettell, 2001).

Death and Life-Review

We have seen that the first of Prof. Borg's dreams involves realization of mortality, which is arguably the trigger for the whole sequence of life-review dreams that follow in the film. In a similar way, we can see a version of life-review in this dream of a 60-year old woman two months before dying:

> FINAL EXAMINATION
> [In the dream] she had entered the hereafter. There was a class going on, and various deceased women friends of hers sat on the front bench. An atmosphere of general expectation prevailed. She looked around for a teacher or lecturer, but could find none. Then it became plain that she herself was the lecturer, for immediately after death people had to give accounts of the total experience of their lives…

The experience of being asked to give an account of one's life matches closely with what is described, in *The Tibetan Book of the Dead*, as the experience of the consciousness after death during the interval known as *bardo* between death and rebirth (Evans-Wentz, 1927). The "Final Examination" dream recalls the memorable, and terrifying, scene in *Wild Strawberries* where the aged Dr. Isak Borg is led into an auditorium and given an academic examination by a stern looking man. Borg, a medical doctor of great professional distinction, fails the test. It turns out that he is unable to identify a specimen in the microscope nor can he decipher the meaning of obscure words on the blackboard. Then, ominously, this good doctor is called upon to examine an unconscious woman patient. Prof. Borg sternly and confidently declares her to be dead. Yet just a moment later the woman wakes up and begins to laugh at him in a mocking voice. The examining inquisitor asks Professor Borg "What is a doctor's first duty?" but Borg cannot answer. "A doctor's first duty," the inquisitor reminds him, "is to ask for forgiveness." Each step along the way Prof. Borg, the distinguished physician, has failed that examination and is finally judged incompetent.

So, too, in the dream "Final Examination" we are presented with an image of the Last Judgment similar to what we find in the Tibetan book of the dead or in more esoteric versions of Western religions. Similar motifs appear in the dreams of those near death (Goelitz, 2007; Bulkeley & Bulkeley, 2006; Kerr et al., 2014). In Prof. Borg's case, a group is assembled in the classroom, reuniting the deceased. The dreamer is telling herself how the soul after death is not judged by God but rather that we judge ourselves: "after death people had to give accounts of the total experience of their lives." As in Prof. Borg's case, it takes a while before the woman grasps what this after death judgment (and punishment) actually means.

"Final Examination" is an anticipation of the afterlife but it is also a message for the living in the spirit of the Sufi aphorism "Die before you die." For both this dreamer and for the "wounded healer" Prof. Borg, we see that the process of life-review takes place not in words or a narrative about the past but in images that reflect the deepest level of the psyche. Life-review unfolds in dreams that call upon us to confront unresolved questions about the ultimate meaning of our lives.

Myron Glucksman (2007) reports the dream of an older woman coming to the end of her professional career who had the following dream, reflecting life-review:

WHAT HAVE I ACCOMPLISHED?
I was with a group of young teachers. They asked me what I had accomplished in my career. I couldn't answer. I felt inadequate, fat, and old. Then I saw an old woman sitting on some steps. She couldn't walk or speak and I felt sorry for her.

The dreamer here has represented her inner state vividly in the dream. With the coming of age, we look back on our lives and wonder, what did it all mean? The dreamer here replies "I couldn't answer." In this dream the old woman sitting on the steps represents herself as one who cannot walk or speak. But the outcome is not entirely negative. The images evoke empathy, and the dreamer feels sorry for the old woman sitting on the steps. Glucksman reports that after this dream the dreamer began to understand why she was so depressed. She was motivated toward more positive reminiscence about her life and career, thinking about past accomplishments, and considering what she might still be capable of contributing to the world.

My Life as a Story

Isak Dinesan said "All the sorrows can be borne if you can put them into a story (as quoted in Arendt, 1998)." In life-review, we tell and retell our life story to ourselves, whether consciously or in our dreams. Dreams of life-review can come not only in old age but at critical ages of transition in adult development, as we have seen in the mid-life case of St. Augustine's *Confessions*. A mid-life example is Bolton Anthony's (2016) dream of life-review prompted in the year he turned 50, the age of eligibility for AARP membership. Anthony's life was at a low point when the following dream came to him:

REWRITING THE SCRIPT

I am a screenwriter who has been asked by a film producer to help rescue a project he fears has become hopelessly bogged down. I'm under some obligation to return a favor. I also know and have admired the director's earlier work, though he is an old man now, and many years have lapsed since his last film.

I follow him about the set during the day. Those times when he talks to me about the film, I find that I am not listening so much to what he is saying as gathering an impression of who he is.

He is inviting me to come into his house. Perhaps he senses that I find the bare, constricted space of the courtyard oppressive, because he tells me how lovely his home is and that his beautiful wife is waiting inside to welcome me. But I am following my own thoughts and interrupt him.

"I have decided I will work with you," I tell him. "I'll rewrite those scenes where I think there are problems and make my best case for the changes. If – after you've looked thoughtfully at my suggestions – you still think things should be handled differently; then I'll write it however you wish." I thought, but did not say: Because I trust you. Because I trust that you know where this needs to go.

This dream suggests reflection on the importance of life-story as a dimension of life-review and adult development: the domain of "narrative gerontology" (Kenyon et al., 2011; Morgan, 2002). Just as in this dream, we are all, like Bolton Anthony, "screenwriters" producing the narrative of our lives: "That's my story and I'm sticking to it," as the saying goes. But Bolton Anthony's story at first appears like his life is heading for a bad ending. He clearly needs help. The "film producer" in this dream represents a Higher Power, as does the "director." These are the agents, after all, the ones responsible for taking a good story, which is the screenwriter's work, and then making it into a good movie, which is the task of the producer. In dream, this "director" in his own psyche is "stuck," just as Bolton himself felt stuck in an uncertain career and an unfulfilling marriage.

This Higher Power in Bolton Anthony's life represents his own Ego Ideal: "someone whose work I knew and admired." Like Bolton, this director is aging – "getting on in years" – and is past his time of success. A key to this dream is the feeling that Bolton has when meeting with the director: he is engaged in "deep listening." Bolton identified the director in this dream with a figure Reb Zalman Schachter called "the elder within," or evolving future self whose wisdom and counsel can be sought. As Bolton Anthony put it, the director in his dream invites the dreamer into "the House of Later Life."

The scene shifts to the director's home, but the dreamer and the director are still standing in that "stark and spare" courtyard, in a mood of claustrophobia that represents where the dreamer's life has come to at the moment: seemingly, with no way out. This "courtyard" or vestibule to the interior life of the director, the Ego Ideal, is just as uninviting as the warm and receptive home would be.

Interestingly enough, the dreamer here never actually has to enter the home, the intimate space of this Higher Power. Just being on the threshold is enough for the breakthrough. In the culminating moment of the dream Bolton Anthony has decided to "rewrite" the story of his life, but he will not do it alone. In the years after this dream, he would be divorced and would change jobs. In the concluding episode in the dream he resolves to work together with the director. In this way the dreamer reclaims agency and responsibility for his life, rewriting "the scenes where I think there are problems." Through this dream he has come to learn to trust this director: "I'll write it however you wish." The final sentiment of the dream is a wonderful statement of ego integrity and hope in the future: "I trust that you know where this [film] needs to go."

As it turns out, that hope was fulfilled, a "dream come true," ten years later when Bolton Anthony met and married Lisa Munsat, who would become his wife: "In my dream a decade earlier, the director, my elder-in-waiting, had invited me into the House of Later Life. He had assured me that it was beautiful inside. But he'd said one other thing – that his beautiful wife waited to welcome me. And here she was." Sometimes our dreams, like a Hollywood movie, have a happy ending.

The Great Work

The medieval alchemists referred to their arcane art of transforming base metals into gold as "the Great Work." In psychological terms, alchemy denotes the process whereby we transform the base metals of our life experience into the more refined precious metal of wisdom (Linden, 2003). That transformation can happen through life-review as a spiritual practice, including life-review in dreams.

Robert King, at the end of his book *Autumn Years: Taking the Contemplative Path* (King & King, 2004) recounts a life-review dream prompted by thoughts about his own mortality, the same trigger we saw in the dreams of Prof. Borg. King began to have dreams about his mother when he realized it had been five years since her death and he wondered if he had fully acknowledged his own grief around her passing. Psychosomatic symptoms suggested to him that this might indeed be the case. Then, the night before he embarked on a meditation retreat, King had the following dream:

SITTING IN CHURCH

In the first part of the dream, I am trying to get to a wedding in the basement of a church, but the girl at the door won't admit me because I don't have a ticket. In the second part, I am directed upstairs and take a seat in the back row of a small, well-lit chapel. As I am sitting there, feeling uncomfortable, several large, open boxes containing grey-haired women laid out in formal attire pass slowly by.

King found this dream disturbing, and he notes that at first he connected the dream to his mother's funeral. He took note of the "wedding" and the presence of the female figure who would not admit him because he did not "have a ticket:" that is, he was inadequate in some respect. This pattern, and prominence of a feminine gate-keeper, suggested to him unreconciled issues of male and female connection, what Jungians describe as images of anima and animus.

But this psychological dimension is not the whole story of this dream. A Zen teacher subsequently pointed out to King that the first part of the dream, in the church, takes place underground, while the second part of the dream takes place in a chapel "upstairs" in the full light of day. Movement from underground to above ground seems to suggest a movement toward greater consciousness, with both parts of the dream in a sacred setting, church or chapel. In the final scene of the dream the dreamer is evidently uncomfortable as he witnessed the "grey-haired women" who were "laid out in formal attire" passing by, as in a funeral. This life-review dream in fact prompted Robert King to undertake a long contemplative automobile trip through many places he had lived earlier in his life. This journey – or sacred pilgrimage, as King himself put it – is something we have seen before in films such as *Wild Strawberries* or *The Trip to Bountiful*, both cases where an aging protagonist feels compelled to return to earlier places representing important stages of life.

In our contemporary world, there are many who have lost traditional religious faith but are searching for a new approach to life, perhaps guided by inspiration from earlier faith traditions. Their situation is addressed by Viktor Frankl in *Man's Search for Ultimate Meaning* (2000). Frankl said "Life is never made unbearable by circumstances, but only by lack of meaning and purpose." German philosopher Arthur Schopenhauer said that life is like a tapestry: we spend the first half of life weaving the fabric, and in the second half of life, we turn the carpet over and discover all the ways in which the threads are connected with one another. That activity of "turning the carpet over" is life-review. It can happen in our dreams, as in this dream of Genevieve Foster (Foster, 1985) at 76-years old, the same age as Dr. Isak Borg in *Wild Strawberries*:

HOMECOMING

I am with a group of people on a safari. The group has many sub-groups and I am affiliated with various family groups (my sister, her husband and children, my nephew, his wife and children, etc.) Our mission has a suprapersonal objective and I am happy to be there. Many of the group are unknown to me.

Since I am too old to take the whole trip, they will drop me off in _____ where I shall stay in my childhood home while they go forward.

When we reach _____, we hear there is some trouble with our bus connection and are advised to start walking, following the bus route so we can pick up the bus if it comes. As we walk, I decide I will not get on the bus at all since I am almost home now. The others can take the bus if it comes.

However, the whole party finally arrives at the old family home which is quite empty. My keys from the distant past do not open the door but I have foreseen that possibility and have designed two new keys to open the two locks on the door. The first key does not function well and I am worried, but the second key opens the door and I am home at last!

As the dream continues, the dreamer meets younger people, including a young man to whom she was attracted. At the end of the dream she remembers that she stands on the porch of "her home" watching the group of young people move on. Finally, I turn to enter the empty and very silent house and tears of reconciliation flow freely as I tell myself, "I am completely alone now but I have come home."

The final lines of this dream recall the great mystic philosopher Plotinus and the words of his masterpiece, *The Enneads*: "The flight of the alone to the Alone." Indeed, the whole of Neoplatonic philosophy can be expressed as a kind of homecoming, precisely the feeling with which Genevieve Foster's dream concludes. Her dream begins with a journey, a safari. Significantly, this trip includes personal ties, her family members, but the dream has a transpersonal mission. Just as in other dreams, we can assume, in the perspective of Gestalt psychology, that all characters in the dream are parts of the dreamer herself. Thus, some parts of the dreamer are waiting to take the bus: that is, waiting to receive support to complete the journey. Yet the dreamer herself understands herself to be "too old" for the whole trip. Yet, paradoxically, she is already "close to home."

The dreamer here, Genevieve Foster, was the author of *The World Was Flooded with Light*, a reminiscence of mystical experience which decisively shaped Foster's later life. As with Dr. Isak Borg, Foster's life-review is a story about a journey and homecoming. For Borg, life-review is a psychological journey which culminates in reconciliation with his estranged son and coming to peace with the memory of his deceased wife, who suffered too much in their marriage. For Foster, life-review is a spiritual journey and her homecoming dream is to arrive at a house (the self) which is empty and silent, just as the mystics describe Ultimate Reality in both Christian and Buddhist doctrine.

Prof. Borg's journey has a positive psychological reconciliation, while Genevieve Foster's reaches an intimation of spiritual transcendence. The duality between psychology and religion is one that deserves deeper reflection. It is sometimes addressed in dreams. For example, Viktor Frankl (2000) cites the case of a dream of a patient in therapy who, on her way to the psychiatrist's office, passed by a particular church. She would often think to herself that she was on her way to God, not through the church building she passed but instead through her psychotherapy appointment. Going to therapy was, in a sense, a "detour" to the church. Then in a dream she found herself entering that very same church she often used to pass by in waking life. Here is her dream:

THE DESERTED CHURCH

The church seems deserted. The church is entirely bombed out; the roof has fallen in, and only the altar remains intact. The blue heavens

Figure 12.1 The Deserted Church
Source: Adapted from Littledale "deserted" church, UK. Photo © John Darch
(cc-by-sa/2.0)

shine through here; the air is free. But above me is still the remainder of the roof, beams that threaten to fall down, and I am afraid of that. And I flee into the open, somewhat disappointed.

Frankl notes that the fact that the church in this dream seems deserted suggests that it is the dreamer who has deserted the church. The imagery of the dream begins to tell us why. Her familiar religious faith is portrayed in this dream as merely a shell, a structure that is "bombed out," with its "roof fallen in." "Only the altar remains intact." The altar, of course, is the center of spiritual life, where the divine mystery unfolds. Above this mysterious center is the path to what is transcendent symbolized by the "blue heavens" and the free air. Frankl suggests that the remaining beams of the structure threaten to fall down on this dreamer because she is afraid of once again being trapped in the debris of a religion that had become only a wrecked shell of what it is supposed to be. Religious institutions have proved disappointing to this dreamer: "I flee into the open, somewhat disappointed." Her disappointment is widely shared since the Catholic Church, like many other religious organizations, has had its share of scandals.

Yet this is this very same Church that has produced figures like John Paul II or Thomas Merton or Mother Theresa, in our own time, or Meister Eckhart and St. John of the Cross in earlier periods. For many sensitive souls during the stage of the spiritual Search, traditional religions can appear as mere wreckage, as in "The Deserted Church" dream. Interestingly, the dreamer in that case had actually experienced ecstatic mystical states. Frankl tells of another dream of where the same dreamer found herself standing in front of the main door of a great Cathedral, only to find that the door was closed. She continued: "In the Cathedral it is dark, but I know God is there." As that dream unfolded, the dream revealed other symbols of the Search: for example, the dreamer kept searching for an entrance into the Cathedral, then found herself looking through a small window, and again running through narrow passages, reminding us of the Gospel verse: "Straight is the gate and narrow the way that leads to Eternal Life."

Transcendence: The Light That Fills the World

The process of life-review, as we saw in the dream "Rewriting the Script," is not limited to old age. Dreams of life-review can come at times of transition and they can even be recurrent dreams. Whatever happens in confronting these voices in the self, there remains a deeper, even inescapable demand to "becoming the person we were meant to be," as Jung described as the process of individuation (Perera, 2013). This process is shown in the following dream, a recurrent dream of Helen Luke recorded in her autobiography, *Such Stuff as Dreams Are Made On* (Luke, 2000):

GOING ALONE

In my dream, I sat on a stone. It was an old milestone such as still exist, or existed in my youth, along many of the roads of England. They always fascinated me: ancient, grey, rounded at the top, telling the miles to the city. The stone of my dreams was a milestone set opposite the last house in a small town or village. It was dusk, the light was grey, the street was completely empty of life, and the windows of the houses were blank. Then an upper window in the house opposite me was thrown open and a hard-faced woman spoke to me in an icily cold voice. She pointed to the desolate road which stretched to my right away from the village. "Get out," she said, "go – you are forbidden to stay here." I looked along the road which ran on a sort of causeway and was lost in the mist, and I knew that I must walk along it alone. I woke in great fear.

Helen Luke's dream contains so many profound images of the life-course: above all, the image of milestones that mark the way through life. As the

Figure 12.2 Helen Luke
Source: Photo by the author. Apple Farm Community, 12291 Hoffman Road, Three Rivers, Michigan

dream opens, Luke sits on a stone, a powerful symbol of stability, the irreducible mineral substance of mother earth. She had always been fascinated by these milestones: for travelers they mark what Kierkegaard would call "stages on life's way." The stone she was sitting on is "set opposite the last house," the final point in the small town in which she was traveling.

"Going Alone" is a recurrent dream; it came to Helen Luke repeatedly, from youth through old age. The setting here is preternatural and uncanny: it is dusk, the light is grey, the street is completely empty. The image of the hard-faced woman is compelling. She delivers a message of departure: "Get out...you are forbidden to stay here." This is the message of individuation: you must go your own way to become an individual. This was the message that Kierkegaard, above all, understood, which is why he would sign his writings as the product of "That Individual."

Let me conclude this overview of dreams and life-review with another powerful dream recorded by Helen Luke, this time at age 78, in her journal (Luke, 2000).

COUNTRY HOUSE

In my dream I was standing outside a country house on a bright, sunny day. It was empty and had been completely repainted – a creamy white, inside and out. The doors stood wide. Someone who was showing it to me suggested I go over to it. I said, "I don't need to do that. I remember it very clearly, every room in it."

Then I remembered that this house (which was a small Georgian type, very gracious) was joined at the back to a much older, dark building; a corridor from the white house's upper story led to a series of rooms, also on two stories, almost like a warren – perhaps stables underneath. It was dark, Tudor-feeling – oak beams, etc.

I thought to myself, "I used to know those dark rooms too," but I could not remember them so clearly as the "white" house in the front, and I wondered if I should go through the latter and explore again those other rooms behind it. I seemed to know they were all clean and empty too, the whole place, front and back, awaiting a new tenant.

The house, as we know, is home, the place where we live. But is the house in this dream Helen Luke's own house, her very own self? The dreamer does not say. She remains detached from the house, a house that is both old and new, both empty and repainted. She has been invited to go into the house again, but she understands that she does not need to enter in at all. For Helen Luke, the process of life-review is already complete: "I remember it very clearly, every room in it."

The house, the self, is joined "at the back" "to a much older, dark building." Like the dark trap door in the labyrinth of my dream "Story Board," this dark building in Helen Luke's dream is somehow familiar to the dreamer. Like the owner of the story board in my dream, this part of ourselves is both known and unknown: familiar but unnamed. The clean and empty house is "awaiting a new tenant," who is the dreamer herself in a new condition, at present unimaginable.

We live on different levels of life. Life-review in dreams makes us understand that the "remembering" in our dreams operates with a different semantic or symbolic code, a form of mental life that Lacan has termed "the Imaginary," and which anthropologist Michele Stephen calls "the Imaginal Mind." In remembering and in narrating our dreams, as in Helen Luke's life and work, we see a bridging of the gap between waking consciousness and the imaginal mind.

Helen Luke's dream is a numinous instance of what Tornstam (2005), termed "gero-transcendence," of letting go of the past and even of everything we take to be ourselves (Moody, 2011). It is a dream of "becoming nobody," as Ram Dass (2001) put it in describing the existential purpose of later life. As in other dreams with the image of a house, the country house here symbolizes Luke's own life, which she knows so well she need not "go over" again, as we might do in some versions of life-review. What Luke cannot quite remember are the "dark rooms" in her house, rooms representing unknown aspects of the self, what the poet Rilke once called "the unlived lines of the body." Perhaps a deeper form of life-review is called for, since the rooms in this vast "house of the self" are now clean and empty, awaiting a "new tenant" in the form of some kind of transcendence.

Life-review, as a kind of autobiography, can include multiple psychological dimensions, such as confronting mortality, dealing with unresolved conflicts, and rewriting the script of my life. As we have seen in the very first autobiography, Augustine's *Confessions*, it can include a dimension of spiritual transcendence, whether in dialogue with organized religion, as in "The Deserted Church" or in the anticipation of inexpressible transcendence, as in "Country House."

Life-review is not a new invention. Perhaps, as we see in some of the dreams discussed here, it is not even about an individual life at all but about reaching a level of transcendence and universality we sometimes glimpse in our most powerful dreams. Although first named and recognized by Robert Butler, life-review is found in cultures all across the world, as in the following verses from an inspiring Inuit song (Thule Expedition, 1924):

And I thought over again
My small adventures
As with a shore wind I drifted out

In my kayak
And thought I was in danger.

My tears,
Those small ones
That I thought so big
For all the vital things
I had to get and to reach.

And yet, there is only
One great thing,
The only thing
To live to see in huts and on journeys
The great day that dawns,
And the light that fills the world.

Inuit Song

Our lives, reviewed or not, are filled with many "small adventures," with things we "thought so big" but that are perhaps not so big when we look back on our past. Something bigger is called for, the "One great thing." This "One great thing" is the transformation alchemists called "the Great Work," and which is nothing less than what our dreams will tell us about "the Light that fills the world."

Figure 12.3 The Light that Fills the World
Source: Sunrise in Bar Harbor, Maine, with Mt. Desert Island in the distance. Photo by Julie Czyzewski/Shutterstock

References

Anthony, B. (2016). *This given life: One Catholic life in context.* CreateSpace Independent Publishing Platform.

Archer, E. (1959). Wild Strawberries (a film review). *Film Quarterly*, 13, 44–47.

Arendt, H. (1998) [1958] *The Human Condition.* Chicago: University of Chicago Press.

Atchley, R.C. (2009). *Spirituality and aging.* Baltimore: Johns Hopkins University Press.

Birren, J. E. & Cochran, C. (2001). *Telling the stories of life through guided autobiography groups.* Baltimore: Johns Hopkins University Press.

Bjorkman, S., Mams, T., & Sima, J. (1970). *Interviews with Ingmar Bergman.* New York: Simon and Schuster.

Boss, M. (1958). *The analysis of dreams* (Pmerans, A. J., trans.). New York: Philosophical Library.

Bulkeley, P. & Bulkeley, K. (2006). *Dreaming beyond death: A guide to pre-death dreams and visions.* Boston, MA: Beacon Press.

Butler, R. N. (1963). The life review: An interpretation of reminiscence in the aged. *Psychiatry*, 26, 65–76.

Butler, R. N. (2002). *Why survive?: Being old in America.* Baltimore: Johns Hopkins University Press.

Butler, R. N. (2017). *Age, death, and life review.* Available at: http://www.hospice foundation.org/teleconference/2002/butler.asp

Clarke, J. H. (2009). The metapsychology of character change: A case study of Ebenezer Scrooge. *Journal of Spirituality in Mental Health*, 11(4), 248–263.

Cohen, G. D. (1993). A tale of two Decembers: The journal of December, 1992 and The case of December, 1843. *American Journal of Geriatric Psychiatry*, 1(2), 91–93.

Cohen-Shalev, A. (1992). The effect of aging on dramatic realization of old age: The example of Ingmar Bergman. *The Gerontologist*, 32(6), December, 739–743.

Coleman, P. G. (1989). Ageing and life history: The meaning of reminiscence in late life. *The Sociological Review*, 37(1).

Conybeare, C. (2016). *The Routledge guidebook to Augustine's confessions.* Abingdon: Routledge.

Eakin, J. P. (2008). *Living Autobiographically: How we create identity in narrative.* Ithaca, NY: Cornell University Press.

Erikson, E. (1978). Reflections of Prof. Borg's life cycle. In E. Erickson (Ed.), *Adulthood* (pp.1–31). New York: W. W. Norton & Company.

Erikson, E. (2017). A life history: Revisitation and reinvolvement. Retrieved from: http://www.haverford.edu/psych/ddavis/p109g/erikson.strawberries.html

Evans-Wentz, W. Y. (Ed.) (Dawa-Samdup, K., trans.) (1927, 1960). *Tibetan book of the dead: Or, the after-death experiences on the bardo plane.* Oxford: Oxford University Press.

Foster, G. W. (1985). *The world was flooded with light: A mystical experience remembered.* Pittsburgh: University of Pittsburgh Press, 80–81.

Frankl, V. E. (2000). *Man's search for ultimate meaning.* New York: Barnes and Noble Books.

French, P. & French, K. (1995). *Wild Strawberries.* London: British Film Institute.

Glucksman, M. L. (2007). *Dreaming: An opportunity for change.* New York: Jason Aronson.

Goelitz, A. (2007). Exploring dream work at end of life. *Dreaming*, 17(3), 159–171.

Halpern, L. (2003). *Dreams on film: The cinematic struggle between art and science.* Jefferson, North Carolina: McFarland & Company.

Hartmann, E. (1998). Nightmare after trauma as paradigm for all dreams. *Psychiatry*, 61, 226.

Heraty, V. L. (2014). *The dream belongs to the dreamer*. Carlsbad, CA: Balboa Press.

Inuit Song from the Kitlinuharmiut (Copper Eskimo). *The report of the fifth Thule expedition, 1921–1924*.

Kenyon, G., Bohlmeijer, E., & Randall, W. L. (Eds.) (2011). *Storying later life: Issues, investigations, and interventions in narrative gerontology*. Oxford: Oxford University Press.

Kerr, C. W., DonnellyJ. P., & Wright, S. T. (2014). End-of-life dreams and visions: A longitudinal study of hospice patients' experiences. *Journal of Palliative Medicine*, 17(3), March 11.

Kettell, M. E. (2001). Reminiscence and the late life search for ego integrity: Ingmar Bergman's *Wild Strawberries*. *Journal of Geriatric Psychiatry*, 34(1), 9–41.

King, R. H. & King, E. M. (2004). *Autumn years: Taking the contemplative path*. London: Continuum: 157.

Linden, S. J. (Ed.) (2003). *The alchemy reader: From Hermes Trismegistus to Isaac Newton*. Cambridge: Cambridge University Press.

Luke, H. (2000). *Such stuff as dreams are made on*. New York: Bell Tower.

Magee, J. J. (2008). Dream analysis as an aid to older adults' life review. *Journal of Gerontological Social Work*, 18, 163–172.

Malmstrom, L. (Trans.) & Kushner, D. (1960). *Four screenplays of Ingmar Bergman*. New York: Simon and Schuster.

Moody, H. R. (1997). *The five stages of the soul*. New York: Doubleday Anchor.

Moody, H. R. (2005). Dreams for the second half of life. *Journal of Gerontological Social Work*, 45(3), 271–292.

Moody, H. R. (2011). Dreams and the coming of age. *Journal of Transpersonal Psychology*, 43(2), 181–207.

Moody, H. R. (2015). Stages of the soul and spirituality in later life. In M. Johnson (Ed.). *Spirituality Dimensions of Ageing*. Cambridge: Cambridge University Press.

Morgan, R. L. (2002). *Remembering your story: Creating your own spiritual autobiography*. Nashville, TN: Upper Room Books.

Olney, J. (1981). *Metaphors of self: The Meaning of autobiography*. Princeton: Princeton University Press.

Perera, S. B. (2013). Circling, dreaming, aging. *Psychological Perspectives*, 56(2), 137–148.

Ram Dass (2001). *Still here: Embracing aging, changing, and dying*. New York: Riverhead Books.

Richter, R. L. (1986). Attaining ego integrity through life review. *Journal of Religion and Aging*, 2(3), 1–11.

Staude, J. R. (2005). Autobiography as a spiritual practice. *Journal of Gerontological Social Work*, 45(3), 249–269.

Thule Expedition. (1927). *Report of the fifth Thule Expedition 1921–24: the Danish expedition to Arctic North America in charge of Knud Rasmussen*. Copenhagen: Gyldendal.

Tornstam, L. (2005). *Gerotranscendence: A developmental theory of positive aging*. New York: Springer.

Vlada, P. (1981). *Film & dreams: An approach to Bergman*. New York: Hippocrene Books.

Webster, J. D. & Haight, B. K. (Eds.) (2002). *Critical advances in reminiscence work: From theory to application*. New York: Springer.

Yeats, W. B. (1939/1996). *Man and the echo in collected poems*. Scribners; and in *The Atlantic*, January, 1939.

Chapter 13

What Does It All Mean?

Observations and Takeaways by a Practical Theologian

H. Peter Kang

EPISCOPAL CHURCH

The Graying of Our Congregations

The chapters in this volume represent important developments in the study of spirituality, religion, and aging. My purpose in this chapter is to step back and ask: "What does it all mean?" I should note that I am not a social scientist by training. I am an active priest in the Episcopal Church, with a doctorate in Religious Studies. I am what some would call a "scholar-priest," or a "practical theologian," vocationally rooted in the daily realities of parish ministry, while benefiting from and contributing to the more specialized discourses of academic research and writing. The observations and takeaways I offer are meant to highlight the valuable resources in this volume for clergy, congregations, and those who have been called to attend to the religious and spiritual lives of older adults.

It is safe to say that most religious leaders in the United States are aware that the landscape of religious and spiritual life in America is changing. This is certainly the case among clergy of my own and other so-called "Mainline Protestant" denominations. We need only look out from the pulpit on Sunday morning, or survey the parish register, to see that the makeup of our congregations has shifted over time. On the whole numbers are down. Attendance is declining, and fewer and fewer young people are actively involved in the life of the church.

The awareness of these changes, most often framed in terms of "church decline," has been the cause of much consternation. Many now contend that mainline protestant congregations in the United States are suffering from what anthropologist Frederic Roberts calls a "collective anxiety attack." "They fear for the future of their individual congregations, their denominations, and even American Christianity. More specifically, they worry about generation gaps in their pews, about their congregations 'dying if they're not growing,' about cultural irrelevance, and about the rise of non-denominational megachurches" (Roberts, 2005, p. 1). Such fears, no doubt, have been the driving force behind the large collection of diagnoses, declension narratives, and manuals for church growth published in recent years. As one commentator blithely observes, "the literature on the church's decline seems to be the only thing growing in North American Protestantism" (Jinkins, 1999, p. 12).

In discussions about the health and future of the church, these changing demographic trends and the increasing prevalence of "graying congregations" are typically presented as problems we should somehow "solve." We seem to have uncritically accepted the fetishization of youth and stigmatization of aging that has become endemic within popular culture. As reported in the first chapter of this volume by Bengtson, Kang, Endacott, Gonzales, and Silverstein, implicit and explicit forms of ageism are common within contemporary congregations. It is not that clergy are intentionally discriminating against older adults. As the authors note, "Clergy members were sincere in expressing the desire to serve their older members." Rather, we have been generally unaware (or perhaps willfully ignorant) of the needs of our seniors, and do not realize how our actions (and inactions) might alienate older church members.

Rarely do we notice the implicit forms of ageism at work within our congregations. Well-intentioned comments and questions that one commonly hears in church leadership meetings – "What can we do to get more kids involved in our youth group?" "How can we attract more young families to the church?" – often trade on problematic stereotypes of older adults and negative associations with aging. To be sure, youth formation and family outreach are important ministries. However, the concentration of resources and initiatives on youth and young adults (who nevertheless remain increasingly absent from our congregations) can blind us to the importance and value of the people who are right in front of us, already sitting in the pews.

As the chapter by Bengtson et al. makes clear, seniors are the most religiously involved of all age groups, and they are the most active and reliable members of our churches today. Yet many older church members report feeling "invisible," "overlooked," and "unappreciated" in congregational life – often as the result of their churches' attempts to become more "youth oriented" and "youth-driven" in ministry. These findings, along with many of the other insights and conclusions provided by the essays of this volume, present a clarion call for clergy and congregational leaders to rethink the way we view older members of our flocks, recognizing not only their value and ability to contribute to the life of the church, but also their changing religious and spiritual needs.

The Figure of Job and the Question of Meaning

It is interesting to note the multiple references to the biblical figure of Job in this collection (see, for example: Coleman & Mills, Chapter 5 in this volume; Manning, Chapter 4 in this volume). Some scholars believe that

Job is the oldest book of the Bible. This is a fascinating idea—suggesting that even before the written accounts of the creation narratives, the exodus from Egypt, or the kingdom of Israel, people shared the puzzling story of Job. Other scholars disagree about the dating of Job's composition, but the fact remains that we find something enduring and timelessly articulated in the book of Job. Thomas Carlyle famously described it as "A noble Book; all men's Book! It is our first, oldest statement of the never-ending Problem,—man's destiny, and God's ways with him here in this earth" (Carlyle, 1876, p. 195). In Job we encounter the primordial question of human suffering—Why? Why are things as they are? What reason can there be for our anguish? Theologically speaking, what Job articulates is the fundamental question of theodicy: if God is good and loving, and if God is all powerful, why do such terrible things happen? Job cries out because he wants to know the reason for his suffering, and the platitudes offered by his friends in the dialogues do not satisfy. Examples of this type of questioning can be found in several of the stories recounted by Coleman and Mills (Chapter 5 this volume).

Stepping back, we might say the problem in Job is not so much the problem of suffering, but rather the problem of meaning. The primary issue is not *that* Job suffers—but that he can find no discernable *reason* for his suffering, and thus no sense of meaning or purpose within it. The philosopher Friedrich Nietzsche observed that the problem of suffering is not suffering itself, but to have no answer to the crying question, "Why do I suffer?" "Man, the bravest of animals and the one most accustomed to suffering, does not repudiate suffering as such; he desires it, he even seeks it out, provided he is shown a meaning for it, a purpose of suffering" (Nietzsche, 2010, p. 162). In this account, what we most desire, what we cry out for from the depths of our being, is meaning, purpose, a sense of coherence that adds intelligibility to our lives, as Manning notes in Chapter 4. Suffering gives rise to these questions. As evidenced by the chapters of this volume, we find that such questioning frequently occurs in later life.

The Quest for Meaning and Role of Religion in Later Life

The Search for Meaning in Later Life

The innate human desire for meaning—or what Linda George, following Aaron Antonovsky (1979), calls a "sense of coherence" in life—is a common theme in these essays (Chapter 7 in this volume). Robert Atchley, referring to the work of Wade Clark Roof (1999), speaks of the "wholeness hunger" felt by a large proportion of American adults, who long for some kind of "unifying experience" to bring together the disparate pieces and relations of one's life (Chapter 3 in this volume). Neal Krause notes that deriving a sense of meaning is one of the fundamental goals not only of religion, but of life itself, and so places "meaning" at the top of his three-tiered model of religion and health (Chapter 8 in this volume).

The essays in this volume also highlight the fact that the basic human longing for a sense of meaning and coherence in life is often heightened among older adults. According to Harry Moody, the search for the ultimate meaning of one's life is the great task of later life (Chapter 12 in this volume). As Malcom Johnson explains, this intensified concern with meaning is often driven by an awareness of finitude that arises among those facing the end of their long lives, people who have likely observed the aging and death of older generations of friends and family (Chapter 11 in this volume). It also seems likely that the larger questions about the meaning and purpose of one's life naturally arise among older adults, like those who are retired, and those whose children have moved away, for whom the demands of raising a family and maintaining a professional career may have previously occupied their primary attention and energies. Generally speaking, in later life, people more often have the time, interest and ability to stop and consider the bigger questions, to finally ask "What's it all about?" As Bengtson et al. note, individuals after retirement are frequently "spiritually curious elders," who "have more time, more money, and often more passion than younger age groups."

While the search for meaning might be a common theme within these essays, what this search entails is not straightforward. The very concept of "meaning" is itself somewhat vague and hard to define. Christel Manning reports that identifying what we mean when we speak of "meaning" has been one of the greatest challenges of her research (Chapter 4 in this volume). This is the sort of meta-theoretical question over which there are longstanding debates among philosophers and critical theorists, which we cannot attempt to resolve here. More important, for our purposes, is Manning's observation that since the scholarly literature defines meaning in different ways, we should not be surprised to find a lack of consensus among the people those scholars study. Simply put, people will continue to define—and also seek—meaning in life in different ways.

Regarding the plurality of approaches to the question of meaning, Manning notes a helpful distinction between discussions of meaning with respect to the past and discussions of meaning in terms of the present. The former is retrospective, looking back at one's life and endeavoring to make sense of, to find a purpose for, past events and experiences—seeking a way to connect, and hold together, the variegated pieces of one's personal history. The latter is more introspective, having to do with one's personal sense of purpose and belonging, often described as a feeling of connection—with others, with nature, or the broader world—recognizing the relationships and activities that contribute a sense of meaningfulness to one's life. Both are important aspects in the search for meaning, and both are variously addressed in the essays of this volume.

Finding Meaning in the Present: Relations and Activities of Social Support

The chapter by Krause highlights the present-tense relational aspect of the search for meaning in life. As he says, "Meaning is not discovered individually. Instead, it is something that people jointly construct with significant others in the process of going through their daily lives" (Chapter 8 in this volume). In particular, Krause focuses on the social dimensions of religious life—the spiritual and emotional support that is provided to and received from others at church, and the more tangible support given and received through formal volunteer programs. These are relationships and activities that contribute a sense of meaningfulness to one's life.

Other chapters in this volume also touch on the importance of social relations and support for finding a sense of purpose and belonging in the present. Though Atchley emphasizes the individualized nature of spiritual journey narratives, he nevertheless affirms a strong need for "small groups within which to seek formation and nurturing of a self-directed spiritual life." As he writes, "The spiritual intimacy that develops within such groups can be strong glue that keeps the groups going." Conversely, Coleman and Mills demonstrate the negative effects that can result from experiencing a lack of spiritual and emotional support in one's religious community, especially in times of bereavement. The authors recount painful stories of people who received poor pastoral care following the death of a loved one, were put off by insensitive comments from members of the clergy, or otherwise felt overlooked and unappreciated by their religious ministers. Understandably, such experiences are associated with a general sense of disillusionment and alienation from the church and the Christian faith in which most of these people were raised. Coleman and Mills conclude by reemphasizing the essential communal element of religious belief, affirming that, "In this perspective we do not stand alone before God but as a people, and a people who should be loving and supportive to one another" (Coleman & Mills, Chapter 5 in this volume). They suggest lessons can be learned from "new age" groups, akin to the small groups Atchley describes, that exist to help form and support the spiritual exploration of their members.

Making Sense of the Past: Life Review and Spiritual Journey Narratives

The chapters by Johnson and Moody each discuss the retrospective practice of "life-review," a term coined by Robert Butler (1963) to describe the activity of evaluating the events of one's personal history in order to find meaning in them, to come to terms with everything that has happened, and thereby make sense of one's life. While Moody focuses on the often-overlooked role that dreams may play in the process of life-review (a point to which I will return later), the conscious activity of storytelling—in autobiography, memoir, oral history, and other forms of media—remains one of the most commonly recognized methods of life-review. According to Manning, telling stories is one of the main ways we make sense of events and thereby create meaning in our lives. Indeed, we often come to know ourselves and who we are through storytelling, and we make sense of our lives and recognize our identities through the stories we tell about ourselves.

Just as stories change and develop over time, so too do our lives and sense of self-understanding in the telling of them. According to Butler (2002), "The goals of life review include the resolution of past conflicts and issues, atonement for past acts or inaction, and reconciliation with family members and friends" (p.6). In other words, the process of looking back and evaluating the past events of one's life, and telling one's story, i.e. setting the events and experiences of one's life within a coherent narrative structure, can actually effectuate a change in one's life in the present. Butler claims life review can lead to greater life satisfaction, psychological well-being, and self-esteem.

> The overall benefit of a life review is that it can engender hard-won serenity, a philosophical acceptance of what has occurred in the past, and wisdom. When people resolve their life conflicts, they have a lively capacity to live in the present. They become able to enjoy basic pleasures such as nature, children, forms, colors, warmth, love, and humor.
>
> (Butler, 2002, p. 6)

These benefits of life review are closely related to the introspective, present tense, aspect of finding meaning in life. On this account, the retrospective evaluation of the past can bring about a more introspective appreciation of the present. One leads to, or at least allows for, the other. I would imagine this notion—that reconciliation and atonement can free us to receive the fullness of life—is familiar to most clergy and congregational leaders.

Though Butler does not explicitly speak of life review in terms of spiritual or religious concerns, the connection seems obvious enough. Moody writes, "We need to appreciate the spiritual dimension of life-review." And Johnson surmises, "The process of life review is essentially a spiritual enterprise." Other researchers find value in making the connection even more explicit. Lewis (2001), for example, introduces the concept of a "spiritual life review" that intentionally integrates "spirituality" in the life review process. This modifies the standard life review process by explicitly inviting participants to re-view their lives through a "spiritual lens," intentionally focusing on the spiritual dimensions of major life events, and drawing attention to any important spiritual experiences they may have had (Lewis, 2001; Stinson, 2013).

The concept of spiritual life review parallels Atchley's account of the practice of presenting spiritual journey narratives in Quaker meetings. Atchley affirms that presenting one's spiritual journey is a useful type of life review. In his words, "spiritual journey narratives often deal with basic 'meaning questions' about life, and coming to grips with these questions in order to present them can be a very daunting yet liberating experience" (Chapter 11 in this volume). Again, we see that the process of looking back and evaluating one's life and sharing one's story can bring about a change in the present. According to Atchley, most people who went through the process of sharing their spiritual journey narratives come away from the experience with a sense of self-esteem and agency. Evaluating one's personal history and past experiences within the context of a spiritual journey might also help make one more consciously aware of the spiritual dimensions of one's life and thus more attuned to the availability of everyday spiritual experiences moving forward.

Religion, Spirituality, and Non-Religious Frameworks of Meaning

Given the many references to "religion" and "spirituality" in this volume, it is worth noting the fact that what people mean when they describe something as religious or spiritual is not always clear. As Manning observes, our conceptual categories are often insufficient to neatly capture the complex realities of people's lives. More often than not, the dividing line between religious and secular is fuzzy. Today, more and more people self-identify as "spiritual but not religious," as Roof notes (Chapter 10 in this volume). Accordingly, Atchley affirms the possibility of having "spiritual experiences without the benefit of religion." Yet, as Bengtson et al. indicate, in recently developed typologies spirituality and religion are not presented as separate binary concepts but instead as linked and related. As the terms are used in the essays in this volume, "religion" appears more closely associated with institutional affiliation and participation in the traditional organized activities of a particular faith community, whereas "spirituality" refers to an amalgam of more individually focused, experientially driven, practices and beliefs.

However one chooses to define the terms, the authors in this volume generally agree that "religion" and "spirituality" are closely associated with the basic human quest for meaning in life. For example, Krause notes that "Religion helps people rediscover and hold on to a sense of meaning in the midst of adversity." Manning similarly describes religion as a powerful source of meaning that provides a readymade set of stories, a framework of meaning that people can adapt to explain what is happening to them in terms that provide coherence and control. And George observes that religion and spirituality are positively associated with a sense of coherence in life.

Some might say that the quest for meaning in life is itself a spiritual endeavor, or at least an act of faith. Toward that end, it is interesting to note the implicit relationship in Krause's chapter between the discussion of seeking meaning in life and the discussion of his own project, a struggle to find a comprehensive theory of religion and health. In one place, he recounts the difficulty of working with messy data, likening the process to listening to an old vinyl record that has been badly scratched, trying to discern a tune amidst the static and noise. From a certain perspective, we might say that Krause's search for a comprehensive theory is an act of faith, proceeding from the belief *that* there is meaning and coherence to be found amidst the messy data, an underlying connection that ties it all together, even though he does not yet know *what* that connection is. So too, in reality, we have messy lives and it is not always easy to see how things fit together, or how to make sense of events. Like listening to a scratchy record, we strain to find meaning amidst the static and the noise, the chaos and confusion of our lives. Such seeking is in essence a matter of faith, proceeding from a belief that there is, in fact, meaning to be found in our lives.

Where does such a belief come from? It could very well be the case that there is no greater meaning or purpose to be found, no deeper reason for the things that happen to us, nothing to unify and hold together the various events and experiences of our lives, that life really is "just one damn thing after another." Why not? I can offer no compelling reason to the contrary aside from the fact that I do not believe it to be so.

From my own theological perspective, I view the matter in the terms articulated by St. Augustine, who confesses to God, "You have made us for yourself, and our heart is restless until it rests in you" (Augustine, 2009, p. 3). According to Augustine, humans have been created to find their fulfillment in the Lord. From this vantage, God is the *telos,* the end and the goal, of our innate human desire and longing for something more, the deeper sense of meaning and purpose and fulfillment within and beyond the creaturely realities of our lives. I think this is what St. Paul is getting at, when he says of Christ, "All things have been created through him and for him. He himself is before all things and in him all things hold together" (Colossians 1:16–17). This is not to say that upon finding and being found by God, one has finally answered the question of life's ultimate meaning, such that one's quest for meaning and understanding thereby comes to an end. As St. Gregory of Nyssa would say, the spiritual life is an endless journey into the infinite mystery of God. From this vantage, Jesus is not so much "the answer" as he is the framework, direction, and guide for living the question. He is "the way, the truth, and the life" (John 14:6), for "in him we live and move and have our being" (Acts 17:28).

What about people who do not share similar theological convictions, those who might not draw upon the resources of religion and spirituality to orient their lives in this way? How do people who are not religious find meaning in life, particularly as they near the end of it? As evidenced by the stories recounted by Coleman and Mills in Chapter 4, some who lose faith in a loving God who providentially orders the course of the universe come to believe more in a cold and uncaring fate, and that the events that happen to a person (for good or ill) are simply attributable to luck. A similar emphasis on the role of luck in determining the course of one's life can be found in Manning's study among both non-religious and (interestingly) religious respondents.

By and large, however, most non-religious people are not nihilists who believe there is no meaning, purpose, or intrinsic value to be found in life. Manning, for one, affirms that it is obvious that she and other nonreligious people can have a meaningful worldview. The essays in this volume describe several different types of resources and narrative frameworks upon which nonreligious people often draw in the search for meaning and a sense of coherence in life. "Science" appears to be the most common response. Indeed, several respondents in the study by Bengtson et al., said they relied on science *as* their religion. People also draw upon the narrative frameworks of popular psychology, mysticism, and free will (voluntarism) to understand and interpret their lives. Ardelt and Wingard (Chapter 9 in this volume) also make the case for philosophy, understood in the classical sense as the "love of wisdom" (*philo-sophia*), as a viable nonreligious resource for achieving a sense of purpose and subjective well-being in the face of death—thus echoing the ancient notion, voiced by Socrates in Plato's *Phaedo*, that philosophy is preparation for death.

Moody introduces the intriguing notion that one's dreams, and the interpretation of them, could offer another helpful resource, which might be considered "spiritual" but not necessarily "religious," for confronting unresolved questions about the ultimate meaning of our lives. Life review is typically understood to be a conscious activity, an intentional evaluation of one's past in words and narratives. Dreams, however, arise from the unconscious, and, as Moody puts it, often present images and events reflecting the deepest level of the psyche. As such, he suggests, dreams can be a powerful vehicle for life-review. Dreams nevertheless require conscious interpretation if they are to serve this function. Moody offers a variety of dream interpretations, drawing upon, and dancing between, the discourses of psychology, spirituality, mysticism, film theory, literary criticism, and the social sciences. In this respect, Moody's interpretive approach reflects the ethos of many "Nones," as described in the chapter by Roof, i.e. "bricoleurs who piece together ideas, practices, religious and spiritual beliefs from many sources."

Non-religious resources and narrative frameworks, from science, psychology, mysticism, philosophy, and dream theory might prove helpful in the retrospective task of evaluating and making sense of the various events and experiences of one's life. Yet, it is unclear what fulfills the role of the present-tense social relationships and activities typically associated with religion that contribute a sense of meaningfulness to one's life. To whom does the nonreligious person turn for the spiritual and emotional support traditionally given (and received) by members of religious communities?

Given the current trends of decreasing levels of religious involvement and affiliation among younger Americans, Idler (Chapter 6 in this volume) predicts that many more people in the US, as elsewhere, will be reaching old age without the traditional social supports that have been there for previous generations. Johnson likewise suggests that many people nearing the end of their lives today might be less well equipped than earlier generations because they lack the vocabulary of spirituality and rituals of faith communities, such as those pertaining to forgiveness and absolution.

In his chapter, Johnson describes the later life phenomenon of what he calls "biographical pain"—"the irremediable anguish which results from profoundly painful recollection of experienced wrongs which can now never be righted." Biographical pain arises from the awareness of ruptures in one's self-narrative. It is the feeling of being helplessly unable to address unresolved conflicts, repair broken relationships, or atone for past misdeeds in one's life. According to Johnson, "pain at the end of life may well be the intolerable result of unheard and unassisted life review."

In many religions, there are established rituals and practices that have traditionally fulfilled the purposes of "life review." In the Christian tradition, for example, we have the gifts and resources of spiritual direction, private confession, holy unction, and rites of reconciliation. Without the benefit of such rituals and practices, care providers today face new challenges and experiences for which they may be ill prepared. Johnson conjectures that learning how to know and resolve one's past life may well become a new zone of engagement with older people. He also signals the increasing need for the sort of "accompanying" presence and nonjudgmental listening offered by chaplains and counselors, and for formal training to prepare them, "if epidemics of silently distraught older people are to be avoided."

Takeaways for Clergy and Congregations

Along with the search for meaning, another common theme among the chapters in this volume is a widespread distrust of clergy and disillusionment with traditional religious institutions. The chapter by Rhys Williams describes how trust in religious leaders has diminished recently, starting in the 1970s, and accelerating rapidly by the televangelist scandals of the late 1990s and the Catholic clerical abuse publicity of the early 2000s. Coleman and Mills also found among their study participants a decreasing confidence in the authority of traditional Christian churches, as well as a reluctance to turn to religious ministers in times of bereavement and religious questioning. So, even though older adults might show an increased interest in religious and spiritual matters, asking broader questions about meaning in life, many might be hesitant to seek guidance from clergy and other traditional religious institutions.

As several of the authors in this volume point out, the baby boom generation highly values individual choice and personal expression. Sometimes this can lead to a kind of spiritual tinkering, or a cafeteria-style approach to religion, in which persons piece together a variety of beliefs and practices from different sources. At the same time, as the research by Roof suggests, as this generation has aged, they have become more settled in their lives and possibly more drawn to a modified "spirituality of dwelling," enriched by the incorporation of a variety of different spiritual practices into their traditional worship services. Roof cites examples enriching spiritual practices such as "centering prayer," medieval chants, mindfulness meditation, and African American spiritual music woven together into the traditional liturgies of congregations. Of course, just what particular spiritual practices might prove effective in any one congregation will have to be locally determined and adapted to the particular needs, interests, and abilities of that congregation.

At the heart of the issue, as articulated by Coleman and Mills, is the reality that churches and other religious bodies cannot expect to enforce their beliefs on people. Rather, people, especially those from the baby boom onwards, want to feel as though they have come to belief on the basis of their own reasoning, and that their feelings and sentiments have been taken into account. As Roof points out, "styles of religiousness and spirituality that are chosen tend to be more deeply committed and energizing." To me, this would suggest that to meet the needs of many older adults today, clergy and congregations might want to consider offering more open-ended exploratory adult formation opportunities, similar to what we do in some youth-oriented curriculums designed to help prepare young people for Confirmation (the sacramental rite in some Christian traditions in which a person, in a sense, takes ownership of their faith, expressing a mature commitment to Christ). The key in such studies is not so much to tell people what they should or must believe to be Christian, but to show them how and why such beliefs are important to your life (as their instructor and guide), while providing them the resources, opportunity and safe environment to see for themselves.

Several chapters in this volume speak about the effectiveness and importance of small groups to help form and support the spiritual explorations of their members. As Roof suggests, this is one of the things that many "mega-churches" do really well, overcoming the divide between the religious and the spiritual by offering within the same institution a large, unifying worship service to bring the community together combined with an array of small groups for discussions and activities. The chapter by Bengtson et al. addresses the effectiveness of programming in churches offering multiple groups for older adults organized loosely around generational cohort and activity level. In light of the research in this volume, we might say that such small groups might effectively be dedicated to activities like assisting members in the process of "spiritual life-review," composing and presenting their spiritual journey narratives, or simply telling stories about their lives and experiences in relation to broader questions about meaning, religion and spirituality. Small groups might also be dedicated to helping members think about the religious and spiritual dimensions of dreams, and what their dreams might help them see and understand about their lives. Yet, more important than the particular content and programming of the small group are the strong social ties that develop over time between members of the group—relations of "spiritual intimacy" that help encourage and support members in their quest for meaning.

Such small groups need not, and perhaps should not, be entirely led by clergy. As the chapter by Bengtson et al. demonstrates, older adults are often highly motivated and "spiritually curious" elders, blessed with an array of gifts and talents, who typically have more time, energy and resources than their younger counterparts. Moreover, many older adults benefit from contributing their time and energies to leading programs with congregations—finding a sense of purpose and value within the work. Older adults given leadership roles, especially in programs that might benefit younger generations, for example through mentorship or storytelling, are less likely to feel "invisible" and "overlooked," and more likely to come to know themselves as the vital and important members of the congregation that they are.

The chapters in this volume also reinforce the need for sensitive pastoral care when engaging in ministry with older adults, especially in times of loss and bereavement, or when individuals might be suffering from "biographical pain." As any good resource for pastoral care will say, in such instances, often what is most important is not trying to offer simplistic platitudes or rationales for the loss or tragic event, but rather listening. People want to know and feel that they have been heard, that their feelings and sentiments are being taken seriously. They want someone to be with them in their pain, not to try to explain that pain away.

This brings us back to the biblical figure of Job mentioned at the start of this exploration. The majority of the book of Job is composed of dialogue and argument between Job and his friends. Job cries out in anguish at the apparent injustice of his suffering and loss. His friends try to explain and rationalize his pain, endeavoring to fit his experience within their ready-made categories and frameworks for understanding God, the world, and humanity's place within it. The problem is, they try to provide an answer to Job's primordial cry for meaning—an answer which they, in truth, do not know and are not fit to give.

Reflected in this volume is a common idea that "religion" is a traditional response to our basic human desire for meaning, that it provides an answer to our longing and desire for a sense of purpose and coherence in life. Yet perhaps this idea is related to the fact that more and more people distrust traditional religious institutions, as well as the ministers and clergy, like myself, who claim to represent and speak on behalf those institutions. As with Job and his friends, they have heard our "answers," our platitudes and rationales, and found them wanting. Perhaps more than anything, what is needed today for clergy and congregational leaders is the courage and humility to admit our ignorance—which does not necessarily mean a lack of faith—but the simple fact that we honestly do not know, and cannot even guess a reason for the horrible events that take place in people's lives.

Speaking from a Christian theological perspective, some might say that God, and not "religion," is the one who hears and responds to our suffering cries for meaning. Even so, God does not respond by trying to explain our suffering, but by sharing it. Through the mystery of the Incarnation, God comes to be with us, in our anguish and confusion, not in some great display of power that would forever "solve" the problem of human suffering, but by becoming one of us, suffering like us, and in so doing, not erasing our pain and suffering, but transforming it into something more, something that is now, and will be, forever meaningful.

Conclusion

In this volume we have seen that it is a mistake to uncritically associate aging with frailty and decline. It is likewise a mistake to associate the "graying" of our congregations with diminished cultural relevance and church decline. Many older adults today lead active, adventuresome lives, with an increased desire to pursue larger questions about purpose and meaning in life. Those called to attend to the religious and spiritual lives of older adults can assist in this latter pursuit. As older adults seek to make sense of their past, we can assist through different activities such as life review and spiritual journey narratives. As they seek meaning in the present, we can foster relations and activities of social, emotional and spiritual support in larger communal and small group settings.

Because of growing distrust of religious leaders and organizations, some might be hesitant to seek guidance from clergy and traditional religious institutions. Today, there are popular "non-religious" resources and narrative frameworks to which older adults might turn, such as science, popular psychology, philosophy, and dream theory. As lines between "religious" and "secular" blur, we might find creative ways to incorporate such resources into the spiritual and religious lives of our communities. At the same time, there remains a pressing need for social support and sensitive pastoral care for aging congregants, especially in times of religious questioning and bereavement. Most importantly, individuals want to feel as though they have come to belief using their own reason, and that their feelings and sentiments have been taken into account.

As aging in America continues to change, so too must our understanding and appreciation of it. If clergy and other ministers are to faithfully respond, we must come to see that aging is not a problem for our churches to solve, but a gift to embrace.

References

Antonovsky, A. (1979). *Health, Stress, and Coping* (1st ed.). San Francisco: Jossey-bass.

Augustine, S. (2009). *Confessions.* (H. Chadwick, Trans.) (1st ed.). Oxford: Oxford University Press.

Butler, R. N. (1963). The Life Review: An Interpretation of Reminiscence in the Aged. *Psychiatry*, 26(1), 65–76.

Butler, R. N. (2002). In K. J. Doka (Ed.), *Living with Grief: Loss in Later Life* (pp. 3–11). Hospice Foundation of America.

Carlyle, T. (1876). *The Carlyle Anthology.* London: H. Holt.

Jinkins, M. (1999). *The Church Faces Death: Ecclesiology in a Post-Modern Context.* New York: Oxford University Press.

Lewis, M. M. (2001). Spirituality, Counseling, and Elderly: An Introduction to the Spiritual Life Review. *Journal of Adult Development*, 8(4), 231–240.

Nietzsche, F. (2010). *On the Genealogy of Morals and Ecce Homo.* Knopf Doubleday Publishing Group.

Roberts, F. M. (2005). *Be Not Afraid! Building Your Church on Faith and Knowledge.* Rowman & Littlefield.

Roof, W. C. (1999). *Spiritual Marketplace: Baby Boomers and the Remaking of American Religion.* Princeton University Press.

Stinson, A. (2013). Spiritual Life Review with Older Adults: Finding Meaning in Late Life Development. *Graduate Theses and Dissertations.* Retrieved from http://scholarcommons.usf.edu/etd/4778

Index